# ANTI-TERRORISM; FORENSIC SCIENCE; PSYCHOLOGY IN POLICE INVESTIGATIONS

First published 1985 by Westview Press

Published 2018 by Routledge
52 Vanderbilt Avenue, New York, NY 10017
2 Park Square, Milton Park, Abingdon, Oxon OX14 4RN

*Routledge is an imprint of the Taylor & Francis Group, an informa business*

Copyright © 1985 by Taylor & Francis

All rights reserved. No part of this book may be reprinted or reproduced or utilised in any form or by any electronic, mechanical, or other means, now known or hereafter invented, including photocopying and recording, or in any information storage or retrieval system, without p ermission in writing fromthe publishers.

Notice:
Product or corporate names may be trademarks or registered trademarks, and are used only for identification and explanation without intent to infringe.

ISBN 13: 978-0-367-00673-0 (hbk)
ISBN 13: 978-0-367-15660-2 (pbk)

NOTE

This volume includes a broad selection of the papers presented at IDENTA '85.

The ideas expressed are not necessarily those of the publisher or the Israel National Police, neither of which takes responsibility for the material.

# CONTENTS

Introduction-M. A. Kaplan, Deputy Commander, Ministry of Police....................................5

Keynote Speech-H. Bar-Lev, Minister of Police, State of Israel....................................7

Keynote Speech-Professor M. Arens, Minister-without-Portfolio State of Israel.......9

The Role of Forensic Science in Criminal Investigations
M. A. Kaplan, Head, Research & Development Unit, Israel National Police (Israel)..................17

## COUNTERING TERRORISM

Facing Unconventional Terrorism
Prof. Y. Dror, Department of Political Science, Hebrew University of Jerusalem (Israel).........26

The Terrorism of Left-Wingers in the Federal Republic of Germany and the Combat against the Terrorists
Dr. W. Steinke (Federal Republic of Germany)....42

Firearms Examinations in a Terrorist Situation
J. Wallace, Northern Ireland Forensic Science Laboratory (United Kingdom).......................52

Documents and Forgery in Terrorist Operations
J. Levinson, Criminal Identification Division, Israel National Police (Israel) ................63

Forensic Ballistics in Counter-Insurgency Warfare
R. Petluck, Criminal Identification Division, Israel National Police (Israel)..................72

## ISRAEL'S EXPERIENCE WITH TERRORISM

Trends in Palestinian Terrorism
T. Prath, Jaffee Center for Strategic Studies, Tel Aviv (Israel).......................................81

The Reemergence of Jewish Terrorism in Israel
E. Sprinzak, Department of Political Science-Hebrew University of Jerusalem (Israel)............................................88

International Terrorism--A New Threat to Information Systems Security
R. Pollak, President, Israel Information System Security Association, (Israel)..................115

Shi'ite Terrorism
N. Kramer, The Dayan Center for Middle Eastern and African Studies (Israel).......................417

## POLICE & TERRORISM

The Israel National Police Bomb Disposal Unit
A. Yakuel, Deputy Head, Bomb Disposal Unit, Israel
National Police (Israel)........................133
Survey of Selected Terrorist Devices
Yosef Sharon, Bomb Disposal Unit, Israel National
Police Northern District (Israel)...............138

## PSYCHOLOGICAL METHODS

A Method for Estimating the Accuracy of Individual
Control Question Tests
G. Barland, Polygraph Examiner, Salt Lake City
(USA)...........................................142
A Built-In Validity in Polygraph Field
Examinations
A. Ginton, Head, Behavioural Science Section,
Criminal Identification Division, Israel National
Police; Department of Criminology, Bar Ilan
Univerisity (Israel)............................148
Validity of the Control Question Test in Two
Levels of the Severity of Crimes
G. Schterzer and E. Elaad, Scientific
Interrogation Laboratory, Criminal Identification
Division, Israel National Police (Israel)......155
Decision Rules in Polygraph Examination
E. Elaad, Scientific Interrogation Laboratory,
Criminal Identification Division, Israel National
Police (Israel).................................167
Computerized Polygraph Interpretations and
Detection of Physical Countermeasures
D. Raskin, J. Kircher, C. Honts, University of
Utah, Salt Lake City (U.S.A)....................179
The Psychological Stress Evaluator: A Validation
Field Study
I. Nachshon, Department of Criminology, Bar Ilan
University, (Israel)............................189
The Effect of Similarity on Psycho-physiological
Responsivity to Pictorial and Verbal Stimuli
I. Ben Shakhar, Department of Psychology, Hebrew
University of Jerusalem (Israel)................194
Hypnosis in Police Investigation: Principles and
Safeguards
Dr. M. Kleinhaus, Ministry of Health, Tel Aviv
(Israel)........................................195

## FORENSIC SCIENCE IN THE FIELD

Field Kits: Forensic Examinations outside the Lab
J. Almog (Israel)......................................206
The Role of the Forensic Clinical Specialist
Dr. H. B. Kean, Police Surgeon, Merseyside Police
and Cheshire Constabulary (U.K.)......................211
Sexual Abuse Field Kits in the United Kingdom
Dr. H. B. Kean (U.K.).................................216
The System for Evidence Collection for Sexual
Assault Victims in Israel
A. Marbach, Head, Biology Laboratory, Criminal
Identification Division, Israel National Police
(Israel)..............................................222
Evidence Technicians : Agents of the Laboratory in
the Field
M. Kaplan (Israel)....................................229

## VOICE IDENTIFICATION

Computer-Based Methods for Forensic Speaker
Recognition
M. Hecker, Head, Handwriting Laboratory,
Kriminaltechnisches Institut, Bundeskriminalamt
(Federal Republic of Germany).........................235
The Current Status of Voice Identification in
Police Investigations in Israel
Y. Tobin, Linguistics Department, Ben Gurion
University of the Negev, (Israel).....................238
Forensic Applications of Automatic Speaker
Verification
Prof. A. Cohen, Department of Electrical
Engineering, BenGurion University of the Negev
(Israel)..............................................246

## FORENSIC SCIENCE

"Hitler Diaries" - Case History, Examination
Results, Handling in Court
Dr. W. Steinke (Federal Republic of Germany)...266
Hitler Diary Forgery
M. Hecker (Federal Republic of Germany)........275
Techniques for Detecting Documents Created by
Photocopy Machines
D. Crown, former President, American Academy of
Forensic Sciences, (USA)..............................281
Surveillance under Adverse Weather Conditions:
Wavelength Filtering Considerations
N. Kopeika, Department of Electrical & Computer
Engineering, Ben Gurion University of the Negev,
(Israel)..............................................288

Analysis of Explosives in the Israel Forensic
Science Laboratory
S. Zitrin, Head, Chemistry & Biology Group,
Criminal Identification Division, Israel National
Police (Israel).....................................307
Recent Advances in Laser Latent Fingerprint
Development
R. Menzel, Center for forensic studies, Texas Tech
University (USA)....................................310
Speedometer Examination for Traffic Accident
Reconstruction
I. Zeldes, South Dakota State Police Crime
Laboratory (USA)...................................316
Determination of Firing Distance by Total Nitrite
M. Ravreby, Criminal Identification Division,
Israel National Police (Israel)....................320
A Simple Adaptation of the Microspectrophotometer
Docuspec TM/A for the Comparison of Small
Quantities of Luminescent Materials
A. Zeichner, Head, Toolmarks & Materials
Laboratory, Criminal Identification Division,
Israel National Police, Jerusalem (Israel).....328
Forgeries of the USSR Drivers License
B. Perelman, Examiner of Questioned Documents,
Jerusalem (Israel).................................335
Handwriting Characteristics of Arabs writing
Hebrew
Y. Yaniv, Examiner of Questioned Documents,
Jerusalem (Israel).................................345

## FORENSIC IDENTIFICATION
Identification of the Dead--Can Chiropodists Help?
Dr. Ivor Doney, Police Medical Officer, Bristol
(U.K.); Paul H. G. Harris, Chiropodist, Bristol
(U.K.).............................................351
Identification of the Seriously Damaged Body using
Non-Dental Data
Dr. M. Rogev, Consultant in Forensic Medicine,
Department of Pathology, Sheba Medical Centre, Tel
Hashomer (Israel)..................................357

## FORENSIC FILES AND COMPUTERIZATION
An Approach to Laboratory Automation
E. Tulloch, E. Kupferschmidt, Royal Canadian
Mounted Police (Canada)............................368

Central Collections of Physical Evidence and
Possibilities of Support Through Use of Computers
Dr. W. Steinke (Federal Republic of Germany)...376
Computerization of the Fraudulent Cheque
Collection
S. Kraus, Head, Laboratories Group, Criminal
Identification Division, Israel National Police
(Israel)........................................387
A Collection of Toolmarks Made by Self-locking
Pliers on Broken Cylinder Locks
N. Agron, Criminal Identification Division, Israel
National Police (Israel)........................391
An Experimental Video-Disc Based Fingerprint
Retrieval System
A. Aperman, Criminal Identification Division,
National Police (Israel)........................395
Automatic Digital Defocus Restoring Filter
N. Ben-Yosef, Applied Physics Division School of
Applied Science and Techonology, The Hebrew Unive.
(Israel)........................................402
Future Priorities in Forensic Science Research and
Development in the Federal Republic of Germany
Dr. W. Steinke (Federal Republic of Germany)...408
Shi'ite Terrorism - N. Kramer, The Dayan Center
for Middle Eastern and African Studies
(Israel)........................................417

## Introduction

IDENTA '85, the 1st International Congress on Technologies for Police Identification & Counter-Terrorism, met in Jerusalem during the week 24-28 February 1985. The conference, held with the assistance of the Israel National Police and under the patronage of the Hebrew University, was attended by over 300 participants from more than twenty-five different countries.

The congress had three main subjects: counter-terrorism, forensic science, and psychology in police operations; and, it was resolved by the International Advisory Board of the conference that these topics should once again constitute the thrust of the programme at IDENTA '87, to be held in Western Europe.

Needless to say, IDENTA '85 would not have been possible without the assistance rendered by a large number of people. The International Advisory Board and Israel Working Committee members played key roles, the Israel Defense Force and the Ministry of Defense rendered support, and the Stier Group of Tel Aviv handled the many administrative details which arose.

I should like, however, to single out certain individuals who were instrumental in various aspects of IDENTA '85: Asher Naim, Aryeh Arazi and Ariela Atari of the Ministry of Foreign Affairs who spent endless hours in helping with the preparations for the conference; Nachum Mendel of the Ministry of Police who served as official spokesman; the late Yaakov Eliav who made IDENTA virtually a personal hobby; Shlomo Aronishky, Arik Yakuel, Esther Tannenbaum and the late Jonathan Licht of the Israel National Police who arranged the conference counter-terrorism exhibition and related segments of the programme; and, Tuvia Livneh who took a special hand in arranging for simultaneous Spanish translation.

Jay Levinson of the Israel National Police served as my "second right hand" and deserves special mention, as does his supervisor, Joseph Almog, who made him available to me and who encouraged the entire Division of Criminal Identification to join the IDENTA '85 effort.

Finally, I should like to thank Minister of Police Haim Bar Lev without whose decisive and active support the IDENTA '85 congress simply would not have happened at all.

M. A. Kaplan, Deputy Commander
Ministry of Police


Jerusalem, 1 September 1985


## INTERNATIONAL ADVISORY BOARD

M.A. KAPLAN (Head, Research & Development Israel Police), Chairman.
BARLAND, G.H., DR. (Utah, U.S.A.)
BRUNELLE, R.L., (Maryland, U.S.A.)
CROWN, D.A., DR. (Virginia, U.S.A.)
CURRY, A.S., DR. (Berkshire, G.B.)
GOBBI, E. (Argentina)
HORVATH, F. PROF. (Michigan, U.S.A.)
KUZMACK, N. (Washington DC., U.S.A.)
MAEHLY, A., DR. (Linkoping, Sweden)
MATHYER, J. PROF. (Lausannes, Switzerland)
MEIER, J., DR. (Zürich, Switzerland)
McWRIGHT, C.G., (Washington D.C., U.S.A.)
RASKIN, D.C., (Utah, U.S.A.)
SAFERSTEIN, R., DR. (New Jersey, U.S.A.)
SEHGAL, V.N., (New Delhi, India)
SUNICO, L.A. (Quezon, Philippines)
STEINKE, W., DR. (Wiesbaden, West Germany)
VILLANOVA, A.C., (Brasilia, Brazil)
WITTE, A.H., DR. (Delft, The Netherlands)
J. LEVINSON,DR., (Israel Police). Executive Secretary

## ISRAEL WORKING COMMITTEE

M. KAPLAN, (Israel Police), Chairman.
ALMOG, Y. DR. (Israel Police)
ALON, I., DR. (Stier Group)
BEN YOSEF, N. PROF. (Hebrew University)
BLOCH, B., DR. (Institute of Forensic Medicine)
GINTON, A., DR. (Israel Police & Bar Ilan University)
J. LEVINSON, DR. (Israel Police), Executive Secretary.
MERARI, A., DR. (Centre for Strategic Studies, Tel Aviv University)
TOBIN, Y., PROF. (Ben Gurion University)

# Keynote Speech

## The Honourable Haim Bar Lev
## Minister of Police
## State of Israel

Modern life has its joys and pleasures as well as its difficulties, and problems. Crime and terrorism are amongst the more serious problems which our modern society has to face. During this fourth quarter of the twentieth century crime has become more sophisticated and complicated, increasingly ruthless, and to a growing degree international. There is no country that does not suffer from the consequences of crime and terrorism, particularly in Western democracies.

How can the countries of the Western world cope with this phenomenom? In my opinion, the fight against crime and terrorism should be based upon four basic elements:

The first of these elements is intelligence. Both ordinary crime as well as terrorism cannot be fought without reliable intelligence. You must know your enemy, his intentions, and his preferences in potential targets. If you do not have the necessary intelligence you are actually acting from blindness.

The second element is what could be broadly termed a strong defense. This is required for ordinary crime and for terrorism as well. You must protect the objects, whether physical property or human life, that can become the victims of terrorism and crime.

Today, the methods to properly secure targets against the possibilities of crime and terrorism are both numerous and sophisticated. In my opiion, all countries share in the goal to thwart criminals and contain terrorism.

The third element is to match a strong defensive posture with an active fight against crime and terrorism. By no means can we giving in to these problems which threaten our modern society and its inherent democratic ideals.

The methods and means of a successful offense are various and often complicated, but without actively fighting terrorism and crime, we stand no chance to limit these problems. To know your enemy and to strengthen your defenses as he plans his attack is not enough. Particularly when terrorism is concerned, the fight to combat it must be aggressive and un-tiring. Crime and terrorism must be attacked; they must be dealt with whenever a reasonable opportunity exists, and not only as an immediate reaction to a specific event.

Whenever and wherever you can strike against terrorism and crime, it is your duty to act! To rely on defense is not enough.

The element of international co-operation in fighting terrorism and crime cannot be stressed adequately. This is a prerequisite for success in modern society, since the phenomena of crime and terrorism today do not recognize national borders. If the battle against them is launched only on a country by country basis, that battle will be most often lost.

As we all know, international co-operation amongst the police of most countries exists in criminal matters within the framework of INTERPOL. On terrorism issues, however, co-operation is limited to bilateral efforts between specific countries.

I am sad to say that the international co-operation needed to fight terrorism actively and successfully does not exist today. Our intentions might be the best, but our efforts are too weak. As I have said, there are links for co-operation between countries, but when compared with the level of activity in INTERPOL, there still is a long way to go.

These are the basic elements with which crime and terrorism can be fought. I am confident that if the forces of law enforcement and civil order in democratic countries really devote the necessary resources and allocate the necessary means, these problems can be solved. A victory against crime and terrorism is a victory for all countries and all mankind.

I wish the participants at IDENTA '85 productive discussions and a fruitful exchange of information. I hope that this conference will be yet another step in furthering co-operation between the twenty-six countries represented here.

# Keynote Speech

### The Honourable Moshe Arens

### Minister without Portfolio
### State of Israel

It's a sign of the times that we have a conference on Techniques for Criminal Identification and Counter-Terrorism. IDENTA '85 is not the only such conference being held; in recent years throughout the free world there have been meetings and consultations on these topics.

The plague of terrorism has become so pervasive in our times that it has taken on worldwide dimensions. The participants here at IDENTA '85 should be commended for having taken the time to come here and discuss the problem of providing better security for people throughout free world.

In many ways, we are living in an age of terror. Today, the incidence of terror and the number of its victims is greater than in any previous period in history, and terrorism has taken on the territorial dimensions of our entire globe. Now, the consequences of terrorism strike virtually every country.

We must undestand the underlying reasons why this terrible affliction of terrorism has spread with such intensity and rapidity.

To my mind, the first part of the answer lays in the area of technology --- the weapons, transportation and communications advances which have been achieved in the modern age and which have inevitably become available to small terrorist groups. The ability to package great force and deliver it with exacting accuracy in a relatively small weapon is characteristic of today's armies, but this capability has unfortunately also fallen into the hands of small terrorist groups.

Modern technology has also provided high density targets were huge financial investment or large numbers of people are concentrated in a limited volume. This has given terrorists targets never known in earlier history. Modern aircraft, for example, cost significant sums of money and carry large numbers of passengers, thus providing the "ideal target" for the terrorist.

A second part of the answer is state supported terrorism, a new phenomenon in our modern age. Today, certain terrorist groups are not merely small underground movements; they are supported by countries and governmental mechanisms. An example of this is when a terrorist group receives financial assistance, weaponry or the use of facilities on the soil of a sovereign country. Some countries have also aided terrorists by providing diplomatic passports and have placed their embassies abroad at the disposal of terrorists, such as recently occurred in an incident in London.

The countries which support and promote terrorism provide directions and instructions to terrorists are unfortunately located primarily in the Middle East. Khomeini's Iran, Iraq, Syria, Libya have all made their embassies abroad available to terrorists, and I assume that they are still doing this as we are meeting here today. These countries, as well as the People's Democratic Republic of Yemen, have trained terrorists on their soil, and they have dispatched terrorists on missions considered to be consistant with national objectives.

There is also the assumption that countries in the Soviet Bloc, and possibly the Soviet Union itself, do promote, encourage and pursue terrorism when it serves political objectives.

A third part of the answer is the existance today of a "world brotherhood" of terrorists. This co-operation and alliance enables terrorist groups whose announced ojectives are divergent and who have no ideological connection to associate together to strike at establishments, governmental interests and embassies, and civilians.

The Red Brigades as well as a long list of other terrorist organizations from the extreme right to the extreme left in terms of their openly voiced ideological statements have been known to associate with each other, co-ordinate and co-operate in carrying out terrorist activities.

Israel has seen the Japanese Red Army stage a terrorist atrocity in this country in clear co-operation with the PLO. We are located in the Middle East, an area where terrorism is endemic and rampant. I suppose that if we were to map terrorist acts in the past decade, we would find that although there are unfortunately incidents throughout the world, there is a heavy concentration of such events in the Middle East.

One indication of this is the assassination of political leaders in the Middle East. There is hardly a Middle Eastern country, of course with the exception of Israel, where there has not been a spate of assassinations and where kings and prime ministers have not been assassinated. Abdullah, the grandfather of the present king of Jordan, was assassinated. We know that King Hussein has been on lists of people targetted for assassination. Completing the geografic circle around Israel, one will find that in Lebanon, Syria, Iraq and Saudi Arabia there have beemn assassinations. In Egypt, only a few years ago, President Sadat who led his country to the peace table was assassinated; In Lebanon, President-elect Bashir Jumayel was assassinated.

Clearly, the Middle East is an area where terrorism is rampant, and we do not have to search for the reason. There is an abundance of both religious and Marxist fanaticism, and in some cases these two varieties are combined. This fanatism breeds brutality and an absence of the values which we have come to cherish in the free world. Therefore, the final result of this fanatism is terrorism.

We in Israel have had to deal with terrorism for many years. I was going to say that we have been dealing with it since the State of Israel was established in 1948, however that would not be accurate; we have had to respond to terrorism even before the state was declared.

As it turns out, by the way, the most prominent victims of terrorism are the people who live in the very countries which originate terrorism.

I have mentioned the assassinations of the leaders in many of our neighbouring countries. Many of the people living in Lebanon, Syria (for example, the city of Hamat which was terrorized by the Syrian army in an act of state-supported terrorism), and Jordan have been the first victims of this scourge.

In talking about the victims of terrorism, the country which most obviously comes to mind is Lebanon. This country is a source of concern to us because it has been used as a base for terrorist activities against Israel. The most prominent victims, of course, have been the Lebanese themselves --- Druze , Sunni, Shiite, Christian. It has been estimated that in the past ten years maybe some 100,000 Lebanese have been killed in fighting that has been essentially between different terrorists groups and the various private milita. Maybe 500,000 other Lebanese have fled the country to escape this terrible tragedy which seems to be consuming their sad country.

Israel has had to go to war because of the terrorism which has come to us from Lebanon. In the years since 1968, when the first attacks started from across our northern border, we have experienced a succession of incidents caused by terrorists who infiltrated our borders, penetrated our country from the sea, or launched rocket and artillery attacks from Lebanese soil. These terrorists took advantage of the reality that the Lebanese government was unable to exercise its jurisdiction and that the Lebanese army was incapable of controling the various local militia forces.

The most prominent terrorist organization (or more accurately an organization encompassing some eight or ten separate terrorist groups, each with its own ideology and patron government providing political and financial support) is the PLO. When the PLO was chased out of Jordan in September, 1970, it emplaced itself in Lebanon from whence it conducted its activities against Israel. These activities, however, have not been only against Israel; the PLO turned Lebanon (and particularly Southern Lebanon into a training ground for terrorist organizations from around the world.

Amongst the documents captured by the Israel Defense Forces (IDF) when they entered Lebanon in June, 1982 were documents attesting to the fact that terrorists from all over the world --- from Europe, from Asia and from Latin America --- had come to Lebanon to receive training from the PLO. Many of the PLO trainees had received the earlier part of their own training in many of the countries of the world, including in the Eastern Bloc. Lebanon had become the training school, the staging ground, the assembly area, the nerve centre where decisions have been taken to stage terrorist activities in many parts of the world.

Israeli military action in Lebanon was probably the greatest blow struck against terrorism in recent years. It destroyed the very large infra-structure which the PLO had built up in Lebanon. It destroyed an international centre for terrorism unequalled since the PLO was forced to evacuate Jordan in September, 1970. It put an end to terrorist activity against Israel's civilian population.

We, in Israel, paid a very high price with the human losses which our army suffered during the fighting and its subsequent deployment in Southern Lebanon. We are now in the process of redeploment. Over a year ago we evacuated the Shuf area controlled by the Druze; today we are leaving some of the areas populated and controlled by the Shia.

As far as we are concerned, the fight against terrorism is far from over. Aside from PLO terrorism, we are now facing what some people consider to be a new brand of violence --- the terrorism of Shia in Southern Lebanon. This is Khomeni terrorism. This is terrorism practised by the most extreme elements amongst the Shia population.

As we so frequently find, the population gets polarized between what you might call the silent majority --- the majority of people who are moderate in their views and actions (in the case of Southern Lebanon, the majority of Christians, Druze, and Shia who feel that they have in common with Israel the interest of keeping terrorism away from their door and not allowing it to run rampant in Southern Lebanon) --- and at the other end of the pole, the extremists who have derived their inspiration and often even their orders from Khomeini's clique in Tehran and from the Syrian intelligence organization, who came into the area first terrorizing the local population, then using the area as a base for terrorist operations against Israel and the IDF.

We have also found that the political leaders, for example in Lebanon, Amin Jumayel (whose brother was assassinated as president elect clearly by orders of Syrian intelligence), Prime Minister Karami, and other leaders have either themselves become addicts and supporters of terrorism; or, as so frequently happens they do not have the courage to stand up to terrorism. Before one can realize it, these leaders have come to mouth the slogans of terrorism against Israel. Here we see the recurring picture of fanatics and terrorists succeeding in intimidating people who should know better, people who had been moderates, people who had constituted the silent majority.

This is the picture of the fight against terrorism, or if you will, the fight of terrorism against the civilized world. Democratic countries who are the targets of terrorism and whose population is the target of terrorism have not always shown themselves to be very strong and effective or, at times, even very courageous in the battle against terrorism.

It is not an accident that there is no terrorism in totalitarian countries. For ideological reasons you would think that to be the arena for terrorist type activities and for actions taken against the establishment, but you will not find terrorism in the Soviet Union or in Syria. The means which totalitarian countries an muster preclude the possibility of any effective terrorist activity on their soil.

The hesitancy and care motivated by values which we in the free world cherish make it possible for terrorists to function in our countries. We must be aware of these limitations, and we must be ready to overcome them so that terrorism does not overcome us.

Clearly, and rightly so, there is an enormous concern in the Western world for human life. In recent years democratic countries have done a great deal in organizing, mobilizing and training themselves to fight terrorism. Here amongst the participants at IDENTA there are probable many who have taken an active part in developing techniques and technology, or in training special units whose expertise it is to deal with terrorist incidents. We in Israel have developed techniques and technologies; we have trained units that have given a very good account of themselves on a number of occasions.

I am telling you that in the democratic countries of the world there is no substitute for an intelligent, determined and relentless policy at the government level in the fight against terrorism. We need mutual co-operation amongst the democratic countries because terrorism is worldwide, because terrorists co-operate amongst themselves, because terrorist groups cross borders. If this international conspiracy of terrorism is not met by international co-operation by the democratic countries who are the targets of terrorism, it will be difficult for us to fight back.

The democratic countries of the world must cease to grant diplomatic immunity to terrorist states and to countries which promote, encourage and support terrorism, countries who lend their passports, diplomatic pouches, and embassies to terrorists. This kind of immunity cannot be enjoyed by Libyans, Iranian, Iraqis and Syrians who, with the aid of their "diplomatic personnel," bring to your countries weapons, terrorists, and acts of terrorism.

If the battle against terrorism is to be carried out effectively, we must share intelligence and information. As the American Secretary of State called for several months ago, there must be pre-emptive action where-ever we have information. We cannot afford to sit and wait for terrorism to strike. If we can obtain information about where terrorists are located or where actions are being planned (and we frequently do obtain this kind of information), preventive action should be taken before terrorists have had a chance to strike.

There is no alternative or substitute for resolute deterrence. We must make it clear to terrorists that blackmail will not work. On the day when terrorist organizations throughout the world realize that this is the unalterable policy of the democratic countries of the world, then we shall see the beginning of the end of terrorism in our age.

Transcribed and edited by Dr. Jay Levinson from recording of keynote speech delivered at IDENTA '85.

KEYNOTE SPEECH:

# THE ROLE OF FORENSIC SCIENCE
## IN
## CRIMINAL INVESTIGATION

M. A. Kaplan, Deputy Commander
Head, Research & Development
Israel National Police

Chairman, IDENTA '85

I should like to discuss the way forensic science has traditionally been operating, and I should llike to suggest different approaches for the future that would make forensic science perhaps more complete as an all-encompassing realm which includes all the sciences, and thus allow forensic science to give a larger answer to the questions which are raised by the courts and by criminal investigations.

Generally, the role of forensic science has been limited to the laboratory examination of physical objects. This limitation does not stem from the fact that the traditional forensic sciences are the only sciences available in criminal investigation. Rather, the limitation emanates from the premise that physical evidence must be the raw material of forensic science.

The situation today is that forensic science serves the criminal investigation. These investigations have two main purposes: (1) determining if a crime has been committed, and (2) identifying the perpetrator of that crime. Thus, forensic science must be contributive to these objectives.

As an example of the first use of forensic science --- to determine if a crime has been committed --- there is the routine laboratory identification of substances of legal interest, such as illicit drugs, poisons, and conflagration accelerants. Determination of the esxistence of these items is usually tantamount to showing that a crime has been committed. For want of a better name, these could be called substantive examinations.

The second category can be called comparative examinations, since it is by comparison that the perpetrator of a crime is identified in the laboratory. The function of determining who committed a specific crime cannot be minimalized, and I want to stress the contributions of the crime laboratory.

Forensic examinations in this area are not substantive; they are comparative. A fingerprint found at the scene of a crime will be compared to a known print in order to link someone to the scene. A ballistics comparison will be made between evidence and a test firing from a weapon to link someone through means of his weapon to the crime. The handwriting on a document will be compared with the known writing of an individual.

These are all examples of marks and impressions, however comparative examinations can also be of materials themselves. Could the blood at the scene of the crime belong to the suspect? Could the semem sample taken from the rape victim have been deposited by the person under suspicion?

Traditionally, forensic science examinations have been limited to the evidence from specific criminal cases, and no comprehensive approach of comparing evidence from different crimes was extensively used. The scientist has addressed the issues previously stated --- was a crime committed; and, if so, by whom. He did so in each case separately, without seriously attempting to connect evidence of identification from various scenes of crimes and determining who the unknown criminal was, and whether different crimes were committed by the same though still unknown criminal on the basis of the comparison and identification of evidence with known samples and the comparison of evidence from different cases.

It seems to us here in Israel that this approach is rather limited. Today we must look for new ways in which forensic science can perform its two basic tasks, and at a later stage assist the courts in their deliberations. Historically, in the sphere of criminalistics, forensic science has stressed the already existing disciplines of chemistry and biology, although other fields of knowledge such as botany and zoology have not been totally ignored.

Chemistry in its broadest sense has been used both for substantive and comparative examinations. In the former area, narcotics examinations could be cited as an example. In the latter area, examples might be the comparison of glass or paint fragments. Biology has provided expertise in examining blood, semen, hair and other items of human origin. It should be noted that there certainly are chemistry and biology by-products which are characteristic of police laboratories, however we should not loose sight of the fact that their scientific basis was established outside the police laboratory.

Forensic science has, on the other hand, also developed its own specific scientific disciplines. Fingerprint comparison is not usually a subject learned in university. Forensic science has not only refined the process of comparison and identification; it has also prepared the scientific basis proving the validity of the precept that no two people can leave the same prints. This scientific groundwork, essentially based in the crime laboratory, has also allowed other fields such as ballistics and handwriting examination to flourish.

The established sciences are not primarily concerned with the question of individuality. Their basic stress tends to be quantitative and/or qualitative analysis, and even classification has become a secondary issue. It has been the police laboratory and the forensic institution which have tackled the broad question of individuality.

Let us now turn to the criminal investigation process. There, one must take all information available and transform it into evidence. After all, the prosecution of a suspect for a crime can be done only on the basis of evidence.

It is my contention that most investigative information is never subjected to scientific scrutiny. Most of the information is from a human source, whether he be a complainant, a victim, a witness, an informer, or even the suspect himself. Until now, information from a human source has always been thought to be outside the pale of criminalistics and forensic science.

I think that this is a limitation which suggests that there is perhaps merit in looking at psychology as a discipline with application in forensic science. This has not been the trational position. Up to now, psychology has not been accepted as a forensic science. Therefore, a large field of investigative information has not been covered by any scientific discipline.

In the Israel National Police it is realized that physical evidence is only a small part of the totality of information which exists in a criminal investigation. I do not want to play with percentages, but I have no reservations in stating that physical evidence usually comprises less than 10% of the information available. Thus, the majority of the information available to the investigator is neglected by science.

There is another problem which confronts all of us today. In modern times we are in a position where criminal investigations cannot be carried out in depth. If you have dozens of burglaries, practically you cannot conduct complete investigations. By definition, investigation means considering something in depth. Today, with the large number of incidents reported, we can no longer allocated the resources required for a full investigation in every case.

In my opinion, however, this problem is not without solution. We must go back to basics. We must once again apply science and technology to the examination and evaluation of existent information from previously reported crimes. My position is nothing new; it is just an expansion of thoughts which are basic in our line of work.

Let us assume that we are going to a burglary. There, based upon experience, we expect to find certain types of evidence. It is not for the police to determine the importance of that evidence; evaluation is a process reserved for the courts.

If we find the perpetrator's fingerprint at the burlary, that is sufficient to convict him. The fact that the perpetrator is unknown today, the fact that we have identified no suspect today ... these factors do not minimalize the absolute value of the discovered evidence.

To cite another example, if the police receives a stolen check with a forged signature written by the thief, this is certainly evidence. When the known handwriting of the thief is obtained, examination of the known and questioned writings can provide scientific findings leading to courtroom conviction. If I do not have the known writing sample today, my problem is not that the evidence does not exist. I just do not have the suspect. I do not even have the time to look for the suspect.

The approach which I am advocating is perhaps new. Take the evidence out of the limited specific incident file and open an active evidence collection where evidence from a large number of incidents is stored. Then, gather comparative specimens from a wide population of possible suspects.

Until now, evidence has been collected, suspects have been identified, and comparisons of suspect to evidence have been effected. I am saying, turn that around. You have the evidence, but you have no suspect; you do not even have the time to investigate to locate the suspect. In Israel we are building active evidence files from previously committed crimes, then the laboratory itself makes comparisons, finds the suspect, and provides the investigator not only with a scientific report, but with a previously unidentified suspect and the evidence by which he can be convicted.

The computer suggests itself for this task of comparing material from different files, and we have used the computer for such a purpose here in Israel. Since most evidence is visual, we have also turned to the video disc. Whether we are dealing with cartridge cases, fingerprints, or handwriting, the information is visual. The video disc is a combination system with computer assisted sorting and retrieval, as well as information in its original visual mode which still allows visual comparison. The approach has many applications, and it is now upon us to take this existing technology and let it aid us in finding practical solutions to the real issues facing us today.

In many ways the police is a prisoner of the legal approach of distinct case units. Until now we have always considered evidence on an incident by incident basis. Perhaps this is because of our basic courtroom orientation. As a result, we have always developed our evidence going case by case. In my opinion, the time has come for us to discard this procedure and consider the alternatives which we have. We have not made spectacular progress in this area in Israel, but we have decided upon a certain direction.

Traditionally, the crime laboratory is a place for receiving evidence, and this has been viewed as a very passive role. Investments have been made in the crime laboratory by trying to recruit higher level personnel and purchasing more sophisticated equipment, but the improvement has not been that great.

Let us consider for a moment the broader view of the laboratory. A sample requiring laboratory examination is discovered, and it is sent from the field to the laboratory where it is processed. The processing can be approved, but there is some-thing which we neglect. Perhaps the sample itself can be improved. Maybe, if we improve the sample, we have improved the possibility of a successful examination ... more than by improving our ability inside the laboratory.

There is a trade-off. Which approach has the greater probability of success? Generally, the laboratory has said that it will examine those samples submitted. Sometimes, the more progres-sive laboratories will say that they have a cer-tain responsibility to give instruction to inves-tigators in the field to giude them in the collec-tion of evidence --- what is desired, where are the hazards, and what to do when certain problems arise.

As far as I know, there has been no serious attempt by the laboratory to say that it is res-ponsible for the whole process of evidence collec-tion. This would include fielding personnel under the supervision of the laboratory for the purpose of evidence collection. It is granted that these people would have backgrounds different from those of people working in the laboratories, but they would nonetheless be working in the same adminis-trative and professional framework as those scien-tists in the crime lab.

In this country we have developed such a working arrangement, but we have not stopped there. We have developed an entire series of field kits to try to bring the technology of the laboratory to the field. We have also trained out field technicians. To cite one example, after an explosion it is now possible for our technicians to use a field kit designed for preliminary screening and sample literally dozens of people within minutes, searching for explosive traces on the hands. The technique was developed in the laboratory, but it should be noted that the close working relationship with field personnel made the laboratory scientists sensitive to operational field needs.

These ideas which I have raised seem to be possible directions for the future, and each will be further developed during the IDENTA '85 congress.

There will be a special session on the use of psychology in criminal investigations, and I should point out that it is the position of the Israel National Police that psychology is a science of great potential value in our work. We feel that we have a responsibility to the courts to scientifically examine information provided to the police by human sources, in addition to the traditional responsibility of examining physical evidence.

A witness under stress in the dark of night views for a few short seconds the commission of a crime, and later he identifies the perpetrator. If the court hears the witness' testimony, it will assign a certain value to the matter, but this totally ignores the scientific validity of the identification. We must raise that issue.

We must also use psychology in a positive sense. How can the Rogues Gallery (Criminal Album) be constructed to show an eyewitness a minimum of pictures yet receive from him a maximum of reliable information? We feel that perhaps psychology should be asked for the answer.

The Israel National Police has used hypnosis quite extensively with willing witnesses to assist them in memory recall. (I should point out that hypnosis is never used with either suspects or hostile witnesses.) It has been thought that after a woman is raped and suffers from a trauma, maybe she could provide more information under hypnosis. We are able to use hypnosis because we have psychologists who are part of our forensic establishment.

In some countries the polygraph is quite controvertial, but in Israel we have found that it has a certain validity ... let me stress again, a certain validity. Only a competant professional can conduct a polygraph examination and evaluate a person's reactions. In Israel we have decided that such a competant professional can only be a graduate psychologist, since he must both formulate the right questions and evaluate the results.

These are three of the fields in psychology (i.e., Rogues Album, hypnosis and polygraph) which we are presently using in the Israel National Police. Each will be discussed in further detail during the special session on psychology here at IDENTA '85.

At another session of IDENTA '85, we shall be taking an intensive look at some of the field kits which have been developed by laboratory personnel to assist technicians in the field. These kits deal with explosives as we have already noted, the handling of firearms, the clandestine flourescent marking of objects, and even the identification of holes made by bullets. We shall also examine the concept of the field technicians themselves, and how they relate to and are controlled by the central laboratory.

Here at IDENTA '85 we shall also be giving special consideration to the concept of active evidence. We have come to value this approach in the Israel National Police, and we want to share it with other police forces throughout the world.

SUMMATION

In summary, forensic science as it is practised today has been limited in a number of ways.

First, the sciences used are essentially the physical sciences and those technologies derived from them or related to them. This has led to the exclusion of non-physical sciences such as psychology, even though most of the information about crimes available to the crime investigator can be categorized as psychological rather than physical evidence.

Another limitation is that forensic science has essentially been a passive police laboratory service. As a basic principle, the laboratory can examine only that evidence which it receives; if potential evidence is not submitted to the laboratory, it obviously cannot be examined. Traditionally, laboratories have not become involved in improving evidence collection so that they might receive exhibits more suitable for examination. Their focus has been on forensic science and not on the possible role of the police laboratory in the evidence collection process.

Forensic science has been influenced by the case system of the courts, as a result of which laboratories have geared their procedures to case by case examinations. Even though one person might commit numerous crimes, the case system precludes laboratories from conducting broader and more constructive examinations.

We must face the issue of introducing psychology into police operations to apply scientific scrutiny to all information collected by the police. The case by case approach to laboratory examinations must be broken down. New evidence files must be developed allowing for retrieval of relevant data from both (a) previous submissions of evidence, and (b) known possible perpetrators.

We can no longer rely on past practice and procedures. If we are to make progress in the fight against crime, we must improve not only our laboratory instrumentation but also expand the scope and contribution of forensic science in the total criminal investigation and the judicial process. Forensic science must also be extended into other hitherto unused scientific disciplines to give a fuller coverage to the application of science in the criminal justice system.


Transcribed and edited by Dr. Jay Levinson based upon the keynote speech delivered at IDENTA '85 by Deputy Commander M. Kaplan.

# FACING UNCONVENTIONAL TERRORISM

Yehezkel Dror
Professor of Political Science & Wolfson Professor
of Public Administration; Director, Center for Security Studies,
The Hebrew University of Jerusalem

Terrorism can become "unconventional" in a number of dimensions: targets, demands, weapons, tactics, format domain, and stategy. Combinations of unconventional dimensions can be very effective in advancing a range of terrorism-goals, as well as attractive in terms of terrorism-motives, which in turn may increase. Also, unconventional terrorism may become an important instrument of "crazy states". Therefore, unconventional terrorism has a high probability, timing and forms depending on "terrorism-innovators" and other stochastic variables. Western Democracies may be expecially vulnerable to some forms of unconventional terrorism, such as psycho-shock-oriented. Consequently, measures against unconventional terrorism are needed. Such measures, however, depend on scarce innovativeness inorganizations, politics, law and international cooperation. Hence, expectations that suitable counter-measures will be adopted after limited unconventional terrorism episodes are optimistic. Professionals must, at least, be ready with good ideas, taking care not to diffuse those to potential terrorists.

PROLOGUE

Correct prediction of mutations in social behavior is
unusual an event, because of unavoidable dependence of fore-
casts on relatively simple and humanly easily recognizable
continuities from the past to the present and into the
future. Therefore, the chances for correctly foreseeing the
shape and implications of future unconventional terrorism are
quite low, all the more so as the future facts of unconventional terrorism are connected to present realities by stochastic and perhaps random links, rather than deterministic patterns. The harsh contradiction which must be faced is that
on the one hand the more innovative unconventional terrorism
may be - the more important it is to predict at least some of
its main contours so as to prepare ourselves to deal with it.
On the other hand, the more innovative unconventional terrorism may be - the harder it is to foresee its shapes, even in
the form of alternative possible futures and scenarios.

The difficulty is compounded by cultural limitations of
Western societies which inhibit comprehension, cognition,
understanding and correct handling of phenomena reflecting
quite different worldviews and behavior patterns. This is
illustrated by the long time it takes Western democracies
to start to realize the emergence of what I have called
elsewhere "Crazy States" (1) and the continuing inability to
handle such countries effectively, despite some learning.
The affinity between some main possible forms of unconventional terorism and "Crazy States" make this case all the
more salient.

This article cannot presume to jump over fundamental
limitations of the Western mind. Still an attempt can be
made to explore some of the factors related to the possible
emergence of unconventional terorism and its accelerated
escalation, with some action implications. This being a
subject widely discussed in literature (2), the present
paper tries to look at it from a different angle. The paper
is speculative in the main, frankly presented as such. Its
aim is to raise some issues and make some points, so as to
sensitize our minds to threatening possibilities and perhaps
to accelerate gearing for such eventualities (3).

TERRORISM AS INNATE IN CONTEMPORARY SOCIETAL PROCESSES

Quite different predictions on the future of terrorism
stem from alternative conceptions of the relations between
terrorism and contemporary societal processes. To put the

matter in a polar form: on one extreme, terrorism can be seen as rather accidental, weakly linked to society, and easily separable from its social bases; on the other extreme, terrorism can be seen as a natural and congenital facet of contemporary societal processes, systemically inbuilt into them, and closely tied in with main social realities.

To be frank, our understanding of fundamental social processes, and in particular of accelerated social change which characterize nearly all of the world now and in the foreseeable future, is all too limited to permit a reliable diagnosis of terrorism as either rather detached or as closely interlocked with social processes (4). Still, I tend more to the second supposition, namely that <u>terrorism is innate in contemporary societal processes</u>.

This conjecture is based on the following main considerations, among others:

*The world as a whole and many countries in particular are in a stage of accelerated social change, accompanied by various disruptions of established institutions and, in many cases, by "marginal-personality" production. These changes and their accompanying hardships are usually not ameliorated by tranquilizing belief-systems, but rather, in quite a number of situations, by search for "enemies" to blame for the difficulties.(5).

*On a more fundamental level, human needs for transpersonal ideologies or religions to cling to as a protection against existential fears and pains (6) provide a motive power for identification with extreme ideologies tied in with terrorism. This is all the more so the case under the destabilizing and even traumatic conditions of many contemporary societies. Even if this applies only to small groups of persons, still these suffice to make terorism endemic to society.

*Also to be taken into account is the lack of roles provided in modern societies for personality types who, in earlier times, would have become explorers, adventurers and saints (7). Some of these can be expected to turn to terrorism as a surrogate life mission.

*The prevalence of violence in all its forms, not to speculate about possibly lasting after-effects of the Nazi period, provide a climate in which violence is a legitimate instrument, up to neo-barbarism. The "routinization" of terror and its de facto acceptance as a part of national and international life further add to this climate, providing a basis for further "terrorism-cultures".

*The power structure of the world and its ideological and economic polarizations encourage terrorism, both directly in the form of providing support, up to state-instigated terrorism; and indirectly, by inhibiting effective global counter-terrorism action. Ideological, political and semantic impossibilities to distinguish clearly between "terrorism" and "freedom fighters" is partly correlated with such fundamental features of international politics (8).

*Within the free world, ideological constraints related to liberal ideologies and human, as well as hu - maine, values hinder adoption of possibly effective counter-terorism strategies (9), especially when combined with overall growing incapacities to govern (10).

*These same features provide many "soft" areas and domains of intense vulnerability to terorism. At least this may be an image easily formed in "terrorism minds", with suffificient a basis in apparent facts to encourage terrorism.

*Many characteristics of the present world make terrorism relatively easy technically, in addition to the already mentioned supportive environment provided by ideological and political features of the global regime. Thus, modern technology provides effective tools for terorism, which can be easily acquired; modern education trains many experts in potential terrorism-technologies; modern freedom of learning and information provides easy access to terorism-relevant data and knowledge; modern transit and communication networks provide easy facilities for terorism-networks, terrorism command and control and terrorism-mobility; and so on.

Additional factors which can reasonably be expected to encourage and support terrorism can be adduced, but they would add little to the list above. No reliable theory of social change being around and no satisfactorily validated model of terrorism-producing variables and processes having been developed till now, despite all the research going on in this area - a reasonable conjecture, as based on the above considerations, is the best that can be provided.

The conjecture supported by the above considerations is, that terrorism is innate in contemporary societal processes. Indeed, metaphorically it may be convenient to think of terrorism in terms of endemic a propensity that should be expected to break out in the form of repetitive, and possibly escalating, pandemics.

Important to add to our tentative analysis is a future dimension: <u>All the terrorism-producing variables can be expected to continue and intensify in the foreseeable future</u> Thus, to take up only a few illustrations from the above mentioned factors:

*Growing gaps between rich and poor countries and endemic unemployment in Western democracies - illustrate factors providing in the foreseeable future a growing basis for terrorism.

*Modern technology will continue and provide more effective tools for terrorism, up to the potentials of bioengineering to provide accessible weapons for mass-lethal terrorism.

*On the fundamental level, I tend to the conjecture that a new epoch of ideological commitments may be in store for significant parts of humanity, with some of the belief-systems being aggressive in nature (11). If this indeed will happen - then terrorism will have quite a different breeding ground (12).

However widespread or limited the effects of the above and related variables may be, it seems quite clear that <u>there will be a continuous propensity for very frustrated groups of true believers to be around and look for ways to have dramatic impacts on reality.</u> This is the stuff which produces and sustains terrorism.

In view of these predictive conjectures, I tend as a minimum to the conclusion that <u>terrorism will remain innate to societal processes in the foreseeable future, with many possibly terrorism-escalating variables on the increase.</u>

TERRORISM-ESCALATION FEASIBILITY

The above analysis indicates a societal propensity towards terrorism, but does not permit any conclusions concerning main modes of future terrorism, not to speak about their probability. But, when <u>feasibility</u> is added to propensities, then some tentative possible futures of terrorism can be derived. Hence, the importance of considering terrorism-escalation feasibility, as distinct from terrorism-propensities, somewhat similar to the "intention" versus "capacity" dimensions of military intelligence estimates.

Taking into account the size, resources, backings and other facilities of present terrorist organizations, quite a number of escalation feasibilities can be postulated, even without assuming significant expansion of terrorist organiztions. In addition, all the variables mentioned above do permit, and probably also encourage, emergence of new terrorist organizations with more initial innovative capacities. In any case, from the perspective of feasibility,escalation can take - and, to some extent, is already taking - the forms of:

*Selection of new targets, including "high-value" and very sensitive ones - such as cultural assets, elites, children, economic critical links and so on.

*Utilization of more effective instruments, ranging from sophisticated electronic devices up to toxic materials, with biological weapons being around the corner, at least for small-scale "demonstration" use.

*"Smart" delivery tools, ranging from suicide-attackers to precision guided munitions.

*Improved tactics, with saturation attacks, combined use of multiple tools, multi-national location of activities, etc.

*Sophisticated strategies, with more effective target selection, negotiation demands, bargaining management, etc.

Especially troublesome are possible combinations between innovations in the above mentioned and additional dimensions, adding up to quantum jumps in terrorism. Counter-terrorism professionals must be very careful not to provide good ideas for terrorists. Therefore, let me limit myself to a sterilized example out of many, without providing concrete scenarios: Selective demonstration of very frightening toxic weapons combined with what may look as credible threats of using them against very sensitive targets - can easily achieve "psycho-shock" effects putting governments under quite a lot of pressure and impairing public order on a large scale, in quite a number of situations.

It seems, therefore, that <u>in terms of feasibility terrorism can escalate a lot.</u> This is true without assuming jumps in availability of novel masslethal instruments, such as new biotoxical agents or nuclear devices, which too cannot be excluded in the foreseeable future.

## THE REAL QUESTION: WHY IS UNCONVENTIONAL TERORISM UNDER-DEVELOPED?

In view of the above discussed propensities and feasibilities, it seems that the appropriate question to ask is not "when will unconventional terorism be around", but rather "why is unconventional terrorism not yet widespread?" Understanding of factors regarding the development of unconventional terrorism may provide a key for predicting its possible appearance, spread and intensification.

Let me take up a number of explanations offered in the literature for explaining, and sometimes even reassuringly predicting, the continuous underdevelopment of unconventional terrorism:

One argument often made is, that "unconventional terrorism is 'irrational' in the instrumental sense, having little chance of achieving its objectives. Therefore, it will not be practiced." This is rather unconvincing a statement, for two main reasons: First, a lot of conventional terrorism also fails in achieving its objectives - so that moving on to unconventional terrorism should be expected as at least a "rational" attempt to try something else, and also as a response to frustration, as well as sometimes quite "rational" learning from failures. Second, some forms of unconventional terrorism may be very effective in achieving select goals, such as mass media attention, governance destabilization, giving-in to some terrorist demands, etc. When the limited power of Western-type cost-benefit analysis for explaining and predicting conventional terrorism is taken into account, the inability of "lack of effectiveness" arguments to satisfactorily answer the question why terrorism is not becoming more unconventional - is quite obvious.

Another argument still sometimes made, though less and less so, is that "unconventional terrorism is not yet feasible". This claim is clearly refuted by the exploration above of the feasibility of terrorism escalation.

A third argument sometimes made is, that "terrorism supporters, and in particular terrorism-supporting states, are afraid that escalating terrorism may bring about harsher retaliation against them by the terrorism-victims". This is more convincing a point, which perhaps explains restraints on those terrorist groups fully, or at least very much, controlled by their master-states. But, this explanation is weak in at least two respects: First, some terrorism-supporting states approximate the "Crazy State" category - which make them very prone to support escalating terrorism; this seems to be already a fact in respect to some terrorist groups. Second, most terrorist organizations are not controlled by any master state, either operating mainly on their own or at least maintaining much autonomy.

A fourth explanation proffered in literature is, that "terrorists think they will loose support by thier 'reference groups' and supportive populations if they escalate beyond a certain point". This may be true in respect to some insurgence-type terrorist groups operating in their own country, who do want to be acceptable to large parts of the population. But: (a) many terrorist groups have no such large client-populations, working on their own or being tied in with very small reference groups; and (b) quite some terrorism-supporting groups may welcome unconventional terrorism, to dramatize their cause and provide hope of meaingful achievements against all odds; or at least provide catharsis for deep frustrations.

Looked at all together, the above "external" answers seem quite inadequte for explaining the underdevelopment of unconventional terrorism. Therefore, a satisfactory answer has to be searched for elsewhere, probably in intra-terrorism processes. Here, the following conjecture can be offered to explain the slowness of movement towards unconventional terrorism:

Terrorist individuals and groups share basic characteristics of human individuals and groups (but not of large organizations, a point to which I shall return soon!), including "operational codes", "groupthink" (13) etc. - which result in tendencies towards conservatism, after a relatively short "innovative" phase. In particular, innovations in terrorism, as in all human activities, depend on "inventors" and "entrepreneurs" - the appearance of whom is, to some extent, a matter of chance, as well as of conditions which are not fully understood.

In other words, my suggestion is to explain the slowness of appearance of unconventional terrorism, at least in part, as a typical case of rigidification and lack of innovativeness caused by variables endogenous to terrorism groups and organizations. At least, this conjecture is offered as an important element in a possibly broader set of causes of absence of rapid movement towards unconventional terrorism, with possible other elements being unknown at present.

## LIMITS OF PREDICTABILITY AND THEIR IMPLICATIONS

The approach proposed above leads to the conclusion, that a main factor determining the emergence of unconventional terrorism is the appearance of terrorism-entrepreneurs. What is, therefore, needed is to try and apply innovation and entrepreneurial theory to the question, if and when this critical variable will enter again the stage and produce terrorism-innovations.

As yet both study of the history of terrorism up till now from the perspective of entrepreneurial theory and innovation processes is missing; and entrepreneurial theory as a whole is too underdeveloped to permit application to terrorism (14). Therefore, it is impossible to predict the appearance of terrorism-entrepreneurs, their timing and the directions of their innovations (15).

Rather, we have here a case of structural uncertainty, where the appearance of unconventional terrorism is socially likely, technically feasible, but with essential ingredients being a matter that must be looked at as a chance event, certainly from the perspective of present knowledge and perhaps inherently. This leads to the conclusion that the appearance of unconventional terrorism is a possibility, but no probabilities can be reliably allocated to it (16).

In other words, this is one of the many cases where structural uncertainties face decision-making, with the consequent need to engage in what I call "policy-gambling" (17). The question must be faced, how much effort to devote to prepare ourselves for unconventional terrorism, with its probabilities and forms being unknowable. It should be added that so-called "intelligence indicators" cannot be relied upon, probably manifesting themselves only shortly before unconventional terrorism incidents occur, all the more so as no clear search patterns for indicators can be prescribed in view of the uncertain shape of terrorism to come and the large variety of its possible modes (18).

Applying standard thinking from decision sciences: When a serious possibility is faced and its negative consequences can be significantly reduced with relatively small cost - then the "principle of minimum regret" leads to the conclusion to prepare for the bad contingency (19).

But a number of caveats must be kept in mind, when the above abstract principle is applied to unconventional terrorism:

. a. Detailed prescription is impossible in view of the uncertain shape of possible future unconventional terrorism incidents. Rather, "broad spectrum" preparations are necessary, such as overall strategies, multi-use instruments, high-quality crisis decision-making capacities, and multiple as well as elastic contingency plans.

b. The costs to be paid for preparations must be relatively small, especially when "value-costs" are involved.

c. Much innovativeness is needed. Indeed, this may well be the scarcest of all resources and the one most essential for gearing towards possible unconventional terrorism. This is a matter well worthy of some further exploration.

## A COMPETITION MODEL OF TERRORISM/COUNTER-TERRORISM INNOVATIVENESS

It follows from the earlier analysis, that the future of unconventional terrorism depends significantly, though not exclusively, on the degrees and forms of innovation within terrorism. If and when terrorism-entrepreneurs, inventors and innovators come around - unconventional terrorism will escalate. As is the case in respect to all forms of innovation, its occurence, timing and forms cannot be reliably predicted and its exact forms are shrouded in rigid uncertainty. Still, taking into account the nature of terrorism as embedded in societal processes and the possibilities of terrorism escalation as discussed above - terrorism-entrepreneurs, inventors and innovators have a high probability of occuring. At least, this is a real possibility - with implications as indicated above.

This leads to a proposed model of terrorism/counter-terrorism innovativeness competition, which can take one of three main forms:

One. Terrorism may innovate much more rapidly than counter-terrorism, with the latter lagging behind in responses.

Two. Counter-terrorism may innovate more rapidly, keeping ahead of terrorism-innovations and maintaining a competitive advantage.

Three. Counter-terrorism may adjust rapidly to escalating terrorism, catching up with it soon.

Full analysis of these possibilities, their conditions and probabilities goes beyond the scope of this paper. But three preliminary considerations permit at least a tentative conjecture, which is very disturbing in its implications:

First, while terrorism too tends towards conservatism and routinization, as indicated above, still its structure in the form of multiple small units related in some overlapping networks, as well as additional of its features, may well be more innovation-prone than the standard organizations in charge of anti-terrorism in most countries, whether more located in the police or in the military (20).

Second, even if select counter-terrorism elite units and islands of innovative counter-terrorism thinking are feasible, and exist in a number of cases, still adjustment to escalating terrorism requires significant governmental and soietal learning and readiness to innovate. Thus, tragic choices may have to be faced on readiness to engage in counter-terrorism activities impairing some liberal values and hurting innocent lives, in order to prevent possibly grievous harm by unconventional terrorism. From all we know - such adjustments are difficult and take a long time.

Third, in particular public opinion and social habits may pose rigid barriers on democratic capacities to innovate essential counter-unconventional-terrorism strategies. This is illustrated by recent discussions in the U.S.A. on more forward counter-terrorism actions and tools adopted by the Reagan administration, once rather unavoidable costs become publicly known. The possibility that popular mood may swing and support rather extreme measures following dramatic terrorism-related incidents, as illustrated in Israel, is of no help either - overreaction being very doubtful a mode of response to terrorism. This point leads to possible disadvantages of democracies in handling terrorism - a point to be taken up later on.

It follows, that at best much lag in adjustment of counter-terrorism strategies after terrorism-innovativeness including unconventional terrorism may well be in store. This, in particular on the level of counter-terrorism activities, especially those involving government and requiring changes in social behavior. All the more so, a strenuous effort is needed to upgrade innovativeness in counter-terrorism thinking. If this can be achieved- then there is a good chance to avoid some "worst cases", involving high social costs, over-reactions, societal destabilization, up to inability to handle effectively unconventional terrorism contributing to the decline of democracy in its competition with effective types of command regimes, which may be much better at using as well as containing terrorism.

## ACTION IMPLICATIONS

The last point is especially disturbing: It is the possibility that unconventional terrorism may combine with other strategic handicaps of democracy and result in dangerous disadvantages of democracies in global competition with some command societies - which makes escalating terrorism into an important security issue. After all, mass killing terrorism is not around the corner and direct effects of somewhat escalating terrorism are by themselves disturbing, but not dangerous. But combined effects of escalating terrorism in conjunction with other security predicaments, especially when used by adverse global forces, justify strenuous counter-efforts; this, in addition to the possibilities of unconventional terrorism itself becoming very costly, which too cannot be ignored.

One recommendation thus clearly emerges from our exploration: The possibilities of unconventional terrorism are real enough and its expected costs high enough to justify some preparations. It is unrealistic, and perhaps unjustified as already noted, to suggest preparatory strategies which involve large costs, in values as well as resources. But, it may well be that relatively small investments can provide meaningful hedgings against unconventional terrorism contingencies. At the very least, intense thinking and contingency planning on handling terrorism-innovations are required. Some efforts in this direction do take place, but - as far as is known to me - are rather inadequate. In particular, the terrorism/counter-terrorism innovativeness competition model leads to a requirement for innovative thinking, as well as preparations for innovative and unconventional action,which is hard to realize within governments, and not easy to assure within Think Tanks and similar structures either (21).

Hence the minimum conclusion, that the spectre of unconventional terrorism is real enough to justify establishment of new types of "islands of excellence" to engage in counter-terrorism contingency planning and preparations. This may sound as a banal conclusion. But, compared to the realities in all governments, with some relatively slight deviations, this recommendation is quite radical and its realization requires strenuous efforts.

How to move ahead in the recommended direction, including design of suitable novel structures, professionals and methods alike (22) this is a subject for another paper.

# FOOTNOTES

1.  Yehezkel Dror, Crazy States: A Counterconventional Strategic Problem (supplemented edition, Millwood, N.Y.: Kraus Reprints, 1980).
2.  E.g., see Robert H. Kupperman & Darrell M. Trent, Terrorism: Threat, Reality, Response (Stanford, CA: Hoover Institution Press, 1978).
3.  For a different, but related, perspective see Yehezkel Dror,"Terrorism as a Challenge to the Democratic Capacity to Govern", in Martha Crenshaw, ed., Terrorism, Legitimacy, and Power: The Consequences of Political Violence (Middletown, CO: Wesleyan University Press, 1983), pp. 65-90.
4.  Very relevant is Raymond Boudon, "Why Theories of Social Change Fail: Some Methodological Thoughts", Public Opinion Quarterly, Vol. 47 (1983), pp. 143-160.
5.  This is a good point for underlining limits of the Western Mind, especially of the liberal type, to understanding some terrorism mentalities and its breeding cultures. Thus, the central role of "enemies" in some conceptions of politics, as fully realized by the German political scientist Carl Schmitt and ignored in modern Western political and social sciences - is crucial for comprehending some terrorism mind sets. See Carl Schmitt, Der Begriff des Politischen (Berlin: Duncker & Hamblot, 1963; first, shorter version published in 1927). It is relevant to mention that this book is not available in English.
6.  Very relevant is Karl Jasper, Psychologie der Weltanschauungen (2nd ed., Berlin: Springer, 1960; first published 1922). This book, also not translated as a whole into English, is essential for trying to analyze the personality-functions fulfilled by various terrorism-supporting Weltanschauungen.
7.  Stimulating for relevant speculations is Donald Weinstein and Rudolph M. Nell, Saints and Society: The Two Worlds of Western Christendom, 1000-1700 (Chicago, IL: University of Chicago Press, 1982).
8.  Therefore, it may be necessary to move to a definition of prohibited levels, targets and forms of violence, rather than engage in futile efforts to agree on a definition of "terrorism". Getting rid of motivational aspects of the definition and rather concentrate on agreeing on forbidden "atrocities" - may also permit cooperation between

the main powers on activities directed at inhibiting the emergence of unconventional terrorism, which may well be in the disinterest of all of them. To move in such a direction, quite some changes in legal approaches to "terrorism" are needed, illustrating the later discussed need for innovativeness. Traditional legal approaches, as still prevalent, for instance, in Alona E. Evans and John F. Murphy, eds., Legal Aspects of International Terrorism (Lexington, MA: D.C. Heath, 1978), are inadequate for facing terrorism escalation possibilities. This dimension of the issue is not further considered in the present paper.

9. Compare Jean-Francois Revel, How Democracies Perish (New York: Doubleday, 1984).

10. Successes of governments in facing terrorism till lately do not serve as an indicator of success probabilities in facing new forms of terrorism, which may be qualitatively quite different. Still, such successes should be kept in mind when evaluating the problematics of unconventional terrorism. See Juliet Lodge, ed., Terrorism: A Challenge to the State (New York: St. Martin's Press, 1981); and Ernest Evans, Calling a Truce to Terror: The American Response to International Terrorism (Westport, CO: Greenwood Press, 1979).

11. In particular, emergence of new types of "political romanticism" may combine with religious millenialism to form a real hotbed for unconventional terrorism. Even if this happens only in a few locations and on a limited scale - this is enough to produce a lot of very innovative terrorism.

12. The difficulties for Western thinking to comprehend innovative "counter-cultural" possibilities, as mentioned also in footnote 11 above, are illustrated by Stephen Sloan, Simulating Terrorism (Norman, OK: University of Oklahoma Press, 1981).

   The author of the present paper has participated in quite a number of terrorism simulations in Western countries; never has he seen real "comprehension" of truly fanatic world pictures and their behavioral consequences, including new modes of terrorism. All the more so, in normal, much less "brainstorming"-oriented counter-terrorism organizations it is nearly impossible to "exit" the paradigms of Western mind sets; but this may be essential for reconnaissance of possible futures of unconventional terrorism. Such inbuilt cognitive and other blinders and incapacities of Western Minds and institutions have far-going implications for the required structure, composition and modes of operation of counter-terrorism intelligence and planning, especially in the face of possible terrorism-escalations, including perhaps quantum-jumps. Needed are abilities to "exit" one's culture and its world maps, its attribution theories, its tacit models, etc. - to be able to imagine, comprehend, and "intuite" possible "counter-conventional" terrorism (and other phenomena).

To return to available methodologies, these are clearly unable to meet such needs without first undergoing far-going transformations. E.g., see Nazli Choucri & Thomas W. Robinson, ed., Forecasting in International Relations (San Francisco: Freeman, 1978): all the methods ably presented in this book are clearly inadequate in the face of possible transincremental terrorism-innovations.

13. E.g,, see Irving L. Janis, Groupthink: Psychological Studies of Policy Decisions and Fiascoes (revised edition, Boston: Houghton Mifflin, 1982).

14. E.g. see Mark Casson, The Entrepreneur: An Economic Theory (Totowa, NJ: Barnes & Noble, 1982); & Eugene Lewis, Public Entrepreneurship: Towards a Theory of Bureaucratic Political Power - The Organizational Lives of Hyman Rickover, J. Edgar Hoover and Robert Moses (Bloomington, IN: Indiana University Press, 1980). Application to terrorism requires quite different theories, with more attention to societal variables, inter alia.

15. To go one step further: present lack of understanding of relevant processes not only inhibits prediction of unconventional terrorism, but leaves open the question whether and how far this is predictable a set of phenomena, or inherently a "loaded random", and even quasi-"chaotic" process. However obscure this question may look to most counter-terrorism "practitioners" - it has important applied implications for the longer-range handling of terrorism, such as the possibilities to rely on intelligence and/or the need to maintain a constant "surprise-expecting" posture.

16. Some experts may nevertheless propose the allocation of "subjective probabilities" in such a case. I think this is a very misleading method which must be strictly avoided, because of its tendency to displace explicated real uncertainty with illusions of predictions.

17. See Yehezkel Dror, Policymaking Under Uncertainty (New Brunswick, NJ: Transaction, 1985), chapter 7,

18. This leads to a number of important problems on the limits of intelligence, even at its best, in the face of structural uncertainties, as illustrated by unconventional terrorism; and consequences for strategic preparations. See Yehezkel Dror,"Intelligence as a Policy-Gambling Aid", in work.

19. For readers unfamiliar with relevant concepts, I recommend Ian Hacking, The Emergence of Probability (Cambridge: Cambridge University Press, 1975), chapter 8 - as preferable as a non-technical introduction with a classical illustration to text books of the usual kind, which require quite some initiation.

20. Relevant is Edward N. Luttwak, The Pentagon and the Art of War (New York: Simon and Schuster, 1984).

21. Relevant inadequacies of Think Tanks are especially disturbing. See Yehezkel Dror, "Required Breakthroughs in Think Tanks", Policy Sciences, Vol. 16 (1984), pp. 199-225.

22. Just to provide some indicative illustrations, let me mention the following ones: Needed is application to our subject of better strategic planning and thinking methods, as illustrated by Albert Clarkson, Toward Effective Strategic Analysis: New Applications of Information Technology (Boulding, CO: Westview, 1981); and, with suitable adjustments, William Ascher & William H. Overholt, Strategic Planning & Forecasting: Political Risk and Economic Opportunity (New York: Wiley, 1983). Much more difficult are needed changes in the professional attitudes and practices of police, military and intelligence staffs - to change their "reflection-in-action" (as discussed in Donald A. Schon, The Reflective Practitioner: How Professionals Think in Action (New York: Basic Books, 1983)).

To be frank, even more innovative designs are needed, as yet unavailable in literature and practice alike. Thus, the "policy-gambling" concept illustrates novel perspectives and approaches needed for considering unconventional terrorism possibilities. In thus bringing out the need for much upgraded security planning and analysis capacities the unconventional terrorism issue constitutes a paradigmatic illustration of a much broader requirement for radically augmented policymaking capacities to handle democratically harsher policy predicaments. The necessity to involve governance as a whole, and society at large, makes needed upgradings in democratic capacity to govern, in the broad sense of that term, all the more demanding.

# THE TERRORISM OF LEFT-WINGERS
# IN THE FEDERAL REPUBLIC OF GERMANY
# AND THE COMBAT AGAINST THE TERRORISTS

Dr. Wolfgang Steinke
Bundeskriminalamt
Viesbaden, Germany


The Federal Republic of Germany has not yet experienced exotic acts of terrorism such as the use of poisons, biochemical materials or ionized rays. Yet, the potential issue cannot be summarily dismissed. In Germany there have been threats of unconventional or unusual terrorist acts. In 1983, 993 illegal acts were committed in which it was tried to extort economic institutions of large sums of money. Mostly public institutions were the object (28.3% --- 14 of the incidents were against the German State Railway, and 9 were against water companies). In 27.4% of the incidents, the objects of extortion were supermarkets. In general, the criminals warned of supposed bomb attacks (48 cases) or poison (13 cases), without specifying details. In 9 cases they warned of fire and/or bombing attacks. This paper gives further details about these acts and addresses the question of appropriate police reaction.

In the Federal Republic of Germany the terrorism of the extreme left-wingers up to today as already during the last years is mainly represented by the terrorist groupings "Red Army Fraction (RAF)", the "Revolutionary Cells (RZ)" and some other groupings of the so-called terrorist surrounding.

The manifestation of their activities essentially are given by:

the severe calculated attacks on individuals normally
with the intention to kill as well as bombing
attacks committed by the "RAF",

the arsons and bombing attacks with the aim of damage
to property committed by the "RZ" whose activities
are concentrated on all areas of social conflicts
and

the actions of other terrorist groups including the so-
called surrounding of the "RAF" ranging from simple
agitations and damage to property up to severe
arsons and bombing attacks.

## RED ARMY FRACTION (RAF)

In the late sixties and since that time most important
grouping, the "RAF" started working. In the beginning
it was called "Baader-Meinhof-Bande". At the same time
great disturbances among the students have taken place
in the Federal Republic of Germany.

The first actions of the grouping have been arsons in
two large stores in Frankfurt committed by Baader and
Ensslin, who later became two of the central members of
the "RAF".

After a phase of activity including lots of bank
robberies, thefts of cars and exchanges of shots with
policemen a first culmination was reached in May, 1972
with bombing attacks in Frankfurt, Munich, Karlsruhe,
Hamburg and Heidelberg. These attacks led to the deaths of
four persons and to severe woundings of a lot of individuals.
At that time already the basic targets of these attacks
have been institutions of the US-forces and buildings of
the police.

The first spectacular murder case occurred in Nov. 1974
when they killed the president of the Supreme Court, von
Drenckmann in Berlin, just one day after Holger Meins died
as a result of his hunger strike. It could not be
evaluated whether von Drenckmann has been killed as he
resisted kidnapping or if his death was a calculated murder.

In February 1975 the president of the parliament of
Berlin, Lorenz, was kidnapped. The terrorists - all of
them could be found and convicted - succeeded to get five
imprisoned set free. They have been released in Yemen but
four of them have been caught again in the meantime.

The second culmination of the activities of the RAF
was reached in 1977, when the general prosecutor of the
Federal Republic, Buback, the banker Ponto and the president
of the employers' federation Schleyer with his
accompanists have been killed.

After that followed a time of low activities interrupted by attack on the US-headquarters in Ramstein and the assassination attempt on the US-general Kroesen in Heidelberg. At the end of 1982 people collecting mushrooms found a hidespot in a forest. The deposits found at that place included firearms, ammunitions, money, personal documents and number plates. Besides that there have been deposited some papers containing important information that - after decoding - led to a dozen of other hidespots all located in forests. Some of them were observed for several weeks. So three of the major terrorists, Klar, Mohnhaupt and Schulz, could be caught, when they attempted to go to one of these places.

These events had weakened the terrorist organisation according to its equipment as well as to its personal capacity. The weakening could be enhanced in 1983 when Dutzi and Winter were arrested and Gunter Maria Rausch surrendered.

In March, 1984 the RAF committed a bank robbery in Wurzburg where they have got more than 170,000.--DM.

In June, 1984 Manuela Happe, suspected to be a member of the "RAF", was arrested after an exchange of shots with policemen in Baden-Wurttemberg. She had looked out for the leading judge of the trial versus Christian Klar.

Further important successes in the combat against the central group of the RAF have been given by the seizures of Christa Eckes, Stefan Frey, Ingrid Jakobsmeier, Helmut Pohl, Barbara Ernst and Ernst Staub. This was on July 2, 1984.

On their seizures as well as in lodging in Karlsruhe have been found extensive papers and documents containing:
information on the actual discussion about the
tactical and political plannings of the "RAF" and
its militant surrounding and
information on the future plannings of attacks.

Especially one paper found in a lodging in Frankfurt cleared up this assessment. This paper deals with the strategy of the "Guerilla" meaning the central part of the RAF itself and the "resistance" meaning the people associated with the RAF as well as the activities of the persons already kept in prison.

Concrete ideas of "lines of aggressions" are developed in this paper:
the first "line" is directed against the legal
authorities as well as against the so-called
"organizations of repression"

the second "line" has to continue the combat against
all institutions of armed forces.

The "offensive" of the "commands outside" meaning the
central group of the "RAF" has to be supported by the
members kept in prison being on hunger strike.

The following areas are shown to be of major interest
according to their offensives:
armed forces (US/NATO/forces of the FRG) as
"institutions of imperialism"
security services as "instruments of imperialistic
politics"
legal authorities as "instruments of repression"
institutions of economy and
politics.

According to the devotions to their plannings to carry
out planned actions even if the police has got knowledge
of their plans in November 1984 two young men have attacked
a store of arms in Rheinland-Pfalz and have carried off 22
handguns and two repeating rifles as well as a lot of
ammunition.

In the beginning of December 1984, 37 imprisoned
members of the RAF gradually went on a hunger strike.
They finished the strike in the beginning of February,
1985. This strike originated a wave of solidarity among
their sympathizers accompanied by a lot of bomb attacks
and of arsons (more than eighty events) against
institutions of the government, of the army of the FRG,
of the allied nations, of the NATO and of economy.

One of the bomb attacks against a school of the NATO
in Oberammergau could be detected giving the opportunity
to take care of 25 kg of explosives of military origin.

The presumed perpetrator could be found out after a
few days, but he is now free, because there was no sure proof.

Another planned bombing attack in Stuttgart ended
with the death of the RAF member Timme and with the
severe wounding of his companion.

On the 1st of February in 1985 the president of the
board of the MTU, a factory involved in arms production,
was killed in his house. The perpetrators have succeeded
to enter the house pretending to bring important letters.

Following this murder that was confessed by the RAF
by letter and by phone, the RAF prisoners gradually
finished their hunger strike.

The political and strategic explanations given in the
above mentioned papers found in several lodgings show
the stability and the continued dangerousness of the

grouping. The authors are supposed to belong to the central members of the RAF.

The activity of the RAF to realize the idea of the "antiimperialistic front" in addition to "military" actions has been expanded on well coordinated militant attacks intending common confessions by both the RAF and the militant groups of their sympathizers.

It seems to be sure that with a view to their logistics the members of the RAF are well equipped with arms, explosives, personal documents, money and so on to allow them to live in the underground and to perform politically motivated actions.

With regard to the number of individuals our experts suppose that the central group of the RAF consists of 15 to 20 persons. The number of their supporters cannot be determined exactly but there are about 200 persons belonging to the group of militant followers.

Beyond it the number of sympathizers who, by the way, also are working on the fields of humanity, will reach several thousands. So for example, 1750 individuals have entered a demonstration on the occasion of the above mentioned hunger strike. Afterwards 200 of them went to the tomb of Timme who has died when he prepared a bombing attack.

## REVOLUTIONARY CELLS (RZ)

In comparison with the "RAF" the "Revolutionary cells" or their womens' groupings "Red Zora" respectively are organized in quite another way according to their concepts and structural organization.

The "RZ" have been formed in 1972.

In contrast to the "RAF" the members of the "RZ" are not operating in the underground. They live as normal citizens in "legality" and build up small groups completely independent of other organizations and also without any relationship to other cells. Living in normal surroundings they plan their activities.

The "RZ" have to be characterized as militant groupings although they avoid attacks on individuals with respect to the wished response to their actions in the population. So, for example, after the minister of trade and commerce of the State of Hessen had been killed, the "RZ" have pointed out that his death had been an accident and not a calculated murder.

The attacks of "RZ" are founded on the so-called "strategy of connections" with existing or supposed conflicts.

The basic patterns of their actions are resistance against the exploitation of mankind and of nature committed by institutions of the State and by private organizations.

Consequently the activities of the "RZ" are widespread and cover very different fields of problems like nuclear energy, pollution, microelectronics, unemployment, feminist movement, US-imperialism and many others.

The attacks of the "RZ" are released by actual reports to one of these areas of problems in the media.

Normally explosives prepared by themselves and not commercial ones are used. The suitable targets for their attacks are selected according to the strategy:

to avoid any risk when they commit the crime and

to avoid any injury of persons.

Since 1973 the "RZ" have committed about 300 arsons or bombings most of them in the areas of Frankfurt, Rhein-Ruhr and Berlin.

In 1984 the activities of the "RZ" have significantly dropped compared with the years before (8 attacks in the first half of the year). In 1983 there have been 27 and in 1982, 36 attacks.

The decrease of attacks in the Frankfurt area and the increase in Nordrhein-Westfalen are remarkable.

The reasons given in claiming responsibility of the "RZ" during the last years:

runway West of the Frankfurt airport

womens' problems

combat against the armament of the Nato

Recently have been expanded onto the areas of modern technology (microelectronics and applications of computers). A rather new area of activity is founded in critics on the situations of people kept in prisons. It is expected that the "RZ" in the future will continue their attacks.

Unfortunately the police investigations in the field of "RZ" have not led to similar successes as in the area of "RAF". Mainly due to their "life in legality" it is very difficult to evaluate the personal structures of the individuals and to get evidence.

But we hope that even in the "RZ" area, we will succeed to join chains of evidences consisting of single information that will lead us to the individuals who have committed the attacks. So it should be possible to be successful in the investigation of these terrorist organizations.

As a first step we succeeded to find connections between different scenes of bombing attacks by analysis of the used explosives. Perpetrators could not be found until now. From the viewpoint of the "RZ" their strategy and tactics are very successful. Therefore, their behavior can be an example for other potential militant groups.

## THE TERRORIST "SURROUNDING"

The so-called "TE-Surrounding" consists of followers of the "RAF" and of other groupings acting in a terrorist way. Several thousands of individuals are estimated to belong to these groupings including sympathizers as well as supporters of terrorists.

The activities of these groupings range from scrawling and damage to property up to severe arson and bomb attacks.

The members of these groupings operate like the "RZ" living in "legality". Mainly in cases of arsons and bomb, attacks they try to realize the ideas of the "RAF" but without accepting the eminent position of the command group of the "RAF".

The reasons that they give for their attacks are widespread and range from fight against imperialism and factories involved in arms production up to fight against factories working with computer systems.

Any uniform ideologies or tactics are not detectable.

Some of these groupings have attempted to gain a foothold in the "peace movement" by use of force but until now without any success.

About 70 bomb attacks of the year 1983 have been committed by militant followers of the "RAF" and some other terrorist groups of the "surrounding". From January to September 1983/4 attacks have been committed by "RAF" followers whereas the other groupings of the "surrounding" have done 17 attacks in the same time.

## SUMMARY OF ARSONS AND BOMBING ATTACKS IN 1984 UNTIL THE END OF SEPTEMBER

Until th e end of September 1984 there have been 128 cases of arson and bombing attacks. 106 of the arsons and 14 bombing attacks cannot be assigned to defined groupings.

The "RZ" have manifested themselves with 7 bombing attacks and one arson whereas the groupings of the "surrounding" have committed 20 attacks, mainly arsons. 4 attacks have been done by terrorists of the extreme right-wing and 4 by foreign groupings.

Targets of the attacks have been building firms,

security services, authorities, financial institutions and other private concerns.

The dramatic increase of the number of attacks in the beginning of 1985 is due to solidarity of the groupings with prisoners being on hunger strike.

## SITUATION OF THE POLICE IN THE COMBAT AGAINST TERRORISM

First, I have to describe the different possibilities for investigations in the field of terrorism given in the Federal Republic of Germany.

The combat against terrorist attacks requires a well functioning collaboration obligate for all organizations of the single states and the Federal Republic.

A planned structuring of the leading organization and the institutions of investigation as well as the clear definition of responsibilities and the lines of informations and orders has proved to be necessary in several cases. The system has been successful in many cases.

An extensive planning ahead has to give to the police the opportunity to start immediately the investigations and searches. They must be able to get an overview and to canalize all tips and traces.

It has proved to be extremely helpful to be supported by data processing. To evaluate all tips and traces it is necessary to establish a central documentation. This documentation in special cases is founded on a permanent documentation where all knowledges about terrorists and their associated persons, institutions, objects and properties are stored. To identify terrorist criminals when caught the Federal Bureau of Investigation in Germany has centrally collected - insofar as possible - all identification data of terrorist for example skin ledge pictures of hands and feet, photographs, motion pictures, laboratory examination results pertaining to blood, hair, saliva, handwriting, sound recordings, dentition, x-rays, description of personal characteristics, habits and behavioral patterns.

To be able to evaluate the papers of terrorists the Bundeskriminalamt has established a central documentation of terrorist writings. With the aid of this documentation and using the data files of "Linguistic Text Analysis", which are still a research project, we intend to get sure informations about the authors of so-called "Confessions" to evaluate connections between writers or actions respectively.

The search for terrorists is done by specially educated investigation groups. The only responsibility of these "target-searching-commands" is the search for one or more individuals of interest.

Concerning the combat against terrorism the so-called "police-observation" is an inalienable kind if investigation. In this field persons of the terrorist surrounding and their motor vehicles can be announced and stored in the investigation data files. Every police office all over the Federal Republic has access to these data files. At the boarders these data files can be accessed by radio with movable terminals.

These measures, that should not be realized by the suspects, shall help to gain further details of suspicion.

Analysis of the behaviors of terrorists have led to systematized investigations, also known as "scanning investigations". Certain knowledges about persons and their habits (for example to rent preferred lodgings in large apartment houses with good connections to traffic lines and to pay the bills of current cash in contrast to common behavior) allow to develop criteria of selection.

With this method it is possible to select a certain group of suspect persons. Further criteria of selection allow to narrow down the number of suspect individuals. These persons than can be observed and by occusion convicted to be involved in a crime.

Inspite of these demonstrated conceptional and programatic measures in the combat against terrorism we may not forget, that especially in this field of crime, careful criminalistic detailed work is of extraordinary value. We have got essential starting points for the investigation by method of searching of traces on a high scientific level. The careful search and collection of traces have made it possible to find evidences in lodgings left by the terrorists, even if they have tried to remove carefully all traces.

These evidences have helped to identify some of the terrorists.

Objects used by the criminals to commit the crime are very carefully determined with respect to their origin.

The police offices all over the Federal Republic have made an arrangement to consult in allimportant cases of terrorist crime the special troup of crime-scene investigation of the Bundeskriminalamt.

We succeded to decode the writings of the "RAF" by time consuming work with rigorous attention to detail. Presupposed was a detailed knowledge of the way of thinking of the "RAF". So for example we were able to discover a lot of depots of the RAF after the finding of the first hidespot as above mentioned. The observation of the conversation of arrested terrorists with their visitors (about 60 of them are observed) makes it sure, that the informations cannot leave the prison. The terrorists try to avoid this by use of codes. But when this happens, the visit will be interrupted.

The activities of the police in the combat against terrorism may not be left isolated. If necessary they have to be supported by decisions of the legislative.

The above-mentioned measures cannot be complete: So for example, the problems of persons who give states evidences according to the italian "lex cossiga" as well as contact persons or undercover agents have to be discussed.

The trustful international collaboration is also helpful for effective combat against terrorism. This collaboration has to be intensified.

To keep terrorist activities on a low level international out-lawing of terrorism according to a world right principle would be very helpful.

But this seems to be nearly impossible for you have to consider that already the definition of the term "terrorism" will not be accepted by all states in the same way.

FIREARMS EXAMINATION IN A TERRORIST SITUATION

Mr. J. S. Wallace
Northern Ireland Forensic Science Laboratory
180 Newtownbreda Road
Belfast-Northern Ireland BT8 4QR

   The current terrorist campaign and the forensic aspects
of firearms examination in Northern Ireland are discussed
and a comparison is made between firearms examination in
a terrorist and a non-terrorist situation.
   Northern Ireland is now and has been for sixteen years,
subjected to a terrorist campaign, however, the rule of law
continues, industry is expanding, tourism is returning to
what it once was and whilst we have terrorist incidents
these incidents cause very little disruption to everyday
life.
   To explain the work of a laboratory dealing with a
terrorist situation it is necessary to give a brief
explanation of the background to terrorism.

Northern Ireland is part of the United Kingdom but it is also part of the island of Ireland. The remainder of Ireland is a Republic and is an independent sovereign nation with no political ties to any other country. Whilst it is the wish of the Government of the Republic to unite the whole of Ireland by political and peaceful means there are people, mostly Catholics, both north and south of Ireland, who wish to expel the British from Ireland by use of the bomb and the bullet.

On the other hand there are people in Northern Ireland, mostly Protestants, who wish to maintain the position of Northern Ireland within the United Kingdom and who will use the bomb and the bullet to further their own ends.

It must be stressed that amongst all these nationalists and unionists it is only a very small number who are involved in terrorism.

The end result of the civil unrest is that there are shootings and bombings both of members of the security forces and of people who are suspected of being associated with one side or the other, and armed robberies to finance the various causes, but I can assure you that we will never be reduced to a state of anarchy.

## NUMBER OF PEOPLE KILLED BY TERRORISM 1969 - 1984

TOTAL DEAD    2410
(727 Security Forces: 1683 Civilians)
(645 Explosives: 1765 Firearms)

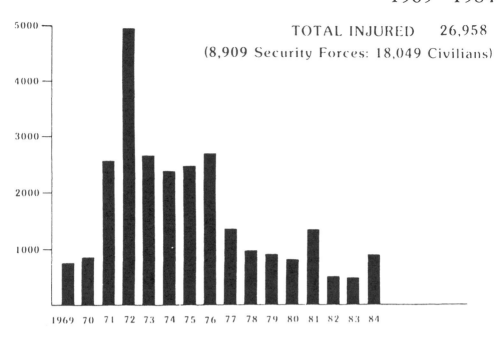

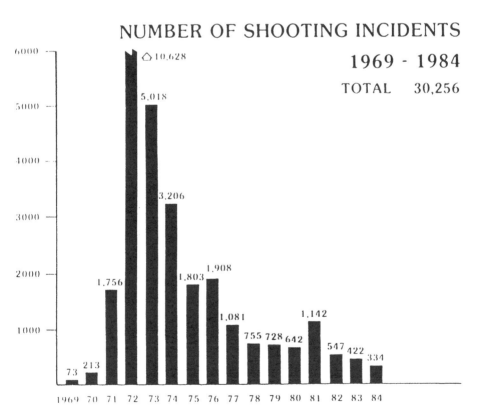

# NUMBER OF EXPLOSIONS 1969 - 1984

TOTAL 7,980

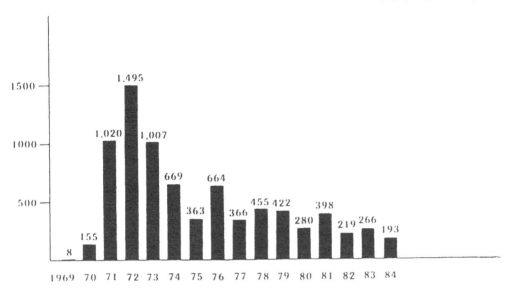

# NUMBER OF ARMED ROBBERIES 1971 - 1984

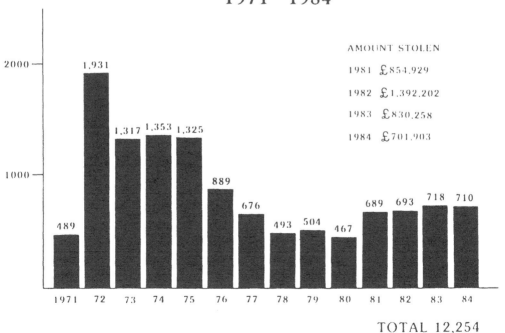

AMOUNT STOLEN
1981 £854,929
1982 £1,392,202
1983 £830,258
1984 £701,903

TOTAL 12,254

|  | ROAD ACCIDENTS 1969 - 1984 | TERRORIST CAMPAIGN 1969 - 1984 |
|---|---|---|
| DEATHS | 4,434 | 2,410 |
| INJURIES | 120,707 | 26,958 |

<u>NORTHERN IRELAND FORENSIC SCIENCE LABORATORY</u>

It is essential for any laboratory dealing with civil unrest to take the firm view that the law of the land is the only yardstick by which all criminal activity is measured and that assassinations, punishment shootings, shootings by the Army and Police, shootings of the Army and Police etc., are all shooting incidents and all demand a full and impartial investigation.

Up to sixteen years ago there was only one person in our laboratory who, in addition to his normal casework as a Chemist, dealt with approximately ten firearms cases per year and these were mainly suicides, accidental discharges or the misuse of legally held firearms. Seldom did we have firearms used in crime.

In 1969 brooding civil unrest unleashed the gunman and the use of firearms in violent crime escalated and at the peak of the trouble the laboratory was dealing with approximately 2,800 firearms cases per year. Apart from the volume of casework the majority of the cases were of a serious nature and many of the examinations were complex.

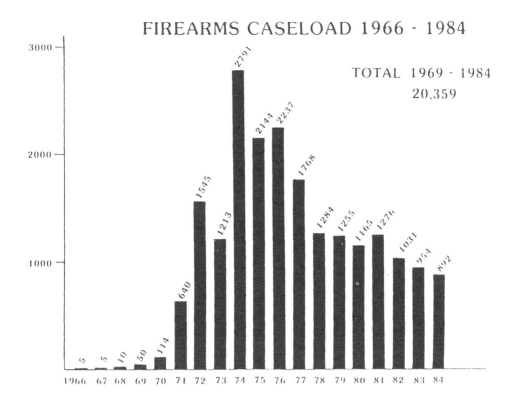

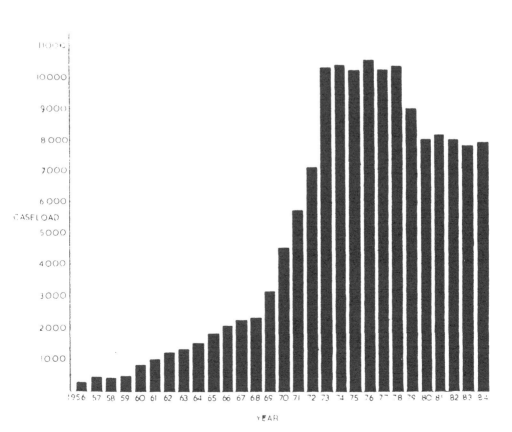

## FIREARMS EXAMINATION

The equipment and methods employed by the firearms section do not differ from those used by other forensic laboratories. The section undertakes all forensic aspects of firearms examination, both chemical and physical.

## MAJOR WORK AREAS OF THE FIREARMS SECTION

### WEAPONS

Examination of firearms, ammunition and associated items.

Examination of firearms and associated items for anything of forensic interest. eg blood, hairs, fibres etc.

Comparison microscopy on spent bullets and spent cartridge cases.

Identification of weapon types from spent cartridge cases.

Serial number restoration.

Research and development projects.

### CHEMICAL

Examination of swabs and clothing from suspects for firearms discharge residue using Scanning Electron Microscopy (SEM MPA)

Examination of clothing and miscellaneous items - identification of bullet holes, differentiation between entry and exit holes, range of fire determination etc.

Identification of bullet strike marks, firing points etc., using SEM MPA and Atomic Absorption Spectrophotometry (AAS)

Chemical comparison of bullet fragments by AAS

Research and development projects.

The section also provides a 24 hour, 7 day a week call-out service to the Security Forces. We are available to attend scenes of crime which are large, controversial or too difficult for the Police Scenes of Crime Officers to deal with. There are aspects of scenes of crime examination that most other laboratories do not experience such as the possibility of booby traps or sniper attack, the scenes are often in hostile areas consequently the time to examine a scene may be very limited and many of the scenes extend over a large area, involve a large number of people and exhibits and are of a controversial nature.

Police have been fired at whilst examining scenes of crime and in one incident two policemen were killed by a booby trapped shotgun when one of them attempted to check if the firearm was loaded. On another occasion a booby-trapped rifle was received at the laboratory but fortunately the explosive device was discovered before the weapon was test fired. We now x-ray all firearms and associated items before examination.

Greater than 80% of our casework involves terrorism and this can be demonstrated by a breakdown of our 1984 caseload.

# FIREARMS CASELOAD 1984

| | | |
|---|---|---|
| SHOOTING INCIDENTS | 219 | |
| ARMED ROBBERY | 41 | |
| PUNISHMENT SHOOTINGS (Kneecappings) | 7 | TERRORIST CONNECTIONS (739) |
| POSSESSION | 28 | |
| ARMS FINDS | 444 | |
| SUICIDES | 43 | |
| MISCELLANEOUS | 110 | |
| TOTAL | 892 | |

A particular firearm can be active over many years in terrorist hands and may or may not be recovered. A link report is a report that connects two or more shooting incidents by comparative microscopy on spent cartridge cases and/or fired bullets and we are often required to provide such reports for court purposes. This can involve a large amount of work as the following case illustrates.

In this case 605 spent cartridge cases and 46 spent bullets had to be examined and in addition to the 27 original reports a further 19 link reports were required for court purposes.

Link reports of this size would rarely be undertaken by other laboratories and are a direct consequence of terrorist activity.

An interesting observation from doing link reports of this nature is that, for firearms used over a number of years, we can nearly always match spent cartridge cases whereas we are frequently unable to match all of the spent bullets. It is our experience that terrorist weapons are generally neglected and that fouling inside the barrel, storage under poor conditions etc., leads to rusting and wear inside the barrel which can substantially alter the striation markings on the bullet.

During the course of the terrorist campaign in Northern Ireland a large number of illegal firearms have been involved, some of which were already in the country from previous terrorist campaigns, some were wartime souvenirs, some were homemade, some were stolen from legal owners but the bulk of them were imported illegally into the country.

# FIREARMS USED
## IN VARIOUS SHOOTING INCIDENTS

| DATE | INCIDENT | ORIGINAL REPORTING OFFICER | WEAPON | | | | | |
|---|---|---|---|---|---|---|---|---|
| | | | 1 | 2 | 3 | 4 | 5 | 6 |
| 5 1 76 | Murder | A | | | | • | | |
| 1 4 76 | Murder | A | | | | • | | |
| 8 4 76 | Explosion | A | | • | | | | |
| 22 8 76 | Shooting | B | | | | | • | |
| 28 8 76 | Att. Murder | C | | | | | • | |
| 4 9 76 | Shooting | A | | | | | | |
| 3 10 76 | Att. Murder | B | | | • | • | | |
| 9 11 76 | Murder | D | • | | | | | |
| 6 12 76 | Att. Murder | D | • | | | | | |
| 26 1 77 | Att. Murder | A | | | | • | | |
| 27 1 77 | Att. Murder | B | | | | • | | |
| 8 2 77 | Shooting | C | | | | • | • | |
| 10 3 77 | Att. Murder | B | | | | • | | |
| 15 3 77 | Murder | A | | | | • | | |
| 20 3 77 | Att. Murder | B | | | | • | | |
| 28 3 77 | Murder | A | • | • | • | • | | |
| 7 4 77 | Shooting | B | | | | • | | |
| 7 4 77 | Att. Murder | B | | • | | | • | |
| 8 4 77 | Murder | A | • | | | | • | |
| 17 4 77 | Att. Murder | A | | | | • | | |
| 22 5 77 | Att. Murder | A | | | | • | | |
| 22 6 77 | Att. Murder | A | | | | • | • | • |
| 6 11 77 | Att. Murder | A | | | | • | | |
| 9 3 78 | Att. Murder | A | | | | | • | |
| 16 4 78 | Att. Murder | B | | | | • | | |
| 11 7 78 | Fatal Shooting | B | | | | • | | |
| 24 1 79 | Shooting | A | | | | | • | |

All link reports done by reporting officer A

WEAPONS

1. .38 Spl. Charter Arms Rev. No 148932    Recovered  8 4 77
2. 9mmP Luger Pistol No 238    Recovered 17 3 78
3. .30-06 M1 Garand No 747314    Recovered 28 5 77
4. .223 Armalite Rifle No removed    Recovered 11 7 78
5. .223 Armalite Rifle No removed    Recovered 24 1 79
6. .223 Armalite Rifle    Not Recovered

# FIREARMS RECOVERED
## 1976 - 1984 = 3,778

| COUNTRY | MANUFACTURE | APPROX% | OBTAINED | APPROX% |
|---|---|---|---|---|
| U.S.A. | 1031 | 27% | 945 | 25% |
| G.B. | 751 | 20% | 137 | 3.5% |
| BELGIUM | 358 | 9% | 186 | 5% |
| N.IRELAND | 269(Homemade) | 7% | 780 | 21% |
| SPAIN | 240 | 6% | — | — |
| GERMANY | 215 | 6% | — | — |
| W.GERMANY | 152 | 4% | — | — |
| ITALY | 142 | 4% | — | — |
| CZECHOSLOVAKIA | 131 | 4% | — | — |
| OTHERS | 448(25 Countries) | 12% | 75(13 Countries) | 2% |
| NOT KNOWN | 41 | 1% | 1655 | 43.5% |

The firearms most frequently used by the terrorist are given below.

# FIREARMS MOST FREQUENTLY USED BY TERRORISTS

|  | TYPE | CALIBRE |
|---|---|---|
| RIFLES | COLT AR15 M16 | .223 |
|  | H&K 91 & 93 | .223 & 7.62NATO |
|  | GARAND | .30-06 |
|  | REMINGTON WOODSMASTER | .308 & .30-06 |
|  | RUGER MINI 14 | .223 |
|  | SKS | 7.62x39 |
|  | AK-47 | 7.62x39 |
|  | M1 CARBINE | .30 |
|  | SAEN | .30-06 |
|  | SIG MANURHIN } Very | 222 & .243 |
|  | ENC } recent | .223 |
| PISTOLS & REVOLVERS | BROWNING HP | 9mmP |
|  | CZ MODEL 70 | 7.65mm |
|  | S&W REVOLVERS | Mainly .38Spl& .357Mag |
|  | COLT 1911 | .45ACP |
| SHOTGUNS | VARIOUS | 12 BORE |
| SUB-MACHINE GUNS | BERETTA MODEL 12 | 9mmP |
|  | VIGNERON | 9mmP |
|  | MP40 | 9mmP |
|  | INGRAM | 9mmP & .45ACP |
| MACHINE GUNS | M-60 | 7.62NATO |
|  | BROWNING | .30-06 |
|  | BROWNING | .50 |

A further sinister aspect of the terrorist campaign is the use of heavy weaponry such as rocket launchers, mortars and heavy machine guns. Items of this nature have been used to attack security force bases and vehicles and on more than one occasion Army helicopters have been struck by large calibre machine gun fire.

## FIREARMS STATISTICS

Firearms and associated items, ammunition, spent bullets and spent cartridge cases recovered over the past 16 years from arms finds, scenes of crime, etc., provide useful information of an intelligence nature.

The majority of the firearms recovered are rifles, revolvers, pistols, shotguns and machine guns but items of a more unusual nature have been recovered including anti-tank rifles, rocket launchers, grenade launchers, flare pistols, air weapons, antiques, starting pistols, toy guns, riot guns, gas guns, humane killers, harpoon guns, industrial nail guns, line throwing guns, replicas, try guns, cross-bows, zip guns, range finding binoculars, telescopic sights, tools, reloading and cleaning equipment, spare parts for a wide range of firearms, silencers, holsters, ammunition belts, etc.

A wide range of items of a ballistics nature have been retained over the years and a large amount of information is stored on a computer. This data base is a valuable aid to police investigating officers and a similar intelligence framework operates for explosives and explosive devices.

Immediately after a shooting incident it is essential that the type of gun used and the history (if any) of the gun is established quickly. This can show which terrorist group last used the gun and the area in which the gun was last used thereby giving the Police an indication of where to look for the culprit and who are the likely suspects. Also in the case of motiveless shootings, if a link can be established with other shootings then the organization responsible may be identified. If a gun has a history of use and suspects are apprehended then the history of the gun opens up a further line of questioning.

Another aspect of intelligence work is the possiblity of tracing firearms or associated items back to the original supplier in another country and through examination of company records, receipts, etc., trace the route of the gun to Ireland. This can lead to information about the purchaser and those involved in gun running and can very occasionally result in prosecutions of those involved. Such prosecutions have taken place in the USA and Australia.

Propaganda is a valuable weapon and has been used effectively by the terrorist. The data base on firearms is frequently used by the Police, Army, Politicians and other official bodies to counter terrorist propaganda. Apart from armed robberies terrorist finance their causes by donations from sympathizers both in Ireland and in other countries and this is one example where facts are essential in order to inform supporters about the deeds and the nature of the persons and organizations that they are financially encouraging.

## SUMMARY

The main differences between firearms examination in a terrorist and non-terrorist situation are that in a terrorist situation more cases tend to be of a serious nature, casework involves a wider variety of firearms and related items, more and larger link reports are required, there are different conditions and more difficulties with scene examination and finally there is an intelligence aspect to the work.

DOCUMENTS & FORGERY
IN
TERRORIST OPERATIONS

Dr. Jay Levinson
Division of Criminal Identification
Israel National Police Headquarters
Jerusalem

Forgery is one of the major tools which international terrorists have used to spread their message and to enable their operations. This paper discusses three uses of forgery: (1) operational use such as forged identify documents, (2) justification for the terrorist to react to an incident described in a forged document (but where the incident never took place), (3) psychological terror, where a forged document alleges an impending (though totally fictititous) danger. Examples are given of each of these uses of forgery, and the question of fabrication without actually surfacing a document is also discussed.

## INTRODUCTION

A serious terrorist incident, such as the 30 May 1972 Japanese Red Army attack on Lod Airport's passenger and baggage processing area, immediately gains headlines in the press. What virtually always is ignored, however, are the careful though not very glamourous stages of planning, logistics and operational support.

It is obvious that a well conceived plan with clear objectives is an important element in the "success" of a terrorist incident, but no terrorist organization can operate without a well run support mechanism. This includes not only the ordinary logistical support associated with purchases of standard items such as weapons or airline tickets; it also encompasses technical operational support such as the supply of forged passports or concealment devices for explosives.

A very small terrorist unit can operate quite adequately without elaborate support, but the natural consequence is a limitation on the type of activities possible. Thus, even in the best organized unit where the members possess a wide range of technical skills, it is still necessary to find a larger support apparatus if activities are to expanded on any large scale.

The natural outgrowth of this support problem is that as smaller terrorist organizations gain sophistication and want to widen their activity base, they are forced to associate if not amalgamate with other larger groups who, if they do not have identical interests, at least have non-conflicting interests. The use of the support facilities is, to be certain, a most saleable commodity, and very often the smaller terrorist group is charged a price, not in common currency, but in services to be rendered.

## THE JRA: AN EXAMPLE AT WORK

An example of this phenomenon at work is the already cited case of the Japanese Red Army, originally a small group of Peking-inspired leftists operating on a very modest scale in Japan. Until their association with the PLO and the Arab cause, one might even say that their internal squabbles and resultant deaths caused more headlines than their actual terrorist activity.

The attraction of the Japanese Red Army to the PLO was not ideological, since their focus was far from the Middle Eastern conflict. Although their basic philosophy did call for a unification of revolutionary forces throughout the world --- a Terrorist International, for want of a better term --- the major benefit of establishing a working relationship went beyond a mere exchange of rhetorical diatribes. The JRA was admitted to the PLO's training bases; it made contact with the international flow of weapons to terrorists, it received the assistance of a large support network, and it was called upon to pay the price...at Lod Airport.

By accepting the training of the PLO, the Japanese received instruction not only in such routine terrorist skills as weapons and explosives; these anxious revoltionaries were exposed to a diet of political thought which they devoured with fervor and zeal in a very understandable desire to earn a welcome with their Palestinian hosts. The side effect, however, was to provide the willing Japanese with indoctrination that would be a critical facet in later operations.

It is still unknown exactly why the Japanese descended upon Lod Airport and opened fire murdering twenty-six innocent travelers and airport workers. In all probability it was a "graduation exercise" with full use of tradecraft, not only to show mastery of terrorist skills, but to finally bring the name of the obscure Japanese Red Army to international headlines on a scale never before thought possible...and to pay that all-important training bill to the PLO.

For a novice or inexperienced terrorist organization the Lod massacre had a number of basic support elements which could only be taught and supplied by a larger group. This included, but was not restricted to, casing of Rome and Lod Airports, weapons concealment techniques and intelligence for border inspection, and forged passports.

## FORGED PASSPORTS: AN EXAMPLE OF SUPPORT

The need for forged documents is a paramount consideration for a terrorist organization and its support mechanism since it is a critical aspect in many phases of work. These documents are not only needed for casing or operational travel; they are needed to rent and manage safe houses; they are also used as convenient tools to hide true names and the records of itinerary of persons traveling to training sites in co-operating countries (such as the USSR, Cuba, North Korea, South Yemen, Syria/Lebanon, etc.).

A more detailed look at the question of the forged passports which the Japanese received can give a better understanding to the entire matter of support.

From all reports available, it is clear that the three Japanese who partook in the Lod action departed for the operation from a training base in Greater Syria, yet no Lebanese or Syrian cachets appeared in the forged Japanese passports with which they were provided. This is only natural; although Israel does admit into the country bearers of passports with Arab state markings, such notations would serve only to raise attention and perhaps intensify border control scrutiny. Therefore, it is clear that the team had to travel on other documentation from the Middle East to Europe. Only in Frankfurt were they provided with their bogus papers.

The preparation of a forged passport is not a simple exercise within the capability of a small group. Not only are materials and a photographic-binding-printing facility required; care and experience in the proper fill-in of the documents coupled with the availability of adequate reference materials can often be the deciding factor in avoiding detection.

For these reasons, the JRA members never enjoyed the use of false documentation during the earlier period of their organization. It was one of the "benefits" of joining forces with the PLO.

In passport forgery, as in many other types of printing, it is first copy off the press that is expensive; further printings of the same item are relatively simple. Hence, it is the first and it is not at all realistic to suppose that the Lebanese based forgery center of the PFLP printed only the three passports used in the Lod operation. Reason and knowledge of other operations dictate that a substantial number of these forgeries were printed for JRA use. It can also be safely assumed that the same center printed forged passports of other nationalities as well.

Although at least one of the three Lod terrorists had surveyed El Al security procedures using his own genuine Japanese passport, it can be shown that two Japanese Red Army members found "casing" Stockholm's Airport had forged Japanese passports; the same forged printing was used in the 1975 JRA attack on the U.S. Embassy in Kuala Lumpur, and in numerous "quiet" operations as well.

It should be noted that even the equipping of the Japanese trio for their final journey to Lod Airport was an activity that took the co-ordinated operational support capable only in a larger organization. The three received their weapons, not at the onset of their journey from Beirut, but at the beginning of the final leg from Rome. This is only reasonable. It would have been pointless to risk discovery of the weapons during border inspection on entry to Germany (where the passports were obtained) or Italy . Thus, the logistical mechanism had to be available to supply both weapons and concealment in two different locations, each at a considerable distance from the home base of the organization.

An aspect of support which should not be overlooked is that it stands very near the "nerve center" of the well-coordinated terrorist apparatus. If compartmentation for good security requires that a forger know an absolute minimum beyond the expertise of his finger skills, a higher echelon must be privy to the details of planned operations so that appropriate documents can be decided upon. A counter-terrorism offensive on this select layer in the general structure is most effective, since it can cause a significant disruption in the flow of appropriate support to operations.

## EXPANDING INTO PROPAGANDA

Although the immediate objective of a forgery operation is the limited function of supplying bogus identification and travel documentation, one of the basic goals of terrorism is to spread a political message. The "success" of Lod was not in the number of persons killed; it was in raising the name of the Japanese Red Army from obscurity to international headlines. Therefore, all appropriate parts of the terrorist apparatus should be geared to maximize their publicity, or propaganda, potential.

In fact, a terrorist act does not have to be true or real. It just has to be believed. When the Voice of Palestine prides itself almost daily on non-existant raids into Israeli territory, the gullable take satisfaction. When a real incident of minor significance is blown totally out of proportion, all the more people can react.

The role of propaganda in terrorism can be best understood by looking at it in context. The actual purposes of transnational terrorism today are several:

> - to force democratic states to respond in a totalitarian fashion (as Uruguay has done to squash the Tupamaro threat, therefore alienating the citizen population
>
> - to raise the cost of defense to an astronomical level, ruining the local economy, and channeling the resultant economic unrest again the government (as happened in Batista's Cuba)
>
> - to weaken international support for a country by highlighting, even through terrorist deeds, the position of a supposedly oppressed minority (a goal of today's PLO)

Thus, properly tuned propaganda can be used to further all three goals.

By stressing the continuous counter-insurgency threat in as many different media as possible (radio, television, newspapers, hand-bills, books, etc.), the true dimensions of the threat are lost, and an over-reaction can be encouraged. When isolated incidents of over-reaction, whether real or notional, are then publicized, citizens often will protest against their own government to show their dis-satisfaction. These protests then serve to further fuel the propaganda mechanism.

Propaganda can be an effective tool in fueling unrest and funneling it against the government. In the sphere of economics, for example, highlighting the successes of terrorism in the press has brought us not only to fear terror in places where it has never happened; it has also encouraged us to make considerable expenditures in insure objectives that just "might" be terrorist targets.

Terrorism certainly has succeeded in raising the "Palestinian issue" into the world headlines, and an effective use by the PLO and other sympathyzing organizations has managed to impress a significant part of the world with a version of conceptions particularly favourable to the Arab point of view. One might well say that Israel has suffered propaganda losses far beyond her few defeats on the field of battle. Today, the question of Palestinians receives worldwide attention while minority populations in countries such as Burma and the Soviet Union go ignored despite a much more factual basis.

Propaganda is a broad subject which cannot be treated adequately in the context of this paper. It can take many forms, but what is relevant here is that very often the support mechanism of the terrorist apparatus is called upon, to assist in both the printing and distribution of materials.

In the early 1970's, for example, terrorists caught in Switerland carried literature justifying their act which was commited in the same freedom fighting spirit that drove William Tell to fight for the liberation of his homeland. The same letter, minus the name of the Swiss national hero, was also used in another terrorist operation, this time in Cyprus. Many terrorist leaflets are distributed locally by a small cell with access to a typewriter and mimeograph machine; the "William Tell Letter," on the other hand, was handled by the much larger formal support unit.

Another type of propaganda which is often encountered is the total forgery of a political document, and just as the support unit provides false passports and identification documents, they frequently manufacture these forgeries as well.

To be certain, the personal skills required to print and fill in a passport are most different from those needed to fabricate materials of political importance. The passport worker can cope with a set routine, and the propagandist must have a fertile imagination matched with a good understanding of basic world trends. But, both types of forgery meet in the printing presses of the support mechanism. Passports are forged to further operational objectives, but political documents are fabricated for other purposes:

        - as an alternative type of propaganda designed to influence the public
        - to provide terrorists with a supposed

(though in fact quite ficticious) incident to which a reaction can be
staged
- as an item which is, in itself, a
threat of terror

## A CUBAN EXAMPLE

An interesting use of forgery that can be
cited as an example of forgery to lay the groundwork to excuse a violent response is the 1958
fabrication by Fidel Castro's rebels of a picture
of one of Batista's aircraft supposedly parked at
the U.S. airbase at Guantanamo. This forgery then
gave Castro the "justification" to strike against
U.S. interests in Cuba. A U.S. military transport
was hijacked, and twenty-eight sailors and ma-
rines were held hostage together with managerial
personnel from an American industrial company.
Raul Castro tried to manoeuver U.S. Ambassador
Earl E.T. Smith to lose face and negociate for the
prisoners' release.

An important aspect here is that forgery and
fabrication were used as a co-ordinated aspect of
terrorist operations. This is a good example
where the forgery was not a document; it was a
picture.

## A FORGERY SURFACED IN INDIA

The Denholm forgery of 1968 is a good example
where the forgery itself posed the threat of terror. A forged letter on U.S. military stationery
was prepared over the photographically lifted
signature of Col. Denholm. The letter, carryiing
the message that supposed deaths from bubonic
plague in the Calcutta area had been linked to
stockpiles of U.S. bacteriological warfare, caused
an anti-American panic as the Indian press picked
up the story.

A parallel to this forgery surfaced in Italy
in the late 1970's. The forgery, written along
the same lines as the Denholm forgery in India,
alleged that the U.S. had stockpiled chemical
warfare in the Naples. This time the effort fell
on deaf ears, but if American reports can be

believed, it was another effort of the Russian KGB support mechanism.

## INTERNATIONAL INVOLVEMENT

The support mechanism of any terrorist operation is a primary target, however the many facets of its operation dictate that no single approach working alone is adequate to thwart its operations. This is complicated by the governmental support given to terrorism by certain countries such as the Soviet Union and Libya. In these cases, the terrorists are only stand-ins for those who assist, supply, and continually re-supply them. Most of these countries do not engage in terrorist operations. They prefer the more discreet support function, and they fully recognize its critical importance.

# FORENSIC BALLISTICS IN COUNTER-INSURGENCY WARFARE

Richard A. Petluck, Superintendent
Israel National Police
Jerusalem

Unfortunately, there have been a number of terrorist actions which have been committed or planned for commission in Israel. This, coupled with materials discovered during the Peace for Galilee Operation, has given the author an up-to-date view of those weapons currently in the hands of terrorists. Some of these weapons are discussed in this paper, and links between terrorist groups throughout the world are made based uupon weapons used. The issue of an international flow of weapons to terrorists is raised, and the author shows clearly the results of forensic bullet examinations done at the scenes of terrorist actions in Israel.

## INTRODUCTION

As counter-insurgency warfare involves hit and run attacks by small armed bands of terroreists, identification of the materials recovered at the scene of incidents must be swift. Unless the area is sealed and air/ground searches instituted immediately, the insurgents, aided and abetted by their local supporters, return by pre-determined escape routes.

The concept proposed by the author involves battle zone ballistics examinations of materials and suspects. This was conceptualized from lessons learned in Vietnam and Northern Ireland several years prior to the recent war in Lebanon.

Vietnam was a massive example of counter-insurgency warfare. It was the first such conflict encountered by the United States, and little was done in the area of scientific examination of both attack scenes and evidence recovered therein. The United States elected to respond with massive retaliation --- the "Iron Fist" --- without including the "Velvet Glove."

The ongoing struggle in Northern Ireland employs the use of forensic examinations of evidence by experts in many fields within the Northern Ireland Constabulary. Unlike Lebanon, this region is more urban than rural, allowing intelligence and forensic experts to function much as they would in normal criminal investigations.

## THE PROBLEM IN LEBANON

Lebanon, on the other hand, had (a little more than a year after the war's start on 6 June 1982) became became more like China under the Warlords or Europe during the Medieval Period, with each combattant group acting like a feudal fiefdom involved in inter-group rivalry and combat as often as engaging the Israeli enemy. It was this fragmentation which permitted the Israel Defense Force (IDF) to determine within each region which terrorist organization was the dominant insurgent group.

Since 1974 the author of this paper had been examining ballistics evidence and military equipment recovered from terrorist incidents within the borders of the State of Israel. During the initial phase of the Lebanese War, he entered Lebanon for brief periods to work closely with the IDF and clear bunkers of huge quantities of weapons and ammunition. When he was not in Lebanon, the author often examined recovered arms and munitions stored in various military warehouses within the State of Israel. This military hardware included many thousands of captured small arms as well as thousands of tons of explosive ordnance and munitions previously captured in the war.

The beginning of the counter-insurgency phase of the war was seen almost immediately following the IDF assult on Beirut. It soon became obvious to parties involved in the Lebanese occupation that this was to be no new War of Attrition. Rather, it was guerilla warfare involving the following types of operations:

(1) Incursions by terrorist bands into the State of Israel

(2) Attacks involving small arms fire, RPG rockets, mortar bombings, and Katyusha fire against fixed IDF positions

(3) The ambushing of mobile patrols in both urban areas and in open terrain through the use of small arms fire, grenades, and anti-tank rockets

(4) The placing of roadside demolition charges

(5) The mining of roads and patrol sectors with both anti-tank and anti-personnel devices

(6) Suicide attack missions involving cars and vans loaded with explosive ordnance

(7) Incursions by bands of insurgents into IDF-controlled territory

By August, 1982 sporadic attacks had begun and materials recovered began to reach the author for examination. These materials included:

(1) Cartridge cases and spent bullets

(2) Captured small arms and materiel (ammunition, pouches, magazines, etc.)

(3) Explosive ordnance which was examined jointly by both the author and by the Explosive Analysis Laboratory of the Israel National Police

## SETTING UP A LABORATORY

By October, 1983 the number of attacks and incursions had increased dramatically, and it was then that the author volunteered to establish a forensic ballistic laboratory within the Lebanese war zone. In most instances materials forwarded to the Jerusalem police laboratory had been taking one or more weeks to be received for examination. Since the time factor in examinations related to counter-insurgency warfare is particularly critical, the author pressed the issue of opening the new field laboratory. After several visits to Southern Lebanon to access the situation, it further became obvious that much of the recovered materials had not been forwarded for examination. The prime reason for these visits was to prepare the physical building where the laboratory was to be located.

A town in south-central Lebanon was selected for the operation. By this time the IDF was solidly entrenched South of the Awali River, so that mechanized transport or helicopter could be utilized to reach any given sitre within occupied territory within minutes.

Agreement on the details of the operation was finally reached in the first days of June, 1984; the author arrived to work in his new quarters on June 7. All necessary equipment was in place and ready. The nucleus of the operation was a Leitz table-top compairison microscope, complete with a large format Polaroid camera. The myriad of police and personal equipment necessary to function as a firearms examiner in occupied territory was entrenched in a billet/office building which had been reconstucted by the IDF to the author's instructions.

The author was to function alone as a firearms examiner with the following duties:

(1) Forensic examination of cartridge cases, bullets, and firearms

(2) The identification of captured materiel and its association to specific terrorist groups

(3) The examination of the scene immediately following an incident

(4) Pinpointing the origin of fire

(5) Accompanying military units on search and seizure missions immediately following terrorist incidents

(6) Co-operating with Explosive Ordnance and Demolition (EOD) personnel when examining explosives, car bombs, boobytraps, road-side charges and sites of attacks involving these items

(7) Use of the Israel National Police's Explosives Test Kit (ETK) to screen suspects, buildings, automobiles and clothing for signs of explosive material

(8) Forwarding of positive ETK results to the Analytical Chemistry Laboratory, Division of Criminal Identification, Israel National Police for laboratory examination and identification. (The samples taken also included propellant powder residues.)

(9) Examination of the hands and clothing of suspects for signs of oil such as that found on weapons or magazines recovered after terrorist attacks

(10) Accompanying IDF units on search and seizure operations involving villages known to harbour active insurgents. This included the methodical searching of as many as forty buildings and homes in a village

By June 8, 1984 the author was actively employed examining over two hundred files which had been awaiting his arrival. The first task was to classify and file cartridge cases recovered from attack scenes, since most of the examinations required were of a "no-gun" nature. (It should be pointed out that the author's professional approach is always to give priority to the filing of spent bullets and cartridge cases before undertaking the examination of weapons. This point is further elaborated in the author's forthcoming ballistics examination book.)

This case load was completed within three weeks, however numerous attacks were taking place on a daily basis, and these required the author's immediate attention. The first successful comparison was of two East German manufactured AKM assault rifles (MPiKM); it was made toward the end of June 1984. Examination determined that both rifles had been involved in three separate attacks. The skepticism which had existed amongst several officers was replaced with enthusiasm and active support.

FUNCTIONING IN THE FIELD

A new wave of terrorist attacks peaked when a three man insurgent band attacked a motorized IDF patrol, killing the commanding officer and seriously damaging an armoured personnel carrier (APC). Two RPG rockets were fired at the patrol, but both went wide of target. Thirty rounds were fired from an assault rifle, but they also missed the target. The effective rounds were fired by a PKM medium machine gun which discharged a complete belt of 100 rounds. One of the two APC's was struck at least six times, and an additional two rounds killed the patrol commander instantly.

Several weeks later the author had occasion to examine a Polish manufactured AKMS assault rifle which had been seized in the home of a suspected terrorist. Comparison was made between this rifle and the thirty cartridge cases recovered from the scene of the aforementioned attack, and it was proven that the cartridge cases had, indeed, been fired from this weapon. Until this scientific finding there had not even been a faint suspicion that the owner of the weapon was a member of an attack team. When the suspect was confronted with the evidence proving participation in the incident, he confessed and provided the names and addresses of his cohorts in the operation. He also provided some thirty additional names of active terrorists. Most of these people were arrested immediately, and over forty firearms and explosive ordnance were seized. Most of the materiel was determined to have been introduced into Southern Lebanon after the initial phase of the war had been completed. Many of the rifles were "factory new"; for the most part, they consisted of late model weaponry of Soviet Bloc, People's Republic of China, and North Korean manufacture. Much of the ammunition recovered had been manufactured in North Korea in 1983.

## A DAY IN SEPTEMBER, 1984

The author quickly established a routine which called for awakening quite early in the morning, usually between 0400-0500. He then prepared for the day's work by first checking with the communications officer for any night-time messages. On September 23, 1984 at 0600 a radio report was received describing the detonation of a roadside charge adjacent to a motorized patrol. Two soldiers had been lightly wounded. At 0640 a second message was received. Another roadside charge had exploded next to a command car in which three infantrymen were lightly wounded.

The two helicopters assigned to the author's base were now in use transporting the wounded to hospital, so when a message was received at 0710 describing yet a third incident, they were not available for response. This message once again described an attack on as command car, however the details of the incident were not clear. After several minutes a follow-up message was received; three members of the patrol had been wounded by RPG and small arms fire. The author hurried to the scene of this third incident, and he arrived only five minutes behind the medical staff which, of course, was given first priority.

The author arrived approximately fifteen minutes after the incident had taken place, and he immediately began to access the ballistics aspects of the situation. While the wounded were being treated by the medical staff, he surveyed the terrain and observed what he believed to be the point from which the weapons fire had emanated, a low hill about fifty meters from the road. Search of the hill yielded a vast number of cartridge cases and an AK magazine. Caution, however, dictated that the magazine could not be immediately examined; the possibility of a boobytrap could not be discounted.

Further search found a fired LAW anti-tank rocket launcher at distance of ten meters. After the author separated the tube from the cover by using a grapnel, he determined that the LAW was the United States manufactured model M72 A1, an early version which was definitely not in use by the IDF. The remainder of the evidence had to wait for collection and examination, since there was a distinct possibility that the terrorists were still in the area. Accompanied by a tracking expert, the author began searching for signs of the insurgents. Two hundred fifty meter from the point of fire, a second (empty) AK magazine was located, and cursory examination showed it to be of PRC manufacture. The search then continued, and the tracker found the footprints of three individuals on a dirt trail.

Air support was requested, and two helicopters were sent --- one to evacuate the wounded, and the other to assist in the search operation. The author then returned to the scene of the ambush. After he recorded the location of all evidence recovered, he was then able to examine the discarded assault rifle magazine. It was also made in the People's Republic of China. Both magazines were in "mint condition" without any obvious signs of wear.

Over seventy cartridge cases recovered from the hill top were examined to determine the number of weapons used, and it was quickly determined that three AK's were involved. This evidence was then placed into bags for shipment back to the laboratory. Within moments a radio report was received claiming the spotting of the three fleeing terrorists, and a hot pursuit followed. After a short exchange of gunfire, pursuit of the terrorists was over.

The author was given the three terrorists' Kalashnikov rifles together with numerous magazines and pouches for examination. Two of the weapons had been manufactured in Bulgaria, and the third was Type 56-1 of PRC manufacture. All of the equipment was found to be in new condition. The ammunition in one of the magazines was the same type as the cartridge cases found at the scene of the ambush. This ammunition, made expressly for Palestinian use, was manufactured in 1983. The author test-fired the three AK's in situ , and after ballistic comparison with a hand loupe, it was certain that these were the weapons which had been fired in the incident.

## CLOSING DOWN & WITHDRAWL

The author continued his service in Southern Lebanon until March 17, 1985. His last major operation in Lebanon was a serise of search and seizure operations. Within one week, three major operations were mounted. Entire villages were sealed off, and the homes of active terrorists were searched for incriminating evidence. The final search in which the author participated was in the house of a known terrorist ... the most active terrorist in the region. The suspect's bedroom contained numerous cartons of propaganda and military training manuals for guerilla warfare, however no weapons were found.

After search of the upper storey was completed, soldiers entered the empty basement of the house. In one corner there was a half meter wide slab resting on the floor. It was moved, and below it was a huge weapons cache the size of the entire house foundation. The author catagorized the materiel as it was removed from the cache. The amount was staggering, and it serves as a good indication of the experiences of the IDF in Southern Lebanon:

(1) 5 107mm Katusha rockets of USSR manufacture

(2) 15 M72 A1 LAW rocket launchers

(3) 2 RPG-18 rocket launchers of East German manufacture

(4) 80 hand grenades made in Lebanon

(5) 5 5kg. cylindrical TNT blocks of PRC manufacture

(6) 100kg. of USSR manufactured TNT demolition blocks

(7) 8 anti-tank mines manufactured in Bulgaria

(8) 10,000 electric detonators manufactured in the USSR

(9) 1000 non-electric detonators in sealed boxes showing USSR labels

(10) 200 anti-personnel and anti-tank rifle grenades of Yugoslav and Hungarian manufacture

(11) 20 stick grenades of PRC manufacture

(12) 1 Czechoslovakian Skorpion sub-machine gun

(13) 1 Unique Bcf 66 pistol with home-made silencer

(14) 1 M-52 sub-machine gun manufactured in Hungary and equipped with home-made silencer

(15) 1 SVD sniper rifle manufactured in the USSR

(16) 1 Franchi police riot shotgun manufactured in Italy

(17) 2 Baikal sporting shotguns of USSR manufacture

(18) 22 Kalachnikov assault rifles, mostly of East German manufacture

(19) 2 Type 73 medium machine guns manufactured in North Korea

(20) Over 15,000 rounds of small arms ammunition in sealed containers

(21) Numerous empty magazines, etc.

Such was the finale of the author's tour of duty in Lebanon --- a tour which was not only extremely interesting but also highly successful. During the tour of duty, the author examined over 2500 weapons and endless rounds of ammunition. This obviously does not include the numerous factory new weapons which, having never been used, cannot be compared with the many "no-gun" cartridge cases on file.

This exercise of performing forensic ballistic examinations on the field of battle proved to be a necessary and successful procedure in counter-insurgency warfare with wide implication for future conflicts.

# THE INTERNATIONAL SECURITY & DEFENCE INSTITUTE
## — ISRAEL —

# OUR EXPERIENCE WILL MAKE YOU AN EXPERT.

Few countries in the world face, on a daily basis, the security problems present in Israel today. For this reason ISDS has established the Institute for security and defence studies in Israel.

Experience is the only teacher. We have that experience.

The Institute offers a range of courses that deal with virtually every aspect of this complex and constantly changing field.

Our courses include theoretical studies, practical training in a variety of environments, and lectures by world renound experts in Security and Defence.

ISDS is directly involved with the latest developments in defence technology and weaponry.

We have specially designed courses for both the private and public sectors.

## PRIVATE- CORPORATION- LAW ENFORCEMENT- MILITARY- AND POLICE SECTORS.

- INTEGRAL SECURITY SYSTEMS — SECURITY OFFICER OF: AIR TRANSPORTATION; BANKING; INDUSTRIAL PLANTS; AGRICULTURAL AREAS; HOTELS; ETC.
- VIP'S AND EXECUTIVES PROTECTION — BODYGUARD AND SECURITY OFFICER PERSONNEL.
- COMMERCIAL AND INDUSTRIAL COUNTER ESPIONAGE.
- SPECIAL TASK FORCE FOR HOSTAGE RELEASE NEGOTIATION.
- SPECIAL UNITS FOR BOMB DISPOSAL
- S.W.A.T. TEAMS

We are aware that each security problem has its specific requirements, and individual programmes may be constructed to suit yours.

| ISRAEL Telex: 361131 ESHED. I.L. | |
| --- | --- |
| Tel: 08-227699 | P.O.Box: 2283 |
| 76122   REHOVOT   ISRAEL | |

אני מאשר בזה את הדפסת הטקסט דלעיל
בספר אידנטה 1985

ליאור לזר

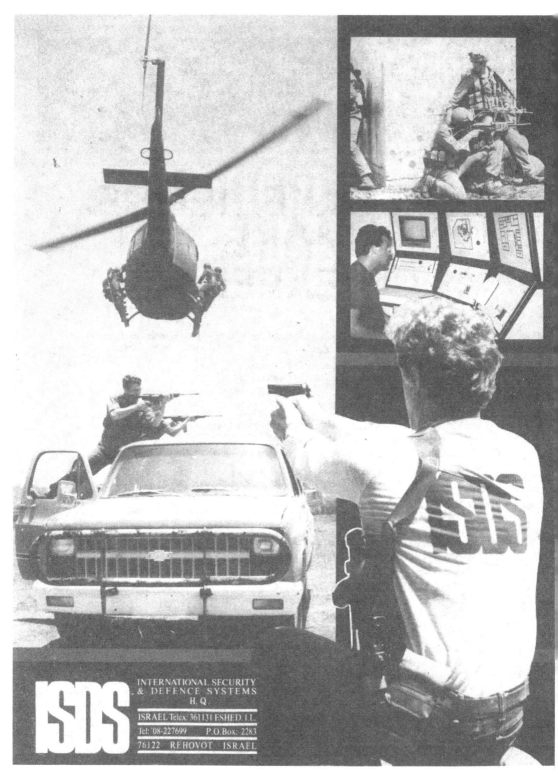

אני מאשר בזה את הדפסת התמונה בספר אידנטה 1985

ליאו גלזר

# TRENDS IN PALESTINIAN TERRORISM

Tamar Prath
Jaffee Center for
Strategic Studies Tel Aviv

The known saying "one man's terrorist is another man's freedom fighter," when translated to the Palestinian context suggests: one man's terrorism is another man's armed struggle.

The concept of armed struggle was the essence of the Palestinian strategy of struggle against Israel when it was first formulated in the 1960s. Since then, it has been the core of Palestinian national identity, having enormous symbolic value.

Armed struggle was the name given by the Palestinian ideologists to the doctrine of guerrilla warfare carried out by the masses and lasting for a long time. The goal of the armed struggle was to destroy the Israeli state and society and bring about the complete liberation of Palestine. This strategy was offered as an alternative to the Arab strategy of carrying out conventional war by the Arab regular armies.

The attempt to implement this strategy in the areas occupied in 1967 failed. The masses were not mobilized and the attacks carried out by the revolutionary vanguard emerged into a pattern of sporadic terrorism which could not seriously endanger Israel's basic security or economy. Attempts were made to establish a guerrilla force based in neighboring countries, mainly in Jordan, which would carry out systematic offensive activities against Israeli targets. Israeli counterinsurgency efforts foiled these attempts by hitting the guerrilla bases directly and by inflicting losses on the host countries which caused them to move against the guerrillas. The 1970 civil war in Jordan caused the Palestinian leaders to realize that they would not be able to develop an effective guerrilla option which would lead to the attainment of the ultimate goal.

Gradually, armed struggle was conceived as a strategy of exerting pressure, aimed at specific goals, e.g., propaganda, rather than as an all-out strategy. It should be noted that the Popular Front for the Liberation of Palestine, led by George Habash, initially conceived armed struggle as the selective use of violence to bring about a specific political goal. Mainly, the goal was to make the world realize the existence of a just Palestinian cause. To that end the group carried out attacks on Israeli targets abroad, as well as on non-Israeli but "Imperialist" targets, e.g., American and European.

Fath adopted this conception only after the failure to launch effective guerrila warfare from the Jordanian border. Fath was then forced to operate abroad. Until then it rejected the attacks abroad carried out by Dr. Habash's Front and other groups because of the damage to the image of the Palestinian liberation movement. But now there was no other arena to operate in and the necessity to continue operating in order to exist was stronger than the gain-loss consideration.

It should be realized that armed struggle was the raison d'etra of the Palestinian groups and it will be so long as they have no other ways to attain their goals, as long as they are a non-state organization.

In an attempt to reduce the cost of the activity abroad, back in the early 1970s Fath refrained from claiming credit for it. But soon it became clear that the activity abroad brought the Palestinian problem to the center of world public opinion and Fath leaders realized that the initially unwelcome strategy was actually most effective. They finally grasped the potential of terror as a dramatic means of conveying messages. Since then, terror has been viewed as serving specific aims posed by the general strategic goal and deduced from specific circumstances.

The general strategic line designed after the international ackowledgement of the Palestinian problem was established was to introduce the PLO as a partner to a settlement. Within this settlement, a Palestinian state would be established in areas of Palestine occupied in 1967. This strategic line implied creating the image of a just national liberation movement and of its leadership as a rational leadership. Of course, international terrorism is counterproductive in this context. But some activity should be carried on to maintain the level of awareness of the severity of the problem. This end was served by attacks carried out in Israel which drew world attention but were considered more legitimate than terror abroad.

It should be noted that even though armed struggle was no longer considered as a general strategy and political struggle was developed alongside it, it still remained at the heart of the Palestinian ethos. The original aim of destruction of Israel was not abandoned and the establishment of a state in areas of Palestine was accepted only as an interim goal. Furthermore, the political strategy and the tactical concessions required by it have been a major point of debate within the PLO. Armed struggle, being a main symbol of national identity and the common factor to all groups, has therefore a very important role in any national strategy. This should be remembered when trying to assess the rationality behind sticking to the armed struggle concept.

To sum up the role of armed struggle in the strategy--armed struggle implemented in the last ten years was directed toward attaining two main goals: on the one hand, to make the world aware of the need to solve the problem politically, with the PLO as the legitimate Palestinian partner; on the other hand, to assure the Palestinians that this political solution is temporary and that the ultimate goal is retained essentially.

The war in Lebanon sharpened the debate within the PLO with regard to the very existence of any legitimate strategy other than armed struggle. It seems the initial position was strengthened in both camps: Arafat was further convinced that the only realistic way to achieve anything is joining the political process, and this caused an open rebellion against his leadership.

All these assumptions on the nature of, reasons and goals of and the rationality behind Palestinian terrorism should be remembered when trying to assess the current trends of Palestinian terrorism.

Now, what are the options of activity of Palestinian terror today? Three basic options are: terror within Israel, terror from borders, and terror abroad.

Terror within Israel has considerable advantages over the other options: it has a relatively legitimate image in international public opinion. It can be described as a spontaneous uprising against an occupying regime; it can be claimed that the targets are military. This consideration of legitimacy is important for Arafat's camp. Another advantage of terrorism within Israel is that it influences more directly the Israeli public: a grenade attack in Tel Aviv terrorizes more Israelis than an attack on an Israeli office abroad.

A third advantage is that terrorism within Israel, launched by people living within the Palestinian local community involves this community in the struggle. Even if the population is not actively involved in the terror, such activity still has a role--to retain the passive support of the local Palestinians and not let them consider a compromise with Israel. The need to strengthen the involvement of the local population increases as years pass and the PLO has failed so far to bring any real fruits for the population living the occupation daily. The last consideration might bring a concentration of efforts for activity in the occupied territories against Jewish targets there. Activity in these territories has yet another advantage. It might raise a sharp public debate in Israel concerning the continuing occupation. The debate is expected to arise as more resources would be required to assure security there. It should be noted that because of these consequences which are grave for any Israeli government, terrorist acts might boomerang: the Israeli government could act decisively against the terrorists deterring the local population from joining them and limiting the basic freedoms of the local population.

As regards what kind of activity-- since terrorism within Israel is expected to serve a central role in the strategy--the more destructive the terror the more effective it will be. Therefore, throwing grenades in crowded places, car bombings, ambushing public transport vehicles and even barricade hostage attacks are expected. The trend to concentrate on more sophisticated activity has already been noted in the passing year.

The main problem with this option is the effectiveness of Israeli security services which till now have foiled most of the attacks and uncovered many of the squads trying to get organized.

This difficulty will lead to attempts to re-establish bases of departure in neighboring countries. Activity from bases in Jordan, Lebanon, and maybe Syria is the second main option.

It is believed that all groups will establish bases in Lebanon and infiltration via the Lebanese border by land or by sea is highly probable. The withdrawal of the IDF from south Lebanon will enable the pro-Syria groups to re-establish bases there. Arafat's loyalists might be more restricted in the south, but for them bases in Tripoli may serve as naval departure bases. It is also believed that attempts will be made to infiltrate Israel through the Jordanian border either by land or across the Red Sea. Pro-Syria groups might try to infiltrate Jordanian territory from Syria and from there launch attacks on Israel, trying to spoil the relationship between Arafat and Hussein. Arafat's loyalists are expected to be more cautious while operating in Jordan. They are expected to try to smuggle personnel and arms through the bridges, but not to infiltrate through the borders in order to avoid clashes with the Jordanian army and tension with the Jordanian regime.

The establishment of bases in Lebanon should be viewed also in the perspective of an attempt to rebuild a secure territorial stronghold in which Palestinian forces will be concentrated and an effective guerrilla option will be built gradually. This option is highly probable for the Pro-Syria groups who argue now that armed struggle is the only strategy left.

While the process of rebuilding the infrastructure might last a long time, the ability to launch sporadic attacks, mainly firing Katyushas into Israel, does not seem improbable in the near future. This kind of activity is much easier, and risks a minimum of personnel compared to sending squads to attack from within Israel. When successful, the firing of Katyushas is expected to affect the Israeli population no less than other activities within Israel.

The more difficult it will be to operate within Israel and from the borders, the more probable is activity abroad.

The clear disadvantage of this activity--the loss of political support--is central for Arafat's camp as long as it strives to join the political process. But if no political process is underway, it might cause this camp to launch activity abroad to push for such a process. In order not to be damaged by the involvement in international terror, it is expected that these attacks will not be claimed by Fath openly, but will be carried out under a cover name.

The radical, anti-Arafat camp is free of any consultation if it decides to operate abroad. Rather, it might decide to do so in order to foil any settlement. Attacks abroad, claimed by Palestinian groups, will make Arafat's claim to be the sole, legitimate representative of the Palestinians seem ridiculous.

The conclusion is that Palestinian international terror is expected to occur relative to the difficulty to act in Israel and from Lebanon and relative to the progress or lack of progress towards a political settlement.

Terror abroad necessitates an infrastructure--that is, links with international groups, safehouses, dormant agents, arms caches, intelligence apparatus, etc. It is expected that those groups which have already operated abroad, e.g., the PFLP, will be able to start operating before other organizations, e.g., Fath rebels. It is expected that all groups will forge links with foreign terrorist groups. The rise of terrorism in Western Europe can move the local groups there to forge links with Palestinian groups which can supply training, arms and personnel. In return, they will supply the Palestinians with operational aids for attacks in Europe. France, West Germany, Belgium, Italy and Portugal are likely arenas for attacks according to this reasoning. Another likely arena in Europe is Greece, whose socialist regime has known links with Arafat, and which has been blamed by the US and Great Britain for being lax with terrorism. This was evident when Greek authorities released a terrorist involved in an attempt to smuggle a suitcase filled with explosives into an El-Al airliner in December 1983. Cyprus is also a likely arena as most Palestinian groups maintain a presence there and some official Palestinian facilities operate openly in Nicosia.

Attacks on Israeli targets are probable also in areas in which there were no attacks in the past. Latin America is one such case. Here the PLO enjoys good links with the Cuban and Nicaraguan regimes. It is known also that recently there have been efforts to organize the local residents of Palestinian descent in Latin American countries. Such an organization can supply both operational aid and cover to terrorist activities. While the eight groups which comprise the PLO have not been engaged in recent years in terrorism abroad, there are other Palestinian organizations outside the PLO, such as Abu Nidal's group, "15 May, Organization", which is linked to Iraq. Those groups have operated abroad in the past and will probably continue to do so.

It is expected, for instance, that the attacks by Abu Nidal's group on British targets will go on as long as the group members who shot Ambassador Argov are imprisoned.

Another likely trend of Palestinian terrorism abroad is that linked with internal rivalry. The two camps have already been engaged in the assassination of rivals and the murder of Kawasmeh is just the latest example. As long as there are internal differences, Palestinian officials are likely targets of attacks. Linked with the Palestinian rivalry is the rivalry between Palestinian groups and distinct Arab states, e.g., Syria and Jordan. It is believed that the interests of these two and other Arab states would be targets for attacks by the two Palestinian camps.

To sum up: "Armed struggle" is a key concept in the strategy of both camps within the Palestinian movement.

The camp which strives to join some political process which will lead to the establishment of a state in the areas occupied in 1967 will use terrorist tactics to push towards a political process. It might consider the intensification of armed struggle within the territories rather than in Israel. It might be expected that the intensification of violence would lead to greater willingness in Israel to hand over these territories because of the high cost of the continued occupation of them. But it is very probable that Israel's stand would be hardened by increasing violence. This also might be considered by Fath strategists.

While the interest in international support makes terror abroad undesirable for this camp, it might be that lack of any progress towards settlement would lead to carrying out terror abroad, though under a cover name.

In any case, even if he opts for political settlement, Arafat cannot stop the armed struggle until he has concrete achievements. He has to maintain an ability to influence the developments in the area, on the one hand, and has to demonstrate to his people that he is not betraying their national interests on the other hand. For these two reasons he cannot stop the armed struggle as long as he has no real political achievements. It is expected then that he will opt for the intensification of armed struggle within Israel or the territories. In order to do this, he might need to re-establish bases in Lebanon which will serve as departure bases.

The rejectionist camp believes in the armed struggle as the only option open. It will intensify terror within Israel and the territories and will concentrate on the re-establishment of the infrastructure for effective force in Lebanon. Meanwhile, sporadic attacks across the Lebanese border are expected. The rejectionists will turn to terror abroad if any real progress towards settlement is made and relative to their success in launching terror in Israel.

In any case, the most important thing to realize about Palestinian terrorism is that it will serve a key role in any strategy as long as 1) the Palestinian movement is a non-state organization which cannot use other measures to coerce its will upon other states or its own members; 2) the Palestinians do not have other symbols of national identity and solidarity. The two conditions are actually one: as long as there is no Palestinian state or at least a very real chance of establishing it, the armed struggle would have a strategic priority even by most moderate groups. It should also be noted that even if a political solution is real, it is still expected that radical elements would go on with armed struggle. And finally, since armed struggle is so essential, it will be carried out in any open arena. Effective countering of it in one arena just makes activity in other arenas more probable.

# THE REEMERGENCE OF JEWISH TERRORISM IN ISRAEL

Dr. Ehud Sprinzak
Department of Political Science
Hebrew University of Jerusalem

At the end of April, 1984 the Israeli public was greatly alarmed by the shocking disclosure of a large scale terrorist plot. A sabotage act of great magnitude aimed at the blowing up of six Arab busses full of passengers was exposed and prevented. Following the arrest of 27 suspects, it was further disclosed that a sophisticated Jewish terrorist organization had existed in Israel since 1980, and its members belonged to the very prestigious settlement and pioneering movement, Gush Emunim (Bloc of the Faithful). The purpose of this paper is to describe and analyse the way in which a very idealistic and non-violent movement has undergone a behavioral process which resulted in the birth of a terrorist underground. Four developmental stages in the evolution of Gush Emunim will be identified: (1) formation of a messianic group eager to settle Judea & Samaria (West Bank of Jordan), (2) crystalization of protest and extra-parliamentary activities against the "sluggish" government (which did not accept the settlement policies), (3) emergence of vigilante activities (against local Arab population) as a result of the government's inability to provide full protection for settlers, (4) transformation of vigilantism into terrorism. The major thesis of the paper is that the emergence of Jewish terrorism was highly probable, since it followed regular evolutionary patterns of illegal idealistic movements.

On Friday, April 27, Kol Yisrael, the Israeli broadcasting service, announced a shocking news report. An act of sabotage of great magnitude, aimed at the blowing up of six Arab buses, packed with passengers, had just been exposed and prevented. During the following week more than twenty men suspected of forming a terrorist network were arrested. In the following weeks, it was further disclosed that the suspects accepted responsibility for the two most spectacular anti-Arab terrorist actions that had taken place in Judea and Samaria (the West Bank of the Jordan, occupied by Israel in 1967) - the assasination attempts on the mayors of three Arab cities in 1980 and the murderous attack on the Islamic College in Hebron in 1983 in which three students were killed and seventeen were wounded. A score of smaller acts of the same nature was also attributed to the suspects and it was further disclosed that a detailed and carefully planned incredible project of blowing up the sacred Moslem mosques on the Temple Mount in Jerusalem was on their planning boards.

However, what shocked many political observers and students of Israeli extremism, was not so much the news about the existence of such a terrorist group, as its identity. The members of the network were identified as hard core members of Gush Emunim (the block of the faithful) a pioneering and religious settlement movement whose members since 1968 have taken upon themselves the task of settling Judea and Samaria. The great shock and surprise about the disclosure of the groups identity was due to the rather non-violent posture, assumed for years by the spokesman and spiritual leaders of Gush Emunim. Though not a peace organization, but rather an aggressive settlement movement and sometimes illegal at that, Gush Emunim never developed openly a brutal ideology of violence. Its Orthodox leaders never argued for the deportation of the local Arab population in the name of the Jewish right to the land - a right in which they strongly believe. Instead, they always argued that a peaceful and productive co-existence with the Arabs was both possible and desirable. To think that any of these highly educated and responsible men, some of whom were ranking Army officers and all of whom were heads of large religious families, were ready and able to resort to systematic terrorist activities, was beyond imagination.

Today, a year after the arrest of the terror network, we know a great deal more about its composition and its modus operandi. The group was not a classical underground or conventional terror organization. Its members, numbering

25, never considered themselves part of a secret organization. If at all they saw themselves as an avenging team responding in kind to Arab terrorism. With the exception of the two outstanding figures of the network, Menachem Livni and Yehuda Etzion and perhaps three or four additional central figures, the members of the group functioned as soldiers. They were convinced that the operations were essential, they trusted the leaders and felt privileged to take part in the missions. All of them are highly religious, devoted members of Gush Emunim and with a few unimportant exceptions, settlers in Judea and Samaria and the Golan Heights.

While the group's first sophisticated strike, the "Mayors operation", took place on June 3, 1980, it appears that already two years earlier, some of its members started thinking about a grand operation . At the beginning, they did not act as a sophisticated operation team and were rather a small circle of religious zealots highly disturbed by the insufficient security provided to the settler community by the government. Their main concern however was the Temple Mount. Highly religious and messianic, these people were totally convinced about the need to remove the Moslem Mosques from the Jewish holiest place. Only a calculated destruction of the mosques could create the proper conditions for the rebuilding of the Third Temple, an act necessary for full national redemption in this generation.

Since the grand operation was historically unprecendented in its magnitude, and potential political effects, a great deal of planning was needed. Theoretical planning required many talks and deliberations about the religious status of the place. Operational planning required topographic surveys, air photographing and surveillance operations. Explosives and ammunition were stolen from army arsenals. During the preparatory stage of the Temple Mount operation a major event in the history of the group took place in Hebron. A murderous attack on Jewish Yeshiva students took place in the beginning of May 1980 in which six people were killed and many wounded. The group, fully backed now by the atmosphere within the settler community decided to strike back. Several additional members were recruited and the "Mayors Operation", an act of great symbolic effect, was committed successfully. The cars of three promiment Arab mayors publically known as unofficial PLO leaders in the West Bank were booby trapped and exploded. Two out of three were severely wounded having their legs amputated. Following the June 3 act which was highly welcomed within the settler community, work on the Temple Mount operation resumed. It is not at all clear why the great plan was never carried out but fortunately it was not. The group, however, was now solidified and was ready for more revenge operations if needed. Following the Arab murder of a Yeshiva student in Hebron in the Spring of 1983 and a score of other anti-Jewish incidents, a massive attack on the Moslem College in Hebron was held on July 26 in which three were killed and 18 wounded. The same pattern was to be repeated in April 1984, when, following a wave of Arab terror attacks, six Arab buses full of passengers were booby trapped. Only an outstanding intelligence work which ended up by the arrest of the network prevented this operation and brought the story of the group to its end.

In view of all the information that has been obtained since the beginning of the trial and as a result of a rereading of some earlier chapters in the history of Gush Emunim, it seems that the previous understanding of this movement and its internal dynamics was greatly lacking. Upon reexamination it now appears that Gush Emunim has not only introduced to Israel's public life a highly successful settlement movement, but also a special fundamentalist mode of thinking and behaving capable of producing-in extreme cases-intense violence and terrorism. It further appears that the observers of the settler community which grew up from Gush Emunim and closer extremist elements, were not aware of the increased process of socialization that it went through. This process has apparently transformed the community and turned it from an idealistic and messianic movement of young zealots into a rugged frontier community highly engaged in active vigillation.

The purpose of the present paper is to reconstruct the process which led to the final emergence of the terror network within Gush Emunim. The general thesis that will be presented here is that today not only Arab terrorism should be conceived as a structural part of the Palestinian-Israeli conflict but also Jewish terrorism. Thus it will be suggested that in the future we are going to see a lot more from both sides.

## POLITICAL HISTORY

Gush Emunim was formed at a founding meeting held early in March 1974 at Kfar Etzion, with about two hundred people participating. It was at that time declared to be an organized faction within the National Religious Party (NRP). The founding meeting was preceded by informal discussions in which a decisive role was played by former students of Rabbi Zvi Yehuda Kook, the spiritual leader of Yeshivat Merkaz ha-Rav. After a short period of intra-NRP existence, the Gush Emunim people left this party in the spring of 1974 and declared their movement to be an independent body. Ever since, they have refused as a group to identify automatically with any Israeli political party and have gained a unique political status on their own account.

From the beginning the Gush Emunim people were dissatisfied with the Israeli government. Against the background of the gloomy public mood and the first territorial concessions in the Sinai Peninsula (in the framework of the first disengagement agreement with Egypt), Gush Emunim's founders felt it their duty to set up a barrier capable of stopping unnecessary territorial concessions. They were particularly wary of the official lukewarm position of the NRP, which was then a partner in the Labor coalition, concerning the future of Judea and Samaria. They also felt that it was necessary to promote Jewish settlement in Judea and Samaria in an organized and vigorous way, and to bring about the extension of Israeli sovereignty to those territories. They regarded extra-parliamentary demonstrations and mobilization of their sympathetic public as effective means to counter the American pressure for concessions.

During the Rabin government (1974-1977) Gush Emunim operated on three planes: it organized protests and demonstrations against the interim agreements with Egypt and Syria and against the political and diplomatic activity related to these agreements; it promoted attention-focusing activities in Judea and Samaria to underscore the Jewish attachment to those parts of Eretz Israel; it carried out settlement operations in the occupied territories.

The power, importance and public influence of the protest actions and the publicity-seeking activities never for a moment obscured for Gush Emunim its deep commitment to the idea of settlement beyond the Green Line. The government of Israel, being pragmatic and subject to pressures from all sides, was not enthusiastic about initiating settlement. Its hesitancy was mostly marked during the period of the negotiations on the interim agreements with Syria and Egypt, talks which were conducted under heavy American time pressure applied by Dr. Kissinger. Gush Emunim did not let up on this matter and its inside pressures, were no less than its external ones. In response to this pressure the government first authorized the settlement at Keshet on the Golan Heights, a military foothold at Tekoa and another at Kochav ha-Shahar. Afterwards Minister of Defence Shimon Peres authorized a workers' camp at Ba'al Hazor, which later became Ofra, a civilian settlement in all respects, including families and children. These activities notwithstanding, the spearhead of Gush Emunim was and remains the core-group of Elon Moreh. This group, which preceded the formal establishment of the Gush, has become the symbol of its fundamental challenge to the guiding conception of the Labor Government, viz., secure borders combined with minimal involvement with the densely populated Arab areas. The founders of this core group have expressed more adamantly than anyone else the determination of Gush Emunim to settle in all parts of Eretz Israel, including the very heart of the Palestinian population. This group tried on seven different occasions to settle in the Nablus-Sebastia region, and each time their attempts were thwarted and the settlements forcibly dismantled by the army. With the eighth attempt, after a very dramatic confrontation, Gush Emunim broke down the government's opposition and achieved the well-known 'Kadoum compromise'. Following two days of tense confrontation it was finally agreed that the members of the core group would leave the site 'on their own accord', pass to a military camp at Kadoum and stay there until a decision was reached about their future location.

The Likud victory in the elections of May 1977 and the declaration of the Prime Minister designate, Menachem Begin, that 'we will have many more Elon Morehs', induced many of Gush Emunim leaders to believe in all sincerity that their extra parliamentary period was over. And indeed, the new regime accorded them full legitimacy. Gush Emunim was in fact never regarded by Menachem Begin as a deviant group. Its young members had always been the Prime Minister's darlings. Many had long been envious of the ease with which the leaders of Gush Emunim could get to speak to Begin and obtain satisfaction from him. Since they had formed their movement in order to achieve the concrete goal of settlement in Judea and Samaria and not in order to add another color to the spectrum of extra-parliamentarism in Israel, many of the Gush Emunim people were happy about the opportunity offered them now to shed the somehow extremist unsympathetic image. Another reason for their satisfaction was the senior position of Rabbi Chayim Drukman, their man who was placed as the number two man in the NRP list to the Ninth Knesset.

The Camp David accords, the Autonomy Plan and the government's commitment to give up the Rafiah Salient struck Gush Emunim like a bolt out of the blue. This was without doubt the lowest point in its short history. Its leaders had had time enough since Sadat's visit to Jerusalem to discern what the future held in store, but the firm belief that history was on its side-which characterized Gush Emunim all along-prevented an early forecast of the dramatic event, and when it happened they were altogether at a loss. The total concession by the 'Greater Israel Faithful', Menachem Begin, the paving of the way for a Palestinian state by the Autonomy Plan and the dismantling of the settlements in the Rafiah Salient left them dumbfounded. The activity of the Gush was paralyzed and its return to normal did not come about easily. The Gush people were simply too weak to manage the organization of an anti-government front by themselves and at that time were greatly assisted by other peripheral elements such as the Herut 'Loyalists Circle', Professor Yuval Ne'eman, members of the Greater Israel Movement, Knesset members Geula Cohen and Moshe Shamir, several former Rafi members and others, who together formed the 'Covenant of the Eretz Israel Faithful'. This new association committed itself to the original platform of the Greater Israel Movement, and by its very founding in effect declared a total war on the Camp David accords. Later on, this whole group founded the Tehiya movement, which took up a decisive position against Begin's determination to carry out the Camp David Accords.

An event of major significance to the history and the consciousness of Gush Emunim took place in the months preceding April 28, 1982. This was the date set by the Israeli Egyptian peace treaty for the final Israeli evacuation of Sinai. The settlers of the Rafiah Salient and the members of Gush Emunim refused to believe that a retreat was at all possible. Together they established a mass movement aimed at frustrating the government's committment. Although the movement was launched in the name of the Sinai Settlers, it was soon taken over by a group of zealots of Gush Emunim. Hundreds of them, perhaps even a thousand settlers in Judea and Samaria, left their newly built homes and moved to Yamit, the new capital of the salient and to its surrounding settlements, in order to stop the retreat with their bodies and by their strong belief. They flocked over with their rabbis, their Yeshivot and even their families, fully convinced that they were Heavenly ordained for the mission. Several of them, the most extreme, seriously considered armed resistance and only a very cautious operation by the army managed miraculously to prevent the eruption of large scale violence.

In the context of discussing the growing frustration of some of Emunim's true believers it is important to stress also some of the great achievements of the movement as a

settlement trust aimed at Israelizing Judea and Samaria.
Following Begin's great electoral success in 1981 the cabinet
which ran Israel's affairs was no longer the same cabinet
that had signed the peace agreements. The dominant axis in
it was composed of Begin, Sharon and Shamir. This was a
hawkish axis, altogether different from the previous one -
Begin, Dayan and Weizman - that was responsible for the spirit
of Camp David. The new axis was limited by the Camp David
framework and the Autonomy Plan, but nevertheless has been
operating at full steam and with considerable aggressiveness
to perpetuate Jewish settlement in Judea and Samaria.
Despite the Gush's disappointment with Sharon's stance during
the period of the Camp David accords, it has become apparent
during the past years that they could not wish for a better
representative in the government. Ariel Sharon has proven to
be a very able minister and has proceeded rapidly towards
the realization of his settlement plan. Sharon always
objected to the Alon Plan, which in one form or another had
guided all the Labor governments. He formulated an all
embracing strategic settlement plan based on Jewish control of
all the dominant roads in the West Bank. By virtue of his
stubborness and aggressiveness he succeeded in carrying out
more of the plan than either his friends and opponents thought
possible. In spite of the difficult personal crises he
encountered in the Likud government, he endured better than
Dayan and Weizman, who were the only ones able to neutralize
him. With Sharon as a dominant figure in the Likud government,
Gush Emunim had no objective need for noisy extra-parliamentarism. The fact they they always kept this option attests
to their great radical potential.

FUNDAMENTALIST IDEOLOGY

Gush Emunim has always been characterized by its
spiritual nature and by the commitment of its leaders to
a unique religiious world view. What escaped most observers
of this movement, however, was the totalistic and
fundamentalist nature of this world-view. The reason for
this is due to the fact that the Gush has been primarily
conceived of as a pragmatic settlement movement identified
with secular aspirations and mundane achievements.
Relatively little attention has been given to the
comprehensive cultural milieu within which the movement has
emerged even before it was formally established and named.
Only recently have a few scholars, prominent among them
Kibbutz intellectual Zvi Raanan and the late Professor Uriel
Tal, identified and characterized the totalistic structure

and the messianic contours of the new ideology. Both Raanan and Tal have shown that in the orthodox and dogmatic cultural system in which the young members of Gush Emunim have grown up, nothing could be done or said without a religious legitimation of a prestigious rabbi. They have convincingly argued that these rabbis because of their spiritial authority were responsible for setting the boundaries of Emunim's sphere of expectations and operations and that these boundaries have in the "messianic age" become almost limitless.

A clue to Emunim's fundamentalist ideology can be found when the fact that all of its spiritual authorities and many of its leaders were educated in Yeshivat Merkaz ha-Rav, is given a proper attention and when it is further remembered that the founder of this Yeshiva, the late Rabbi Avraham Yitzkah ha-Cohen Kook, the first Chief Rabbi of the Jews of Eretz Yisrael, was an original messianic thinker. It now appears that the unique kabbalistic interpretation of the late Rabbi Kook has assumed since 1967 a manifest and popular character and has become not only the esoteric property of a selected few, but the forensic ideology of many and a guide-line for political action. Several of the cardinal points of this all embracing belief system warrants closer scrutiny:

REDEMPTION

Rabbi Kook believed that the Jewish people of his day existed in an era in which the birth pangs of redemption had already begun. This was attested, according to his interpretation, by the rise of modern Zionism, the political gains of the movement, the Balfour Declaration and the entire Zionist enterprise in Palestine. For many years the students in his small yeshiva were educated in this spirit and when he died the tradition was passed on especially to his only son, Rabbi Zvi Yehuda Kook. Until 1967, the Kooks' special interpretation was kept on a rather esoteric level. Like a classical kabbalistic thinker, the elder Rabbi Kook was equivocal on many issues, vague on others and was said to have different scholarly interpretations. His teaching did not become a fountain for earthly activities and mundane operations. The Six Day War and the great Israeli victory however, transformed the status of Rabbi Kook's theology. Suddenly it was clear to his students, and eventually to others that they were living in a truely messianic age and that it was their calling to deliver the message to the rest of the nation. Empirical reality has assumed a sacred aspect and every event was shown to incorporate a theological meaning and to be part of a matahistorical process of redemption.

Though shared by many rabbis and religious authorities, the new interpretation was most vocally preached by Rabbi Zvi Yehuda Kook. He, the present head of Yeshivat Merkaz haRav, has defined the State of Israel as the halachic Kingdom of Israel and the Kingdom of Israel as the Kingdom of heaven on earth. Total holiness was now extended to each and every Jew living in Israel and all phenomenon including secular ones were said to eventually be taken over by this holiness. From this study's point of view, the significance of the new mystical status bestowed upon present reality has been its operational meaning. No more was the new interpretation preserved in esoteric Kabbalistic writings. It has become the order of the day. Even before the gathering of Gush Emunim, individual yeshiva students and activists have begun talking in the new language but after the official establishment, the new theology has become the practical property of a whole movement. No ordinary discourse with the members of this movement was now possible without repeated references to grand national resurrection, historical meanings of ordinary events, the building of the third temple and redemption. Gush Emunim thus assumed its fundamentalist nature. All the Biblical rules regarding the Kingdom of Israel, the nation and the land were now literally applicable and strict Halachic instructions concerning national behavior in the messianic age were now said to be valid.

THE SANCTITY OF THE LAND OF ISRAEL

According to the fundamentalist conception of reality which is espoused by the new school, not only the time dimension of the Jewish nation but also the space dimension has been metaphysically transformed. The essence of this transformation amounts to the total holiness of the land of Israel and every concrete grain of its soil. "This holiness", writes Professor Tal, "does not replace the physical substance but inversely, the physical substance is itself becoming sacred until total holiness is achieved. Thus no individual can escape holiness and every place upon which a Jewish foot is set is holy. The historical symbols are transformed from mere symbols to a concrete substance. Not the single individual but the place is holy and not the place as a symbol for holiness, but the physical

place: trees, stones, graves, walls and other places as
well. They all are sacred in themselves." It should
perhaps be stressed that the belief that the Jewish people
and the land of Israel in its entirety are one and the
same, goes back to Rabbi Kook's mystical interpretation of
distinguished religious authorities, but in this case, too,
an immense epistemological leap has taken place since 1967.
From that time on and as a result of the concretization of
messianism in Israel, the whole issue of the borders of
the land has assumed an unprecedented seriousness. In
countless religious symposia and learned essays the question
of the genuine borders of the Land has been discussed and
debated. While the secular proponents of the greater Israeli
idea have started to survey the borders according to security
considerations or legal historical ones, the religious
messianic proponents have only had in mind one consideration:
the Biblical covenant and the promise made by God to
Abraham. In that context it was soon discovered that the
territory under consideration was not restricted to the
vast area taken by the Israeli army in the Six Day War, but
extended to the Euphratus on the northeast and to part of
the Nile on the southwest. While no unanimity on the
operational meaning of the new Biblical map has been reached,
not a single one of the fundamentalist authorities was
ready to consider giving back even a single square inch for
either peace or security considerations. Some of the
extremists do even believe that further territorial
annexations are timely. Rabbi Israel Ariel the former
head of Yamit's (the evacuated city in the Rafia Salient)
yeshiva is a typical example of a stiff fundamentalist mind.
In a private interview with this writer, he did not disclose
his opinion that our time is a high time for Israel to wage
a War of conquest. When asked about current political
constraints and diplomatic limitations, the Rabbi
responded by saying that Joshua who waged an immense war
of conquest in Canaan had far worse political constraints
and limitation. When pressed further about potential
casualties and national losses the fundamentalist rabbi
responded by referring to a Biblical ruling that in case of
a holy war no question about casualties is legitimate
until one fifth of the nation is extinct.

    Not all the rabbis of the new school or the members
of Gush Emunim would go all the way with Rabbi Ariel and so
far his is clearly a minority opinion. The fact that such
an argumentation is heard today and is legitimate is
however indicative. Thus, Israel's chief Rabbinate-which
has formally nothing to do with Gush Emunim-had in 1976

issued an official halachic ruling about the holiness of the Jewish territories and the consequent holiness of the political sovereignty over them. And in 1979 this distinguished national institution which is sanctioned by a state law had ruled that no part of the holyland could be returned even in the context of a peace treaty. "According to our holy Torah and the unequivocal and decisive halachic rulings there exists a severe prohibition to pass to foreigners the ownership of any piece of the land of Israel since it was made sacred by the Brit Bein ha-Betarim (Abraham's Covenant)".

The totalistic and uncompromising position of the messianic school and its operational translation in the daily life of the members and supporters of Gush Emunim is highly helpful in the explanation of several events in the last decade. It explains for example the stubborn opposition to Israel's retreat from Sinai and the belief held until the last moments of April 28, that God was about to intervene directly in order to prevent Begin's national crime. It also explains the high welcome accorded by Gush Emunim to the Israeli conquest of Southern Lebanon. This territory belonged in Biblical times to the tribes of Asher and Naftali and no reason in the world existed not to free it from the hostile Arabs and reclaim it forever.

## THE ARABS

A key operational question that stems from the monopolistic approach of Emunim fundamentalists to the issue of the Land of Israel concerns the Arabs. What is the role accorded to the Palestinian Arabs in the age of Jewish redemption? What right if at all should they maintain in the holy land of Israel? For many years the spokesmen of the movement had stuck to the formal "three alternatives" answer. According to it every Arab living in the land would be presented with three alternatives: to acknowledge publicly the legitimacy of the Zionist doctrine (the Gush Emunim's version) and to receive full civil rights, including the right to elect and be elected to the Knesset (and serve in the army); to obey the laws of the state without formal recognition of Zionism and be in return granted full rights of resident alien (but not political rights); to be offered economic incentives to immigrate to Arab countries.

While not excessively liberal the "three alternative" proposition makes at least some political sense. In a context of a peace settlement and an agreed upon borders it may even be appealing to some non Gush Emunim Israelis. The problem with this position is that it never really exhausted the full range of attitudes on the status of non-Jewish foreigner's expressed in the theoretical deliberations of the fundamentalist school. It is only when examined in view of the conceptions of redemption and the sanctity of the land that these attitudes are becoming clear. Basically as the late Professor Tal has shown, the entire issue is a question of human and civil rights. Tal has accurately phrased the issue by saying that "if the time and the space are two total existential categories, then no room can be left to foreigners. As we have seen the question is not limited to a bunch of crazy prophets that lost control or to an unimportant marginal minority but pertains to a dogmatic and highly elaborated philosophy. This system leads to a policy which cannot coexist with civil and human rights and in the final analysis it does not leave room for toleration." Following Tal it is possible to identify in the fundamentalist school three positions on the civil and human rights of the non-Jewish person: limitation of rights, denial of rights and in the most extreme and isolated end - a Torah based preachings for genocide. Each of the positions, it should be stressed, is anchored in an authoritative interpretation of the Holy Scriptures. The first position is relatively moderate. It stems from the conviction that the notion of universal equal human rights is a foreign ideal which like other European, non-Jewish values, has no meaning in the context of the Holy Land. The status accorded to non-Jewish residents in the Bible is the status of resident aliens who may enjoy partial privileges but never obtain full equal rights to the Jews. Emunim's three alternative propositions reflect this rather moderate position and may be seen as its political translation.

The second approach to the question of human rights amounts to a denial of those rights since the very existence of the Jews in Israel depends on Arab emigration. The ruling regarding conquest of the land according to Rabbi Shlomo Aviner, in his essay "The Messianic Realism", stands above 'moral-human' consideration of the national rights of the Gentiles in our Land. The people of Israel, according to this interpretation, were ordered to be sacred but not to be moral. Alien moral considerations do not obtain in the case of the Chosen People. The practical meaning of this interpretation is that in times of war no distinction should be made between enemy soldiers and civilians since both are of the category of people who do not belong in the land. The most extreme position, that of genocide, was expressed in an essay by Rabbi Israel Hess under the title "The Genocide Ruling of Torah". In his essay, published in the official magazine of Bar Ilan University students, Rabbi Hess likens the Arabs to the Amalekites about whom it was decisively ruled in the Bible that they deserve annihilation. The historical Amalekites were according to Hess both socially and militarily treacherous and cruel. Their relation to the Jew is like the relation of darkness to light; i.e., one of total contradiction. The Arabs who live today in the land of Israel and who are constantly waging a terroristic and treacherous war against the Jews are direct descendants of the Amalekites and the correct solution to the problem is genocide.

Discussing the delicate issue of the Arabs it is important to maintain that Hess' position is an isolated minority position and that even the second "denial" approach is not very often discussed. Nevertheless, the issue at stake is that in the context of the present fundamentalist discourse, these positions are taken without being considered illegitimate or disgusting. And what is of greater importance is the fact that none of them has so far been ruled out as totally erroneous by high religious authorities. Since the cultural atmosphere of the fundamentalist milieu is not open and pluralistic, but rather socially monolitic and hierarchal, there is a serious reason for concern. It is not at all clear whether the silence on the extreme positions is a sign of disapproval or an indication for a tactical underplay born out of political prudence.

Some indication for the awareness of Gush Emunim to the great political sensitivity of the extreme talk on the Arabs is provided by the present refusal of its leaders to comment meaningfully on the future of the Arabs in Judea and Samaria following the "expected" annexation to Israel. Emunim's standard answer on this issue is that their mission is not to solve the Arab question (the Palestinian problem does not exist!) but the Jewish question. When hardly pressed, Emunim's spokesman always maintain that in due time All-Mighty God would provide the right answer. The evolution of Emunim's frontier vigillantism and anti-Arab terrorism does not leave much room for the imagination.

## THE RELATION TO DEMOCRACY AND THE RULE OF LAW

A key issue in the understanding of the politics of Gush Emunim is the attitude of the movement and its fundamentalist cultural infrastructure towards democracy and the rule of Law. A historical examination of the movement's record is rather incriminating. During its formative years, the days of the Rabin administration, Gush Emunim had clearly satisfied an image of an anti-democratic organization. It initiated illicit settlements, affronted the democratically elected government and was on balance intensively illegal. In the case of the retreat from Sinai in 1982, the movement had again demonstrated its great disorderly potential. In its refusal to respect the peace treaties with Egypt, Gush Emunim did not just oppose the government but came out directly against Israel's legislature, the Knesset, which overwhelmingly approved the treaty. Many of Emunim's settlers have over the years been involved in anti-Arab vigillante activity which eventually culminated in the sophisticated terror network exposed in 1982.

Not only the past operations of Emunim's members are of dubious "democratic" nature, but also the cultural milieu of its spiritual authorities. There can be little doubt that the fundamentalist beliefs of the rabbis mentioned above are undemocratic. Their totalistic conception of redemption, their understanding of the existential dimension of time and space and their interpretation of the laws of Torah are totally alien to modern democracy and to the principles of legal positivism. Nor else but on the issue of human and civil rights of the non-Israeli residents, is this position so clearly expressed.

But is it the entire story? Do the past illegal operations of Emunim's settlers and the totalistic conceptions of their rabbis exhaust the subject? An empirical examination indicates that there is more to it. Thus, despite their rather impressive illegal record, the leaders and theoreticians of Gush Emunim are surprisingly not defensive about the issue of democracy. Their rather interesting argument is that they and their school should not be judged in the context of the abstract notion of democracy, but in the context of the Israeli political system which is a democracy. They point out to the fact that they have always had great respect for the secular institutional expressions of Israel's soveriegnty-the the government, the Knesset and the army.

Upon a close examination, much of Emunim's argument

is sustained by the facts. The movement has never developed a blunt anti-democratic ideology and in a general historical Israeli context has not displayed an exceptionally undemocratic behavior. Its main problem with democracy is that with respect to the one issue that truely concerns Gush Emunim, namely Eretz Yisrael, the movement has adopted a very restrictive and doctrinaire attitude. According to its interpretation the only legitimizing principle in whose name the State of Israel, its democratic regime and its legal system were established, is Zionist settlement in all parts of Eretz Israel. In this view, democracy is a reasonable system provided it exists within a truely Zionist community. Should the two collide, Zionism takes precedence. If the majority, as represented by the Knesset of Israel, rules against it, then it must be a momentary political majority, manipulative and misleading. It must be consequently fought at all costs. It is the right and the duty of every Jew in Eretz Israel to struggle against any tendency to compromise on the issue of settlement in the land even if it is proposed by the majority. When Gush Emunim people are asked how is it that they, who show so much respect for the state, are prepared to act against the government's order and guidlines, they reply that the existing government coalition and its legal framework do not represent the true spirit of the state. Government actions that prevent settlement may be legal but they are illegitimate. A government that prevents settlement undercuts its own legitimacy and places itself in the same position as the British Mandatory government, which undermined its legitimacy by enacting the policy of the infamous White Paper of 1939. During the period of the White Paper, illegal acts of settlement by secular Zionists were altogether legitimate; the same obtains today, and that does not imply a general anti-democratic orientation.

A final judgement about Gush Emunim, democracy and the rule of law should thus be held in abeyance. There exists many indications that the fundamentalist structure of their thinking and thier limited commitment to the democratic procedures would, in time of high pressure, drive many members of Gush Emunim to a total confrontation with the democratic system. There are on the other hand some indications that many elements within the movement will not opt for such a confrontation. These elements will put a high premium on the interpretation that the present state of Israel, despite all its follies, is both the halachic kingdom of Israel and the culmination of the Zionist dream. Its rulers should perhaps be strongly criticized but finally obeyed. I would consequently risk the proposition that in a situation of extreme pressure about critical issues such as the surrender of Judea and Samaria, Gush Emunim and the fundamentalist school will split.

## FROM VIGILANTISM TO TERRORISM

Almost since its establishment, Gush Emunim excelled itself as an extraparliamentary movement. Its leaders left the parliamentary N.R.P. never to return, waged intensive demonstrations against the government, and made it clear that no legal power on earth could stop their effort to settle Judea and Samaria. Although they were careful not to be involved in an anti governmental violence, expressing constantly their principled respect for the institutions of national sovereignty, they have developed effective methods of civic disobedience and passive resistance. In a historic retrospect, it is clear today that their collective self consciousness was shaped in those years not only by their youthful pioneering but by a spirit of lawlessness as well. Their dual relations with Menachem Begin is a case in point. Menachem Begin was, as a leader of the opposition in 1974-1977, a great supporter. No man could be closer to the young zealots than the man who said that "never will Eretz Israel be repartitioned". Nevertheless, when the same man became Israel's Prime Minister, who could not, for considerations of high politics follow Emunim's conception of settlement chapter and verse, the members of the Gush were but again on the hills of Samaria staging symbolic illicit settlements.

The dual orientation of Gush Emunim towards the law and the prevailing legal system was greatly perpetuated in the years of its institutional legalization. In those years which started under the Begin administration, Gush Emunim invested a great deal in gaining permanence and public respectability. In 1978 Amana (Covenant) was established as an official settlement organization, recognized by the World Zionist Organization. In addition another organization was established, the Yesha Council, which was to become the political organ of the Jewish settlements in Judea, Samaria and Gaza. Having been so successfully legalized, the movement tried now to dissociate itself from the name Gush Emunim which retained the image of an illicit extremist movement. This attempt was not successful. The Emunist philosophy was so central in the daily spirit of the settler community that its marks could not be erased by tactical arbitrary decision.

Legalization, was not the only process undergone by Gush Emunim in the late nineteen seventies. Another process whose features were not clearly visible at the beginning of the period also took place; an evolution of increased agressiveness towards the local Arab population.

Gush Emunim was not the first to introduce Jewish violent conceptions and violent behavior to the complex relationships between Jews and Arabs. Long before some of its people had started to think and act in such a way. Another extremist, Rabbi Meir Kahane, introduced the new style. Kahane, the former founder of the Jewish Defense League in the U.S., had started since 1974 to talk about T.N.T. (Terror Neged Terror), which meant Jewish terror against Arab terror. He argued that the Israeli government had to respond in kind to PLO terrorism and if the government was not ready to do it, individual Israelis had to. Since he also thought that all the non-combatant Arab people had to be expelled from Israel, his concept of T.N.T. was very soon extended to local Arabs. The Arabs, according to the extreme rabbi, were bound to ruin the Jewish character of the State of Israel so in order to survive the nation had to strike first. Intimidation and terrorism according to this view were proper means for achieving the goal.

The members of Gush Emunim were never enthusiastic about Meir Kahane and his violent supporters. He was not one of them, did not share their philosophy and was a high priest of anti-Arab hooliganism which they despised. They preached violence and eventually terrorism by way of an inintended process whose beginnings they were not aware of and whose end was very shocking to many moderate people within them. The beginning was indeed peaceful, since all Emunim members wanted was co-existence with the local population. They sincerely believed that the local Palestinians could accept Jewish hegemony in Judea and Samaria as they accepted prior to the 1967 war, Jordanian hegemony. They were convinced that there was sufficient room in the West Bank to both Jews and Arabs. The fly in the ointment however was that the local Arabs were never asked about this concept of coexistence and its operational meanings. Since the Six Day War and its results most of the Arab inhabitants of the West Bank considered the Israeli take over as an unjust conquest. The ideological among them talked about brutal colonialism and all of them identified completely with the PLO. As long as the number of Jewish settlements was relatively small and their location was not within densely populated Arab areas, the Arab animosity could be contained. PLO guerilla and terror operations were fought agsinst by the military and civil Jewish-Arab friction was minor. It pertained, if at all, to certain conflicts in Hebron where settlers demands over the holy Cave of the Patriarchs collided with similar Arab claims. But in 1977 and 1978 things have changed a great deal. The Begin government authorized a non-selective Jewish settlement all over Judea and Samaria including settlement in populated Arab areas. First moves were taken in order to renew Jewish settlement of Hebron. Now, in addition to news about settlement developments in the West Bank, news about Jewish-Arab communal collisions had started to pop up. They included information about Arab road stonings and about settlers violent reactions. Though these news were scattered and greatly minimized by all the elements involved, they had slowly contributed to a changing image of the settler community. The typical settler started to appear as a rougged frontier man rather than a youthful pioneer. But not until 1981 was this image put to an official test.

In March 1981, a letter signed by some of Israel's most prominent law professors was sent to the State Attorney General. In the letter a demand was made for an official investigation of alleged violent acts of the settler community against the local Arabs. Following this letter and a strong supreme court denunciation of the undecisive prosecution of Jews involved in anti-Arab acts, the State Attorney General, Mr. Zamir, asked his deputy Mrs. Corp to head a distinguished investigation committee of the whole affair. When a year later the committee submitted its report, the conclusions were shocking. Not only did the Corp report confirm for the first time the existence of Jewish anti-Arab vigilante activity but it stated that most of the vigilante acts remained unattended. Out of 70 cases reviewed by the committee, and which involved killings, woundings, physical assault, property damaging and application of armed and non-armed threats, 53 ended in no action. 43 of the files were closed for lack of suspect's identification, 7 because of the existence of no official complaint and 3 because of a lack of public interest to justify prosecution. The committee did not study each case in detail but a random examination indicated rather a general sloppy investigation. In several cases investigation was only reopened after a decisive committee demand.

A typical case examined by the committee was the case of Beit Hadassah (Hadassah House). Beit Hadassah, a well known site in Hebron, has always been a prime target for the Jewish settlers of Kiryat Arba (the adjacent Jewish city to Hebron, established after 1967). Referring to it as to an old Jewish property-forsaken by the Jews of Hebron in 1929 after a brutal Arab pogrom which ended the Jewish presence in the city-the settler community under its leader Rabbi Moshe Levinger, has long been asking for its resettlement. Since such an act meant a beginning of a Jewish takeover of the Arab city of Hebron, the government of Israel was very reluctant. Under these circumstances, Levinger's men have gone back to the old tactics of Gush Emunim of illicit acts and the creation of accomplished facts . The inhabitants of Beit Hadassah were harassed ocassionally and finally the building was ilegally taken over by the wives of the settlers under Mrs. Levinger in 1981. The committee had no say about this process of creeping annexation because it was already accomplished and legalised by Begin's government. It rather adrened itself to continued acts of harrassments by the Jewish dwellers of the house. These people were not satisfied with the original takeover. They were now out to intimidate all the Arab neighbors, so that Jewish control of the area be completed. The Corp committee investigated a complaint of an Arab upholsterer who had a shop in the outskirt of the building. The man was a subject of constant prenures to leave. Upon coming back one morning he found the ceiling of his shop destroyed. Following a complaint he filed with the military government he was assaulted again by the settlers. While they had made it plainly clear that he had better leave, the response of the military authorities to his complaint was slow and ineffective. The committee expressed its great dissatisfaction with the whole event including its improper investigation. A score of similar cases had convinced the committee that sloppy investigation of vigilante activities has become a common usage and that a tacit complicity between the wrongdoers and the authorities was responsible for it.

The most severe finding of the Corp report had to do with its public exposition of the total refusal of the settler community to cooperate with the police. The leaders of the community insisted that unlike the Arabs, they were only accountable to the military government and that they were not available for any routine police investigation. That insistance made it clear that in view of the settler community two standards of justice were to be obtained in Judea and Samaria; Jewish justice and an Arab one. The committee which included legal experts and high officials came under severe attack by the settlers for its "partial and unballanced" view. Indeed the settlers had all the reasons for their inconvenience. In one of its most incriminating passages the Corp report stated that vigilante incidents were not investigated, "because of intervention of politicians, including senior members of the government coalition, who have caused investigations to be called off by intervening with authorities".

Today and following the Corp report as well as other information verified and published since, the vigilantism of the settler community is an established fact. A report by the Israeli International Center for Peace in the Middle East enumerated in the period between May 1979 and July 1983. 55 reported cases of vigilantism. The acts included shooting (resulted sometimes in killing) of Arab demonstrators, window smashing (of houses and cars), severe beating, road blocking, fire setting and various kinds of intimidation. Since many Arab complaints are not made for fear of settler reprisals and others are not reported, it can be assumed that the actual number of vigilante activities is higher.

A pioneering study of the vigilantism of Emunim's settlers has been done in 1983 by David Weisbard. Weisbard, a criminologist by profession, had systematically examined the involvement of the settlers in anti-Arab vigilantism and the attitude of the entire community towards this phenomenon. His results are remarkable indeed. Weisbard found that 28 percent of male settlers and 5 percent of female settlers out of a sample of 500 admitted of having participated in some type of vigilante activity. An even more relevant finding has been the fact that 68 percent of Weisbard's respondents agreed with the statement that "It is necessary for the settlers to respond quickly and independently to Arab harrassments of settlers and settlements". Following another finding, that only 13% of the settlers questioned disapproved of vigilantism, Weisbard concluded that Emunim's support of vigilantism "represents community sentiment, not the view of a small group of radicals or trouble makers".

In the context of discussing Jewish vigilantism it should be mentioned that the greatest part of the settlers vigilantism was triggered by a previous Arab harrassment like road stonings or individual anti-Jewish assaults. But in most of these cases not a simple complaint was filed. The settlers have apparently developed a vigilante philosophy whose gist was stated to Weisbard by one settlement leader:

> Our attitude has been that we cannot afford to allow any actions of hostility by the Arabs to go unanswered...If during the day or night a rock was thrown by x amount of Arabs (at a car)...we will go out and react. Now, what reaction means really

depends on the situation. We sometimes go talk to the Muktor (the village head) and warn him, sometimes we try to catch the kids or the people, whoever it was responsible for what was done. The general idea, as I have said, is that we found that if we don't react, the Arabs will translate this as a sign of weakness. And once we are in that situation, we really don't have any point of strength to make sure this won't happen again.

Richard Maxwell Brown has defined vigilante movement as an organized extralegal movement which takes the law into its own hand. A close examination of Emunim's vigilantism indicates that the behavioral patterns developed by the settler's community fit the definition very adequately. Thus it is clear that the movement does not see itself as lawless or in a state of conflict with the prevailing legal system. Its main argument is that no sufficient security is provided by the government to the settlers of Judea and Samaria who perform a national mission of the first degree. In such a situation of lack of satisfying degree of law enforcement they must take the law into their own hands. Action which is born out of the principle of self defense is both legal and just. And, it must be done quickly and decisively so that no doubt regarding the desirable order of things remains in the Arab minds.

Over the years an additional pillar to the vigilante philosophy has been added, the image of the Arab who stands on the other side. When talking about the Arabs both individually and collectively, the settlers talk about the Arab mentality which explains the necessity for constant settler vigilance. One of Weisbard's interviewees says: "There have to be good relations with the Arabs as far as possible. But one has to show firmness if they make trouble. Because the mentality of the Arabs is such that they are used to the situation that people with power have to show their power. If someone throws a stone at you, you don't walk over and say Shalom etc... Rather first of all, you throw two stones at him and afterwards Sulhah (meeting of reconciliation)"

Having this image of the Arab in mind vigilantism is becoming a way of life. If the Arabs need all the time to be shown force, very little chance is left for effective ordinary law enforcement.

A full understanding of the vigilante activity of the settler community cannot be achieved until another factor in its life is accounted for; the official involvement of the settlers in the military security of the area. Almost from the beginning of the Israeli occupation of the West Bank, there were security problems in the area. Many anti-Jewish terrorist and guerilla operations took place in the early years and the settlements were consequently defined in the military jargon as "confrontation settlements". In those "border settlements" according to Military Order 432 and other orders, guards were authorized to excercise force and among other things to open fire under necessary circumstances. Many residents of the West Bank have, in fact, been conscripts "on extended leave", mainly religious students combining military service with rabbinical studies. In every settlement a settler has been appointed "security officer" and received a salary from the Ministry of Defense or from the Israeli police. The result of this system is a very intensive involvement of the settler community in official defense and security matters.

In 1978 a great change in the prevailing security system of Judea and Samaria took place. Israel's chief of staff, general Raphael Eitan initiated a new defense concept under the title Territorial Defense. According to the new concept, the settler community was now assigned the entire job of protecting the area and defending itself. Hundreds of settlers were removed from their former infantry units and transfered to the West Bank. In addition to their own settlements they were to secure cultivated fields, access roads and commercial and general community facilities. Every settlement was bound to have in it an alloted number of fit combatants including officers. They were to perform their active duty on a part-time basis while leading a normal civilian life. The new system also established large regional mobile forces equipped with armored personnel carriers. The task of these units was defined as "current security" activities which in the military jargon means policing the Palestinian population in their proper regions.

There exists today many indications that some of the anti-Arab violent operations have been initiated by reserve soldiers on duty. These indications have led West Bank expert Dr. Benverish to state that "the quasi-independence of ideologically motivated armed settlers, serving part time under their own commander has led to various vigilante activities, including the smashing of cars and harassment of the Arab population". A special notoriety in these actions has been obtained by the "Judea Company" of the regional defense system consisting of settlers in the Hebron Mountains. Taking all these facts into consideration, David Weisbard has reached the conclusion that settler vigilantism not only exists in Judea and

Samaria but is has become part of a total "system of rational social control". Such a system has in it, according to Weisbard, four essential ingredients; the failure of traditional social control, legitimacy, effectiveness of vigilantism and perception of its low costs. His total conclusion warrants consequently a special attention.

The vigilantism of Gush Emunim settlers is part of an organized strategy of social control calculated to maintain order in the West Bank. Though a minority of settlers actually participate in vigilante acts, they are not isolated nor deviant figures in this settlement movement. Rather, those vigilantes are agents of the Gush Emunim community as a whole. They carry out a strategy of control that is broadly discussed and supported.

Had the vigilante activities of the settlers been limited to minor operations like road blocking or retaliatory stoning of Arab cars and property, they would have had to do very little with terrorism. Terrorism, i.e. operations that combine atrocious and unconventional violence with the purpose of creating extreme fear in the victim, is not synonimous with retaliatory harrassment or window breaking. There are many indications however that the settlers vigilantism often exceeded that low degree of harrassment. On several ocassions there have been cases of actual killing or mortal woundings of civilian Arabs. These acts were initiated in order to terrorize the local population and to prevent a further anti-Jewish activities. When several distinguished members of Kiryat Arba shocked by the PLO murderous attack on the Yeshiva students in Hebron, had convened in early May 1980 they had no doubt in mind that previous "conventional" vigilantism was foiled. Only terror could counterbalance terror. While the number of people who actually operated was rather small, there exists today sufficient evidence to warrant the proposition that they had strong support. A legitimate vigilantism has thus slowly given way to a legitimate terrorism.

## TOWARDS A BUILT IN JEWISH TERRORISM

In view of the evolution of Jewish vigilantism and terrorism in the last decade as described above, it appears that our previous avoidance of the facts had led us to a misunderstanding of the nature of present day Jewish violence in Israel. For many years Israeli students of violence were convinced that Jews in their country were bound to terrorism free. Terrorism, a very atrocious form of political combat, was first and foremost an Arab phenomenon with which the civilized Jews had nothing to do. The task of fighting Arab terrorism was assigned, according to this conception, to the state's legitimate agencies; the army and the secret services, and no spontaneous citizens terrorism was either desired or expected. Students with long memory could well remember the prestate days when anti-Arab counterterrorism was indeed in existence in the form of the Irgun and later on the Stern Gang, but they were convinced that this terrorism was a matter of the past. After all these existed in the 1930's and the 1940's, no sovereign Jewish entity, and the Arabs were determined to prevent the very establishment of a Jewish state by all means. In addition, it was emphasized that even under the prestate worst conditions, only a tiny minority resorted to terrorism. No Jewish terrorism was to have a place in modern Israel. In contrast to this "non terroristic" self image which prevailed for years, it now appears that since the conquest of the West Bank in 1967, and especially since the beginning of its non-selective settlement process, conditions for permanent Jewish terrorism had emerged. The major fact in the terrorist arena, and it should be greatly stressed, was and remains to be Palestinian terrorism. The PLO and other Palestinian organizations never for one moment gave away the method of systematic terrorism. They had no reason for doing it because the only way to having the state of Israel and attract world attention have been a strategic application of guerilla warfare and terrorism. However, as long as Jewish settlement in Judea and Samaria was meager and confined to unpopulated areas there existed a real chance of preventing illicit Jewish terrorism. As in the past the job of combating Arab internal violence could well be accomplished by the army and the intelligence agencies. Indeed there was almost no Jewish terrorism until the mid-Seventies.

Jewish terrorism, in its embrionic form of vigilantism, started to evolve in 1976-1977 when Jews, especially members of Gush Emunim, had started a non selective settlement process under the Likud government. The new agressive settlement in densely populated Arab areas had made a very significant contribution to the tension in the region. Stoning of Jewish vehicles on the roads started to prevail and violent clashes took place in special locations in which Jews and Arabs met daily. Most outstanding has been the Old City of Hebron which was claimed by the settlers to be a holy city open for Jewish settlement. While small scale unorganized violence could be expected anyways, the fact that PLO strategists were determined to take advantage of the new situation has greatly contributed to the flare up. The way for massive Jewish retaliation was now full open.

In view of the knowledge commanded today it is clear that Jewish terrorism - broadly defined - was not confined to the major operations of the underground exposed last April. There were, since the late 1970's, other violent operations which bore all the identifying marks of terrorism. They were waged in order to create extreme fear in the Arabs and they involved extreme violence. The fact that the damages inflicted by these acts were rather small do not attest to the non-terroristic nature of the operations as much as to the incompetence of the actors. Kach people, for example, nurtured by the notion of T.N.T. (Jewish terror against Arab terror) were involved in occassional anti-Arab brutal acts. Meir Kahane and another associate of his were detained in 1980 in an administrative arrest for more than six months. While details of the conspiracy have never been disclosed, it has been widely rumored that the arrest had to do with an immense project of blowing up the Moslem Mosques on the Temple Mount. Two other fringe groups, though highly detached and incompetent, were also caught and charged with anti-Arab acts and great sabotage plans.

What all this information amounts to is a conclusion that under the conditions obtaining today, there exists very little chance that the Arab-Jewish cycle of terrorism will be stopped. No indication or political rational exists today for an end of Palestinian terrorism. The PLO warlords are fully convinced that without this tactic their case in the West Bank will be lost. Their anti-Jewish terrorism can be seen in this respect as a very rational means of staying politically alive.

In view of this very reality, future settler terrorism is also highly probable. No indication for the ability of the IDF to totally eliminate Arab harrassment of Jewish life in the West Bank exists today. Fully convinced in their legal ownership of the area and in their right to live there in peace, the settlers are bound to retaliate and in fact, to overreact. All of the settlers, we should remember, are armed to their teeth and are allowed according to the prevailing military regulations, to use their arms for self defense. All of them are convinced that they know better than the government what should be done and are certain in addition that the Arabs only "understand force". Under those conditions a large extension of the concept of self defense is inevitable.

The recent reaction of the settler community to the soldiers-terrorists exchanged with Gibril's terror organization is a case in point. As a result of Israel's government incredible deal to free 3 Israeli soldiers for 1, 150 Palestinian terrorists, including several very brutal murderers, the settler community made it clear that it would independently act for the expulsion of all the terrorists who were allowed to return in their homes in Judea and Samaria. An immediate release of the members of the Jewish underground was also demanded. Both announcements were made publically and were supported according to opinion polls by more than 70% of the Israeli population. Statements of support for the two demands were not limited this time to marginal political extremists or peripheral elements. They were voiced by some of Israel's most prominent politicians including deputy premier Itzak Shamir.

The last decade of violence and especially the recent trends add up to a very special Israeli reality. I can not but name it a built in structural terrorism. In such a situation the imminent conditions for terrorism are not only objective- political, social, psychological, etc., but also subjective. On both sides of the Palestinian Jewish fence there exists today two very determined communities ready and capable of systematic atrocities. We can identify on both sides three viable elements for terrorism: skillful and armed potential actors, legitimizing spiritual authorities and highly sympathetic communities. Very little else is needed for a terror vicious circle. I would risk the proposition that in the future not only Arab terrorism but also Jewish terrorism will cross the "green line" and spill over into "smaller Israel".

# INTERNATIONAL TERRORISM
## A NEW THREAT TO
## INFORMATION SYSTEMS SECURITY

Raoul Pollak

Explosive bombings and arson attacks on information systems by international terrorist organizations pose a new threat to data processing personnel, data bases and communications newtworks. The author estimates that to date, over 200 terrorist attacks against computer targets and data processing personnel have been committed. One hundred twenty-four published cases from nineteen countries are listed in this paper. Thirty-eigth of these attacks were launched against American companies, mostly abroad. These attacks emanate from the Red Brigades' ideology, according to which, "destruction of computer centers and data processing personnel is one of the main goals within their terrorist activities." Other terrorist organizations follow this idea. Vulnerability and security measures are analysed. Counter measures are recommended, with references for practical application.

This Paper is the basis of the lecture presented at the International Congress on Techniques for Criminal Identification and Counter Terrorism, IDENTA - '85, organized by the Stier Group with the assistance of the Israel National Police and under the patronage of the Hebrew University of Jerusalem, in Jerusalem 24-28 February, 1985.

It is a revision and extension of the Paper accepted for presentation at INFOCOM '83 session on Security and Privacy by IEEE Computer Society, the Institute of Electrical and Electronic Engineers, Inc., at San Diego, April, 1983.

Explosive bombing and arson attacks on information systems by international terrorist organizations pose a new threat to DP personnel, Data Bases and Communication networks. The author estimates that to date, over 200 terrorist attacks against computer targets and DP personnel were committed. 125 published cases are listed in this paper. Many of these attacks were launched against American companies, mostly abroad. These attacks emanate from the ideology of international terrorist organizations according to which, "destruction of Computer Centers and DP personnel is one of the main goals within their activities". Vulnerability and security measures are analysed. Counter measures are recommended with references for practical application. Planning of artificial intelligence expert systems for physical security and crisis management are recommended.

## VULNERABILITY OF INFORMATION SYSTEMS

Terrorist attacks on computers and DP personnel are no longer isolated incidents. When carefully analysed, they indicate part of Soviet direct and indirect efforts to damage and weaken Western Democracies from within, and are especially aimed at American corporations abroad.

The issue of vulnerability has not escaped the attention of nations such as Sweden, France, Italy, Germany, Spain, Norway, Canada and Israel which were voicing concerns that centralized systems are open to terrorist attacks.

In the United States, vulnerability and security of information systems is on the agenda of Congressional Committees, the National Security Agency, FBI, the Defense Department, the Congressional Office of Technology assessment and many other government, corporate and private security institutions and experts. The emphasis is, however, on national emergency situations and it is generally accepted that the priority given to vulnerability emanating from terrorist actions is relatively low.

It is the purpose of this paper to emphasize the evergrowing danger from terrorist attacks on information systems - worldwide and the threat to the lives of DP personnel. In comparison with other types of threats (such as computer crime), little has been written or published on the subject of terrorism against computer installations and DP personnel, although many attacks of such nature have been made. The reason may lie in the fact that attacks on computers were often reported as "terrorist bombings", aimed at certain companies or targets in general. The fact that computers and Data Processing personnel were the terrorists' primary target, has either been unknown to the press and other media or the information was deliberately withheld by the companies themselves.

"Companies hit by computer crime believe that the less the public knows about their misfortunes, the better it is for business".[1]

Since little is known about the real number of terroris attacks and the resulting damage incurred, management and DP personnel are not aware of the real danger emanating from those attacks in the future. Therefore, companies which by nature of their business, ownership and location may be exposed to terrorist attacks, should carefully review their security measures. The specific targets of terrorist attacks on information systems, as analysed in the 125 cases listed have one thing in common: they are chosen in such a way as to obtain maximum publicity on radio, T.V. and in the press. They included destruction of installations, bombing of backup sites, killing and wounding of DP personnel with bombs and machine-gun fire, in commando-type attacks.

In most cases, inside information was provided on sensitivity of installation, backup location and security.

## Computer Crime - Terrorist's Aspect

Another aspect of terrorist activities against information systems is computer crime, committed by an insider at a DP installation, in order to raise money for terrorist activities. Two such cases are known in Europe. The DP professional can commit the crime either because of political sympathy for the terrorist movement, or because he, or his family, may be threatened by terrorists.[2]

## TERRORIST ATTACKS ON INFORMATION SYSTEMS

1. Types of Computer Attacks by Terrorists
   The following attacks of international terrorist organisations have been witnessed, and most of them will be found in the 125 cases listed in Part II:
   a. Bombing of computer installations.
   b. Bombing complex Information Systems. Such Information Systems and their backups, consists of:
      1. hardware (computers)
      2. firmware (in the area of micro electronics)
      3. software (operating systems and application programs)
      4. peopleware (vendors, users and data processing programs)
      5. netware (all types of communications)
      6. brainware (data, knowledge and information)
   c. Premeditated killing of personnel.
   d. Spying via data processing records and intelligence gathering through insiders, political accomplices

or through blackmail, threats and pressure on knowledgeable data processing personnel.

e. Murder by computer.
f. Money theft, especially in the field of Transborder Data Flow and interbank transfers.
g. Destruction of communication lines.
h. Technoterrorism.
i. Gaining valuable information on military, economic and political matters.
j. Information from police files.

2. Attacks by Terrorists on Information Systems

How many attacks have been actually executed worldwide against Information Systems, Data Processing personnel and Installations? Very few estimates exist at all, and so far no estimates have been published. Except for Italy, where figures for the years 1976-1979 were provided by a private source, no statistics are available.

Based on material gathered and analyzed, the author estimates that by the end of 1984, over 200 terrorist attacks against computer targets or DP personnel were committed. This estimate contradicts the general belief of those engaged with information systems' security, that the danger of terrorist attacks against those targets is low, "since terrorists are not sophisticated enough or interested enough to attack computer targets".

In this paper, documents are listed proving that terrorist organizations see, in the destruction of computer systems and DP personnel, their primary target. The 125 cases of terrorist attacks against information systems, as listed in Part II, are the first known effort to collect, document and illustrate this serious type of threat.

The threat of terrorist attacks on information systems is of particular interest to American companies abroad. Out of the 125 cases cited, many attacks were directed against American companies established in other countries.

CASES OF TERRORIST ATTACKS
ON COMPUTER TARGETS IN 19 COUNTRIES
1969-1984

| ARGENTINA | 4 | KUWAIT | 3 |
|---|---|---|---|
| AUSTRALIA | 1 | LEBANON | 3 |
| CANADA | 1 | MEXICO | 8 |
| EL SALVADOR | 1 | NEW ZEALAND | 1 |
| FRANCE | 16 | S. AFRICA | 1 |
| W. GERMANY | 15 | SPAIN | 2 |
| HOLLAND | 1 | SWEDEN | 5 |
| IRAN | 4 | U.K. | 2 |
| N. IRELAND | 2 | U.S.A. | 26 |
| ITALY | 29 | Total: | 125 |

## TERRORIST ATTACKS ON COMPUTER TARGETS
### 1969-1984

| | |
|---|---|
| 1969 | 2 |
| 1970 | 3 |
| 1971 | 1 |
| 1972 | 5 |
| 1973 | 7 |
| 1974 | 1 |
| 1975 | - |
| 1976 | 6 |
| 1977 | 12 |
| 1978 | 13 |
| 1979 | 10 |
| 1980 | 18 |
| 1981 | 3 |
| 1982 | 12 |
| 1983 | 13 |
| 1984 | 19 |
| Total: | 125 |

## TERRORIST ORGANIZATIONS RESPONSIBLE FOR ATTACKS ON INFORMATION SYSTEMS - 1969-1984

ITALY - 29 - ATTACKS
-Brigate Rosse (Red Brigades)
- Unita Combatenti Communiste
-Action Directe
-Ultra-left Group
FRANCE - 16 - ATTACKS
- "CLODO" - Committee for liquidation and arson against
   computers
-"OAD" - Action group 27-28 March (linked to Red Brigades)
-Action Directe
WEST GERMANY - 15 - ATTACKS
-Baader-Meinhof Group I, II and III generation
-RAF- Rote Armee Fraktion (Red Army Faction)
-Ultra Rote Zellen
SOUTH AFRICA - 1 - ATTACK
-African National Congress
UNITED KINGDOM - 2 - ATTACKS
-"CRANK" - Anticomputer Establishment Group
IRAN - 4 - ATTACKS
-Radical students
-Revolutionary & dissident groups

-Anti-Vietnam groups
-SDS - Radical students for a democratic society (Pro-Fatah, (Pro-Ira)
-Underground for Freedom of Puerto-Rico
-United Freedom Federation
-Armed Resistance Unit
-The Revolutionary Puerto-Rican Independence Movement

## THE IDEOLOGICAL AND THEORETICAL BACKGROUND FOR ATTACKS ON COMPUTERS BY INTERNATIONAL TERRORISTS

A. The first theoretical record for attacking computers in Harvey Matusow's book, "The Beast for Business" London 1968, which is a record of computer atrocities. Background on investigations concerning the subject can be found in "Strategy and Tactics of World Communism - The Significance of the Matusow Case", the hearing before the Subcommittee to investigate the administration of the Internal Security Act and other internal security laws of the committee on the judiciary, United States Senate First Session - pursuant to S. Res. 58 February 21, 1955.

Part I - Testimony pages 1-763
Part II- April 19, 1955 - pages 827 onward
Following are excerpts of the book "The Beast of Business":

Human beings of the world, unite !
The computers are taking over - and from now on it's got to be them or us.

This book is a record of their atrocities against the human race...

....and a guerilla warfare manual for striking back.

Do it now - before it's too late!

Fight the creeping computer menace!  Learn how to:
  -De-magnetise your cheques
  -Add millions to your computerised bank statement
  -Get ten tons of broken biscuits delivered to
   people you don't like
  -Worry a computer
  -Confuse a computer
  -Wreck a computer.

B.  Red Brigades'"Strategic Direction Resolution"
In Italy, the Red Brigades produced a document in February 1978, "Risoluzione della Direzione Strategica", which presented the ideological and theoretical-political background and "justification" for attacks on computer centers and DP personnel.

Although cases of destruction of computer systems by terrorists occured ten years before this "Resolution" was published, it was the first time that a written terrorist document called for attack, and destruction of data processing <u>personnel</u>.

<u>THE RED BRIGADES' STRATEGIC DIRECTION RESOLUTION</u>
(translation from the Italian)
February 1978.

-Red Brigades identify computers as the foremost instruments of both the ability of multinationals to succeed and as the most dangerous instrument to be used against them in terms of files and cross referencing.

-While the material focuses on Italy, it also makes it clear that the activities of all urban guerillas in Europe are linked with common leadership to some extent.

-The material quotes from a NATO document as follows: "It is important to mention the use of computer technology in the development of anti-terrorist strategies and techniques. The use of computerised systems and of computer networks, permits the realization of the plan of anti-terrorist activities".

-We (The Red Brigade), must not underestimate the use of computer technology in the repression of the class war, as the efficiency of computers is supported by the ideology and by the technical-military personnel responsible for their functions.

-Computer systems are the monopoly of the American multinations and, in addition to ensuring the USA hegemony on world economy (The electronic sector is the strategic sector of advanced capitalism), they also guarantee the exportation of forms of control, of police methods and they also export the highest levels of repression, ripened in the strongest link of imperialism.

In fact, the export of these "systems" is not only export of advanced technology, it is the American "filing system", ruling the control structures of all the states of the imperialistic chain and, exactly because of this, it is also the creation of a layer of technicians-policemen in charge of preventitive and total espionage of the people". You see, computers are identified as the symbol, the highest profile target. <u>"It is important to destroy their mesh, to disrupt these systems, beginning from the technical-military</u>

personnel which directs them, instructs them, and makes them functional, against the proletariat." [3]

C. MAA - The Anti-Imperialistic Military Movement

After an attack on a Honeywell installation in Italy (date not published), the MAA (Movimento Armato Anti-Imperialista) left behind the following leaflet, (translation from the Italian):

MAA
(the Anti-Imperialistic Military Movement)

"Today we have hit and destroyed another counter-revolutionary and anti-proletarian center of the government which stored information and names.

We have shown the true face and the imperialistic design of the multinational Honeywell, engaged in the process of infiltration and leading to the center of data information of the bourgeois state.

The power of the repressive and counter-revolutionary system is today based upon friendships and technical collaboration between the bourgeois apparatus and United States imperialism.

Gendarmes, police and other uniformed slaves use the electronic information systems, in particular the Honeywell system.

The methods have changed, the goals remain the same: Yesterday the CIA system, today the multi-nationals.

The target remains: exploitation and oppression.

The chase after the imperialistic structure, until their successful destruction, is being continued by the militant forces.

Smash and destroy the product of contrarevolution of the United States multinations!

We are building the movement of anti-imperialistic resistance! !

Signed:

The Anti-Imperialistic Military Movement[4]

D. Attacks on Computers by Terrorists in the U.S.A.

The following communique, dated August 17th, 1983, from the Armed Resistance Unit, after bombing a navy computer, was left by the terrorists:

"Communique No. 2

Tonight we attacked the computer operations complex at the <u>Washington Navy Yard</u>.

We have acted in solidarity with the revolutionary struggles of the peoples of Central America and the Caribbean. We hope that this act of proletarian internationalism is just one of a growing number by anti-imperialists in the country determined to show that there will be no blocade between the struggle of oppressed peoples around the world, and those here inside U. S. borders ...."

"...the computer complex at the Washington Navy Yard is used to train high-ranking officials of the naval war college. They simulate massive naval battles, practicing how to sacrifice the lives of millions -- perhaps hundreds of millions -- for the interest of the U.S. ruling class..."

The computers are part of the technology of death that the U.S. government employs to try to defeat the struggle of peoples around the world.

-Defend the Nicaraguan revolution.
-Victory to the FMLN/FDR!
-Independence and socialism for Puerto Rico!
-Build a revolutionary resistance movement!
-Fight U.S. imperialism!
-Sabotage the <u>technology</u>!

E. The Ideology of CLODO and Action Direct Organization

Another group, calling itself 'CLODO' or 'Committee for the Liquidation and Misappropriation of Computers' claimed that it and "Direct Action Organization" were responsible for the raid on Philips Data-Systems premises. In a statement to the left-wing newspaper, "Liberation", France, it said:

"We are computer workers and therefore well placed to know the present and future dangers of computer systems. Computers are the favourite instrument of the powerful. They are used to classify, to control and to repress. We do not want to be shut up in ghettos or programs and organizational patterns."

They threatened more attacks on other computer outfits throughout France which they believed processed information for 'the Defence Ministry and the counter-espionage service'. The group went on to say that it would authenticate its actions in future with the letters "OAD" on the floor of computer rooms they raided.

F. The Ideology of PLO Concerning Destruction of Communications

In June 1982, the Israeli Defense Forces captured in Lebanon a document which is a manual of instructions for sabotaging communication systems. It is written in Spanish by the Organizacion Para La Liberacion de Palestina, Mision Permanente en Cuba La Habana, which is the permanent PLO mission in Cuba. The document is marked "Top Secret 0076".

The document enclosed detailed technical instructions for the sabotage of communications and electrical power supply. It enclosed 18 detailed technical pages with the following chapters:

- Chapter 117, 118 and 119: Top Secret - Sabotage of Communications.
- Chapter 120, 121 and 122: — Sabotage of Motor Vehicles
- Chapter 123: Detailed instructions for sabotage of telephone communications:
    1. external telephone and telegraph communications;
    2. underground telephone and telegraph cables;
    3. telephone and telegraph centers.

G. The Ideology of the CCC - Belgium

The CCC - Cellules Communistes Combattantes (fighting Communist Cells) claimed responsibility for 11 bombings between October 1984 and January 1985, including Honeywell and Litton Industries.

They issued the following communique in Brussels, January 1985:

"Further actions could kill Yankee military and their accomplices...

Human life is not an absolute in itself, a mysterious value. It holds no sacred character for us."

## SUMMARY OF ANTI-COMPUTER TERRORISTS' IDEOLOGICAL DOCUMENTS

A. 1968 Great Britain - Harvey Matusow:
"A GUERILLA WARFARE MANUAL"
Wreck computers.

B. 1978 Italy - Red Brigades:
"STRATEGIC DIRECTION RESOLUTION"
Destroy, disrupt computer systems and personnel.

C. 1978 Italy - M.A.A.
"TODAY WE HAVE HIT AND DESTROYED ANOTHER COUNTER REVOLUTIONARY AND ANOTHER PROLETARIAN CENTER OF THE GOVERNMENT WHICH STORED INFORMATION AND NAMES."

D.  1983 U.S.A. - Armed Resistance Unit:
       "SABOTAGE U.S. COMPUTERS - THE TECHNOLOGY OF DEATH.'
E.  1980 France - CLODO and Action Direct Organization
F.  1982 Lebanon - PLO
       Concerned with the destruction of telephone and
       telegraph communication networks.
       Detailed technical instructions for sabotage in
       Spanish by the permanent PLO Mission in Cuba.
G.  1984 Belgium - CCC
       "KILL YANKEE MILITARY AND THEIR ACCOMPLICES".
       Fighting communist cells.

## ATTACKS ON AMERICAN COMPANIES AND PERSONNEL ABROAD

"...certain nationalities are particularly at risk as
targets of international terrorism.  The U.S.A. is regarded
in the terrorist ideology of most of the New-Marxist
revolutionary groups as the arch-enemy, the embodiment of
'capitalist imperialism', and hence its representatives,
businessmen and citizens are seen to be appropriate targets...
Between 1968 and 1977 more than 200 U.S. diplomats and more
than 500 private citizens and businessmen were victims of
terrorist incidents abroad.  Fifty Americans were assassinated."[5]

## SECURITY MEASURES

The security measures against terrorist attacks on
information systems consist of three different levels of
security, the third level being new even to professionals
who deal with Information Systems security.
FIRST LEVEL:   Security on the political, military and
               intelligence level.
SECOND LEVEL: This level is directly involved with DP
               installation and includes:
               - Physical security.
               - Personnel security.
               - Backup of hardware, software and personnel.
               - Risk analysis.
               - Disaster recovery planning.
THIRD LEVEL:   Expert systems for personnel investigation,
               physical security and crisis management.
The First Level
       Dealing with security on the political, military and
intelligence levels.  This level deals with active fighting of
terrorism and was defined in the Jerusalem Conference on
International Terrorism in 1979 [6] as follows:
       "In fighting terrorism we have to follow several basic
       rules:

- There should never be a surrender to terrorism.
- We must have an elaborate intelligence system apparatus, a well organized early warning system, and properly trained people. Only these can nullify the terrorist advantage of surprise and indiscriminate attack.
- We must fight terrorists not only in the operational field, but also on the psychological one...
- Terror has become international and must be fought internationally. The terrorists consider most free nations and people as their enemies; counter measures must therefore be internationally co-ordinated. The earlier this is done, the better will be the anti-terror operation. Since terror is carried out in the dark and clandestinely it cannot be met squarely in the open field; its tactic of surprise must be met by a well-prepared strategy of surprise on the part of the international community."

As part of anti-terrorist activities, French President Mitterand announced on August 17, 1982, use of anti-terrorist Data Base by French police and security agencies, which are modelled after the Data Base in operation in Austria.[7]

The Second Level

Should be structured in a manner which should anticipate explosive bombing and arson, as the most probable type of terrorist attack. An important factor must be taken into consideration: the analysis of previous bombing attacks and arson against computer installations and personnel show a clear indication that the terrorists had inside information, emanating from professional DP personnel. This indicates that they knew where, how and when to place the bomb, in order to cause maximum damage. In some cases remote backup sites were also destroyed.

1. Therefore, protective measures which are included in physical security must be executed in such a way as to prevent terrorists' access to a computer installation and minimize the damage in case of attack. Recommended references on computer security are James Martin's book[8] and Donn Parker's manual[9]. Excellent practical handbooks for Data Base, Data Center and Data Communication security are by Jerry Fitzgerald[10,11] the Plagman Group[12] and by J. Kuong[13,19] including 10 publications by R. Pollak.

2. Personnel Security
   a. Personnel security includes protection of all

DP personnel and, in particular, those individuals who may be chosen as targets for terrorist attacks or extortion, because of their special function: <u>Data Base Administrators</u> (see description of function in (14), <u>Data Security Officers</u> and <u>Data Coordinators</u>, who are responsible for enduser created software security controls and data management.[15,19]

b.  Distributing the centralized functions of Data Base administrator
One method to decrease the security burden on on the DBA and decrease the vulnerability and damage the installation if the DBA is attacked, is to decentralize his functions. This may be achieved by a method in which "a multiuser data base permits users to selectively share data while retaining the ability to restrict data accesses."[16]

c.  Personnel security includes very deep and detailed investigation of the personnel background, in order to find someone who might cooperate and supply information to terrorists from inside. Personnel security includes also protection of DP personnel from: physical attacks - threats of extortion. It also calls for backup of sensitive DP personnel functions.

3.  The <u>backup</u> of hardware and software should be provided on off-site facilities, since it must be anticipated that the original installation may be destroyed. (See James Martin, ref. (8) p. 332.)

4.  Risk analysis cannot take the classic path of evaluation of various risk possibilities. The risk from terrorism is evident and clear. What must be evaluated are the alternatives of locations of the systems, in order to decentralize systems and diminish concentration of DP facilities in one place. Distributed systems have an obvious advantage over centralized ones, when anti-terrorist security is concerned.

5.  <u>Disaster Recovery</u> facilities must be of such a nature as to enable recovery of the information systems from total destruction. This increases the cost of security budgets, because it calls for almost full replacement of hardware, software and peripheral equipment. If the personnel is safe, this is the minimum cost which organizations must

bear in order to keep their vital information systems operating.[17]

6. Artificial intelligence expert systems for personnel investigations, physical security and crisis management. (See Expert Systems)

## ARTIFICIAL INTELLIGENCE EXPERT SYSTEMS FOR INFORMATION SYSTEMS SECURITY

The future of any security system (including Information System Security) lies with Expert Systems.

Artificial intelligence Expert Systems, will not replace computer security officers, but they will assist them in executing their difficult tasks more efficiently, quicker and punctually. Expert systems help security officers in the decision making processes in complex situations where time factors are critical, such as decisions in crisis management.

Expert Systems will, within the near future, find applications in fighting terrorism and computer security. They will be applied in the following fields:
- Risk analysis
- Disaster recovery
- Contingency planning
- Personnel investigation
- Fire protection
- Insurance
- Computer auditing and control

Following is a short description of three security Expert Systems originated by Raoul Pollak:

1. "SAPEX" - in process of prototyping
2. "FIPREX" - developed with BMB Security Knowledge Systems Ltd.
3. "INSUREX" - developed with BMB Security Knowledge Systems Ltd.

A. SAPEX - Security Assessment Personnel Expert System
An Expert System for hiring procedures and monitoring of DP Personnel.

1. This expert system will evaluate and monitor background information on DP personnel, in order to increase security and decrease hazards emanating from intentional criminal acts.

2. This expert system can be utilized in three stages of security evaluation:
   a. before hiring procedure
   b. during various stages of employment; before promotion and increasing authorization and responsibility; in periodical security tests.

c. before employment <u>termination</u> and after the person
      has left the company in regard to its activities
      in the company.
3. This expert system can act as stand alone system but
   can also be extended and combined with additional
   expert systems (such as Contingency Planning and
   Disaster Recovery).
4. Although the authors have originally planned this
   expert system for implementation in DP installations,
   the actual potential use of the expert system is much
   wider. It can be used for personnel security,
   monitoring and evaluation in practically any
   installation and applied to almost every profession in
   which a high degree of personal integrity is required,
   such as bank officials, government employees,
   military, etc.

B. FIPREX - Fire Protection Expert System

An Expert System designed for managing a "crisis situation".

FIPREX will assist in managing rescue and disaster recover
operations when fires occur. <u>FIPREX</u> will be invaluable to
fire brigades, military, police, hospitals, city-rescue teams
and others involved in the EFFICIENT MANAGEMENT AND CO-
ORDINATION OF RESCUE OPERATIONS in situations under stress
and in crisis. In such situations, time and catastrophy
constraints force management to make OPTIMUM decisions often
under changing circumstances and within critical time
limitations and lack of relevant, updated information.

Making the optimum decision in such situations is almost
"Mission Impossible" for even the best trained and experienced
brains - without the assistance of a computer-driven expert
system.

The difference between using FIPREX in FIRE PROTECTION and
disaster recover, or relying on the classical "state of the
art" approach ("... now let's keep our heads calm...don't
panic...let's see how to get out of this mess..") can mean
the difference between life and death, the difference between
salvage or destruction of property, libraries and art
treasures.

FIPREX may save lives and property when fire disaster
strike.

FIPREX will cover large populated areas, industrial
complexes and installations.

FIPREX will be used as stand alone system or as part of
many connected systems, integrated into a large FIPREX
network.

FIPREX will have two versions: STATIC-STRATEGIC versions
and MOBILE OPERATIONAL version.

C. INSUREX

An expert system for Insurance Companies

INSUREX will help Insurance companies to make decisions on underwriting and insuring properties against all types of vulnerabilities. It will also help insurance companies to upgrade their security measures in various types of industries against fire and destruction in accordance with pre-determined insurance standards.

## THE VULNERABILITIES OF COMPUTERIZED SOCIETY IN SWEDEN (THE SARK REPORT) [18]

One of the few countries where legislation has advanced Information Systems Security on a national level, is Sweden. Here are some abstracts.

SARK Legislation

- On May 1977 Sweden's Ministry of Defence Established the Committee on the Vulnerability of Computer Systems - SARK - to investigate the vulnerability of the Swedish computerized society and to propose measures to reduce it.
- In December 1979 SARK Report was published
- In July 1981 the Swedish Government accepted the SARK Report
- In 1982, the Swedish Minister of Defence directed that an Advisory Board be appointed, with representatives from Government Agencies and the business community.
- The Board prioritized vulnerabilities to support the 1982 Total Defence Bill and Data Policy Bill.
- The Board is now drawing up proposals for more permanent measures and was to have completed its work by July 1984.

External Vulnerability to Information Systems as defined by SARK Report

1. Criminal offences
2. Sabotage, espionage and crimes against property
3. Political terrorism as means of aggression between countries
4. Blockade against import
5. Espionage and sabotage by maintenance technologists
6. Electromagnetic pulse (EMP) from nuclear explosions
7. Natural and intentionally caused destruction

# REFERENCES

1. "Computer Crime Skeletons", Editorial, Computerworld, Nov. 29, 1982.

2. "Computer-related Crime, Methods & Detection", Computer Crime - Criminal Justice Resource Manual Bureau of Justice Statistics, U.S. Department of Justice, Washington, DC 20531 1979. pp. 9-29

3. DSH, Inc. (Data Security Holdings, Inc.) - International Operations (internal report).

4. Ibid.

5. "Terrorism: International Dimensions" - answering the challenge, by Professor Paul Wilkinson, University of Aberdeen, Scotland. Conflict Studies No. 113, Nov. 1979, published by the Institute for the Study of Conflict, 12/12A, Golden Square, London W1R 3AF. Quoted by permission of the author.

6. "International Terrorism: Challenge and Response", proceedings of the Jerusalem Conference on International Terrorism. Editor: Binyamin Netanyahu The Jonathan Institute, Jerusalem, 1981 Distributed by Transaction Books. ISBN 0-87855-456-4.

7. Computerworld, August 23, 1982.

8. Security, Accuracy and Privacy in Computer Systems by James Martin, 1973. Prentice-Hall, Inc., Chapter 27: Sabotage, p. 323.

9. "Computer Security: The Best Method for Attacking the Real Problems", Donn B. Parker, SRI International Jan., 1981.

10. Designing Controls into Computerized Systems, Dr. Jerry Fitzgerald, 1981 (101 individual control lists that contain over 2,500 specific controls).

11. Internal Controls for Computerized Systems, Dr. Jerry Fitzgerald, 1978. Library of Congress Cat. No. 78-

69677 ISBN 0-932410-04-9 Chap. 8: "Physical Security Control Matrices".

12. The Data Base Environment: Audit & Control published by the Plagman Group, Inc., 1981 New York.

13. COM - S.A.C. Computer Auditing and Control,published by Javier F. Kuong, Management Advisory Publications, P.O.B. 151, 44, Washington St., Wellesley Hills, Mass 02181.

14. Principles of Data-Base Management, by James Martin. Prentice Hall Inc., 1976, Englewood Cliffs, New Jersey. ISBN 0-13-708917-1, Chapters 21: Data Administration and 22: Security and Privacy.

15. Application Development without Programmers, by James Martin. Prentice-Hall Inc. 1982. ISBN 0-13-038943-9 Data Administration, p. 267 Data Coordinator pp. 313-314

16. An Authorization Mechanism for a Data-Base, Arditi, Joel & Zukovsky, Eli - Computer Center Weizman Institute of Science, Rehovot, Israel. Academic Press Inc. ISBN 0-12-642150-1.

17. EDP Disaster Recovery Workshop, Michael I. Sobol, MIS Associates, 12 Juniper Lane, Framingham, Mass. 01701

18. Fighting Computer Crime (1983) by Don Parker, Ch. 37. 1002 721.

# THE ISRAEL NATIONAL POLICE
## BOMB DISPOSAL UNIT

Arik Yakuel, Superintendent
Deputy Head of the Unit

To better deal with the serious terrorist threat, the Israel National Police was charged with the responsibility of dealing with security problems within the country proper. A major portion of this responsibility falls upon the Bomb Disposal Unit which was created in 1976 as an autonymous unit in the Operations Department. The unit has administrative center in the National Headquarters and field units which are distributed country-wide as required. The paper deals with the structure and functions of the Bomb Disposal Unit, then a general survey of terrorist activity in Israel is given: factors effecting terrorist activities, mode of terrorist operations, etc.

Essentially there are two different types of terrorism - external and internal. This paper will concentrate on counter-terrorism inside the borders of Israel, although that terrorism most often begins with a border infiltration from a neighboring region.

Infiltration into Israel has been tried by air, sea and land. An example of an attempt by terrorists to penetrate Israel's borders by air is the glider on display in the exhibit in the corridor. The commando boat also on display is an attempt by terrorists to gain access into the country from the sea and carry out an attack on Nahariya.

There is no shortage of examples where terrorists have tried to enter Israel across our land borders. History can unfortunately tell of too many attempts. The tragic events several years ago at Maalot are only one example. Favorite targest of terrorists for land infiltration have also been Kiryat Shemonah and, in earlier days, Bet Shean.

The main task of the Israel Bomb Disposal Unit begins after the terrorist is already in the country. The unit's responsibilities can be divided into work in the following categories: (a) explosives and boobytraps, (b) throwing of hand grenades and incendiary bottles (more informally known as Molotov Cocktails), (c) mining, (d) terrorist motivated arson, (e) firing of rockets and artillery missles, and (f) hoax bombs or false charges. There are, of course, other means of terrorist attack such as the use of standard fire arms; however only the subjects listed fall within the area of the units operating framework.

Before we proceed any further, I should like to mention that false charges are a common aspect of the bomb disposal unit's work, and we treat these with maximum caution. Every false charge is treated as though it were a highly sophisticated Improvised Explosive Device (IED), until its true nature is definitively ascertained.

Chart No. I gives a good indication of those targets most often used by terrorists for attack. As the other chart shows, terrorists have preferred commercial buses, bus stations, markets and other public installations where large numbers of people gather. Tourists and tourist sites have been terrorist objectives, as have been military and police facilities and personnel.

The second chart shows the relative quantity of terrorist attacks since 1977. Considerable time has been spent analysing the reasons for the increase or decrease of terrorist activity in any given period, and some of our conclusions are quite obvious.

It is felt, for example, that major political events, whether they be of a domestic nature such as elections, or of an international nature such as the signing of a political agreement, are important causes in determining the height of terrorist activity. Internal strife within terrorist organizations is also a major factor, since groups fighting among themselves have very little time to conduct other activities.

An evaluation of the number of IED's against Israeli targets will show that a marked decrease was experienced with the commencement of the Peace for Galilee Operation. On the one hand, terrorists were tied down to a conventional war against Israel coupled with internal fighting between rival groups; on the other hand, however, the terrorist infra-structure was dealt a serious blow, and the availability of sophisticated explosive materials and the trained personnel to use them was severely reduced.

There has been a marked increase in the throwing of Molotov cocktails. In 1977 there were only 26 incidents recorded; however in 1984 this number was in excess of 125. The primary reason for the increase is felt to be the fact that these are simple incendiary devices which can be made by relatively inexperienced personnel within the confines of a private dwelling. Our experience has shown that today a much higher percentage of terrorist attacks is conducted with less sophisticated equipment.

Obviously, although casualties are the most memorable statistic after a terrorist event, they are a poor guage of the intensivity of terrorist activity. A single terrorist incident involving one sophisticated IED can cause numerous casualties, while a long list of incidents using simple methods can result in no significant injury.

A geographic analysis of terrorist incidents in Israel has shown that during the past few years there have been markedly fewer incidents within the pre-1967 borders of the country. This has led us to conclude that the preventive measures which we have been undertaking have been, for the most part, quite successful.

Clearly, it is easier for terrorists to operate in the Arab areas of Judea, Samaria and Gaza, hence the figures for these regions are higher.

In order to deal with the terrorist threat, the Israel National Police has established a country-wide program including the Anti-Terror Unit (Yamam), the Citizens Guard, and the Bomb Disposal Unit. Other government agencies involved in the fight against terrorism are the Israel Defense Forces (IDF), the Mossad, and the General Security Service.

One of the key elements in the fight against terrorism is outside this official framework. It is the Israeli public. The Bomb Disposal Unit encourages the public to summon assistance every time a suspect parcel is delivered, every time that an unidentified package is found. One hundred false alarms are better than one incident that could have been prevented (1).

The nerve center of the Bomb Disposal Unit is at Israel National Police Headquarters in Jerusalem. Several key units are located in the headquarters building: Research & Development, Equipment Maintenance, Intelligence, Bomb Disposal Laboratories, Training, Israel Bomb Data Center (IBDC), and Staff Psychologist.

The unit's Research & Development Section is tasked with providing those working resources needed by technicians in the field. It might sound simple to open a car door, but in the Bomb Disposal Unit this is often required to be done quickly while the person opening it remains at a safe distance. Developing the equipment to solve this problem is just one request made of R&D.

Once of the most serious mistakes an organization can make is to concentrate exclusively on the difficulties of today and ignore the problems of tomorrow. So, another function of Research & Development is to look to the future, not only to identify possible problems, but also to confront the question of solutions.

The basic philosophy of the Bomb Disposal Unit is that it must work independently, and for this reason it has established the Equipment Maintenance Section. If it purchases a robot and it malfunctions, the section will fix it. The Bomb Disposal Unit does not want to send it back to the manufacturer who might repair it at his leisure.

Perhaps the best approach to defending against terrorism is to understand the terrorist, and here intelligence is a key factor. The Intelligence Section of the Bomb Disposal Unit is a working partner in Israel's Intelligence Community. It provides technicians in the field with all of the necessary background knowledge available, so that whenever possible IED's can be dismantled as objects whose inner workings are known and not as totally unknown puzzles.

The four Bomb Disposal Laboratories located in key cities in Israel are responsible for the analysis of all explosive devices found in Israel and for the dissemination of written reports both to technicians and to the courts as required.

The Bomb Disposal Unit views training as the backbone of the organization. Sending a technically unqualified technician to dismantle an IED is nothing other than an open invitation to tragedy. For this reason, the Training Section was created. It takes full responsibility for training of technicians, from their enlistment in the police to their departure from the force. This training includes not only initial basics; it also includes periodic updating sessions and refresher courses.

The IBDC is one of seven similar centers located in different countries throughout the world. These centers work in close co-operation with each other, exchanging data and sharing information. It was realized long ago that terrorism is an international threat against which the combined resources of key countries are most effective.

A staff psychologist might at first seem like a strange partner in the Bomb Disposal Unit; however, his contribution to the effort is quite important. Before personnel are hired, the psychologist screens them to determine factors such as manual dexterity. It would be foolish to consider a man "with 10 thumbs" as a candidate for the exacting work of dismantling a bomb. The psychologist also assists staff as problems arise during their employment.

The field structure of the Bomb Disposal Unit closely follows the general structure of the Israel National Police. Israel is divided into four police districts (North, Central, Tel Aviv, South), and it is further divided into 11 sub-districts. The Bomb Disposal Unit is represented in each one of these regional divisions, with size of staff dictated by factors such as case requirements, geographic area covered, and population density.

All field units are equipped to respond to all emergencies which might occur in their areas. In the major cities of Israel, response time is usually no more than 10 minutes. Responses to the presence of suspicious vehicles or parcels are the potentially sensational aspect of their work; however not to be ignored is the increasing number of preventive tasks performed.

In order to have an efficient field force, the Bomb Disposal Unit has emphasized proper equipment, sound training, learning from past mistakes and close co-operation between responsible government agencies. Hopefully with this approach, the war against terrorism will be won.

Note: This summary was written by Dr. Jay Levinson from the lecture presented by Arik Yakuel at IDENTA '85.

Footnote:

(1) At the very time that this paper was being delivered at IDENTA '85, two bombs were being dismantled in Jerusalem after police had been summoned by private citizens.

# SURVEY OF SELECTED
# TERRORIST DEVICES

Joseph Sharon, Head
Northern District Bomb Disposal Laboratory
Israel National Police

An Improvised Explosive Device (IED) contains three main components: (a) explosives, (b) an initiator, and (c) a firing mechanism.

## EXPLOSIVES

In cases in the Northern Police District during the past several years, we have encountered two basic types of explo ives. When standard explosives have been used in IED's, they have been accompanied by gaseous releases and blast effects. Common explosives in this category have been plastics (usually in multiples of 2.5 kilogramme packages), TNT blocks (most of Soviet manufacture and found in packages of 200 or 400 grammes), and RDX.

Industrial explosives, such as dynamites or gelatins, have been encountered as well, but with much less frequency. Usually, these have been found in sticks ranging from 100 to 250 grammes each.

The other major group of explosives which we have seen in common use by terrorists is the improvised, or homemade, type. These are made with two basic components: (a) oxidizers, and (b) agents. The manufacture is extremely simple, since these components are readily available. These improvised explosives do not "explode" like the standard variety; rather, they deflagrate or burn. To obtain this effect, they must be kept inside a closed container.

## INITIATORS

Initiators can also be divided into similar categories of standard and improvised. The standard initiator is a detonator, either simple or electrical and most often made using an aluminum sleeve with two layers: (a) PETN explosive, and (b) lead azide. Activation is by the use of a flame, often introduced in conjunction with a safety cord.

In an electrical detonator activation is accomplished, not by a standard flame, but by the use of electrical current.

Improvised initiators are commonly built on the basis of bulbs of either the simple or flash variety. They create heat or flame which then activate improvised explosives. These bulbs, however, cannot be used to activate standard explosives.

## FIRING MECHANISM

In discussing firing mechanisms, two factors must be taken into consideration: (a) delayed time devices, and (b) boobytraps.

Electrical delayed time devices are usually watches or clocks, and in PLO cases which we have experienced, we have seen examples ranging from standard wrist watches to much larger clocks. In terrorist cases the time delay is usually no more than one hour , so the Bomb Disposal Unit must act quickly when a bomb is found.

Chemical delayed time devices are most often based upon sulfuric acid. To cite one example from our case work, a wire causing detonation was set to be released once the chemical reaction with sulfuric acid would have set it free.

In practical terms, another terrorist device which was discovered before detonation can be cited as an example of chemical delay. Sulfuric acid was placed in a glass tube sealed by a cork, on the other side of which there were match heads and a blasting cap. When the tube is turned upside down, the sulfuric acid begins to penetrate the cork, and when it reaches the match heads a flame is achieved.

Mechanical delay devices are based upon metal fatigue. Clasically, when a safety pin is released, mechanical force is applied to a piece of metal holding a striker. Metal fatigue eventually allows the striker to make contact leading to detonation.

Boobytraps usually fall into one of several categories: (a) mechanical pressure, (b) electrical pressure, (c) pressure release.

An example of electrical pressure would be the presence of two unconnected plates. The IED is constructed in such fashion that if it is moved casually, the two plates make contact with each other, closing an electrical circuit and achieving detonation.

In several cases where pressure release boobytraps were discovered in the Northern Polic District, a camouflaged battery was found fastened atop a lead box. Beneath the battery there is a pressure release switch similar to the one used inside refirgerator doors to control the light. When an unsuspecting person removes the battery thinking that he has dismantled the bomb, he has, in fact, released the pressure switch controlling the true electrical circuit.

In one common variation, a relay is used, and when the wires fastening the battery to the box are cut, the electrical circuit is then completed.

Another boobytrap used in Israel is based upon a glass tube containing mercury and two electrical contacts. When the tube is inverted, the mercury closes the electrical circuit, and detonation is achieved.

Explosives, detonator, and firing device - if any one of these components is missing, the IED cannot function. There are, however, two additional components which are optional in an IED: (a) fragments, and (b) camouflage.

## FRAGMENTS

In some cases fragments are a result of a covering around the explosive. For example, if explosives are housed in a metal pipe, that pipe will fragment after detonation of the IE. Fragments from the pipe can even be scattered over a large area. In Israel it is no problem to buy pipes, and terrorists have used them quite often, both with standard and improvised explosives.

Sharp pieces of metal, and nails in particular, can be used in conjunction with an IE. It should be pointed out that in the terrorist bombing of the No. 18 bus in Jerusalem, a large quantity of nails was placed next to the explosive.

## CAMOUFLAGE

Many times it is necessary to hide an IED or have the device "blend into the scenery" in order to prevent discovery. In the area of camouflage, terrorists have been quite inventive.

A small mine-like device was placed in an empty cigarette package and left on the ground. It was intended that when someone stepped on the package, either not noticing it or thinking it to be litter, detonation and resultant injury would occur.

The list of camouflages used by terrorists is truly endless. A number of years ago an IED was hidden in a book whose pages had been carved out - what more common item than a book found in the National Library Building in Jerusalem! Terrorists have also used egg cartons, flower pots, industrial sized cans of salad oil, loaves of bread, ...

This has been an overview of some of the experiences of the Northern Police District's Bomb Disposal Laboratory. A number of the IED's encountered and described can be found in the IDENTA '85 Exhibition of Terrorist Devices.

Note: This summary was prepared by Dr. Jay Levinson of the Israel National Police, based upon the lecture delivered by Joseph Sharon at IDENTA '85.

Illustration I

Boobytrapped book found at Hebrew University, and typical pipe bomb.

Illustration II

Camouflaged IED in fire extinguisher, and reconstruction of IED found in Jerusalem hidden in artificial sweetner bottle.

# A METHOD FOR ESTIMATING THE ACCURACY OF INDIVIDUAL CONTROL QUESTION TESTS

Gordon H. Barland, Ph.D.

The type of polygraph examination most commonly used in criminal investigations in the U.S. is the control question test. Although many experts agree that it is generally about 90% accurate under optimal conditions, no method has been available to the field examiner to estimate the probability of an error associated with specific control question polygraph examinations. Polygraph charts obtained in laboratory research involving mock crimes were numerically scored using field techniques. Normative tables were derived from the distribution of the scores of the "guilty" and "innocent" subjects. Given any three-chart score from polygraph charts obtained and scored under similar conditions, the probability of false positive and false negative errors can be estimated by reference to the tables. It would be premature to apply this method to criminal investigations until similar tables have been developed from verified real-life cases.

The federal scoring system for evaluating single issue control question tests in the field requires a final test score of +6 or higher for a decision of truthfulness and -6 or lower for a decision of deception. Scores between +/-5, inclusive, are inconclusive. Although many experts agree that numerically scored control question tests are about ninety percent accurate when criminal suspects are examined under appropriate conditions, there exists no method by which the field examiner can estimate the accuracy of individual control question tests. Once the score exceeds the threshold required for a decision, the accuracy is assumed to be about ninety percent. However, if the scores of the innocent and guilty suspect populations are distributed in anything approaching a normal distribution, it would follow that the more extreme the score is, the more accurate the decision is likely to be. Conversely, the closer the score approaches zero, the greater the possibility of an error if a decision is made.

This study tested that assumption and, using data from mock crimes, developed a table which lists the estimated probability of an error for each polygraph test score irrespective of what the base rates are for truth and deception.

Data from mock crimes were used in order to obtain ground truth about whether the subjects were truthful or deceptive on the relevant questions. Data from three sources were pooled in order to have as large an N as possible. The pooling of data would be expected to increase the variance of the scores, which would make the resulting probabilities more robust, increasing the generalizability of the results. It is better for the probabilities generated by this research to overstate rather than understate the probability of error. The three sources included two mock theft studies (Barland & Raskin, 1975; Dawson, 1977) and a variety of mock crimes committed for the polygraph training course of the Canadian Police College.[1] The data consisted of the numerical scores obtained from the first three charts of the federal zone comparison control question test, in which three physiological measures were scored: respiration, skin resistance and cardiovascular activity as measured by a pressurized arm cuff.

The pooled data included 120 truthful and 74 deceptive subjects. The mean scores were +6.9 for the truthful group and -8.3 for the deceptive group, with standard deviations of 8.65 and 8.78, respectively. As can be seen in Figure 1, 122 (63%) of the examiners' decisions were correct, 10 (5%) were incorrect, and 62 (32%) of the polygraph examinations were inconclusive. Excluding the inconclusive results, 92% of the decisions were correct. There was a 9% false positive error rate and a 5% false negative error rate. Some 96% of the truthful decisions and 88% of the deceptive decisions were correct.

Each of the two frequency distribution curves was separately grouped into intervals of five. The differences between the observed frequencies and the frequencies expected if the distribution were normal were compared using the chi square goodness of fit test (Downie and Heath, 1974). The differences were significant neither for the innocent group

$(x^2 = 3.1187$, df $= 4$) nor for the guilty group $(x^2 = 5.2652$ df $= 3$). Because neither curve was significantly different from a normal distribution, the raw polygraph scores were converted to standard scores for each group separately, based upon its mean and standard deviation, and the probability associated with each of the standard scores was obtained from standard tables. These are presented in Table 2. Column 3 lists the probabilities that a guilty subject could score as high or higher than the 3-chart polygraph scores in column 1. Column 5 lists the probabilities that an innocent subject could score as low or lower than the scores in column

There are several approaches that can be taken when estimating the probability of errors associated with individual control question tests. One method would be to determine the ratio of the frequencies of the innocent versus the guilty subjects at each polygraph score. For example, if exactly nine times as many guilty subjects obtain any given score as do innocent subjects, then the ratio of 9:1 implies that there is a 10% chance of a false positive error if all subjects with that score were called deceptive.

A related approach would be to compare the ratio of the areas under the two curves which are at or beyond a given score. As in the previous method, if 90% of the areas under the two curves at or beyond a given score are under the guilty curve and 10% is under the innocent curve, then there is a 10% chance of a false positive error if all subjects with that score were called deceptive. There are two problems with these approaches, however. First, they are sensitive to distortions caused whenever the base rate for guilt is different from whatever it is assumed to be, which is customarily assumed to be 50%. Since the base rate for guilt is difficult to estimate in real life situations, techniques which are sensitive to base rate fluctuations are problematic. Second, whenever the polygraph score is so extreme that it falls above or below the bulk of both curves, the probability of error estimated by both methods approaches 50%, which is obviously incorrect.

The approach detailed in this paper is not subject to either problem. The proportion of cases falling at or beyond any given score is essentially the same regardless of the number of subjects in the population. So long as only one curve is selected for use without reference to the other curve, base rate fluctuations cause no problem. As one approaches the appropriate tail of each curve, the estimated probability of an error approaches the infinitesimal. In conceptualizing the problem of estimating errors in polygraph tests, it is important to note the distinction between reporting "The probability of an error is..." or "The probability that the subject is guilty (or innocent)is ..." versus "The probability that a deceptive subject will score as high or higher than a given score is..." The first two statements are affected by base rates of guilt and innocence; the third is not. When the base rate for innocence is 100%, there is no chance of a false negative error, but that does not affect the accuracy of the third statement. The approach used here is that of estimating the probability of an error if the person is in fact guilty (or innocent).

The probabilities shown in Table 1 are carried out to only one decimal place, except in the tails where two significant figures are shown. To display more detailed probabilities would imply a precision not justified by the size of the data base. Even were the data base much larger, it would seem presumptuous to show more than three significant figures in the extreme tails when estimating the

TABLE 1

POLYGRAPH OUTCOME FOR INNOCENT AND GUILTY SUBJECTS

Polygraph Outcome

|  |  | T | D | ? | Total |
|---|---|---|---|---|---|
| Ground | Innocent | 70 | 7 | 43 | 120 |
|  | Guilty | 3 | 52 | 19 | 74 |
| Truth | Total | 73 | 59 | 62 | 194 |

Note:  T = truthful;  D = deceptive;  ? = inconclusive

probability of an error with an individual result due to the vagaries of the human mind.

It is hardly necessary to point out that the table of probabilities published here is generated from subjects in a mock crime paradigm. The psychodynamics of actual criminal suspects undergoing polygraph examinations are no doubt quite different. It would therefore be inappropriate for the probabilities listed in this table to be applied to criminal investigations. In order to develop a table for use in criminal investigations it would be necessary to use a data base obtained from the examination of criminal suspects. The purpose of this article was not to generate a table for use in criminal investigations, but rather to suggest the methodology by which such a table could be generated.

REFERENCES

Barland, G. H. & Raskin, D.C. (1975). An evaluation of field techniques in detection of deception Psychophysiology, 12, 321-330.

Dawson, M. E. (1977). Detection of deception: An analysis of psychophysiological component processes. Psychophysiology, 14, 86. (Abstract).

Downie, N. M. & Heath, R. W. (1974). Basic Statistical Methods (4th ed.). New York: Harper and Row.

The author is greatly indebted to Michael E. Dawson, Ph.D. and Brian Lynch, M.S. for the raw data they so generously provided.

## Table

### for estimating error rates

### of control question polygraph tests

| 3-Chart Polygraph Score | z-Scores from 74 "Guilty" Subjects | Probability that a guilty S will score this high or higher is < | z-Scores from 120 Innocent" Subjects | Probability that an innocent S will score this low or lower is < |
|---|---|---|---|---|
| 36 | 5.045715 | .01 | 3.363076 | 1 |
| 35 | 4.931844 | .01 | 3.247407 | 1 |
| 34 | 4.817973 | .01 | 3.131738 | 1 |
| 33 | 4.704102 | .01 | 3.016069 | 1 |
| 32 | 4.590231 | .01 | 2.900400 | 1 |
| 31 | 4.476360 | .01 | 2.784731 | 1 |
| 30 | 4.362489 | .01 | 2.669062 | 1 |
| 29 | 4.248618 | .01 | 2.553393 | 1 |
| 28 | 4.134747 | .01 | 2.437724 | 1 |
| 27 | 4.020876 | .01 | 2.322055 | 1 |
| 26 | 3.907005 | .01 | 2.206386 | 1 |
| 25 | 3.793134 | .01 | 2.090717 | 1 |
| 24 | 3.679263 | .01 | 1.975048 | 1 |
| 23 | 3.565392 | .01 | 1.859379 | 1 |
| 22 | 3.451521 | .01 | 1.743710 | 1 |
| 21 | 3.337650 | .01 | 1.628041 | .95 |
| 20 | 3.223779 | .01 | 1.512372 | .95 |
| 19 | 3.109908 | .01 | 1.396703 | .95 |
| 18 | 2.996037 | .01 | 1.281034 | .9 |
| 17 | 2.882166 | .01 | 1.165365 | .9 |
| 16 | 2.768295 | .01 | 1.049696 | .9 |
| 15 | 2.654424 | .01 | .9340270 | .9 |
| 14 | 2.540553 | .01 | .8183581 | .8 |
| 13 | 2.426682 | .01 | .7026891 | .8 |
| 12 | 2.312812 | .05 | .5870201 | .8 |
| 11 | 2.198941 | .05 | .4713511 | .7 |
| 10 | 2.085070 | .05 | .3556821 | .7 |
| 9 | 1.971199 | .05 | .2400131 | .6 |
| 8 | 1.857328 | .05 | .1243442 | .6 |
| 7 | 1.743457 | .05 | .0086752 | .6 |
| 6 | 1.629586 | .1 | -.106994 | .5 |
| 5 | 1.515715 | .1 | -.222663 | .5 |
| 4 | 1.401844 | .1 | -.338332 | .4 |
| 3 | 1.287973 | .2 | -.454001 | .4 |
| 2 | 1.174102 | .2 | -.569670 | .3 |
| 1 | 1.060231 | .2 | -.685339 | .3 |
| 0 | .9463599 | .2 | -.801008 | .3 |
| -1 | .8324890 | .3 | -.916677 | .2 |
| -2 | .7186180 | .3 | -1.03235 | .2 |
| -3 | .6047471 | .3 | -1.14801 | .2 |
| -4 | .4908761 | .4 | -1.26368 | .2 |
| -5 | .3770051 | .4 | -1.37935 | .1 |
| -6 | .2631342 | .4 | -1.49502 | .1 |
| -7 | .1492632 | .5 | -1.61069 | .1 |
| -8 | .0353922 | .5 | -1.72636 | .05 |
| -9 | -.078479 | .6 | -1.84203 | .05 |
| -10 | -.192350 | .6 | -1.95770 | .05 |
| -11 | -.306221 | .7 | -2.07337 | .05 |
| -12 | -.420092 | .7 | -2.18904 | .05 |
| -13 | -.533963 | .8 | -2.30470 | .05 |
| -14 | -.647834 | .8 | -2.42037 | .01 |
| -15 | -.761705 | .8 | -2.53604 | .01 |
| -16 | -.875575 | .9 | -2.65171 | .01 |
| -17 | -.989446 | .9 | -2.76738 | .01 |
| -18 | -1.10332 | .9 | -2.88305 | .01 |
| -19 | -1.21719 | .9 | -2.99872 | .01 |
| -20 | -1.33106 | .95 | -3.11439 | .01 |
| -21 | -1.44493 | .95 | -3.23006 | .01 |
| -22 | -1.55880 | .95 | -3.34573 | .01 |
| -23 | -1.67267 | 1 | -3.46139 | .01 |
| -24 | -1.78654 | 1 | -3.57706 | .01 |

# A BUILT-IN VALIDITY IN POLYGRAPH FIELD EXAMINATIONS [1]

Avital Ginton
Behavioral Sciences Section Criminal Identification Division
Israel Police Headquarters &
Criminology Department, Bar-Ilan University, Israel

> An estimate of the validity of polygraph field examinations was developed using a new strategy. Forty-two pairs of real life cases (mostly unverified), each consisting of two examinees who accused each other of being deceptive about certain clear cut points, were used. The eighty four polygraph examinations were scored by experienced examiners. The examiners were completely blind as to the cases involved, nor did they identify the pairs. Assuming that in each pair there must be one deceptive and one truthful subject, it was clear that each pair which had been scored either as two deceptive or two truthful subjects must include an error. Also, it was clear that a pair which had been scored as one deceptive and one truthful subject means either two hits or two errors. Based on these assumptions the error rate was computed. Results indicated an error rate of 19.5%. The problem of generalizing these results to polygraph field examinations as a whole was discussed.

Validity studies of polygraph examinations are basically divided into two categories. Either they are based on real life situations and examinations (field studies), or on some sort of laboratory experimental setting (analog studies).

The two categories suffer from different methodological weaknesses. The problems in field studies stem mainly from the difficulties in obtaining a reliable criterion against which the polygraph results can be validated, as well as in avoiding a substantial sampling bias (Oren, 1975, Ginton et al. 1982). While these weaknesses are usually controlled in analog studies, it is the lack of realistic fear of failure on the test which questions the usefulness of this type of studies for assessing the validity of polygraph examinations in real criminal investigations (Orne, 1975, Ginton et al. 1982).

To overcome these methodological handicaps is almost an impossible mission within the conventional approach (but, see Ginton et al. 1982), especially if one considers the limitations presented by ethical standards.

The present study tries to reduce the above mentioned pitfalls by adopting a completely new approach. The study is based on field examinations conducted in cases where two opposing versions regarding the occurrence of specific events were presented by two examinees in each case. Selecting only the cases in which it was practically impossible to assume that the two parties were telling their subjective truth or that the two of them were lying, it was possible to estimate the validity of the tests by mathematical computations based upon the proportions of the various results obtained by the polygraph examinations per-se. Thus there was no need to rely upon confessions, convictions or any other sort of so-called verifications, which usually result in a substantial sampling bias.

## METHOD

Eighty-four records of control question polygraph examinations that had been conducted in the two main polygraph laboratories of the Israel National Police during the years 1982-1984 were selected for this study. The 84 records refer to 42 cases with a pair of examinations per case. Each pair consisted of one examinee who put some sort of a blame on the other, who totally denied it, accusing the first examinee of fabricating the accusation. These 42 cases were the only cases that survived a selection procedure in which a careful content analysis of all the details involved in the controversies resulted in a conclusion that it is almost impossible to expect the two parties to be either both deceptive or both telling the truth regarding the relevant questions. There were 11 cases of minor sexual offence, two cases of theft, six cases of fraud, seven cases of police brutality and 16 cases of miscellaneous issues.

The 84 records were numerically scored by six experienced examiners using a seven point scale per comparison ranging from +3 to -3. Each record was scored by two examiners and using the Latin square design, each examiner scored a total of 28 records. The scorers were completely blind as to the cases involved nor could they identify the pairs.

For detailed explanation of the numerical scoring technique the reader is referred to Barland and Raskin, 1975. Nevertheless, it is important to mention that in this technique each record receives a final numerical score. A negative score signifies that the autonomic responses to the relevant questions were on the whole stronger than to the control questions, thus indicating deception to the relevant issue. On the other hand, positive final scores indicate truthfulness. In case of 1$\emptyset\emptyset$% accuracy, the outcomes of each pair should be one positive and one negative score (opposite outcomes). However since we might expect errors, some pairs might produce either two positive or two negative scores (identical outcomes).

## MATHEMATICAL ANALYSIS

Let us define the probability of having a correct decision as P(correct)=X, and the probability of having an incorrect decision as P(incorrect)=Y. Since a decision must be made whether correct or wrong, it is clear that P(correct) +P(incorrect)=X+Y=1.

Assuming that the examinations of the two parties in each pair were conducted independently, the probability of having correct decisions for both parties equal to $X^2$. Following the same logic it is clear that the probability of having incorrect decisions for both parties is equal to $Y^2$, while 2XY expresses the probability of having one correct and one incorrect decision (see table 1).

### Table 1

A model of the distribution of outcomes in paired examinations of opposing versions. X=P (correct decision); Y=P (incorrect decision).

#### VERSION B

| | Probability of Correct Decision | Probability of Incorrect Decision | Total |
|---|---|---|---|
| Probability of correct decision | $X^2$ | XY | X |
| Probability of incorrect decision | XY | $Y^2$ | Y |
| Total | X | Y | 1.0 |

The precentage of pairs which had two identical outcomes (i.e., two positive or two negative scores per pair) is equal to the probability of having one correct and one incorrect decision (2XY). Similarly, the percentage of pairs which had two opposite outcomes (i.e., one positive and one negative score per pair) may be regarded as the joint probability of having two correct or two incorrect decisions per pair $(X^2+Y^2)$.

Hence, given the percentage of identical and opposite outcomes it is possible to compute the values of X and Y which indicate the accuracy rate of detection of deception by polygraph examinations.

## RESULTS

As mentioned above, each record was scored blindly by two examiners. The correlation between the two scores over the 84 records which indicates the reliability was found to be $0.85$. Of the 84 records there were seven records from seven different pairs for which the two scorers gave opposite final scores. These records were considered as inconclusive, and for the purpose of the present study they were eliminated from further computations. Thus, only 35 pairs (70 records) were left.

In 24 pairs the two parties received opposite scores (i.e., one positive and one negative) and in 11 pairs the scores were identical (three pairs with positive scores for both sides, and eight pairs with negative scores). The above data lead to the following equations:

$$X^2 + Y^2 = \frac{24}{35} = 0.686$$

$$2XY = \frac{11}{35} = 0.314$$

By a simple computation the solution which was obtained is:

$$X = 0.805 \text{ and } Y = 0.195. \tag{2}$$

Inspection of the various types of offences in this study revealed that cases of police brutality contributed a disproportionate number of errors. When this category was eliminated, 35 pairs remained, of which six were regarded as inconclusive, leaving 29 pairs (58 polygraph records) for computation. The results for these 29 pairs were:

$$X^2+Y^2 = \frac{22}{29} = \emptyset.759.$$

$$2XY = \frac{7}{29} = \emptyset.241$$

$$X = \emptyset.86, \; Y = \emptyset.14$$

Possible explanations for the higher proportion of errors in the cases of police brutality, are beyond the scope of the present article, and will be presented elswhere.

## DISCUSSION

The internal validity of the accuracy rate found in this study ($8\emptyset.5\%$) depends heavily on the assumption that the two examinations in each pair were conducted independently. Thus, one can raise the question that knowledge of the result of the first examination in each pair might influence the manner in which the second examination is conducted, leading to an articial increase in the probability of obtaining an opposite outcome. This is especially acute when the two parties are tested by the same examiner. While it is impossible to ignore this danger, there are some indications that this is not the case. In the present study $2\emptyset$ pairs of examinations were originally conducted by two differ ent examiners per pair, and only 22 pairs were conducted by one examiner per pair. Table 2 gives the distribution of the blind evaluation outcomes in these two categories. It seems that there is not a substantial difference between the pairs of examinations conducted by a single examiner and those which were conducted by two different examiners. It should be mentioned that in most cases in which two examiners were involved, the examinations were actually conducted parallel in time, eliminating any possible influence of one outcome on the other.

## Table 2

The distribution of outcomes in paired examinations conducted by a single examiner per pair or two different examiners.

|  | ONE EXAMINER | TWO EXAMINERS | TOTAL |
|---|---|---|---|
| OPPOSITE OUTCOMES | 13 | 11 | 24 |
| IDENTICAL OUTCOMES | 5 | 6 | 11 |
| INCONCLUSIVE OUTCOMES | 4 | 3 | 7 |
| TOTAL | 22 | 20 | 42 |

Another important question which stems from the present study is the generalizability of the results to polygraph field examinations as a whole. I believe that the very fact that an innocent person is confronted with a direct accusation by another person increases his level of tension and anxiety more than in the usual situation in which a person is confronted with a circumstantial suspicion. Thus the present situations are prone to a higher rate of false positive errors than usual. On the other hand if a guilty person is confronted with such a direct accusation there is a high probability of confession before a polygraph examination takes place. Thus the guilty persons who took these examinations may be "better liers" on the average than the normal population, and therefore a higher rate of false negatives is also expected. In conclusion, I believe that the present result is an underestimation of the general accuracy of polygraph examinations as a whole.

Finally, it should be noted that among the 11 pairs with identical outcomes there were three with false negatives and eight with false positives, which can be used as a gross estimation of the distribution of error types. (3)

NOTES

(1) This article is only a condensed presentation of the study. A more detailed version will be published elsewhere in the near future.

(2) - Inspection of the various types of offences in this study revealed that cases of police brutality contributed a disproportionate number of errors. When this category was eliminated, 35 pairs remained, of which six were regarded as inconclusive, leaving 29 pairs (58 polygraph records) for computation. The results for these 29 pairs were:

(3) A more precise computation of the two different error rates will appear in the detailed version of this study.

REFERENCES

Barland, G.H. & Raskin, D.C. An evaluation of field techniques in detection of deception. Psychophysiology, 1975, 12, 321-330.

Ginton, A., Daie, N., Elaad, E., & Ben Shakhar G. A method of evaluating the use of the polygraph in a real life situation. Journal of Applied Psychology, 1983, 67, 131-137.

Orne, M. T. Implications of laboratory research for the detection of deception. In: Ansley, N., (Ed.) Legal Admissibility of the Polygraph, 1975, Charles C. Thomas, Springfield, Illinois, U.S.A. pp. 94-119.

# VALIDITY OF THE CONTROL QUESTION TEST IN TWO LEVELS OF THE SEVERITY OF CRIMES

Gideon Shterzer and Eitan Elaad
Scientific Interrogation Unit, Criminal Identification Division
Israel Police Headquarters, Jerusalem, Israel

Two samples of verified Control Questions Technique (CQT) records were blindly scored by 8 experienced polygraph examiners. One sample consisted of murder and attempted murder (severe crime) cases and the other of theft and burglary (minor crime) cases. The area under the ROC curve (an index of the diagnostic value of a test) for the two samples was computed, providiing areas of 0.880 and 0.829 (against chance level of 0.5) for the severe and minor crime samples respectively. This indicates that the CQT was highly accurate in discriminating between deceptive and truthful subjects. The two areas were not significantly different, meaning that the efficiency of the CQT was not influenced by the severity of the crime. It was also hypothysized that when comparing the two samples, subjects who face severe charges will be more concerned about the consequences of being found guilty than subjects who face less severe charges. They will tend to respond more to relevant questions. Referring to this claim, an arbitrary decision rule not used in the field procedure was selected. That rule defines every record scored less than 0 as "deception indicated" (DI); and, when it was applied to the severe crime sample, 22 of 51 truthful records (43.14%) yielded a DI score. The minor crime sample yielded only 7 of 30 (23.33%) false positive errors. The difference between the two samples was significant, indicating that the subjects who faced severe charges are prone to false positive errors more than those who faced minor charges.

It was further found that when applying a decision rule which defines every record scored less than 0 as deceptive and every record scored equal or greater than 0 as truthfull, innocent subjects of the minor crimes sample are prone to present truthful results in a larger proportion than innocent subjects of the severe crimes sample. It was suggested, therefore, that Lykkens' prediction that most subjects will respond more to relevant questions can not be applied to innocent subjects responses without taking into account intervening factors like the severity of the crime of which the subject is accused.

The Control Question Test (CQT) (Reid & Inbau 1977) is the most preferred technique in field polygraphy. Basically, in the CQT procedure, relevant questions which refer directly to the investigated crime are compared to control questions which introduces an issue of the same nature in a more general way. It is assumed that the control questions present a greater threat to the innocent than to the guilty subject because the innocent subject knows he is truthful regarding the relevant questions, but he is concerned that he is likely to be found deceptive to the control questions and therefore fail the test. A guilty subject, on the other hand, who knows he is deceptive to the relevant questions, feels that those questions are a threat to his welfare and thus will ignore the control questions and focus his attention solely on the relevant questions.

Lykken 1979, disagreed with these assumptions and claimed that most subjects, whether they answer deceptively or truthfully, will respond more to the presentation of relevant questions than to controls because the former refer directly to the source of their immediate jeopardy. Consequently, the CQT should yield a high false positve error rate.

To support his arguments, Lykken presented the results of two field studies (Horvath 1977, Barland and Raskin (1976) which used drawn ex post facto polygraph records where ground truth was established by confessions, for a blind interpretation to exclude the influence of clinical judgement.

Relatively low accuracy of the CQT and a high rate of false positive errors were presented in these two studies, however Raskin (1978) argued that Lykken misquoted the results of Barland and Raskin, while the results of Horvath should be considered with caution because of the poor training in numerical scoring of the polygraph examiners who scored the records.

In short, more data concerning the validity of the CQT employing real life criminal examinations is needed. Polygraph records should be scored blindly by experienced polygraph examiners who routinely use the objective numerical scoring technique (Barland and Raskin 1975), and are well-trained in chart interpretation. This was the first purpose of the present study.

The second purpose of this study was to investigate the claim put forward by Lykken regarding the tendency of most subjects to respond more to relevant than to control questions leading to a high false positive error rate.

Finally, the third purpose of this study refers to Lykken's (1974) suggestion, that subjects of the polygraph CQT will differ in their individual fear of the consequences of being found guilty. That difference, according to Lykken, contributed to the final outcome. Extending this claim from the individual to the group, it was hypothesized that innocent subjects who face severe charges, such as murder or attempted murder, will be more concerned about the consequences of being found guilty than innocent subjects who are accused of minor crimes (MC). Therefore, the severe crimes (SC) group will tend to yield a higher false positive error proportion than the MC group.

## METHOD

Two samples of real life criminal polygraph records were randomly drawn from the Israel Scientific Interrogation Unit's pool of verified polygraph tests. The drawing was random with the exception that for one sample only minor crimes such as theft, burglary, fraud, etc. were selected, and only severe crimes such as murder or attempted murder were selected for the second sample. The MC sample consisted of 60 records of polygraph examinations conducted during the years 1979-1984, 30 of which were verified by confessions obtained from guilty subjects and the remaining records were verified by confession of another person clearing the innocent of involvement with the crime. The 69 records selected for the SC sample were of examinations conducted during the years 1977 - 1982. Eighteen of the records were of the subject involved by commission or at least participation. The remaining 51 records were verified by confession and/or conviction in trial of another person clearing the subject from involvement.

All the records of both samples were of polygraph examinations conducted by trained field examiners according to standard control question techniques (see Reid & Inbau 1977, Backster 1969).

## RECORD ANALYSIS

Eight experienced polygraph examiners interpreted, independently, the MC sample records using the objective numerical scoring technique (Barland and Raskin 1975). Ten examiners did the same for the SC sample records. While scoring the records, the examiners were blind to the guilt or innocence of the subject, to the frequency of deceptive and truthful records in the sample, and to the criminal case the record referred to.

The polygraph examiners compared the responses to each relevant question with those to adjacent control question, separately for each response channel (respiration, skin resistance, and cardiovascular) and scored the difference. The scoring was done on a 7 point scale, ranging from +3 to -3. When the response to a control question was evaluated stronger than the response to the relevant, a score with a positive sign was introduced and its size was determined by the difference magnitude. When the response to the relevant question was judged to be stronger a negative score was assigned and its size was determined by the difference magnitude. A zero was assigned when no decision about the stronger response could be made by the examiner.

Every record was scored by three polygraph examiners assigned randomly with the exception that no examiner was to score a record of an examination originally conducted by himself. The composition of the three scores changed from one record to another according to a latin square design.

Every polygraph examiner scored about 30 records.[1]

## RESULTS

### Agreement in record scoring

In order to find the interscorer agreement rate for the numerical scoring technique, the final scores obtained were condensed into 5 agreement regions according to the 5 main results of the field tests used for the polygraph examinations of the Israel police. For the present study purposes, the two extreme points gathered all final scores less than -7 (clear deception results) or larger than +7 (clear truthful results). In the 2nd region, all final scores between -3 and -7 inclusive, were gathered (reserved deception results). Similarly, in the 4th region all final scores between +3 and +7 inclusive, were gathered (reserved truthful results). The 3rd region gathered all final scores between -2 and +2 inclusive (inconclusive results).

In order to compute the interscorer agreement rate, the difference (d) between every pair of examiners who scored the same record was determined. The lowest value of such difference was 0 (two final scores in the same region) whereas the largest value that could have been computed for such a difference was 4 (two scores in extreme opposite regions). The (d) score was subtracted from the largest value of 4 in order to compute the agreement score (a) of that pair. The largest possible difference (d=4) was then multiplied by the total number of pairs, defining the highest possible difference score (Hd).

The (Hd) scores computed for the SC and MC samples were: 4(3x69) = 828 and 4(3x60) = 720, respectively. The ratio between the sum of all (a) scores and (Hd), determined the interscorer agreement rate.

The interscorer agreement rates and percentages computed separately for the two levels of crime severity, are presented in table 1.

Table 1
Interscorer Agreement in Polygraph Record Analysis

|  | Severe Crimes sample (SC) N=828 | Minor Crimes sample (MC) N=720 | Marginal N=1548 |
|---|---|---|---|
| Agreement |  |  |  |
| Score | 708 | 630 | 1338 |
| Percent | 85. 05 | 87. 5 | 86. 4 |

Both agreement rates are fairly high indicating that the scorings of both samples were done in a reliable manner. When comparing the two samples (MC and SC), Table 1 reveals almost identical agreement rates.

MC and SC field validity

An index of the diagnostic value of the CQT was computed using the signal detection approach. This is considered the most appropriate means to be applied to this type of data and has been used in the past with regard to polygraphic data analysis (Lieblich et al. 1970; Ben Shakhar 1977). The signal detection approach uses the area under the receiver operating characteristic (ROC) curve as an index. The ROC curves, in the present study, consists of 19 consecutive cutoff points, each representing the cumulative percentage of correct detections of guilty subjects when compared to the cumulative percent of false positive errors.

The areas under the ROC curves computed separately for the MC and the SC samples are presented in table 2.

In order to determine if the two areas are significantly different, 95% confidence intervals were computed. The confidence intervals, presented in table 2, indicate that the two areas are not significantly different.

Table 2

The Area Under the Receiver Operating Characteristic (ROC) Curves and 95% Confidence Intervals Computed for the Two Levels of Crime Severity

|  | Severe Crimes Sample (SC) | Minor Crimes Sample (MC) |
|---|---|---|
| ROC Area | .88Ø | .829 |
| 95% Confidence Interval | .786-.973 | .722-.936 |

Table 2 reveals that both areas under the ROC curves are quite large indicating that the CQT is a valid procedure for discriminating between guilty and innocent subjects.

**Comparison of response magnitude to relevant and control questions for one selected cutoff point**

In order to find out if the claim that most subjects will respond more to relevant than to control questions leading to a very high false positive error rate, is correct, only one cutoff point on the ROC curve was selected. This point divides the mean scores which are less than 0 and those which are equal or greater than 0, defining a decision rule according to which responses to relevant questions stronger than those to controls are regarded as deception indicated (DI), while equal or stronger responses to control questions are regarded as no deception indicated (NDI). The results in each of the two crime severity samples are presented in table 3.

Table 3

Frequencies of Truthful (NDI) and Deceptive (DI) Decisions According to a Zero Cutoff for Actually Guilty and Actually Innocent Subjects and for the Two Levels of Crime Severity

| Criterion | Actually Guilty | | Actually Innocent | | |
|---|---|---|---|---|---|
| Decisions | DI | NDI | DI | NDI | Marginal Sum |
| Crime    MC | 23 | 7 | 7 | 23 | 60 |
| Severity  SC | 17 | 1 | 22 | 29 | 69 |
| Marginal Sum | 40 | 8 | 29 | 52 | 129 |

According to Lykken (1979) it was expected that regardless of the crime severity, more than half of the innocent subjects should yield deceptive results. Table 3 reveals that this is not the case, and innocent subjects produce more truthful than deceptive results. Furthermore, according to Lykken, a much higher false positive error rate will be found when compared with the false negative error rate. Table 3 shows that it is true for the SC sample in which 22 out of 51 (43.14%) records of actually innocent subjects yielded scores higher than 0. Using the normal approximation to the binomal distribution procedure, the difference was found highly significant (z=11.72, p .001). However, when the MC sample is refered to, an identical false positive and false negative error rate, 7 out of 30 (23.33%) was found.

It was further hypothesized that the SC group will yield a larger proportion of false positive errors than would the MC group. Table 3 reveals that this is actually the case. The difference between the percent of correct decisions for the innocent subjects in the SC group (56.86%) and the percent of correct decisions for the innocent subjects in the MC group (76.67) is significant (z=2.19, p .05).

DISCUSSION

The debate about the rationale underlying the CQT and its validity in real life criminal polygraphy, is based on insufficient empirical data. The main purpose of this study was to enrich the empirical data concerning the validity of the real life CQT with two samples of polygraph records verified by confession of the guilty party and/or by conviction in trial. The two samples selected differ in the severity of the crimes of which the subjects were accused. The records were blindly scored by well trained polygraph examiners yielding a reasonably high interscorer agreement rate. Furthermore, the agreement rates for the two samples were almost identical, indicating that the differences between the two samples are independent of the scoring technique.

The results for the validity of the CQT, when the area under the ROC curve function as an index, present rather high figures for the two samples indicating, that the CQT is an accurate means of discriminating between guilty and innocent subjects. The results have special meaning because they refer to two independent samples which relate to completely different crimes but yield almost the same accuracy rate.

Unlike the polygraph decision making practice in the field, the signal detection approach utilizes an index which combines many possible decision rules (many cutoff points on the ROC curve).

To create field like decision conditions, only one classification rule, which best reflect Lykkens' argument against the validity of the CQT, was selected. Thus, the selected cutoff point divided between the responses scored less than 0 and those scored equal or greater than 0. Contrary to Lykkens' claim, innocent subjects responses to relevant questions were not more frequent than the responses to control questions.

When we refer to a less extreme statement of a high proportion of innocent subjects who yield false positive errors, as compared to much lower proportion of guilty subjects yielding false negative errors, it is true only when the most severe crimes are addressed. When less severe crimes are investigated, it seems that the errors are distributed evenly between the two types. One possible explanation for these findings refers to the attention which the subject allocates to the various stimuli in the CQT setting. The attention of any subject is drawn to questions which are salient as an immediate threat to his welfare. In the SC sample, because of the strength of the stimulus, many innocent subjects perceive the relevant questions as most threatening while in the MC sample more subjects are free to attend to less salient control questions, realize their significance, and respond to them.

It must be noted, however, that the selected 0 cutoff point is by no means the best classification rule by which innocent and guilty subjects should be classified. In real life polygraphy, an inconclusive region is added which decreases the error rate on the expense of a lower correct detection rate.

The use of confessions as validity criterion of the guilt or innocence of CQT examinees may introduce a sampling bias since there may be a relationship between the polygraph results and the probability that a subject will confess (Ginton et al. 1982). This could be detrimental for results of guilty subjects but should not affect the innocent. It is suggested, therefore, that only the innocent subjects in the present study should be regarded as free of this sampling bias.

To conclude, more studies concerning the validity of the CQT should be presented before the theoretical claims of Lykken can be based on solid empirical ground. It is suggested that Lykkens' generalizations about the responses of innocent subjects to relevant questions in the CQT, should be considered cautiously because, as this study showed, there are intervening factors which influence subjects' responses. More empirical attention should be given to these factors.

FOOTNOTES

1. In the SC sample every polygraph examiner scored 33-34 records. In the MC sample, five examiners scored 30 records each, while the remaining 30 records were scored by 3 examiners.

REFERENCES

1. Backster, C. Technique fundamentals of the tri-zone polygraph test. New York: Backster Research Foundation, Inc. 1969.

2. Barland, G. H., & Raskin, D.C. Validity and reliability of polygraph examinations of criminal suspects (U.S. Department of Justice Report No. 76-1, Contract 75-NI-99-0001). Salt Lake City: University of Utah, Department of Psychology, March 1976.

3. Barland, G. H. & Raskin, D. C. An evaluation of field techniques in detection of deception. Psychophysiology 1975, 12 321-330.

4. Ben Shakhar, G. A further study of the dichotomization theory in detection of information. Psychophysiology, 1977, 14, 408 -413.

5. Ginton, A., Daie, N., Elaad, E., and Ben Shakhar G. A method for evaluating the use of the polygraph in a real life situation. Journal of Applied Psychology, 1982, 67, 131-137.

6. Horvath, F. S. The effect of selected variables on interpretation of polygraph records. Journal of Applied Psychology, 1977, 62, 127-136.

7. Lieblich, I., Ben Shakhar, G., & Kugelmass, S. Efficiency of GSR detection of Information as a function of stimulus set size. Psychophysiology, 1970, 6, 601-608.

8. Lykken, D. T. Psychology and the lie detector industry. American Psychologist, 1974, 29, 725-739.

9. Lykken, D. T. The detection of deception. Psychological Bulletin, 1979, 86, 47-53.

10. Raskin, D. C. Scientific assessment of the accuracy of detection of deception: A reply to Lykken. Psychophysiology, 1978, 15, 143-147

11. Reid, J. E., & Inbau, F. E. Truth and deception: The polygraph ("lie detection") technique. 2nd ed. Baltimore: Williams & Wilkins, 1977

Comment by Dr. Avital Ginton to the study by Sterzer and Elaad:

## Assessing Polygraph Accuracy:
### The importance of choosing an evaluation technique which is compatible with the way the examinations were conducted

Sterzer and Elaad in their study found that using a zero cutoff point with no inclusive zone results in false positive (FP) error rates of 23.33% for the minor crime sample (MC) and 43.14% for the severe crime sample (SC). The difference between these two error rates, which was found to be significant, was attributed to the different levels of threat presented by the relevant questions in the two levels of crime severity.

Another factor, however, might have contributed to the difference in FP error rates. During the year 1979, the Israel National Police Polygraph Laboratory went through a substantial change regarding the conduct and evaluation of polygraph examinations. The basic change was from a considerable reliance on the behavioral symptoms of the examinee and a global evaluation of the polygraph records (as recommended by certain schools of thought), towards a major reliance upon an objective numerical scoring technique, which had by then become widespread. It was soon found that the change in the way information from the polygraph examinations is considered and evaluated, brought upon a change in the manner in which the examinations were conducted, including a tendency to stress, during the pre-test interview and between charts, the control questions more than had been done previously. This tendency resulted in a considerable increase of the physiological reactions to control questions.

Hence, in the SC sample, when comparing the records of the 18 innocent examinees who were examined before 1979 (i.e., during 1977-1978) to those of the 22 innocent examinees who were examined after the change took place (i.e., during 1980-1982)* it was found that in the earlier group, 55.6% of the records received negative numerical scores, as opposed to only 31.8% in the later one. Using the normal approximation to the binomal distribution, it was found that the probability associated with this difference is $P \leq 0.065$ (Z=1.487, one tailed), which is very close to an acceptable level of significance.

In contrast, the MC sample was taken on the whole (27 of 30 records) from examinations conducted in the 1980's (1980-1984), and the percentage of negative scores for these 27 records was 18.5%.

It seems that in order to obtain an estimate of the effect of crime sevirity on FP error rates in this study, only examinations conducted in the 1980's should be considered. When relating to only these examinations, it was found that the difference between the MC and SC samples regarding the FP error rates (with no inconclusive zone) is associated with the probability of P≤ 0.142 (Z=1.07, one tailed), which is far from any acceptable level of significance.

As correctly mentioned by Sterzer and Elaad, in real life decision making, a safeguard against FP (as well as FN) is practised, using an inconclusive zone. It was, therefore, recommended by Barland and Raskin (1975) as well as by others that only records which received negative scores of at least -6 should be considered as deception indicating records.

Applying this rule to the 1980's sub-samples of of innocent examinees yields FP error rates of only 11.7% (2 errors in 17 conclusive records) and 8% (2 errors in 24 conclusive records) for the SC and MC samples respectively.

Following this analysis, it turns out that the factor of crime severity has only little, if any, effect upon the FP error rates.

The main reason for this comment is more general. It demonstates that one cannot estimate the accuracy of polygraph examinations by using an evaluation technique at odds with the way in which the examinations were conducted. Thus, examinations whose conduct was geared to the global evaluation and behavioral symptoms approach might be unsuitable for analysis by the objective numerical scoring technique, or even by a blind global evaluation which is not accompanied by behavioral symptoms analysis. This point has been, unfortunately, overlooked in many studies in the past, leading to unreliable and conflicting results.

Footnote

* The SC sample also included 11 records of innocent examinees who were examined in 1979, the year in which the change took place.

References

Barland, G. H. and Raskin, D.C., An Evaluation of Field Techniques in Detection of Deception, Psychophysiology, 1975, 12, 321-330.

# DECISION RULES IN POLYGRAPH EXAMINATION

Eitan Elaad
Scientific Interrogation Unit
Criminal Identification Division
Israel Police Headquarter, Jerusalem

Analysis of polygraph examination charts is done in two basic steps: the identification of signals which will be relevant to reaching a decision of result, and analysis of those signals. The accepted method of chart analysis recognizes a clear distinction between the two stages. The examiner assign a numerical value between −3 and +3 for every comparison between the responses to relevant questions and the reactions to standards. In the second stage he summarizes the numerical values which were recorded, and this constitutes a basis for arriving at a result in the examination. Another accepted system of analysis is the system of global values. This is a less systematic approach, but it still recognizes the two stages of examination. The examiner collects reactions which are liable to be of help in reaching a result; he then selects relevant responses and reaches a decision based upon appropriate blatant factors, remaining through the selection. Based upon two polygraph examinations where the results were verified for accuracy (confession by the guilty and conviction in court) --- in one case murder and attempted murder, and in the second case a crime of property --- an attempt was made to reach the best level of certainty between the two aforementioned analysis systems. This paper examines the results of this test.

Polygraph records conducted with the control question test (CQT) (Reid & Inbau 1977) are usually interpreted according to one of two main methods. The first is the objective numerical scoring (ONS) technique (Barland & Raskin 1974) with which the data is analyzed in a sequence of two stages. First, relevant data are gathered by systematically addressing every comparison point (a single comparison of response magnitude between a relevant and a control question for a single channel by one examiner) and assigning a numerical score to this comparison. Second, all comparison point scores are summed up to one total score which should present an estimate to the direction (truth or deception) and magnitude (confidence in the result) of the polygraph record outcomes. While the first stage of noting relevant data and gathering them has the advantage that all possible information is referred to in a most reliable manner (when conducted by well trained polygraph examiners), the second stage, which integrates the information, suffers from oversimplicity. Thus, all three physiological measures are given the same weight, no attention is paid to dynamic changes in the subjects' responses during the test session, consistency of responses over time is not considered, etc.

Another method of CQT record analysis is the global record evaluation (GRE) in which the evaluator studies the record and notes any significant changes in response patterns between the relevant and control questions. This type of data analysis presents the opportunity to treat the record as a whole rather than a combination of all its components. However, the GRE is based mainly on the subjective impression of the evaluator, and since evaluators differ in the weight they place on various physiological measures (Orne et al 1972), and in their emphasis on the dynamic changes during the test, no definite decision rules are applied and the evaluator makes the data selection while collecting them. Consequently, the final result is based on some few salient cues which pass the selection process and this exhibits relatively poor interevaluator reliability (Podlesny & Raskin 1977).

The purpose of this article is to introduce some desision rules which exhibit improvement of the CQT detection rate, while using the ONS and the GRE techniques on data collected from two independent, and completely different samples of verified polygraph records.

METHOD

Since the present article follows, in many respects,

the procedure employed in a previous study (Shterzer & Elaad, 1985), only the main details of the procedure are described in this article.

Two samples of real life criminal polygraph records, used in a previous study (Shterzer & Elaad, 1985), which were verified by confession and/or conviction of the guilty party, were utilized for the purposes of the present analysis. The two samples were randomly drawn and consisted of 60 and 69 records of minor crimes (MC) and of severe crimes (SC), respectively. The MC sample was divided evenly between actually guilty and actually innocent subjects' records (30 in each) while the SC sample consisted of 51 innocent and 18 guilty subjects' records.

All the records were of polygraph examinations conducted by trained field examiners according to the standard control question techniques (Reid & Inbau 1977, Backster 1969). Three physiological measures were present on each test record. The first, recorded thoracic and abdominal respiration. The second recorded skin resistance (GSR), and the third recorded the cardiovascular activity (e.g. blood pressure, blood volume and heart rate).

## POLYGRAPH RECORD ANALYSIS

The records were independently analyzed by eight (MD) or 10 (SC) experienced polygraph examiners. This was done twice, in two counterbalanced sessions separated in time. First, the evaluator was asked to make a blind interpretation of the record according to the objective numerical scoring technique. (A more detailed description of the technique is presented in Shterzer & Elaad 1985). Second, the same polygraph examiners were asked to analyze the records according to the global record evaluation method, in which the evaluator was asked to make an overall decision regarding each relevant question in the record. The overall decision was expressed on a five-point scale which defines at its extreme points strong confidence in the truthful or deceptive result, at the second and fourth points low confidence in the results and on the third point an inconclusive decision. On the second analysis of the record the examiner did not know the results of his previous analysis.

RESULTS AND DISCUSSION

i. THE INCONCLUSIVE REGION:

First, a comparison will be made between a two decision region design with a zero cutoff point, and a three
decision region design which includes an inconclusive region. The inclusion of an inconclusive region was suggested
by Barland & Raskin (1975), and is used routinely in field
polygraphy.

Table 1 presents the results for both the MC and SC
groups with and without the inclusion of the inconclusive
region. The inconclusive regions were selected by searching
for the optimal discrimination between guilty and innocent
subjects; thus, its boundaries are asymmetrical around zero
and are skewed in the direction of the negative scores for
both MC and SC samples.

Table 1

Distribution of Raw ONS Scores for the two Samples in Two and Three

Decision Regions According to the Ground Truth

| Sample | | Severe crimes | | | Minor crimes | | |
|---|---|---|---|---|---|---|---|
| Decision | | DI | INC −4 / −1 | NDI | DI | INC −3 / 0 | NDI |
| Actually guilty | 2 | 17 | | 1 | 23 | | 7 |
| | 3 | 14 | 3 | 1 | 20 | 5 | 5 |
| Actually Innocent | 2 | 22 | | 29 | 7 | | 23 |
| | 3 | 5 | 17 | 29 | 4 | 4 | 22 |

2 = Two decision regions with a zero cutoff score.

3 = Three decision regions with inconclusive region included.

Table 1 reveals the importance of the inconclusive region for reducing false positive error rate. This is manifested in both SC and MC samples. When the SC sample is considered, the inclusion of the inconclusive region eliminates 17 out of 22 (77%) false positive errors without any loss of true negative decisions. Regarding the MC sample, three out of seven (43%) of the false positive errors were shifted into the inconclusive region, while only one out of 23 (4%) true negative decisions was lost. The results for the false negative decisions are not as impressive. For the SC sample the inclusion of the inconclusive region did not affect the single false negative decision; however it reduced the true positive decisions from 17 to 14 (-18%).

For the MC sample, two of seven (29%) false negative decisions wers shifted into the inconclusive region and the same happened to three out of 23 (13%) true positive decisions.

## ii MEAN PER COMPARISON POINT:

The ONS technique is a procedure to note and gather data in a reliable manner but is not necessarily the optimal method to integrate this data. Table 2 presents the frequencies and percentages of the comparison point scores, with positive, negative and zero signs, gathered from two collections of data for guilty and innocent subjects separately.

Table 2 reveals that zero scores are consistently more than 40% of all scores assigned to the polygraph records. For the guilty subjects, over the severity of the crime, scores with negative signs exceed the scores with positive signs by more than 20% while for the innocent subjects the positive scores are only 10% more than the negative scores. A closer look at Table 2 reveals that the difference originates from the severe crime sample where the guilty subjects produce about 25% more negative scores than positive scores and the innocent group produce about positive scores in excess of negative ones by only 6%. The very high proportion of negative scores in the innocent group implies that a relatively minor deviation from the average may have serious consequences.

The minor crimes sample seems to be less vulnerable. It presents similar but opposite figures for guilty and innocent subjects with about a 15% difference between them.

Table 3 sums up the figures of Table 2 into percentages of agreement and disagreement with the ground truth and separates them into the three physiological measures.

## Table 2

Comparison Point Score Signs for Guilty and Innocent Subjects
of the Two Crime Samples

| Criterion | Actually Innocent | | | Actually Guilty | | |
|---|---|---|---|---|---|---|
| Score sign | − | 0 | + | − | 0 | + |
| Severe Crimes | Total=4749 | | | Total=1674 | | |
| Number | 1146 | 2165 | 1438 | 693 | 704 | 277 |
| Percent | 24.1 | 45.6 | 30.3 | 41.4 | 42.1 | 16.6 |
| Minor Crimes | Total=2784 | | | Total=2928 | | |
| Number | 620 | 1159 | 1005 | 1081 | 1232 | 615 |
| Percent | 22.3 | 41.6 | 36.1 | 36.9 | 42.1 | 21.0 |
| Marginal Mean Percent | 23.2 | 43.6 | 33.2 | 39.2 | 42.1 | 18.8 |

## Table 3

Agreement (Percent) Between the Ground truth and Comparison
Point Score Sign for the Two Levels of Crime Severity and
the Three physiological measures.

| | Severe Crimes | | | Minor Crimes | | |
|---|---|---|---|---|---|---|
| | Agreement % | Zero Scores % | Dis Agreement % | Agreement % | Zero Scores % | Dis Agreement % |
| Measures | | | | | | |
| Respir. | 38.35 | 35.73 | 25.92 | 44.54 | 32.83 | 22.64 |
| GSR | 26.34 | 54.65 | 19.01 | 32.72 | 49.16 | 18.12 |
| Cardio | 34.84 | 43.62 | 21.53 | 32.30 | 43.59 | 24.11 |
| Marginal Mean | 33.18 | 44.67 | 22.15 | 36.52 | 41.86 | 21.62 |

The results of the two samples, over physiological measures, are very similar: About 36% of the responses in the MC sample and 33% in the SC sample are scored in accordance with the actual state of the subject toward the investigated crime. About 22% of the responses in the two samples are in the opposite direction. This means that the decision is based, on the average, on 13% of the responses in the test. When the different physiological measures are regarded individually, Table 3 shows that for severe crimes a difference of 13% is preserved for the respiration and cardio measures but for the GSR the difference decreased to only 7%. The difference for the GSR in the MC sample is 14%, but for respiration it increases to 22% and for the cardio it decreases to only 8%. The zero scores percents for the two samples are very similar, with a relatively large proportion of these scores for the GSR (about half of the scores) and a relatively low percent for respiration.

In light of the results presented in Tables 2 and 3, the widespread use of raw scores sums to determine polygraph outcomes should be reconsidered. Many polygraph records exhibit a small difference between the number of positive and negative scores and the use of raw scores sums may lead to a decision based on a record which is not clear enough. The problem is not acute for short records since the raw scores sum will probably be assigned to the inconclusive region. Records with many comparison points and a small difference between the percentages of positive and negative scores, increas the probability that the raw score sum will fall in a decision region.

To demonstrate the long records problem, the records of both MC and SC samples were divided into two groups according to the length of the record. The cutoff point was 27 comparisons. Consequently, the SC sample was divided into 35 short and 34 long records and the MC sample was divided into 26 short and 34 long records.

The distribution of raw scores results for actually guilty and actually innocent subjects according to the length of the records is presented in Table 4.
Table 4 presents a strong connection between long records and false decision probability. All six false positive and false negative decisions in the SC sample, and all nine errors of both types in the MC sampel are found in long records. It seems that when a clear result is manifested on the record after three repetitions of the question battery the polygraph examiner tend to end the test and report the result. When the decision is not clear the examiner tends to continue with the test hoping that the forthcoming repe-

Table 4

Distribution of Raw ONS Scores for the Two Samples in Three
Decision Regions According to the Ground Truth and Length of
the Records.

| Sample | | Severe crimes | | | Minor crimes | | |
|---|---|---|---|---|---|---|---|
| Decision Region | | DI | INC -4 / -1 | NDI | DI | INC -3 / 0 | NDI |
| Actually Guilty | L | 9 | 0 | 1 | 9 | 4 | 5 |
| | S | 5 | 3 | 0 | 11 | 1 | 0 |
| Actually Innocent | L | 5 | 5 | 14 | 4 | 1 | 11 |
| | S | 0 | 12 | 15 | 0 | 3 | 11 |

L = Long records        S = Short records

titions would clarify the result. Unfortunately, this approach may lead to false decisions.

To overcome the problem, the raw score sum was replaced with the mean score per comparison point (MCP). The MCP is considered as a single score assigned by one scorer to one comparison of responses to adjacent relevant and control questions in a single physiological measure. The theoretical maximum MCP is 3.00 and will occur only when all three examiners decide that the responses to all control questions are greater than those to all adjacent relevants and the difference is judged to have the maximum value (+3). This should occur in all three measures for all the questions in the record. In general, a positive mean score indicates a relatively stronger response to the control questions. Conversely, -3.00 is the theoretical minimum score possible, and negative mean score indicates that the responses to the relevant questions in a given record are stronger than those to the adjacent controls. In order to compare the validity of the MCP with that of the ONS raw scores, the MCP score for each record was computed.

The optimal inconclusive region for the MC sample has boundaries of -.2 and +.1. Thus, all MCP scores less than -.2 are considered as deception indicators (DI), while all MCP scores greater than =.1 are considered as no deception indicators (NDI). All other MCP scores are considered inconclusive. Similarly, the optimal inconclusive region for the SC group was determined. The region has boundaries of -.2 and $\emptyset$. Table 5 presents the distribution of MCP scores in each of the three decision regions for both SC and MC groups.

Table 5

Distribution of MCP Scores According to the Optimal Inconclusive Regions for the Two Samples.

| Sample | | Severe crimes | | | Minor crimes | | |
|---|---|---|---|---|---|---|---|
| Decision | | DI | Inc. -.2 / 0.0 | NDI | DI | Inc. -.2 / +.1 | NDI |
| Actually Guilty | | 12 | 5 | 1 | 17 | 9 | 4 |
| Actually Innocent | | 1 | 21 | 29 | 2 | 9 | 19 |
| Sum | | 13 | 26 | 30 | 19 | 18 | 23 |

Table 5 reveals that the distribution of MCP scores in the three decision regions eliminate many of the false positive decisions found for the raw score sums. This is true for both MC and SC groups. When the SC groups is considered, four out of five (80%) false positive decisions were shifted into the inconclusive region while none of the 29 true negative decisions were affected. For the MC group, two out of four (50%) false positive decisions were included in the inconclusive region at the price of three out of 22 (14%) true negative decisions. In the actually guilty subject group, the only false negative decision in the SC sample was unaffected by the change from ONS raw scores to MCP scores, but two out of 14 (14%) true positive decisions were shifted into the inconclusive region. For the MC group a similar percent of false negative (one out of five, (20%) and true positive (three out of 20 (15%)) decisions were changed to inconclusives.

Table 6

Distribution of MCP Scores in the Three Decision Regions for
the Two Samples after Applying the Intersection Decision Rule.

| Sample | Severe Crimes | | | Minor Crimes | | |
|---|---|---|---|---|---|---|
| Decision Criterion | DI | Inc. | NDI | DI | Inc. | NDI |
| Actually Guilty | 11 | 6 | 1 | 17 | 11 | 2 |
| Actually Innocent | 0 | 30 | 21 | 1 | 10 | 19 |
| Sum | 11 | 36 | 22 | 18 | 21 | 21 |

### iii THE INTERSECTION RULE:

The effect of a hybrid method, based on the ONS technique and the GRE method of record interpretation, upon correct and incorrect decision rates, was investigated. For this purpose, the evaluations of the three evaluators on the five-point scale were summed up yielding a 13 point continuum in which the first score (3) reflects a unanimous decision of the three evaluators that the subject is undoubtably deceptive, while the last (15) reflects a consensus about a strong truthful decision. The 13 point continuum was divided into three decision regions which best discriminate between guilty and innocent subjects. The first consisted of the five extreme DI evaluations (sums of 3 to 7 inclusive). The second gathered all evaluation sums between 8 and 10 inclusive (inconclusive region), and the third consisted of all the sums greater than or equal to 11 (NDI region).

A new decision rule was now defined, according to which a result would be considered truthful only if it is included in both ONS and GRE NDI regions. The same rule was applied to the deceptive results. All other decisions which did not meet the demands of the intersection rule were regarded as inconclusives.

Table 6 presents the distribution of MCP scores in the three decision regions after applying the intersection decision rule.

Table 6 reveals that for the MC group the intersection rule eliminated three out of six (5∅%) errors (1 false positive and 2 false negative errors). Furthermore, the rule has no effect on the correct detection rate of both true positive and true negative decisions. When the SC group is considered, the decision rule shifted the only false positive error to the inconclusive region but did the same to eight out of 29 (28%) true negative decisions. For the guilty group of subjects, the intersection rule reduced the true positive decisions from 12 to 11 (-8%). While not being impressive, even the results for the SC group seem to justify the use of the intersection rule.

For both samples the decision rule eliminated half of the errors. The price in reduction of correct decisions was relatively low (∅% in the MC group and 22% in the SC group).

## iv  FINAL REMARKS

The external validity of the present results lean on the fact that the reported decision rules apply to two independent and completely different samples of polygraph records. On this ground it is recommended to use both objective numerical scoring and global record evaluation techniques. For each, an inconclusive region should be included because, as the present analyses show, such a region considerably reduces both false positive and false negative errors, at a price of relatively lower reduction of the correct decisions. The inconclusive region boundaries seem to be slightly skewed in the direction of the negative scores, and this tendency is somewhat stronger for the SC group when compared to the MC group. It is further recommended to replace the ONS raw scores sums with MCP scores which standardize results of records with varied length and eliminate many of the errors which result from this variation. Finally, it is suggested to apply an intersection decision rule to both MCP and GRE results. This may lead to a further substantial reduction of both false positive and false negative errors from a rate of about 1∅% to a rate of about 5%. At the same time the inconclusive region is expected to grow from about 3∅% to about 4∅%.

It must be noted, however, that the present results are based on polygraph records verified by confessions and/or by conviction in trial. This may introduce a sampling bias since the confession is not independent of the polygraph outcomes. Furthermore, the verified sample is not representative of the population of polygraph examinations (Elaad and Schachar, 1978).

NOTES

The author would like to thank Chief Superintendent Dr. Avital Ginton, head of the Behavioral Science Section and the Scientific Interrogation Unit, for reviewing this article, and Superintendent Murray Kleiner for his help in improving the presentation in English of this article.

## REFERENCES

Backster, C. Technique fundamentals of the tri-zone polygraph test. New York: Backster Research Foundation, Inc. 1969.

Barland, G.H. & Raskin, D.C. An evaluation of field techniques in detection of deception. Psychophysiology, 1975, 12 321-330.

Elaad, E. & Schachar, E. Polygraph field validity, Crime and Social Deviance, 1978, 6, 16-24. (Hebrew)

Orne, M.T., Thackray, R.I. & Paskevitz, D.A. On the detection of deception. In: Handbook of psychophysiology. Greenfield & Sternbach (Eds.) Holt, Rinehart and Winston, Inc. N.Y. 1972.

Podlesny, J.A., & Raskin, D.C. Physiological measures and the detection of deception. Psychological Bulletin, 1977, 84, 782-799.

Reid, J.E., & Inbau, F.E. Truth and deception: The polygraph ("lie detection") technique. 2nd ed. Baltimore: Williams & Wilkins, 1977.

Shterzer, G. & Elaad, E. Validity of the control question test in two levels of the severity of crimes. Paper presented at the IDENTA 85 conference in Jerusalem, Israel on February 27, 1985.

# COMPUTERIZED POLYGRAPH INTERPRETATIONS
## AND DETECTION OF PHYSICAL COUNTERMEASURES

David C. Raskin, John C. Kircher, & Charles R. Honts
University of Utah, Salt Lake City, U.S.A.

Accuracy of polygraph chart interpretation is a major problem in using polygraph techniques to detect deception. Training, ability, and subjective factors may influence the examiner's diagnosis. We have developed computer methods which automatically analyse the physiological recordings and provide a probability of the subject's truthfulness in answering the questions. Using discriminant analysis and statistical decision models, we have obtained accuracy rates similar to those of highly experienced psychologist-examiners who used unemerical scoring based on psychophysiological principles and data. In a mock-crime experiment, accuracy of decisions was 94% for the computer and 97% for numerical scorer. We also trained college students to employ the countermeasures of tongue-biting and toe-pressing to attempt to beat the polygraph test in a mock-theft situation. Numerical evaluation yielded 50% errors in the countermeasure group and 10% errors in the guilty control group. However, muscle potential (EMG) recordings from temporal and calf muscles enabled the interpreter to identify 90% of the countermeasure users with 0% error on the guilty controls. We expect that the computer can be programmed to do as well or better when EMG measures are incorporated into the discriminant function. The results indicate that physical countermeasures pose a serious problem for polygraph applications, but special measures can be used to detect such attempts. Computer methods appear to be capable of providing powerful ways to overcome problems of examiner training and subjective influences as well as countermeasure attempts.

The accuracy of polygraph chart interpretation is a major problem in applications of polygraph techniques for the detection of deception and the verification of truthfulness. Although there is considerable scientific knowledge concerning methods and criteria for maximizing the accuracy of diagnoses based upon the physiological recordings obtained in polygraph examinations (e.g., Kircher, Raskin, & Honts, 1985; Raskin, 1979; Raskin, Barland, & Podlesny, 1978), many polygraph examiners are either untrained or unable to apply those techniques with a high degree of accuracy. Field polygraph examiners often rely on the subjective or intuitive methods advocated by Reid (Reid & Inbau, 1977) or the more objectionable methods advocated by Arther (1975). Unfortunately, even the numerical methods developed by Backster (1983) and the U.S. Army (Decker, 1978) are seriously deficient in terms of their reliance on misconceptions of psychophysiological processes and incorporation of procedures which violate basic psychometric principles.

A celebrated example of the problems which arise from deficiencies in diagnostic approaches is the case of Floyd Fay who was convicted of a homicide of which he was later exonerated (Raskin, 1981). Prior to his trial, Fay was administered two stipulated polygraph examinations. The first test was given by an Ohio law enforcement examiner trained by the U.S. Army in numerical evaluation, and the second was given by a private examiner trained and employed by Lynn Marcy who practices global and intuitive approaches to polygraph diagnosis. Both of those examiners reported Fay as deceptive. The Army-trained examiner based the decision on his assignment of a numerical score of -6, using a scale where +6 is required for a truthful outcome and -6 is needed for a deceptive outcome. The Marcy examiner based his decision on some unknown mixture of case facts, behavioral observations, and inspection of the physiological recordings.

Following his imprisonment, Fay obtained independent evaluations from four experts, all of whom held doctoral degrees. Psychologist and Army-trained polygraph examiner Gordon Barland reported an inconclusive numerical evaluation of +1, criminologist and Reid-trained polygraph examiner Frank Horvath evaluated the result as inconclusive and suggested a retest, and psychologist David Lykken who has no polygraph training reported that such tests are essentially meaningless for any purpose. Only a University of Utah psychologist experienced in polygraph techniques correctly evaluated Fay as truthful by using scientific methods of chart interpretation which yielded a numberical score of +7. Subsequent investigation led to the apprehension of the actual perpetrators and the eventual exoneration of Fay. In this unfortunate case, diagnostic approches commonly employed by field examiners did not produce a truthful outcome, and only the scientifically-based numerical method developed at the University of Utah produced a correct result. This example underscores the need for objective and automated methods of diagnosis in order to overcome widespread deficiencies in methods, training, and application, even among polygraph examiners who possess doctoral degrees in psychology and criminology.

A second major problem in the application of polygraph techniques involves the potential for training individuals to defeat the polygraph test. Virtually all so-called authorities among polygraph practitioners, including those holding doctoral degrees, claim that it is not possible to use countermeasures to beat the polygraph test. However, research from our laboratory has clearly demonstrated that it is relatively simple to train guilty subjects to produce truthful-appearing polygraph recordings by careful application of the simple physical maneuvers of tongue-biting and toe-pressing during and following the control questions (Honts, Hodes, & Raskin, 1985; Honts, Raskin & Kircher, 1983). As many as 70% of our trained subjects were able to beat the test, and even parapsycholigst Cleve Backster was able to identify only 25% of the countermeasure users (Honts & Hodes, 1983). It is obvious that these results pose a serious problem in the application of polygraph techniques, especially for national security purposes where hostile infiltrators have the greatest opportunities to receive training in countermeasure techniques.

In order to address the problems of inadequate training and competence among polygraph examiners who render diagnoses of truth and deception and the potential problems posed by infiltrators who are trained and skilled in polygraph counter-measures; our laboratory at the University of Utah has been working for 10 years on the development of computer evaluation methods and physiological measures which will automatically render highly accurate decisions and will also detect those who are attempting to defeat the test by the use of physical countermeasures. We have made a great deal of progress toward both of those objectives, and this paper briefly reports the techniques we have developed and the results we have obtained with those techniques.

The best method available for the evaluation of polygraph techniques is the mock-crime paradigm, and the best method currently available for polygraph chart interpretation and diagnosis is numerical scoring (Raskin, 1982). Using those procedures applied by highly experienced psychologist-polygraph examiners, we conducted an experiment to develop an operational system of computerized polygraph diagnosis. One hundred male subjects were recruited from the local community by newspaper advertisements. They were paid for their participation and were offered a substantial monetary bonus if they could produce a truthful polygraph result. Half of the subjects were assigned to the guilty condition in which they enacted a mock theft, and the other half were innocent and were simply informed about the general nature of the theft. All of the subjects were given a polygraph examination by a psychologist who was trained in the procedures for proper application of the control question test. He was blind with regard to the guilt/innocence status of each subject.

The polygraph recordings were obtained on a Beckman Dynograph which measured thoracic and abdominal respiration, skin conductance (GSR), relative blood pressure (cardio), finger pulse amplitude and blood volume (plethysmograph), heart rate, and electrocardiogram. During each presentation of the 11-question sequence, which included three relevant and three control questions, the physiological measures were recorded on paper charts and simultaneously digitized and analyzed by a laboratory computer. After the examination was concluded, two methods were employed to render a diagnosis. The polygraph charts were subjected to a blind numerical evaluation by another psychologist who was experienced in the conduct and interpretation of polygraph examinations using the methods developed in our laboratory. The physiological recordings were also subjected to an automatic and objective computer analysis which utilized software which we had previously developed (Kircher & Raskin, 1981).

The numerical evaluation consisted of a series of systematic comparisons of the reactions obsered to each pair of control and relevant questions for each of the physiological components (respiration, skin conductance, relative blood pressure, and vasomotor activity). Criteria for the assignment of numerical scores were based upon a series of laboratory and field studies (Raskin, et al., 1978; Rovner, Raskin, & Kircher, 1979).Criteria for skin conductance responses were increase in amplitude, duration and complexity of responses; for respiration they were decrease in amplitude, apnea, slowing, and baseline increase; for blood pressure they were increase in diastolic level and duration; and for vasomotor activity they were decrease in amplitude and duration of constriction. For each comparison, a score was assigned according to the relative strength of the reactions to the control and relevant questions using a 7-point scale. If the control question produced a stronger reaction, then a score ranging from +1 to -3 was assigned as a function of the magnitude of the difference between the two reactions. If the relevant question produced a stronger reaction, then a score ranging from -1 to -3 was assigned. I there was no noticeable difference in the two reactions, then a ) was assigned. The scores were then summed across physiolocal components, pairs of questions and repetitions of the question sequence to obtain a total score for the examination. If the total score was +6 or higher, the test outcome was .considered truthful; if it was -6 or lower, the result was considered deception; and scores of less than 6 in either direction were inconclusive.

The computer performed by analysis (Kircher & Raskin, 1985) which began with the extraction of features from which the strength of the physiological responses to the control and relevant questions could be measured and compared. For each feature extracted from the physiological recordings, the computer converted the raw physiological measures for each subject to standard scores for the control and relevant questions for all of the presentations of the question sequence. Those standard scores were summed separately for each feature, and the sum of the standard scores for the relevant questions was subtracted from the sum of the standard scores for the control questions. Those differences in total standard scores for each of the major physiological components were subjected to a discriminant analysis and internally validated in order to select the most useful measures and to combine them in an optimal manner. The resulting function included three measures of skin conductance amplitude and temporal characteristics, blood pressure increase, and a measure of respiratory activity which reflected decreases in breathing amplitude and rate. A single discriminant score was obtained for each subject by applying that function to the differences in standard scores for control and relevant questions. The likelihoods that such a score would have been produced by a guilty or an innocent subject were then entered into a statistical decision model to calculate the probability that the subject was truthful on the polygraph test. Probabilities of truthfulness greater than 9.90 were considered to be definite truthful outcomes, probabilities less than 0.10 were considered to be definite deceptive outcomes, and probabilities between 0.10 and 9.90 were considered inconclusive.

The accuracy of classifications made by the computer method were compared to those obtained from the blind numerical evaluations, and the results are shown in Table 1. It can be seen that there was very little difference in accuracy

## Table 1

## Classifications by Numerical and Computer Evaluations

|  | Correct | Wrong | Inconclusive | Decisions Correc |
|---|---|---|---|---|
| Guilty Subjects |  |  |  |  |
| Numerical | 88 | 6 | 6 | 93.6 |
| Computer | 84 | 6 | 10 | 93.3 |
| Innocent Subjects |  |  |  |  |
| Numerical | 86 | 6 | 8 | 93.5 |
| Computer | 86 | 4 | 10 | 95.6 |
| Combined |  |  |  |  |
| Numerical | 87 | 6 | 7 | 93.5 |
| Computer | 85 | 5 | 10 | 94.4 |

or inconclusive rates for interpretations made by the experienced numerical scorer and the computer method. Since the numerical evaluations were made blindly by a psychophysiologist who had 12 years experience as a field polygraph examiner and 15 years of research experience with those techniques, and the scoring method employed was based on a systematic application of the latest scientific data, the accuracy of the numerical evaluations in this study is likely to be as high as can be attained in the field situation. In fact, the report by the Office of Technology Assessment of the U.S. Congress (1983) indicates that typical performance of polygraph examiners in the field is substantially lower than the 93.5% accuracy achieved with numerical scoring in this study.

The computer method also achieved a very high accuracy of 94.4%, which is greater than what appears to be characteristic of the performance of field polygraph examiners. If accuracy in the field were to reach the high level attained with the computer, several major improvements would result. First, the accuracy of diagnosis of truth and deception in field applications would undoubtedly be increased over the levels currently achieved. Second, the influence of subjective factors, inadequate training, and incompetence which are common among field polygraph examiners would be minimized by this totally objective and reliable system. Third, differing expert opinions, such as those which were manifested in the Fay case, would be eliminated. Fourth , a computer method of diagnosis has the advantage of producing a result in the form of a probability which indicates the degree of confidence that can be placed in the result rather than the relatively crude three-category outcome provided by numerical scoring. Finally, we have strong evidence (described below) that computer and multivariate statistical techniques may be used to differentiate between bona fide physiological reactions to control questions characteristically produced by innocent individuals and reactions created by guilty subjects who employ physical or other maneuvers in efforts to defeat the test.

After we were convinced by our earlier data that up to 70% of guilty subjects can be trained to produce truthful polygraph outcomes by biting their tongues and pressing their toes down against the floor, we began to search for methods to detect such activities. In our first such attempt (Honts et al., 1983) we recorded muscle potentials (EMG) from the temporalis and gastrocnemius areas in order to detect the occurrence of movements associated with tongue-biting and toe-pressing. When the EMG recordings were blindly evaluated by procedures analogous to numerical scoring of standard polygraph charts, we were able to identify 90% of the physical countermeasure users without any misidentifications of those subjects who were not engaging in such maneuvers.

Our success in identifying countermeasure users by means of EMG measures was encouraging. However, there are two major problems in relying on that approach in field applications. First, a well-trained agent of a hostile organization could engage in covert muscular activities from body areas which were not being monitored by EMG electrodes, thereby defeating the purpose of EMG recordings. Second, the EMG measuring equipment is not available on field polygraph instruments, and field polygraph examiners have no experience with its use. In light of those significant obstacles to the successful use of EMG countermeasure detectors, we began to explore the possibility that our previously-developed computer techniques may be used to discriminate between bona fide reactions to control questions and those produced by deliberate physical maneuvers designed to beat the polygraph test.

We are currently in the process of collecting data in a large-scale mock-crime experiment designed to investigate the effectiveness of physical and mental countermeasures and the ability of our computer diagnostic methods to discriminate between countermeasure users and other subjects. In addition to the standard innocent and guilty groups, we trained different groups of subjects to use physical and cognitive countermeasures. So far we have collected data from 71 countermeasure-trained guilty subjects. Using numerical scoring, the polygraph examiner has made 55% false negative errors on those subjects. However, our computer analysis has made only 18% errors on the same subjects. It should be noted that the superiority of the computer method of evaluation was attained without any modifications of the model designed to take account of the specific possibility of countermeasure usage. When the data have been fully collected, we expect to improve the computer performance substantially by developing a new model which incorporates measures which capitalize on the characteristic differences between bona fide and voluntarily manufactured physiological reactions.

Our most recent results confirm our earlier findings with regard to the effectiveness of simple physical countermeasures, but they also indicate that mental as well as physical countermeasures may be effective in defeating a control question polygraph test. This is a very distrubing prospect for those who rely on polygraph techniques in counterintelligence applications as well as in criminal investigation. However, preliminary results indicate that our computer methods for diagnosing truth and deception from physiological recordings may be adapted to minimize the errors produced by countermeasure usage. We expect that in the near future we shall have the methods perfected to the point where they will be highly effective and readily available to the law enforcement and intelligence communites. We hope to be able to report such results by the next meeting of IDENTA.

## REFERENCES

Arther, R.O. (1975). _Observing gestures_. Unpublished manuscript.

Backster, C. (1983). _Backster zone comparison technique_. San Diego: Author.

Decker, R.E. (1978). _Chart interpretation_. Ft. McClellan, AL: U.S. Army Military Police School.

Honts, C.R., & Hodes, R.L. (1983). The detection of physical countermeasures. _Polygraph, 12_, 7-17.

Honts, C.R., Hodes, R.L., & Raskin, D.C. (1985). Effects of physical countermeasures on the physiological detection of deception. _Journal of Applied Psychology, 70_, 177-187.

Honts, C.R., Raskin, D.C., & Kircher, J.C. (1983). Detection of deception: Effectiveness of physical countermeasures under high motivation conditions. _Psychophysiology, 20_, 446-447. (Abstract)

Kircher, J.C., & Raskin, D.C. (1981). Computerized decision-making in the detection of deception. _Psychophysiology_, 18, 204-205. (Abstract)

Kircher, J.C., & Raskin, D.C. (1985). _Computerized decision-making in the psychophysiological detection of deception_. Manuscript submitted for publication.

Kircher, J.C., Raskin, D.C., & Honts, C.R. (1985). _Clinical versus statistical lie detection reexamined: An evaluation of three methods of diagnosing truth and deception_. Manuscript submitted for publication.

Office of Technology Assessment. (1983). _Scientific validity of polygraph testing: A research review and evaluation_. Washington, DC: U.S. Congress.

Raskin, D.C. (1979). Orienting and defensive reflexes in the detection of deception. In H.D. Kimmel, E.H. van

Olst, & J. F. Orlebecke (Eds), The orienting reflex in humans. Hillsdale, NJ: Erlbaum.

Raskin, D.C. (1981). Science, competence, and polygraph techniques. Criminal Defense, 8(3), 11-18.

Raskin, D.C. (1982). The scientific basis of polygraph techniques and their uses in the judicial process. In A. Trankell (Ed.), Reconstructing the past: The role of psychologists in criminal trials. Stockholm: Norstedt & Soners.

Raskin, D.C., Barland, G.H., & Podlesny, J.A. (1978). Validity and reliability of the detection of deception. Washington, DC: U.S. Government Printing Office.

Reif, J.E., & Inbau, F.E. (1977). Truth and deception: The polygraph ("lie detector") technique. Baltimore: Williams & Wilkins.

Rovner, L.I., Raskin, D.C., & Kircher, J.C. (1979). Effects of information and practice on detection of deception. Psychophysiology, 16, 197-198. (Abstract).

# THE PSYCHOLOGICAL STRESS EVALUATOR: A VALIDATION FIELD STUDY

Israel Nachshon
Department of Criminology
Bar Ilan University
Ramat Gan, Israel

Eitan Elaad
Unit for Scientific Interrogation
Division of Criminal Identification
Israel Police Headquarters
Jerusalem, Israel

Tuvia Amsel
Interrogation and Investigation
Tel Aviv, Israel

The Psychological Stress Evaluator (PSE) is a device for detecting vocal cues of stress, such as those prevalent during a criminal interrogation. Validation studies of the PSE have yielded conflicting results. One of the assumptions offered to reconcile the existing contradictions was that the PSE is valid for detecting high stress cues only. This assumption was investigated in the present study on 40 criminal suspects who underwent polygraph examinations, while their vocal responses were recorded for PSE analysis. Six polygraph examiners and one PSE examiner evaluated the charts. Immediately following the examination, a final decision was made by the original examiner. Subsequently, blind e-valuations of pairs of adjacent relevant and control questions were made twice. Data analysis showed about 89% reliablity in the PSE chart evaluations, and about 78%-93% reliability in polygraph chart evaluation. Correspondence of PSE and polygraph decisions based on blind evaluations ranged from 33% to 55% for the various channels. Overall correspondence between blind PSE evaluations and conclusive final polygraph decisions reached about 57%. Finally, overall agreement between conclusive PSE and conclusive polygraph final decisions was about 95% for truth tellers and about 33% for deceivers, when polygraph final decisions served as criterion. It was concluded that the PSE might be valid for detecting truth tellers and about 33% for deceivers, when polygraph final decisions served as criterion. It was concluded that the PSE might be valid for detecting truth tellers in criminal interrogations. However, the differential contributions of the various factors affecting the evaluator's final decision need further study.

The Psychological Stress Evaluator (PSE) is a device for detecting vocal cues of stress, such as those prevalent during a criminal interrogation (Dektor, 1974). Validation studies of the PSE conducted during the last decade have yielded, however, conflicting results (see Nachshon and Feldman, 1980). Yet most studies showing negative results have been conducted under experimentally controlled conditions (e.g., Nachshon and Feldman, 1980). Since laboratory situations are clearly less stress-provoking than field situations (Abrams, 1972), it is conceivable that while the PSE may be invalid for low-stress (experimental) situations, it may be rather sensitive for high-stress (field) situations (Barland, 1978; Nachshon and Feldman, 1980; Rockwell et al., 1979). However, in three independent attempts (Barland, 1975; Nachshon and Feldman, 1980; Virginia State Police, cited in Horvath; 1982) to test PSE applicability as a lie detector in criminal interrogations, no significant correspondence between PSE and polygraph-based decisions (which served as criteria) have been found.

However, consistent though insignificant trends of higher reliability and validity scores for high-stress than for low-stress situations found in one of those studies (Nachshon and

Feldman, 1980), coupled with methodological criticisms levelled against the study (Nachshon, Elaad and Amsel, 1985), suggested the desirability of an additional, rigorously controlled field validation study of the PSE.

## METHOD

Forty criminal suspects undergoing polygraph examinations at the Israel Police Headquarters in Jerusalem served as subjects. They were examined individually by five experienced polygraphers who used control-question procedures. Subjects' verbal responses were recorded (and subsequently analyzed) by a PSE expert (Tuvia Amsel) who participated in the interrogation and observed the polygraph examination through a one-way mirror.

## RESULTS

Six polygraph examiners and the PSE examiner evaluated the charts. Immediately following the examination, final decisions were made independently by the polygraph and the PSE examiners. Subsequently, blind evaluations of pairs of adjacent relevant and control questions were made twice.

Charts of six subjects were excluded from analysis due to technical defects. Data analyses were therefore performed on the charts of the remaining 34 subjects. Preliminary analysis showed about 78% -93% reliability in polygraph chart evaluations, and about 89% reliability in the PSE chart evaluations. Correspondence of PSE and polygraph decisions based on blind evaluations ranged from 33% through 55% for the various channels. Overall correspondence between blind PSE evaluations and conclusive final polygraph decisions reached about 57%.

In the last analysis, validity of the PSE conclusive final decisions was checked against the polygraph conclusive final decisions, which served as criteria. In 17 of the 34 cases, both polygraph and PSE decisions were without reservations. Among those, in 16 cases (94%) the decisions corresponded to each other. Concerning all 34 subjects, nine deceivers were detected by the polygraph, only three of whom (33.33%) were also found to be deceivers by the PSE. By contrast, of the 23 truth-tellers detected by the polygraph (in two cases polygraph decisions were inconclusive), 22 (96%) were also found truthful by the PSE (for further details see Nachshon, Elaad and Amsel, 1985).

DISCUSSION

The data of the present study show first that PSE validity may be evaluated on the basis of final decisions only, since, as the preliminary analyses revealed, blind chart evaluations are valid indices neither for the polygraph nor for the PSE.

Concerning final decisions, very high correspondence between polygraph and PSE-based decisions were found for truth-tellers. This result clearly contradicts previous findings (Nachshon and Feldman, 1980) showing no significant correspondence between polygraph- and PSE-based decisions under field conditions. This inconsistency might, however, be due to a number of situational differences between the two studies; in particular, the differential level of expertise shown by the evaluators who participated in those studies. Presumably, the non-expert evaluators in Nachshon and Feldman's (1980) study gave the interrogated suspects an a-priori 50% chance to be regarded as truth-tellers or as deceivers. By contrast, wishing to avoid false positive errors, the experienced PSE expert in the present study, when in doubt presumably tended to decide that a given suspect was a truth-teller rather than a deceiver. Since most suspects agreeing to undergo criminal polygraph examinations eventually turn out to be truth-tellers (Elaad and Schachar, 1978), the chances of correspondence between the decisions of the PSE expert and those of the polygraph experts were considerably higher than 50% for the truth-tellers and considerably lower than 50% for the deceivers -- as indeed found in the present study.

In conclusion, the present study showed that when conducted expertly, and when evaluated globally, field PSE examinations might be valid for the detection of truth-tellers who undergo criminal interrogations. However, the fact that the PSE expert actually witnessed the polygraph examinations makes it virtually impossible to single out the effect of the PSE alone on the decision made by the PSE evaluator. Therefore, more research is needed before a final conclusion concerning the PSE validity, its scope of applicability, and the differential contributions of the factors affecting final decisions (PSE charts, examiner's expertise) can be reached.

## REFERENCES

1. Abrams, S. The polygraph: Laboratory vs field research. Polygraph, 1972, 1, 145-150.

2. Barland, G. Detection of deception in criminal suspects: A field validation study. Unpublished Ph.D. Dissertation, University of Utah, Salt Lake City, Utah, 1975.

3. Barland, G.H. Use of voice changes in the detection of deception. Polygraph, 1978, 17, 129-140

4. Dektor Counter Intelligence and Security, Inc. Psychological Stress Evaluator, In: Committee on Government Operations, House of Representatives. The use of polygraph and similar devices by federal agencies, 1974; 238-241.

5. Elaad, E. and Schachar, E. Polygraph and field validity. Crime and Social Deviance, 1978, 6, 16-24. (Hebrew).

6. Horvath, F. Detecting deception: The promise and the reality of the voice stress analysis. Journal of Forensic Sciences, 1982, 27, 340-351

7. Nachshon, I. and Feldman, B. Vocal indices of psychological stress: A validation study of the Psychological Stress Evaluator. Journal of Police Science and Administration, 1980, 8, 40-53

8. Nachshon, I., Elaad, E., and Amsel, T. Validity of the Psychological Stress Evaluator: A field study. Submitted for publication, 1985.

9. Rockwell, D., Hodgson, M., and Cook, D. Psychological Stress Evaluator: An attempt at validation. Unpublished manuscript, 1979

The authors acknowledge the help given by Deputy Commander Meir Kaplan, Head, Division of Research and Development, and Chief Superintendant Dr. Avital Ginton, Head, Section for Scientific Interrogation, Israel Police Headquarters, Jerusalem

# THE EFFECT OF SIMILARITY ON PSYCHOPHYSIOLOGICAL RESPONSITIVITY TO PICTORIAL AND VERBAL STIMULI

Gershon Ben-Shakhar & Itamar Gati
Department of Psychology
Hebrew University
Jerusalem

The present study is an attempt to relate stimulus similarity to psychophysiological responsivity. Tversky's contrast model, which assumes that similarity judgements between stimuli are determined by their common and distinctive features, served as the guiding approach for the study. The main goal was to try to examine whether a systematic manipulation of the common and distinctive features among stimuli would effect the autonomic responsivity evoked by these stimuli.

The study utilized the information detection paradigm. Compound stimuli were used, each being a combination of four components. Two experiments employed pictorial stimuli (schematic faces, with beard, glasses, and hat) and two employed verbal stimuli (descriptions of people in terms of occupation, city of residence, hobby, and a personality trait).

Skin conductance responses were measured while the stimuli were presented to the subjects. In each experiment, four independent groups of 30 subjects were compared with respect to the efficiency of detecting the critical stimulus by skin conductance changes.

The four experimental groups differed in the number of common and distinctive features of the relevant and the critical stimulus (presented to the subject in the detection phase).

The results indicated that (a) detection efficiency increases as a function of the number of common components shared by the critical and the relevant stimuli, and (b) detection efficiency was lower for pictorial stimuli than for verbal stimuli. The results are discussed in light of the contrast model, with possible implications for the application of the Guilty Knowledge technique.

# HYPNOSIS IN POLICE INVESTIGATION:
## PRINCIPLES AND SAFEGUARDS

Moris Kleinhauz, M.D.
Tel-Aviv University

Hypnosis can be utilized as a powerful tool to enhance the memory of witnesses in the course of police investigation through the direct manipulation of memory processes (hyper-amnesia) and through the utilization of phenomena such as disociation of mental and emotional processes, hallucinations, age regression, dream induction. In this paper I shall focus on three main areas with which we have to cope whenever hypnosis is used in the frame of police investigation. First, the degree of reliability of the recalled material is explored to highlight the ways in which processes intrinsic to the nature of hypnosis may distort the recollection of the "facts" of a witnesses event. Second, the degree of the clinical responsibility of the hypnotist towards the subject is discussed. The amnestic processes may have been mobilized as a defense mechanism to cope with the anxiety awakened by conscious or unconscious conflicts triggered by the witnessed experience. In this case the hypnotic manipulation of memory and bypass of amnesia may have potential psychopathological implications which call for proper decisions between the interests of the investigation and the well-being of the subject. They call also for proper clinical and psychotherapeutic intervention whenever such a need arises. Third, we shall explore the ethical dilemmas

> and problems of civil rights in-
> volved in using hypnosis for crimi-
> nal investigations. Safeguards to
> protect the validity of the recol-
> lected information, safeguards to
> protect the right of the subject
> for his well being and safeguards
> to protect the civil rights will be
> proposed.

Although there is controversy concerning the theoretical foundation of hypnosis, there is much agreement among scientists concerning the ways in which the hypnotic state can be induced, and the changes in human behavior as a result of hypnotic suggestion. For many years, hypnosis has been used by clinicians interested in facilitating their patient's recall of previously forgotten experiences. Psychotherapists can achieve this through the direct suggestive manipulation of memory processes (hypermnesia) or through the utilization of more subtle, indirect techniques in order to unfold the concealed material. Among this hypnotic procedure we may mention the eliciting of age regression and revivification; the dissociation of mental and emotional processes in order to neutralize the anxiety concomitant with the forgotten material (thus facilitating its open manifestation) and the utilization of hallucinations, dream induction, automatic writing and other less frequently used proceedings. These same techniques can be utilized as powerful tools in order to enhance the memory of witnesses in the course of police investigation. In this paper we will focus on three main areas that we have to cope whenever using hypnosis in the frame of police investigation.

First, the degree of reliability of the recalled material is explored in order to highlight the ways in which processes intrinsic in the nature of hypnosis may distort the recollection of the "facts" of a witnessed event. Second, the degree of the clinical responsibility of the hypnotist towards the subject: The amnestic processes may have been mobilized as a defense mechanism in order to cope with the anxiety awakened by conscious or unconscious conflicts that have been triggered by the witnessed experience. In this case the hypnotic manipulation of memory and bypass of amnesia may have potential psychopa- thological implications that calls for proper decisions

between the interests of the investigation and the well being
of the subject.  It calls also for proper clinical and
psychotherapeutic intervention whenever such a need arises.
Third, we shall explore the ethical dilemmas and problems
of civil rights involved in using hypnosis for criminal
investigation. Safeguards to protect the validity of the
recollected information, safeguards to protect the right
of the subject for his well being and safeguards to protect
the civil rights will be proposed.

RELIABILITY OF RECALLED MATERIAL:

In a forensic context, hypnotic techniques can be used
in an attempt to uncover information which has been
blocked by some disruption or repression of memory in an
apparently healthy individual because of psychological
causes.  Retrospectively, if hypermnesia or recall occurs
under hypnosis, it can be hypothesized that psychological
dynamic factors underlie the amnesia.  Although specific
research would be needed to confirm this involvement, the
clinician is justified in using it as a working
assumption.
Criminal Investigations often rely on the reports of
witnesses as a basis for collecting information about a
crime.  However, sometimes potential witnesses report that
they are unable to remember what they saw or experienced.
In these cases, investigators are turning more and more
often to the use of hypnosis to stimulate recall that has
been blocked.

CASE 1

A seventeen year-old girl was threatened at knife
point by a previously unknown assailant and cruelly raped.
Despite the fact that they had spent a few hours together
prior to the attack, she could not describe, under routine
police questioning, either her assailant or the scene of the
crime.  However, under hypnosis, she was able to reconstruct
an identi-kit portrait of the suspect and guided the police
to the scene of the crime where they recovered the knife
which was used to threaten her.  The identi-kit portrait was
accurate enought to lead to the arrest of a suspect who
later confessed to several similar rapes, including the cruel
attack on the same young girl.

## CASE 2

Two buses in Northern Israel were found to contain hidden bombs, one of which later exploded. When questioning the bus drivers, who served a constant itinerary with more or less the same passengers, the police concentrated on having the drivers try to recall suspicious looking passengers carrying parcels. Under routine questioning, it was impossible for the bus drivers to recall any significant details. However, when under hypnosis, one of the drivers was able to revivify and so reconstruct the entire route and to report every small event and detail which took place. He reported that upon arriving at a certain bus stop a dark-skinned youth, unknown to him from his previous rides, entered the bus carrying a parcel. When the driver handed him his change, he noticed a cold sweat on the young man's palm. Although the driver only faced the youth for the short period of time needed to sell him a ticket, he was able to construct an identi-kit portrait. At a later date, a suspect, whose description perfectly fitted the identi-kit portrait, was arrested and confessed to the crime.

## CASE 3

An Israeli soldier was reported missing from his base. The testimony given by two witnesses was contradictory. One of them stated that the soldier left the base in a certain vehicle travelling north. A second witness testified that he saw the missing soldier in the base after the same vehicle had allegedly left the base. It was of crucial importance to the investigating team to determine the correct version in order to begin the search for the missing soldier. Both witnesses were questioned under hypnosis. The first retracted his original statement, saying that the soldier he saw in the vehicle was not the soldier in question, but one who resembled him. The second witness confirmed his original statement. The body of the missing slldier was later found near his base, a fact which corroborated the results of the questioning under hypnosis.

Although such dramatic and accurate reports are to be found, their existence tend to produce in the investigator the misconcept of seeing all information recalled under hypnosis as genuine and to perceive hypnosis as an almighty methodology in the investigative process. It is the clinician's responsibility to constantly warn the investigator and legal officers of the Court of the potential nonfactual elements which may stem from psycho-dynamic emotional needs. There is a significant body of information from laboratory and from field investigators that information retrieved through hypnosis is frequently nonfactual and may be fantasized, confabulated, distorted, simulated (consciously and intentional) or created in order to comply with the hypnotist expectations as the subject understands them from verbal, paraverbal and nonverbal clues provided (consciously or unconsciously) by the hypnotist. All this arises the question of the psychological dynamic forces underlying the amnesia and memory recall and the nature of memory as a storehouse of sequentially recorded events or as an active process in which there is constant and continual restructuring of material. In any case, it is essential that recovered material be tested against other objective and independent evidence in order to test its authenticity. Only such confirmation proves factuality, while lack of objective evidence simply cast doubt even on material which may be true, although unusable; or false.

## CASE 4

In an investigation of a murder, one witness stated to the police that he had seen a person leaving the place where the body was found. Hypnotically induced recall (using time regression) enabled the witness to provide a detailed account of events. Timing in this case was crucial, and the event was described as happening on a Monday. However, later independent information and a subsequent confession confirmed that the hypnotically recalled events had actually occurred on a Tuesday. In this case the distortion of the recalled material could have caused serious trouble to an innocent man.

An example of contamination of data recalled under hypnosis is manifest in:

## CASE 5

A youngster who had witnessed the kidnapping of a second child described the car of the kidnapper in detail under hypnosis, stating that the gas-rationing decal on the car's window had the number 3 on it. Following independent investigation the kidnapper was located and apprehended. His car was as described by the youngster, except that there was no number 3 on the decal.

## CASE 6

A man reported to the police that he had killed a girl and buried her body by the sea. On first check the police were unable to locate the body and requested that the suspect undergo hypnosis in order to pinpoint the site. Preliminary psychiatric evaluation did not reveal evidence of gross psychopathology, and hypnosis was induced. Under hypnosis the subject produced a lucid, detailed account of the murder and a clear description of the place where the body was buried. However, a night-long on-site investigation assisted by dogs and a bulldozer failed to uncover any sign of murder or traces of a body. Lack of confirming evidence added doubts regarding the mental stability of the man. He was referred for intensive and comprehensive psychiatric evaluation and ultimately diagnosed as delusional and psychotic. Thus, in this case the material supposedly recalled had been fantasized entirely.

A hypnotist directed to seek specific information may ask a question in such a way that it stimulates a response based on the desire of the subject to meet the request rather than true recall. Such an example is:

## CASE 7

A post office van containing a large shipment of money was robbed by three armed men, who used a car to stop the van before robbing it. In order to enhance the memory of the driver of the van, hypnosis was used to elicit a description of the car that had blocked his path. He was asked to visualize the license plate of the car and to "read off the number". Apparently this was a "leading question", since the number which was readily provided proved later to be the license number of a car unconnected to the crime.

## CLINICAL RESPONSIBILITY OF THE HYPNOTIST:

The hypnotist eliciting information needed by the police must also be careful to function as a clinician responsible for the present and future well-being of the subject.

Particularly because of the psychological implications of amnesia itself as a defense mechanism, the clinician must be alert to the possibility that removing or overcoming the amnesia may create problems for the subject. Unlike the police, whose task is to uncover useful facts, the hypnotist must function both as investigator and as a clinician. Amnesia following a crime may stem from three major psychological factors. First, the experience itself may cause the individual involved acute emotional trauma, especially if he was the victim. Second, the experience may take on a symbolic meaning for the individual, in the context of a long-standing prior psychodynamic conflict. Lastly, recall of material criminal evidence may place the witness in an actual existential conflict, since it may have ramifications for his future. Psychological conflict may result from expressing that which can be used as testimony.

Some crimes, such as assault or rape, are intense traumatic experiences for the victim. In Case No. 1 (of the young girl raped at knifepoint) the hypnotic recall was accurate and useful and from the point of view of the investigation a success. However, despite the techniques used in order to attempt an emotional detachment, the girl abreacted strongly under hypnosis and consequent to the hypnotic session, strong depressive anxiety outbursts occurred, and limited therapeutic intervention was necessary.

Another case illustrates the manner in which an experience can take on symbolic meaning if linked to prior repressed conflicts.

## CASE 8

A man was held up by an armed assailant while parking his car. He acquiesced to the demands of the robber by handing over his money and then allowing the robber to espace with no attempt o impede his departure. Subsequently, he experienced amnesia for the details of the event. Under hypnosis, hypermnesia was induced and the subject was able to cooperate in constructing an identi-kit picture of his assailant and a detailed timetable for the event. Both were accurate, as confirmed independently. However, during and after the proceedings, the subject manifested evident signs of distress and anxiety. During proper clinical intervention the subject stated that his behavior at the time of the robbing, had been "cowardly and shameful" and inappropriate for "his father's son". His father was a well known war hero. Apparently, both the amnesia for the details of the event and the anxiety during and after the recall were connected to the prior psychodynamic conflicts concerning his relationship with his father and the symbolic meaning of failure to resist the assailant. At the conclusion of the hypnotic intervention the anxiety and guilt persisted, since the subject could no longer resolve them with amnesia (although amnesia was suggested). Follow-up clinical intervention was suggested.

As noted, the actual process of recalling significant evidential material may place the potential witness into an actual existential conflict situation, which amnesia had been preventing:

## CASE 9

Following the discovery of the body of a murdered girl, a witness came forward to report that he had seen two men force the girl, who lived in his neighborhood, into a car in the vicinity of his home. However, he was unable to remember what the men or the car had looked like. Under hypnosis he was able to recall the scene and describe the car. He noted that the men were neighbors and known to him and was able to name them. Immediately after the termination of the hypnotic procedures he became tense about having identified the men and stated that he feared that they might take revenge and kill him, since they were members of the criminal underworld.

Thus, in this instance, hypnotic hypermnesia removed the defensive amnesia and, in fact, may have put the subject's life in danger. Although consciously he had wanted to cooperate, his amnesia had been protecting him from the conflict between cooperation and fear for his own life. Hypnotic recall made this solution untenable.

In this situation, which is by no means unique, the responsibility of the hypnotist is not a clear clinical matter. The risk to the subject is real and has been heightened by the hypnotist by stimulating recall. This puts the hypnotist into an ethical conflict: To whom does he owe responsibility, and how should he balance these conflicting responsibilities. Asked to perform a specific task for the police, the information he unfolds is "property" of the police. Even should he claim "medical confidentiality" when the subject asks not to impart the information, the police would be justified in suspecting that important evidence has been uncovered. Indeed, they may even suspect that the hypnotist is withholding information incrinimatory to the subject, and the investigation may take an unwarranted turn. This type of dilemma has no easy solution, and leads us to the next section.

ETHICAL DILEMMAS AND CIVIL RIGHTS:

Hypnotically induced recall may produce many ethically complicated issues. Following on the example just cited, there are other times when the clinical hypnotist is placed in a situation of seemingly insoluble conflict. For example, according to accepted procedure, hypnosis should not be used with a suspect but when it is requested by the suspect and in the presence of his lawyer. This is obviously designed to protect the accused person from any situation in which he might unknowingly incriminate himself. However, the line between witness and suspect is not always defined well, especially in the early stages of the investigation:

CASE 10

In one murder case, a person reported to the police that he may well have been the last person to see the victim alive. The police requested that he be placed under hypnosis to enhance his recall of the circumstances under which he had seen the victim. Material so recalled by the subject seemed to implicate him in the crime and directed the investigation toward this assumption. Later on, following independent investigation, the real murderer was caught and confessed to the crime.

It is clearly not the function of the hypnotist to decide when material being recalled under hypnosis is, in fact, self-incriminatory. Legal safeguards must be established to protect the basic right against self-incrimination. It should be the task of the professional hypnotist to alert the legal profession to the need to clarify the point in time at which a person requires legal councel prior to the hypnotic intervention.

It is clear that a hypnotist participating in a criminal investigation should be protected against any knowledge of the case, except the minimal pertinent information to direct the recall to the specific areas in which information is needed by the police. Moreover, the hypnotist must establish a "contract" with his subject so that he raise no issues extraneous to those requested by the police. We know of one investigation of a serious crime in which the hypnotist noticed that the subject manifested anxiety reactions to certain stimuli which he interpreted as indicative of homosexual tendencies. The police had not requested information regarding the subject's sexual inclination, and the subject did not expect to be examined in this area. Following the session, in his report to the police, the hypnotist stated that the subject was probably a homosexual. This report had unexpectedly important ramifications, given the nature of the crime in investigation, and the gratuitously discovered reactions of the subject as interpreted by the hypnotist proved to be self-incriminatory.

## SAFEGUARDS:

We have discussed a number of practical and ethical considerations which may arise with the use of hypnosis during forensic investigations. We have provided illustrations taken from an extensive clinical background in some of the ways in which implications so derived can effect both the course of the investigation and the welfare of the patient. It is important that the effort to develop legal and clinical safeguards be continued and in view of our presentation we would like to stress the following:

I.  Safeguards to protect the validity of the recollected information:

    a.  All material recalled under hypnosis must be regarded as nonfactual unless and until independent corroboration is obtained. Police and legal agencies should be aware that the information obtained may have been totally or partly fantasized, confabulated, distorted, given in order to comply with the operator's expectations or, for reasons of his own, simulated by the subject.

    b.  Since the clinical hypnotist is aware of all the ways in which a subject may interpret and attempt to conform to the hypnotist's intentions and preconceived notions, he must insist that he receive only the minimal pertinent prior information, limited to the specific goals of the investigation as related to his subject.

    c.  All prior information, and the entire encounter between hypnotist and subject, must be recorded, or preferably video-taped, to permit independent evaluation.

II. Safeguards to protect the right of the subject for his well-being:

   a. Since the process of hypnotic recall to overcome amnesia following a criminal event may have psychological implications for the subject, and the psychological dynamics and clinical manifestations may require immediate professional intervention, the hypnotist participating in forensic investigations should be a psychiatrist or clinical psychologist trained in hypnosis.

   b. Clinical psychological evaluation of the subject must be provided prior to hypnosis, preferably by the clinician who is to perform the hypnosis.

   c. Clinical psychological evaluation should be performed after the hypnotic intervention. Counseling and care services should be available.

III. Safeguards to protect the civil rights of the subject:

   a. The clinical hypnotist participating in a forensic investigation should maintain a direct focus on the subject as a human being and attempt to guard his human and civil rights.

   b. Hypnosis must be undertaken only with witnesses or victims who have expressed full and explicit willingness to undergo hypnosis.

   c. Hypnosis must not be induced in any person who is a suspect in an investigation, except when it is at his request and aimed at the elicitation of material in his interest. In this case the hypnotic intervention should be conducted only in the presence of his attorney.

   d. The hypnotist must not raise any matter unrelated to the case with the subject or draw or report any conclusions extraneous to the information requested.

We believe that hypnosis is an important tool in forensic investigations. It is for this reason that we encourage the continuing development of safeguards such as these, which will enhance its utility while protecting the rights of the individual.

# FIELD KITS - FORENSIC EXAMINATIONS OUTSIDE THE LAB

### JOSEPH ALMOG

The Israel National Police has invested much time and effort to develop and improve a number of diagnostic examinations for forensic purposes. Their aim is to find clues to assist investigations (and not to provide evidence for court). Such clues become evidence when they are confirmed by the laboratory. In general these are scientific examinations for non-scientists. Some of the advantages are: (a) they do not require scientists, (b) they can be carried out anywhere, and (c) they can be performed before the evidence has deteriorated. Four forensic field tests that were developed in Israel have been found to be very useful, and they will be demonstrated and discussed. Case examples will be given. These tests are ETK (Explosives Testing Kit), BTK (Bullethole Testing Kit), Ferroprint (fire-arms imprints on hands of suspects), and Nomark (long lasting invisible marking of objects and persons).

In December 1984 a 5 year period of evaluation of our field-test concept was completed. During this period, a series of field kits specially designed for our field technicians were tested under actual working conditions. Although we have not yet fully analyzed the results, primary findings indicate that the project was very successful. With a relatively small investment in manpower and materials we have developed a variety of forensic aids that are now considered indispensable. The new kits have achieved an impressive number of successes, some of which I shall describe later. The kits have also greatly improved the motivation and self-confidence of our field-technicians.

Field kits are devices that help utilize Locard's Contact Law. They were designed to collect, preserve and examine evidence which is unseen to the naked eye because it is either latent (and needs to be developed) or microscopic.

I shall demonstrate three of the ten kits which are discussed. Before doing so I must emphasize that the aim of these examinations is to find clues or presumptive evidence to assist an investigation and not to provide evidence for court. Such clues will only become evidence once they are verified in the laboratory.

Other basic characteristics of these field kits are that the tests are not necessarily carried out by scientists (I think that in most Western countries the field technicians or scene-of-crime officers are not scientists), and that testing can be conducted outside the laboratory, without laboratory instruments, at the crime scene, in the suspect's home or elsewhere.

I wish now to show three of the kits, and afterwords we shall hopefully arrive at the same conclusions.

## ETK (EXPLOSIVES TESTING KIT)

The past several years have seen an alarming increase in the use of explosives in criminal and terrorist activities. In such circumstances, many suspects must be quickly screened for recent contact with explosives, and police, customs, and other security agencies must be able to determine on the spot whether a suspected substance is an explosive.

Explosive vapor detectors are relatively complicated and expensive; dogs require an elaborate and expensive logistical system of training, and they are not always reliable; and, other chemical kits are time-consuming, relatively complicated, and require technical training. Thus, there was an obvious need for a simple, quick, reliable, and inexpensive device for field detection of traces of all standard explosives. ETK, however, eliminates those problems. It consists of certain "detection buttons", a coarse filter paper, and two small reagent tubes. Detection is based on a very sensitive, visible chemical reaction with traces of the explosive compounds that may be left on the hands.

In order to perform the test, the suspect's palms and fingers are thoroughly rubbed with the filter paper (the "detection buttons" are particularly suitable for fingertips). The reagents are then added to the paper at the sampling site. The appearance of certain colors indicates the presence of explosives. Suspicious objects or materials are similarly tested.

This kit can be successfully used by police and law enforcement agencies in screening suspects. It can also be used by security officers and customs services to check suspicious objects (such as the innocuous-looking explosive "Detasheet") and determine whether they are made of explosive material.

Recently, after a request from the United States, we added to ETK a third reagent that detects home-made explosives based on inorganic nitrates as well.

## FERROPRINT: DEVELOPMENT OF FIREARM IMPRINTS ON HANDS

While investigating crimes involving handling or use of firearms, it would be of great advantage if the police could develop the imprints of the weapon on the hand of the suspect regardless of whether the gun has been fired. Until recently there was no efficient method for this, the oxine-test (the procedure for detecting metallic traces on hands) having been considered obsolete for years for its lack of sensitivity. In the Israel National Police Laboratories, a reagent has been developed that provides a visualization of a firearm's imprint on a suspect's hands, a test so sensitive that ballistics experts can frequently tell the type of weapon used from the shape of the imprint.

When one is holding a weapon, the perspiration of the hand dissolves some of the iron oxide from the metallic surface. Detection of such marks depends on the shape of the weapon and location of the metallic parts exposed to the person's touch, the amount of perspiration on the person's hand, the duration of handling and the intensity of contact with the weapon, the time elapsed since contact, and the way the weapon has been maintained (a well-kept and greased weapon leaves weaker imprints than a poorly maintained and rusted one).

## NO-MARK: LONG-LASTING INVISIBLE MARKING OF OBJECTS AND PERSONS

Objects which are tagged with fluorescent materials, so that offenders who come in contact with them can be identified later by ultra-violet light. This is an interesting example of Locard's Contact Law. Under such circumstances can we not only detect the traces that a person leaves on the object (i.e., fingerprints) but also the invisible traces that the object leaves on the person (namely the fluorescent marker). Thus by using an appropriate fluorescent taggant we are able to "assist" Locard's Law.

Commercial devices for invisible marking leave on the surgace a thin, invisible layer of powder that will stick to the person's hand upon contact and can be detected afterward under an ultra-violet illumination. The previously available commercial fluorescent powders or sprays required that the suspect be screened within several hours after touching a tagged object to assure that he had not wiped or washed the invisible residue off his hands.

The most important advantage of "No-mark" is that it remains on the hands at least two days after contact, thereby permitting efficient and convenient detection. Invisible marks made by this non-toxic, non-corrosive formulation are stable on tagged objects for several weeks and on hands touching the marked objects for several days, even after washing. The marks are detected by their strong fluorescence under ultra-violet light.

This formulation can be easily used by all police and law enforcement agencies, as well as security officers, postal services, customs, and private security personnel.

The list of field kits developed during this project includes all of the following:
1. BTK - Bullet-Hole Testing Kit.
2. Onprint - Latent fingerprint development from paper and other porous surfaces.
3. GSR - Collection of gun-shot residues for SEM examination.
4. A kit for sampling victims of Sex crimes evidence
5. Cannabispray - detection of traces of cannabinoids on hands
6. Field sampling of fire debris.
7. A portable unit for restoration of obliterated numbers.

And now to the conclusions:

Such field tests are particularly valuable because:

When, if time is wasted, there is a risk of losing those items of evidence that are liable to deteriorate rapidly (i.e. traces on suspects hands);

When there is a large number of suspects and the majority of them can be rapidly eliminated through a quick field test; and, when the discovery of a specific substance proves that a crime was committed (for example, field tests to determine whether a fire was started accidentally or is the result of arson; traces of metals in bullet-holes etc.)

## ADVANTAGES OF FIELD EXAMINATIONS:

First and foremost, they don't require scientists. As the tests are not designed to provide evidence, it's not necessary that the person making the tests understand the chemical causes of the reaction involved. In Israel, however, only qualified persons can carry out the tests, which guarantees a certain level of competence. Field tests also give immediate results, are relatively inexpensive, require no special equipment and can be carried out anywhere-before the evidence has deteriorated. In addition, they reduce the scientific and administrative workload of the laboratory (recording evidence, tagging. etc.) and are extremely useful for examination that would be impossible or impractical to conduct in the lab, i.e., testing the hands of 100 suspects in under an hour. Finally, such tests have a beneficial psychological effect; the suspect often feels compelled to confess if he is shown the visible results of the examination immediately.

Forensic science laboratory techniques are often developed with no regard for the problems that may arise in the field and no attempt being made to devise better methods for field use. In fact, many of the difficulties connected with field testing can be solved quite easily if the appropriate research is undertaken.

# THE ROLE OF THE FORENSIC/CLINICAL SPECIALIST (POLICE SURGEON)

H. B. Kean, Police Surgeon
Merseyside Police
U.K.

The training and work of the clinical forensic specialist is discussed along with his responsibilities to the police authority and to the complainant and accused (prisoner). The value of medical examination and collection of forensic specimens from victims and accused persons by a specialist medical practitioner is emphasized. Details of medical examination and methods of collection of specimens for forensic examination, the storage and transport of these specimens are given, with special reference to sexual assault. The age and origin of wounds and the estimation of time of death is briefly discussed. The content of a sexual offense kit will be shown and discussed.

It is suggested that there should be a Police Surgeon appointed for every 100,000 persons in the United Kingdom. The title 'Police Surgeon' is maintained for historical reasons but is misleading. I am neither a Policeman nor a Surgeon. In Northern Ireland the term 'Medical Examiner' has been adopted, but we can properly be described as Forensic/Clinical Specialists.

There is no National or State police force in the United Kingdom and each Metropolitan or County area has its own police force and its own appointed Police Surgeons and Deputies.

The amount of undergraduate teaching in forensic medicine varies from one medical school to another. It does not enable the graduate to practice forensic medicine efficiently.

Those doctors wishing to do clinical/forensic work apply for appointment as Deputy Police Surgeons in their local force.

In recent years the Association of Police Surgeons of Great Britain has encouraged a rise in the standards of practice. There are now many meetings about medical judisprudence and forensic medicine which prepare candidates for the Diploma of Medical Judisprudence (D.M.J.). There is a clinical and pathological section of this exam. Most large centers have a Medico-Legal Society, many Police Surgeons are members of the Forensic Society and other kindred and national groups.

The Police Surgeon is in receipt of an annual retainer and is paid for items of service on a negotiated scale. Income is derived also from Courts and from Social Service Departments.

As most crimes associate with alcohol excess, the practitioner must be prepared to work late at night and in the early hours of the morning.

We work mainly in medical rooms which are found in most Police Stations in the United Kingdom. Efforts have been made to bring these rooms up to a good standard of furnishing and equipment. We also attend on request at Hospitals, at the scene of the incident, and occasionally, at the home of a victim.

Our remit is to assist the Police on request by examination of victims, or suspects of crime, as soon as possible after an incident. We also advise on drugs, medication or medical care of those in Police custody. We examine injured members of the police force, we render medical assistance by direct treatment of minor injuries and illness, or by the appropriate referall.

The extent of any assault is determined and the forensic evidence collected, and reported in writing to the Police, and thence to the Court if charges are preferred. If required we attend Court to give evidence, usually as a Professional Witness to the Fact, but occasionally as an expert witness. Our independent status allows the production and interpretation of evidence on behalf oft the defence as well as for the prosecution.

The standard of evidence produced and the manner in which it is reported and later verbally given to the Court is of the utmost importance. The Doctor must be a good witness, able through instruction and practice to withstand aggresive and skilled cross-examination. He or she must impress the Magistrate or Jury with impartiality and professionalism. Some prosecutions have withered away on the inconstancy on the cross-examination, of competent and well-meaning medical specialists.

In the Western countries medical staff often move from job to job and it is often inconvenient for them to give evidence at short notice. The Police Surgeon is permanently and almost immediately available to the Court.

The following Table indicates the nature of the cases I attended during 44 weeks of the year 1984:

| | |
|---|---:|
| Fit Custody: | 192 |
| Assaults: | 101 |
| Assaults on Police (Victim): | 61 |
| Assaults on Police (Suspect): | 61 |
| Sexual offences: | |
| (Victims and Suspects) | 62 |
| Driving under the influence of | 63 |
| alcohol and/or drugs | |
| Drug addiction: | 39 |
| Suspicious and/or Sudden Death: | 35 |
| Child Abuse (physical): | 31 |
| Police Injuries or illness on | |
| duty: | 12 |
| Forensic sampling: | 10 |
| Allegation against Police: | 6 |
| Murder (attendance at scene or | |
| examination of Suspect): | 5 |
| Treatment: | 3 |
| Kidnapping: | 2 |
| Arson: | 1 |
| Unclassified: | 19 |
| **TOTAL:** | 712 |

Consent must always be obtained before examination and sampling. If the client is a minor (less than 16 years of age or mentally handicapped) the consent of a Parent or Guardian must be obtained. Once this is received a patient/Doctor relationship has been established. The victim or suspect must realise that medical and forensic evidence obtained may be used in a future Court proceeding.

If examination is refused, observations e.g. of demeanour, clothes, injuries, may be made, but I do not believe that these observations should be disclosed without permission of the client or direction from a Court.

A history is taken from the victim and if indicated from the suspect. Emotional and mental states are noted, together with the evidence of alcohol or drug intoxication. An impression is formed of the accuracy and reliability of the story. Factors concerned especially with sexual offences will be mentioned in the next paper. In general any moving and packing of clothing and collection of forensic samples for trace evidence should be done before detailed examination. Clothing should not if possible be removed by the Police before examination as tears and stains on the clothing can often be related to underlying features on the body. The clothing is packed in plastic bags, except for socks and shoes which go into brown paper envelopes. Wet, or wet-blood-stained clothing should be dried before packing.

The client stands on a large brown paper sheet. Appropriate forms are completed as each article is removed to avoid mistakes. The brown paper sheet is folded and packed. A paper gown is provided for the client. General physical and sexual development, together with blemishes, tattoo's, and for example injection sites, operation or burn scars can be noted. Body diagrams should be used.

Wounds are accurately described and categorised, e.g. bruise or abrasion, shape, size, color and situation, relating the injury to a fixed object e.g. 3" below the point of the right elbow. An opinion of the causation and age of the injury should be formed.

Hair should be removed by combing and plucking. Foreign bodies in the hair are best obtained by combing after a layer of cottonwool has been applied to the base of the teeth of the comb. Dirt marks are sampled by special cellotape which is afterwards placed on a clear thin, plastic sheet. Blood stains can be sampled with 6" pieces of white cotton thread (not nylon thread) and dried before packing. For dried stains the cotton can be moistened with water, preferably distilled water. In either case a Control Swab, dry or moistened, should be submitted. Semen stains are sampled by plain swabs, dry or moist, again with Control Swabs.

In assault, wounding or murder, a venous blood sample is often required. A sample for blood/alcohol estimation is always worthwhile taking.

Any fibers of foreign bodies, e.g. grass, is removed. from the person and packed and labelled. Nail clippings, or if the nails are bitten down nail scrapings, may be taken from each hand separately.

If the client is a drug addict, or one suspects is a
hepatitis carrier, samples must be clearly labelled to
this effect.

The height/weight, hair color/eye color, are noted.
Minor injuries or illness are treated. Withdrawal symptoms
are alleviated.

In addition to diagram, photographs (for personal
recall) may be obtained with permission of the client and
Police Officer in charge. Direct Ultra-Violet light and UV
light photography may show up older injuries which are not
otherwise evident.

The report must be accurate and the terminology must
be non-technical, e.g. it is better to say there is a
round, blue bruise 1" in diameter with slight swelling 3"
above the boney prominence on the outside of the left ankle,
than to write this bruise is 3 " above the left external
malleolus, unless an explanation follows.

In Court evidence should be similarly clear. One can
step out of the witness box to indicate situations of wounds
on ones own person. The Judge may ask for copies of the
diagrams you have made at the time of examination to be
distributed.

Injuries made by specific objects have typical appearance
and with careful observations and experience the probable
causation can be stated. Too dogmatic an estimate of the
age of an injury can lead one into great difficulty,
usually with experience a worthwhile opinion can be given.

Attendance at the scene of an incident, e.g. at a
suspicious or sudden death, is often requested. Foul play
should be ruled out only after careful consideration of
the factors, including if necessary, some suggestion of the
possible time when death occurred, if evidence on this
point is not forthcoming, or is incompatible with the
state of the body.

If foul play is a possibility, after pronouncing that
death has occurred, the clinical examiner should avoid
further contact with and contamination of the scene.

If possible, victims and suspect are examined by
different Doctors in different rooms to avoid cross-
contamination. This restriction should also apply to Police
Officers. If this is not feasible, e.g. if there are many
suspects, the examiner can wear gloves, a gown and hat.
If only blood, saliva or nail clippings are required, or
if there is a week between examinations, these restrictions
can be relaxed.

The Forensic Science Laboratories can easily be
overwhelmed with useless samples. It is of no value for
example to obtain scalp hair samples if victim and suspect
have been recently co-habiting and the crime took place

# SEXUAL ABUSE FIELD KITS IN THE UNITED KINGDOM

H. B. Kean, Police Surgeon
Merseyside Police-U.K.

An analysis of the types of sexual offenses dealt with by the clinical forensic specialist is presented. The number of offenses in England and Wales and in the Merseyside Police Area (whose population is approximately 1.5 million) is shown. The method of examination of victim and offender and the sexual offense kits used for the examination are described with special reference to forensic identificaiton of the offender. It is emphasized that general body examination and sampling is at least as important as inspection of the specimens taken from genital organs.

Before describing the contents and use of the Kit, I would like briefly to discuss the interview with and the examination of the victims and suspects in sexual offence cases.

In the U.K. at present most examinations of the victim are carried out in the Medical Room of the Police Station. A minority are done in the hospital, but in all cases the Police Surgeon is the examiner. Obviously, urgent treatment has priority and will be carried out in the hospital by the Gynecologist or other specialist. The latter would not proceed however to the forensic examination. We look for the early establishment of Sexual Offence Centers where examination, comprehensive care and follow-up can be carried out along with research into the many facets of sexual offence.

Tables 1 and 2 illustrate the incidence and type of recorded sexual offences in the United Kingdom as a whole, 1982, and in Merseyside in 1983. You will note the high number of victims under the age of 16 years. Fortunately, most Indecent Assaults are of a minor nature and there is little forensic content in the investigation. Absence of injury does not of course rule out the possibility of detrimental and emotional consequences. Often in the case of young children these involve the parents rather than the child victim.

The examination is essentially as described in the previous paper. The history from a female victim includes details such as marital state, boyfriends, menarche, last menstrual period, nature of menses, number of children, contraception, date and time of previous intercourse, whether washed or passed urine. Any history of venereal disease or hepatitis, amount of alcohol consumed. Questions are asked about clothes, e.g. are they all present? Were any worn previous to the assault and discarded or lost at the scene or subsequently donned?

One should note whilst the victim is undressing on a brown paper sheet how easy or difficult it is to remove clothing, e.g. if she is wearing a very tight pair of jeans. The clothing should be examined for marks and stains to relate to the underlying body, tears or missing buttons should be noted.

### ENGLAND & WALES 1982 RECORDED

#### TABLE I

| | |
|---|---|
| Buggery | 516 |
| Indecent Assault (M) | 2082 |
| Indecent Assault (M/M) | 1104 |
| Rape | 1336 |
| Indecent Assault (F) | 11156 |
| Unlawful Sexual Intercourse-13 yrs. | 223 |
| Unlawful Sexual Intercourse-16yrs. | 2791 |
| Incest | 230 |

### MERSEYSIDE 1983 RECORDED

#### TABLE II

| | |
|---|---|
| Buggery | 8 |
| Indecent Assault (M) | 77 |
| Indecent Assault (M/M) | 19 |
| Rape | 41 |
| Indecent Assault (F) | 286 |
| Unlawful Sexual Intercourse-13 yrs. | - |
| Unlawful Sexual Intercourse-16 yrs. | 39 |
| Incest | 7 |
| Gross Indec. Child | 28 |

(M) - On male  (M/M) - Between Males  (F) - On Female

Clothes from the genital and anal area should be taken as soon as a client has undressed. A vaginal speculum should be used to obtain high vaginal samples. Pubic and scalp hair is combed and plucked. Blood and saliva samples are taken. Additional specimens may include swabs from the skin if it has been bitten or sucked and mouth swabs if oral intercourse is suspected. The examination couch sheet should be submitted along with the floor sheet. Sanitary towels, tampons and contraceptives, e.g. cap, should be submitted if obtained. General and genital injuries are noted and samples are taken as described in the previous paper and as listed in appendix B. Vaginal swabs should still be taken in the presence of menstrual or traumatic bleeding.

The procedure for the examination of the male victim of a homosexual attack, and for the suspects in sexual offences, follow similar lines. The submission of anal and penile swabs may be of more significance in these cases.

Samples must be packed and stored correctly and continuity must be ensured.

SPECIMEN STORAGE:

Freeze: Vaginal, penile and anal swabs, and saliva (semen or saliva stained articles if possible).

Refrigerate: Blood and urine.

In the United Kingdom laboratories do not request that slides be made of vaginal or anal swabs.

A sexual Offence Form, detailing briefly the circumstances of the Assault, and the specimens submitted, is completed. It is in triplicate. One copy goes to the Laboratory. One is retained by the C.I.D. (Police),and the other by the examiner. The submission of the Form does not preclude the completion of a more detailed report for the Police.

The Police Surgeon may also complete a further Form when he feels the victim should be referred to his/her General Practitioner or to the hospital for pregnancy and/or sexually transmitted disease screening, and psychological assessment, follow-up and treatment.

The Home Office sexual offence kit has been designed to provide in the hands of the skilled examiner the optimum amount of evidence for the investigating Police.

The contents of the kit is shown in Appendix I. The sexual offence Examination Form is illustrated in Appendix II.

APPENDIX 1

HOME OFFICE FORENSIC SCIENCE SERVICE

# MEDICAL EXAMINATION KIT

### For use in Sexual Offence Examination

ECONOMY — Please ensure that all unused items are placed in the bag provided and returned to the laboratory. The box must also be returned.

This kit can be used to examine the complainant or suspect.

## CONTENTS

3 Copies of the Sexual Offences Examination Form.

Large sheet of paper in a polythene bag.

2 medical cleansing towelettes, 2 Monovette syringes, 2 needles, Elastoplast.

Bottle for saliva sample.

8 plain sterile cotton wool swabs.

2 cocktail sticks in small self seal polythene bags for fingernail samples.

2 combs in printed polythene bags for hair combings.

15 printed polythene bags.

1 roll of Sellotape.

1 pair of disposable polythene gloves.

Packing materials for clothing will be made available by the police.

The following notes by a senior police surgeon and a forensic scientist may assist in the examination and are for guidance:

## GENERAL INFORMATION

Should cover:

1. The mental state of the person for evidence of shock or distress.

2. General state of development.

3. If the person looks older or younger than the given age.

4. Degree of intelligence.

5. The state of the clothing, disarrangement, tears, earth or vegetation, blood, seminal stains or lubricants.

## EXAMINATION FORM

This form should be completed at the time of the medical examination. The top copy is for the laboratory; additional self carbon copies are provided for the police surgeon and for the police.

Persons being examined should stand on the large sheet of clean paper whilst undressing and any fallen debris collected by folding the paper, returning it to its self-seal bag.

Please record the order in which the items of clothing were worn, for example it is not unusual for two pairs of pants to be worn.

Please indicate which items were:

    (a)   worn during the offence.

    (b)   removed before the offence and not replaced.

    (c)   removed before the offence and replaced afterwards.

If a sanitary towel/tampon was used after the offence this should be submitted.

Any damp patches noticed on clothing should be marked and also noted on the examination form, as their position could be important if they are subsequently found to be semen.

219

APPENDIX 1

## PHYSICAL EXAMINATION

A complete examination of the body should now be made and notes taken of any bruises, scratches, gravel marks, etc. Those relevant to the complaint should be fully described and measured. If you consider that photographs would be of assistance the attendance of a police photographer should be requested. Arrangements will subsequently be made for their production in court as exhibits.

## SWABS

Before any further medical examination is carried out, the following swabs should be taken as appropriate:

Vaginal — maximum of 3 (at least 1 external and 1 internal).

Anal — 1 external and 1 internal.

Penile — for vaginal material, if within 2 days of the offence,
1 external, preferably from the coronal sulcus,
1 external if faeces visible or lubricant suspected.

Semen found on the body surface should be collected on to a sterile swab.

An unused swab should be labelled "control swab".

Slides should not be made from the swabs.

Sufficient swabs are included to cover every eventuality.

BLOOD 2-10 mls in the Monovette syringe which serves as a container.

SALIVA 2-10 mls in the bottle provided.

Blood and saliva are needed from both complainants and suspects.

## FINGERNAIL SAMPLES

Take only if circumstances suggest blood or fibres present. Cuttings are preferred but scrapings using one cocktail stick per hand can be taken. Pack in the polythene bags provided.

## HAIRS

As many hairs as possible should be combed from the head and pubis using the combs provided and additional hairs should be pulled and packed separately. A total of not less than 25 head hairs and 25 pubic hairs should be collected. (The combs will also be examined for foreign hairs and fibres).

In cases of buggery the anal region should be examined for foreign hairs. Other hair samples (facial, chest etc.) should be taken where appropriate.

Should there be any matting of the pubic hair then this area should be cut off and submitted as a sample.

## IDENTIFYING THE SAMPLES

The self seal polythene bags included in the kit are printed as a police exhibit label. This should be signed, dated and exhibit number and description of the exhibit inserted. Each of the samples taken, including swabs, blood samples, hair, fingernails etc., should be placed in an individual polythene bag. Brief details should be marked on blood and swab containers sufficient to confirm that it has been placed in the correct polythene bag.

## GENERAL NOTES

Precautions should always be taken to avoid the risk of contact trace materials from victim and suspect and their clothing being cross-transferred in the examination room.

The person's name should be clearly written on all samples.

For details regarding medical aspects of the examination, "The New Police Surgeon, A Practical Guide", published by the Association of Police Surgeons of Great Britain, is recommended.

At the completion of the examination the cardboard insert should be removed from the box and discarded. The box is then a suitable container for the transport of samples to the laboratory.

APPENDIX 2

Home Office Forensic Science Laboratory

## SEXUAL OFFENCES FORM   5323 /C

To be submitted to the Laboratory with the Lab. Form in all cases (1 per person).

---

NAME AND ADDRESS OF DOCTOR

Your reference
Our reference
Date

---

**PART 1: INFORMATION REQUESTED FROM THE MEDICAL EXAMINATION**

Name and age of Victim/Suspect                                    Male/Female

Date and Time of Alleged Incident

Date and Time of Examination

---

**SPECIFIC INFORMATION:** (give details in the space below if additional information is indicated)

Contraceptive: None/sheath/pill/other (specify)          Bleeding: None/Menstrual

Lubricant used: No/Yes (type if known)                   Traumatic Bleeding: No/Details

Is/Is Not suffering from VD/other infectious disease (specify)    Has/Has not washed/bathed since offence

Buggery victim has/has not defaecated since offence      Male has/has not been vasectomised (date)

---

Date and times of other relevant intercourse within two weeks

Contraceptive used  Yes/No  Type

---

**PART 2: SAMPLES AND STORAGE**

Person being examined stood on large sheet of paper whilst undressing (for fallen debris)    Yes/No

Person lay on clean paper during examination (for falling debris)    Yes/No

SWABS    control included    ☐

Vaginal external    ☐          Use only plain dry sterile cottonwool swabs with tubes:
        internal    ☐          no others are suitable.

Anal    external    ☐          An unused swab should be included as a control.
        internal    ☐

Penile    ☐                    For vaginal material: 1 external, preferably from coronal sulcus;
                               1 external if faeces visible or lubricant suspected.

HAIRS    Head    ☐
         Pubic   ☐             Take combings and pulled samples (at least 25 hairs)

FINGERNAILS    Left    ☐
               Right   ☐       Take only if circumstances suggest blood or fibres present.
                               Cuttings are preferred but scrapings using one cocktail stick per hand
BLOOD    ☐                     can be taken.

SALIVA    ☐                    To be taken from victims and suspects: 2-10 ml in the container provided.

OTHERSAMPLES please specify

If sanitary towel/tampon was used before or after the offence it should be submitted.

Slides, examination gloves and vaginal aspirates are not usually required.

Completed by_____

---

**STORAGE**

Placing samples in a refrigerator used for food can present a health risk. Where this is unavoidable, place the samples in a sealed bag before putting in the refrigerator.

**BLOOD SAMPLES** - Store in a refrigerator (DO NOT FREEZE).

**SALIVA SAMPLES** - Place sample in a freezer (ice box) and keep frozen until arrival at the laboratory. If this is not possible boil in a water bath for at least 10 minutes as soon as possible after sampling.

**SWABS**          - Should be put into a freezer (ice box).

Place shoes in brown paper bags and dried clothing in brown paper bags or polythene bags as recommended by the laboratory. If the clothing is wet or damp, place in a polythene bag and bring to the Laboratory with minimum delay. The receiving officer at the Laboratory must be informed of its condition.

If these storage conditions cannot be complied with, your Laboratory should be consulted.

# THE SYSTEM FOR EVIDENCE COLLECTION FROM SEXUAL ASSAULT VICTIMS IN ISRAEL

A. Marbach, Ph.D.-Head
Forensic Biology Laboratory
Israel Police
Jerusalem, Israel

A rape or sexual assault victim is, in addition to the human point of view, a part of the crime scene. Access to a victim's body for the collection of evidence is restricted to medical personnel and should not be done by the police technicians or investigators. Unfortunately, in Israel there are no designated police surgeons, and in the past physical evidence from sexual assault cases was not routinely collected. Today, physicians are acting as mediators between the physical evidence on the victim's body and the Israel National Police Biology Laboratory where the evidence is examined. Treatment for sexual assault victims is now becoming standardized throughout Israel. The victims are received at a public hospital where he/she is treated by the appropriate physician (e.g. gynecologist for female, pediatrician for children). During the examination physical evidence from the victim's body is also collected. Sixteen hospitals are participating in this evidence collection project. Although each hospital serves a regional population, it will treat any sexual assault victim regardless of his/her home address or the geographical location of the assault. Now every police station has an address to which victims can be taken for treatment. To improve

> and standardize the evidence collection process, a sex crime evidence collection kit was developed by the I.P.F.B.L. and supplied to each of the sixteen regional hospitals. The multi-lateral connections between the police investigator, the attending physician and the personnel in the biology laboratory will be described. The sex crime evidence collection kit will be presented, and its contents and the factors considered in its development will be described.

Treatment for sexual assault victims is now becoming standardized throughout Israel. A sex crime evidence collection kits are supplied to the hospitals participating in this project. The multilateral connections among the police, the hospital, volunteer organisations and the victims are described. Data about the quantity and quality of usage of the kits are presented. The significance of the data and the modular characteristics of the system are discussed.

The Israeli system for the treatment of sexual assault victims has been run for about four years. This is not too long a time to remember what was the situation before, and yet it is long enough to have a preliminary summary in order to evaluate this set-up and to draw some conclusions for the future.

Such a system although it was set up to cope with Israel's needs, can be regarded as a model for other countries sharing the same problems.

A sex crime differs from other crimes by the fact that the victim's body is part of the scene of the crime, and some times it is even the only available source of evidence. The access to a victim's body for the collection of evidence is, restricted to medical personnel, and quite understandably cannot be done by scene of crime officers or police investigators. Examination by police surgeon is one way to overcome this difficulty, but as we do not have police surgeons in Israel, and there was no alternative way four years ago, sex crime cases were seldom accompanied by evidence collected from the victim's body.

In order to solve this problem we decided to base our solution on the already existing medical support which is quite elaborate in Israel. It is well known that mere goodwill from medical personnel is not enough. We must also support them with a sex crime evidence collection kit to help them with their examinations.

We ran a test project for one year in the Jerusalem area with strong cooperation from "Shaarei Zedek" hospital. When we found that our prototype kit satisfied the needs of medical examinations, and the liaison between the police and the hospital was working well, we expanded use of the kit throughout the country.

The current system is based on the cooperation of eighteen hospitals in Israel. These hospitals were chosen according to the following technical criteria:

a. The hospital must have a gynecological examination room open twenty four hours a day, with gynecologists and other medical experts available.

b. The hospital must be able to provide psychological assistance to the victim as the need arises.

To these two criteria we added consideration of geography and the demography of the areas which they serve.

Last but not least the attitude of the medical staff to this "job" was considered. It should be emphasized that our connections with the hospitals are based only on "goodwill". The medical staff taking part in this project, was convinced by us that doing "police work" does not contradict their "humane medical work".

We realized that getting the acceptance of the hospitals should be strengthened by working equipment and a clear set of procedures for using it. So, a sex crime evidence collection kit which could be used by the examining gynecologist, was developed (Fig. 1).

The kit contains only the envelopes and containers for the samples taken by the examiner - swabs, microscope slides, pads for blood and saliva etc. We did not add instruments such as speculum, gloves, and syringes. This is because our kit was planned to be used in an emergency room which is already supplied with these instruments.

The kit also contains a form to be filled by the examining doctor. In the form the doctor is directed to ask the victim certain details about the case. What kind of a sexual contact was there? Where did the ejaculation take place? etc. Later, there is a check-list of actions that the examiner should follow, for example: taking vaginal swabs from different areas, taking blood sample on a gause pad, looking for motile spermatozoa, etc.

The advantages of the kit are:

a. It standardizes the sampling taken in different hospitals and by doctors with different levels of experience.

b. It helps and forces the examiner to keep the right procedures in case of tiredness or work pressure in the emergency room.

c. It ensures to the Forensic Biology Laboratory that the samples were collected according to its requirements, that nothing was forgotten and every sample was collected correctly.

A complicated network of interactions between the police station, the local hospital and the Forensic Biology Laboratory was established. The police station is responsible to bring the complainant to the local hospital, to receive the kit from the hospital and to send it to the laboratory at National Police Headquarters.

The hospital is responsible for the examination using the kit, to give the entire kit to a policeman from the local police station and to inform the laboratory when more kits are needed for stock.

The laboratory is responsible to examine the evidence collected in the kit, to supply the hospitals with unused kits according to need and to oversee the whole system.

The police is also helped by volunteer social workers and members of the rape crisis centers.

The overall picture of the system for treatment of a sex assault victim in Israel can be compared to a triangle. Police is in one corner, the hospital is in the second one and the volunteer organisations are in the third.

The main problem in sex crimes is the low number of complaints as compared to the believed actual number of cases. We hope that through this triangle we can cover as much area as possible, and give the victim more than one address to which she can complain.

The most common procedure is for the victim to file a complaint at the local police station which will then bring her to the hospital and the volunteer organisation. For the victim who wants only a medical examination, there is a way to go directly to the hospital. Later on the examining physician would suggest to the victim that she contact the police. For those victims who prefer the intimate atmosphere of a volunteer organisation, they can contact such groups and later they will be advised to complain in the police station, too, and to have a medical examination.

It is important to emphasize that although the project was established mainly for Forensic purposes there is also a broader benefit, because the victims receive an ordinary medical examination as well. Hence, not only the project can be justified from a law enforcement point of view, it also contributes to the public hygene.

Quantity and quality of usage of the kit by the medical examiners and the police investigators was evaluated. During the years 1982, 1983 and 1984 an average of 49%, nearly half of the sex crime cases which were submitted to our laboratory included kits as exhibits (Fig 2, sections 1 and 2).

A thorough analysis has been completed for the years 1982 and 1983 which were the first and the second years of running the project. In those years 18% of the cases had kits as the only exhibit (Fig. 2, section 2). That means that if there had been no kit, 18% of the cases would have been with no exhibits at all, and thus lost.

We found that in general the examining physicians used the kit according to the instructions in the form. Some minute mistakes that we found have been brought to the attention of the medical staff by personal meetings and letters.

In 51% of the cases evidence was forwarded for laboratory examination but the kits were not used (Fig. 2 sections 3-6). Through analysis we decided whether in our opinion there was or was not justification for not using the kit.

In 17% of the cases without kits, there was a justification for not using the kit (Fig. 2, section 3). The main reasons that justified not using the kit were ejaculation not on the body, or more than three days having elapsed between the sexual act and the time of complaint.

In another 17% of the cases without kits there was no justification for not using the kit (Fig. 2, section 4). The kit was not used although the sexual act was within three days or less of the complaint, and the ejaculation place was unknown or known to be on the body.

In another 13% we could not reach an opinion about the necessity of using the kit due to a lack of detailed information about the case (Fig. 2, section 5).

In most of the cases where the kit was not used, it was because the complainant was not send to the medical examination (Fig. 2 sections 3-5). Thus it is a fault caused by police investigators and not by medical examiners. Only in 4% was there a medical examination but no kit taken. The reasons for this are several and different (Fig. 2 section 6).

Our analysis emphasizes the importance of the police investigator in achieving the goal of sex crime evidence collection. In accordance with our findings we recommended that thorough oral and written guidlines concerning the appropriate circumstances for use of the kit must be given to police investigators.

We also asked police investigators to advise the complainant to get the medical examination even in those cases when it is too late for using the kit.

We regard the project as a modular example because it can be established in one place in a regional hospital, independent from other regions. There is no need to have it in use at the same time all over the country, later it can be expanded to other regions as well. The system is relatively easy to build and it is not expensive because the medical network already exists.

The system must be followed by a kit for evidence collection if we want to keep the examinations and evidence collections on an acceptable professional level.

Introducing the system to the hospitals and the police stations must include thorough training not only of medical staff but also of police investigators, in order to ensure a high percentage of usage of the kit.

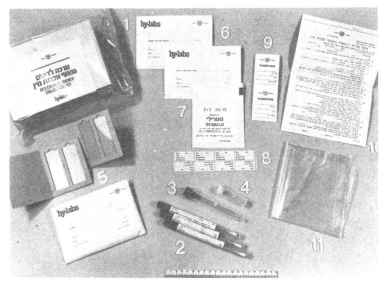

Fig. 1. The Sex Evidence Collection Kit and its contents.

1. Unused, factory sealed kit.
2. Sterile cotton swabs.
3. Test tube for whole blood sample.
4. Small test tube for fingernails' clippings.
5. Envelope with cardboard slide holders and microscope slides
6. Envelope with sterile gauze pad for saliva sample.
7. Envelope with sterile gauze pad for blood sample.
8. Specimens seals.
9. Evidence seals.
10. Sexual offences Examination Form (3 copies).
11. Polythene bag for underwear and debris.

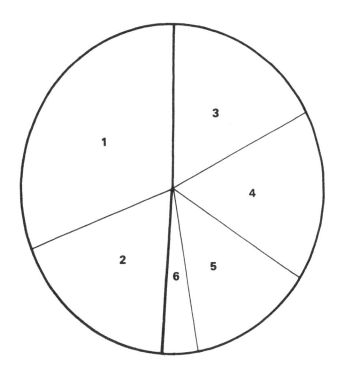

Fig. 2. Use of the kits in sexual offence cases.

1. Cases containing kits and other exhibits (31%)
2. Cases containing kits only (18%).
3. Cases without kit with justification for not using (17%).
4. Cases without kit without justification for not using (17%).
5. Cases without kit but not possible to evaluate lack of use (13%).
6. Cases where medical examination was made without the kit (4%).

# EVIDENCE TECHNICIANS

M. A. Kaplan, Deputy Commander
Israel National Police
Jerusalem

Laboratory results can be no better than the sample of evidence recovered in the field. Hence, the Israel National Police has made a major effort to develop a corps of evidence technicians trained to maximize the recovery from scenes of crime of potentially valuable evidence. These technicians are screened carefully before employment, and after they have finished their special course of instruction, their record is constantly under review. Based upon this review, they are ranked; those technicians performing under standard are transferred out of the program. Successful technicians are given periodic advanced training in the technical collection of physical evidence which they forward for laboratory examination. The technicians do not appear as expert witnesses in court, however they are called to describe their activities as they relate to the chain of evidence. In summation, these technicians can be considered "agents of the laboratories in the field."

I should like to elaborate this morning on one of the points which I mentioned in my keynote speech at yesterday's openning session of IDENTA '85. I am speaking of the function of the evidence technicians in the forensic process. These technicians do their work in the field, but they constitute a key to the effective functioning of the central forensic laboratory.

The purpose of the institutionalization of the evidence technician is to optimalize the entire forensic science operation by bringing representatives of the laboratory into the field. The technicians have three functions:

(1) Locating the sample of potential evidence

(2) Collecting the sample through such technical procedures as photography and casting, amongst others

(3) As has been happening recently in the Israel National Police, performing certain examinations of evidence hitherto conducted in the laboratory but found practical to be done outside the central laboratory

As a consequence particularly of this latter point, the evidence technicians have also been giving expert testimony in courts of law on the results of the examinations which they have been performing.

There are two basic alternatives to this system:

(1) Examinations at crime scenes could be performed by non-laboratory personnel with a minimal involvement by the laboratory in terms of determining what the laboratory requirements are for subsequent processing of evidence

or

(2) Dispatching central laboratory scientists to the scenes of crime (hardly realistic except in the most serious of crimes)

We in the Israel National Police feel that we have developed a middle of the road solution. The evidence technician is not a laboratory worker; nonetheless, he is closely related to the central forensic laboratory, and he represents the labotatory in the field units.

In the Israel National Police, the forensic science laboratories are in the Division of Criminal Identification. This division, today, is responsible for selecting the technicians, and training and supervising their technical work.

The technicians are scattered throughout the country, and they are an extention of the central forensic laboratory. There is a very strong working relationship between the technician and the staff of the central laboratories which take full technical responsibility the quality of his work (even though he is in the direct administrative chain of command of an investigatory unit). In other words, there is technical professional responsibility which comes from the central laborator and supervising responsibility which is the function of the commander at the unit.

Professional responsibility is exercised to the extent that the central laboratory can determine that a particular individual must stop working as a technician because his work is technically inadequate. There are standards of performance, and the work of the technicians is reviewed according to these standards.

The work of the evidence technician is actually conducted in three places: (1) at scene of the crime, (2) in his own "laboratory," and (3) in the courts. In his "laboratory" he is readily available to investigators for consultation, a function difficult for the central laboratories which are located only at National Headquarters in Jerusalem.

Outside his own laboratory the technician can perform a variety of preliminary examinations involving blood, explosive traces, gunshot residues, He is also tasked with the detection and development of fingerprints, and the clandestine marking of objects (using flourescent powders and NOMARK, a spray developed by the Israel National Police).

Many evidence technicians also have responsibilities in the area of technical surveillance, which is alsodone outside the laboratory.

What does the technician do in the laboratory? Clearly, there is administrative work. The technician also does the photography and fingerprinting of suspects in his laboratory. Additionally, he photographs exhibits, operates the rogues gallery, and composes IDENTI-KIT portraits for the investigative units. The technician is capable of photographing latent fingerprints and the IDENTI-KIT portraits which he has made.

The technician develops erased numbers on metal and determines the validity of the marking on automobiles. In other words, these are subjects which, in Israel, cannot be easily handled from the central laboratory, so technicians throughout the country have been trained to do this work in the name of the central laboratory.

When the technicians have special problems, they will of course consult with the laboratory, or they will even bring the exhibit in question into the laboratory.

Over the past few years we have added a new task for selected evidence technicians. They now conduct examinations to determine the presence of hashish. This determination is required by the courts but it is not necessary to use the time of the central laboratory for these routine cases. Nor does it need a high level of scientific expertise to conduct the standard tests involved.

Hashish examinations are done only by those technicians specially selected and brought to the central laboratory for training. Their work is supervised, and if there is any difficulty in court (which so far has not happened) a scientific expert from the central laboratory will be called in to assist.

This is the theory supporting the concept of the evidence technician, and so far the system has been working very well.

There are about 165 approved technicians throughout the country in 37 technician units. These units are attached to the 11 police sub-districts. Each sub-district has a supervisory evidence technician of officer rank.

The 37 technician units are under the administrative control of the investigations unit in the host police station. Thus, they are told to go to the scene of crime by the investigative officer. The technical aspect of their work, however, is under the control of the central forensic laboratory.

There are 44 photography groups in the evidence technician network. Each of the 37 technician units has a photography group, and in addition there are seven photography units which work independently. Twenty of these groups have dark rooms; the others do photography, but they rely on external laboratory facilities for photographic processing.

The equipment needed by the evidence technicians is provided through the central laboratory which has its own supply center. There is a great deal of equipment --- cameras, technical surveillance gear, etc. These items are not only initially supplied; they are serviced for repairs and replaced when beyond repair or obsolete.

The central laboratory also has responsibility for the special vehicles used by the evidence technicians. There are 21 vans and an additional number of smaller vehicles.

As I have already mentioned, the central laboratory recruits the technicians, and in order to do this, special standards have been designed. There even are proficiency tests to determine who shows the best potential to be a good technician.

Believe it or not, it was discovered that a good sense of orientation is very important for a technician, because looking for fingerprints at the scene of a crime often depends on having a sense of orientation and putting oneself in the steps of the person who committed the crime.

When the proficiency tests were initiated, we did not know the best or most important qualities required. We divided our technicians into two groups: one group of technicians who were considered to be very good, and another group of technicians who were not performing as well. All of the technicians were put through a battery of tests to find out which tests would correspond to our own opinion of the people being examined. In this way a proceedure was developed for examining these future applicants.

Now, new technicians are recruited by the central laboratory, and they given a special 10 week course. After a period of on the job training they are recognized as qualified evidence technicians.

Refresher courses and instruction in advanced techniques are not forgotten. Only after technicians take a special course are they allowed to perform special functions. For example, only a technician who has successfully passed a course in hashish examination will be authorized to work in that area. Courses are conducted in the central laboratory.

Supervison of the evidence technician units is carried out by a special department in the Division of Criminal Identificaton, the home divison of the central laboratories. This special department deals with questions of training and technical advancement, promotion, co-ordination, supervision and control.

There are periodic meetings. The heads of units are called in to the central laboratory, and problems are discussed with them. Reports are received by the Division of Criminal Identification from the technicians in the field, and the central laboratory itself checks on work. All evidence technician units are visited by headquarters personnel at least once a year.

The technical unit in Headquarters is also involved in the logistical problems of the unit in the field --- building facilities vehicles, determination of equipment standards.

As I have said, recommendations are made to the commanders of the various police districts and sub-districts. If any of the evidence technicians excels, the laboratory is often in a better position to know it than the technician's own commanders. The laboratory has standards for the number of fingerprint identifications per visits to scenes of crime. In how many cases do you expect to find a fingerprint which could be matched with a true suspect? If a man goes to a certain number of crime scenes without finding fingerprints that lead to an identification, then he is deficient in this area. He is warned, and if he does not improve, he is transferred from this job to another one in the police.

The laboratory also tries to help people who are below standard by teaching them techniques used by people who are doing well. Thus, everyone can benefit from the successes of the best technicians.

In summation, evidence technicians are a very useful adjunct to the central laboratory. I should note, however, that although a great deal of their work relates to fingerprints, they are not sent to court on this subject because of the crucial significance of fingerprints in the determination of guilt inmodern courts. The tentative comparisons of fingerprints are sent to the central laboratory which examines the comparison, reviews and signs on the court opinion if it approves. Only the experts from the central laboratory appear in court as experts on fingerprint identification.

In the Israel National Police, we have also found that evidence technicians have strong motivation in connection with cases they have handled. If a man is working at the scene of the crime, he comes back to his office with the drive to search his local fingerprint collection. "I saw this fingerprint before. Now, just where?"

The local level in an investigation is very important. The technician, sitting in the local station, makes the work of the central laboratory more fruitful, and he places the central laboratory in a better positon to serve investigative units.

# COMPUTER-BASED METHODS FOR FORENSIC SPEAKER RECOGNITION

M. Hecker
Scientific Director
Head Handwriting Laboratory, BKA

In a number of criminal offences such as kidnapping, extortion, intimidation and nuisance calls the human voice or speech transmitted via telephone plays a devisive role. Thus, in the forensic field there is a growing demand for information on speakers in order to delimit the number of suspects or to identify the perpetrator. This applies to both police investigations and court procedures.

Two kinds of tasks may be distinguished in forensic speaker identification:

a. There is only one speech sample. In this case, a voice analysis is to be performed in order to delimit age, dialect, and social status of a speaker. This task is frequent in police investigations.

b. There is at least one speech sample recorded in the course of a criminal act and a sample for comparison with one or more suspects. This is the basis for a classical voice comparison task.

The aim of voice comparison is to show whether or not two samples pertain to the same individual. In this respect we cannot speak of "prints" such as, for instance, fingerprints which are definable in mathematical terms. We rather have to stress that a "voice-print" does not exist simply because speech is not a reproducible phenomenon: nobody can repeat a word twice in exactly the same fashion. A recording depends on many external conditions. Strictly speaking, only statistical statements may be made in forensic voice comparison.

In the last few years, great progress has been achieved in nearly all fields of speech processing using modern computer facilities. As far as speaker recognition is concerned the technological state of the art has lead to first industrial applications such as access control systems.

At first sight it may seem that techniques developed in the course of these activities should be able to show up a way to solve the problem of forensic speaker recognition, too. There is, however, a fundamental difference between the commercial and forensic situations, since for the latter the set of side conditions is highly different.

As far as commercial applications are concerned, speakers are co-operative, i.e. they want to be recognised in order to gain access to money or informations. Thus they are prepared to repeat a given standard text. The psychological state of these persons may be assumed to remain constant from one sample to the next, and samples are directly fed into the speech processing system via microphone.

In forensic voice comparisons, however, speakers normally are not co-operative, and may even disguise their voices. There are also vast differences in terms of the so-called speaking situation. Furthermore, speech samples are attained by background noise and distortions due to the telephone channel. In order to account for varying side conditions the task of forensic voice comparison will exploit all informations available from the tape recordings, that is: many forms of evidence, both measurable and non-measurable features will have to be assessed so that ultimately an auditory investigation and an objective comparison on the basis of computer results merge into one expert report.

An auditory analysis by the trained ear of a speech scientist should not be dispensed with since its results wil not be obtained by any computerised techniques in the fore-seeable future. Such features are, for instance, peculia-rities or habits of pronunciation, assessment of regional accent or idiolectal features, pathological features, emotions etc. On the other hand, measurable features such as pitch, spectral properties or the temporal structure of speech may be investigated using computer facilities, highly sophisticated instrumentation and signal analysis techniques Both classes of features yield a chain of cues for police investigations and expert testimony.

Since side conditions differ from one case to another it is not appropriate to dispose of only one technique. There rather has to be a bundle of different methods adapted to the individual situations. For this reason a vast number of instruments for the presentation and analysis of speech have been established, such as:

1. digitisation of speech, acoustic and graphic presentation of tape recordings
2. digital filtering techniques
3. analysis and compensation of background noise and distortions introduced through telephone trans-mission (speech enhancement) including the correction of recording speed, adaptive decon-volution, comb filtering and spectral subtraction techniques
4. tape authentication and channel identification
5. technique for the definition of beginning and ending of acoustic events (speech segmentation)
6. temporal parameters such as closure duration of plosives (e.g. German p,t,k,b,d,g), duration of

aspiration of these sounds, duration of voicing
7. short-time spectrum analysis, that is the continuous analysis and presentation of the energy level in the frequency domain as a function of time. A particular variety of this procedure is called "sonagraphy" and is used mainly for the visual documentation of auditory findings.
8. long-time spectral analysis
9. short-time and long-time cepstral analysis
10. linear prediction of speech (LPC analysis)
11. technique for the equalisation of speech tempo differences
12. assessment of objective similarity values between different speech samples

Prior to computerised voice comparison tape recordings are digitised. Sections of the speech signal are selected using a high resolution segmentation system. Speaker specific features are then gained from these portions using the above-mentioned techniques. In order to obtain reliable and quantitative values of similarity between two samples the following steps are necessary:
1. assessment of side conditions and noise
2. elimination/compensation of perturbations
3. selection of features which are resistant to perturbations under the given circumstances

Then, similarity values obtained are evaluated with respect to the actual side conditions and to empirical knowledge (background statistics) gained from large experiments and interpreted for an expert report.

In order to establish a statistical base for a reliable interpretation of the data large experiments will have to be performed, investigating the behavior of speaker-specific features under various conditions such as speaking situation, voice disguise, background noise, etc. When in an actual case a set of external conditions is given, evaluation of the data presupposes either the compensation of perturbations or the investigation of the individual statistical background.

Thus the fundamental task in the development of a computer-aided forensic voice comparison system is to check individual methods using large data bases under real-world conditions in order to supply a reliable interpretation for forensic argumentation. Experiments in view of this aim are currently being performed at the BKA. The project will be terminated by the end of 1984.

# THE CURRENT STATUS OF VOICE IDENTIFICATION
## IN POLICE INVESTIGATION IN ISRAEL

Yishai Tobin, Chairman
Department of Foreign Literatures and Linguistics
Ben-Gurion University of the Negev
Be'er Sheva
Israel

and

Sima Segev, Head
Voice Identification Unit
Criminal Identification Division
Israel National Police

> This paper summarizes the spectrographic method of voice identification currently used by the Israel National Police from the scientific, practical and forensic points of view. Questions regarding the validity, execution and the admissibility of the spectrographic method of voice identification are discussed in light of specific cases (e.g., the Oron Yarden kidnaping) in which the method has been successfully employed by the Israel National Police.

This paper represents an assessment of our cooperative work in the Voice Identification Unit of the Criminal Identification Division of the Israel Police over the past ten years. Our work in voice identification includes over one hundred and fifty voice identification cases (from Israel and abroad) of various degrees of complexity of extortion, threats, kidnapping, drugs, and obscene anonymous telephone calls combined with preliminary research in the search for suitable, operational and optimal features and combinations of features as valid cues for voice identification (Tobin and Segev 1982, 1983a,b, 1984a,b). Our work in voice identification has exposed us to all the classical problems traditionally associated with forensic voice identification: the use of the telephone, the presence of background noise, attempts at disguising the voice, identical texts of various lengths as well as non-identical texts.

What makes the Voice Identification Unit of the Israel Police "unique" or "special" -- at least in our view -- is the close cooperation between both the academic and the forensic aspects of voice identification. We might even go as far as to say that we have enjoyed a very successful "professional marriage" between the academic side of voice identification in the fields of articulatory and acoustic phonetics and linguistics as well as the forensic side where we are doing most of our research on actual forensic cases and not just in a laboratory situation. We feel that this is very unique to the Israel Police where we have been working hand in hand for the past ten years using actual data from forensic cases as the basis for our preliminary research. In our preliminary research we have taken our successful cases and used them as a data source in our search for linguistic and phonological features which have been and could be used in the field of voice identification. In addition to the phonetic, phonological and spectrographic research we have done ourselves, we have also consistently maintained close contact with computer-oriented/semi-automatic voice verification and identification research being done in Israel (cf. Arnon Cohen of the Ben-Gurion University of the Negev (this volume) in an attempt to have each of these three complementary aspects of voice identification contribute to an optimal and operational eclectic method of voice identification.

After having worked actively in this very controversial field of voice identification, both theoretically and method-ologically, in experimental and forensic situations, we can safely say that we have developed a "realistic" view of the current possibilities of voice identification in the forensic field. Specifically, we are not "naively optimistic" on the one hand . Nor, must I add, are we "overtly, condescendingly or presumptuously pessimistic", on the other. We try to maintain what we view as a "sober, realistic" view of the field in light of our experience combined with our awareness of all the theoretical and methodological limitations involved in voice identification.

Our work in the voice identification unit is based on the auditory and visual spectrographic method -- with all its well-known limitations -- as it was originally developed in the joint work of Professor Oscar Tosi and the Michigan State Police in the United States (Tosi 1979). We have, of course, over the years, adopted and adapted this particular method to the specific needs of the Israel Police, both linguistically and operationally for our specific forensic purposes. It is our belief, that this method, with all its limitations which you become acutely aware of in ten years, when used cautiously, carefully and responsibly -- works! We will certainly not claim here that it is the "best", the "only", or the "ultimate" method. Nor will we make exaggerated claims for (and against) its basic reliability in experimental situations as have been done over the years in various academic forums. The purpose of this paper is merely to share our own experience in this field with you in order to give you a clearer picture of what is involved in the forensic area of voice identification.

In short, our experience is the following: We have taken the basic spectrographic method of voice identification, adapted it to our local needs, made it operative bearing in mind its fundamental limitations, used it actively and operationally, applied it to acoustic, articulatory and applied experimental phonetic and phonological research, using real proven cases for data, applied it to the computer as well, in order to fit what seems to be not an "ideal" method, but a method we have found workable, rather reliable when you work within its limitations and look at it realistically, in order to adapt a particular method which will meet the needs of the Israel Police.

In our view there are two fundamental and basic issues which are related to all the work in voice identification and possibly all forensic work in general:

1.  the interface of "objective" versus "subjective" cognitive processes in the process of reaching a decision, and
2.  the plethora of possible, potential criteria needed in order to be able to reach a reliable and responsible decision.

In all forensic work we have an expert who is making a "subjective" decision based on his evaluation of "objective" variables. His decision is an abstract conclusion or set of conclusions reached from concrete sensory (auditory or visual) data. This decision, therefore, is never totally "subjective" nor totally "objective" but lies somewhere in between a continuum of abstract subjectivity and concrete objectivity.

The particular problem of voice identification is the greater number of necessary and sufficient criteria needed in order to reach a reasonable and reliable decision. I think the complex problems of determining the particular features of voice identification are greater for voice identification than in the other forensic laboratories. Taking fingerprints as the most objective member on our continuum, voice spectrograms are not comparable to "voice prints" for the following reasons:

1.  While fingerprints represent a direct 1:1 representation of unchanging physiological features which reoccur, voice spectrograms represent an indirect

240

graph of the entire vocal tract (from the diaphragm to the lips) and the auditory perceptual processes.

2. Every sound cannot be repeated in the exact same way each time it is produced nor can it be reduced to the exact same set of distinctive features reducible to a limited number of points of comparison.

Thus, spectrograms are much more complex and indirect graphical representations of both physical and acoustical properties which are relatively unstable compared with the more direct and limited fingerprints on an objective basis.

If we were to take handwriting analysis as the opposite or most subjective member of the continuum we have outlined above, we can see that voice identification is basically different and more complex here as well:

1. Handwriting comparisons involve physiological criteria which are also indirect and subjective: pressure of holding pen, a more involved physical process, kinds of paper or writing instruments similar to recording media and quality, etc., which makes it more similar to voice identification. It still represents a more direct indication of a less complex physical process to be observed visually, without taking the acoustic or auditory characteristics into account as does voice identification.

2. The effect of context, i.e., what precedes and follows, may also be crucial in handwriting analysis in a similar way that letters, like sounds, are never exactly identical each time they are made. Here, once again, however, the voice analyst relies on acoustic (auditory) as well as visual (spectrographic) data to reach a decision. Thus, even on the subjective plane, the voice analysis is more complex than handwriting analysis because it based on more complicated and a larger amount of objective data from different sensory channels.

If we view the subjective-objective continuum from the point of view of the abstract versus the concrete, voice identification is even more problematic, cognitively speaking, than handwriting analysis as well. Speakers of a language are not aware of the actual way they pronounce specific sounds, but are cognitively aware of the idealized abstract repetoire of communicatively significant sounds in their language. For example, there is no /p/ sound in English but rather at least four alternative pronunciations of a hypothetical target of articulatory and acoustic features we assume to be /p/:

1. a highly aspirated /p/-like sound before stressed vowels: e.g., the /p/ in the word pony or pot;

2. a less aspirated /p/-like sound which appears before non-stressed vowels or syllables: e.g., the /p/ in the word pyjama  or happy,
3. a non-aspirated /p/-like sound which appears after another consonant: e.g., in the word speed,
4. a non-released /p/-like sound which occurs at the end of a word or utterance: e.g., in the word stop.

All speakers of English believe that they know what a /p/ is, but they are only aware of an idealized sound and are actually shocked by the fact that there are so many different concrete realized individual /p/-like sounds which they actually produce and are totally unaware of. This gap between the abstract and idealized hypothetical sounds versus the specific concrete and contextually determined variations of this ideal invariant make the very process of speech production and perception underlying voice identification a most complex and arduous task. It is no wonder then that so much research has been devoted to uncover those specific features necessary and sufficient to effective forensic voice identification.

On the practical level, the dichotomy existing between the abstract asounds or targets that only exist in our minds and the actual sounds we produce is most relevant for our work in voice analysis. The recordings we deal with are only presenting us with the concrete data, the invariants based on hundreds of possible articulatory and acoustic features which are not only difficult to measure but vary according to linguistic and situational contexts and are affected by different media or means of recording. We are aware, however, of the abstract target sound which does not exist, and not of the different invariant concrete renderings of the sound each time it is made. We are thus dealing with those features which are constantly changing, are not fixed and are produced by almost an infinite number of alternative strategies each and every time they are produced by the same speaker as well as different speakers. Thus, it may very well be that from the point of view of sub- jective versus objective cognitive processes involved in expert decision making, based on the fundamental concepts of underlying abstract invariants versus concrete context-dependent variants, voice identification is the most difficult and complex area of forensic work.

In addition to the hundreds of articulatory and acoustic features involved in the speech act of producing individual sounds we also have a whole set of further areas of difficulty in voice identification:
1. Besides the actual segmentable sounds which we can recognize and distinguish as individual entities,

we have all the acoustic suprasegmental features of
speech which go beyond these individual sounds and
are most difficult to ascertain and measure. These
suprasegmental features include, pitch, stress,
accent, rhythm, intonation, etc., all of which are
essential for communication and crucial to voice
identification. These suprasegmental areas of speech
production and perception further complicate the
process of voice identification in a most basic and
fundamental way adding to the number of potential
necessary and sufficient features in a geometric
rather than an arithmetic ratio.

2. Variation in speech, different dialects, be they regional,
   social, e.g., upper versus middle versus lower class
   speech, gender-oriented, male versus female speech,
   age-oriented, old versus young versus middle aged
   habits of speech, ethnic, e.g., foreign accents, or
   speech traits associated to specific ethnic groups,
   all of these sociolinguistic variables which help us
   recognize speech groups and individual speakers within
   these groups all further complicate the task of the
   voice analyst.

3. In the particular forensic situation we have the
   additional problems of attempts to disguise or
   camouflage the voice, the problem of mimicry or trying
   to impersonate another speaker, and all sorts of
   attempts to alter the voice.

4. In actual voice identification cases we usually deal
   with telephone conversations, not always recorded under
   ideal conditions by expert technicians using superior
   equipment. Thus, oftentimes, much of the acoustic
   material necessary to provide sufficient and necessary
   information is often lost.

5. Furthermore, very often the amount of recorded data may
   be lacking and/or the possibility of receiving voice
   samples under identical recording conditions using
   an identical text where the role of context influencing
   the speech is severely limited. This, in turn,
   makes the task of voice identification even more
   difficult.

Thus, in addition to the hundreds of articulatory and
acoustic features of segmentable sounds and all the other
problems involved in speech production, perception and voice
identification in general and for forensic purposes we have
just outlined above, we have a further difficulty in that
linguistics, phonetics, phonology, speech act theory,
communication theory and all the other non-hard sciences

related to voice identification are not as well developed nor as exact as the harder sciences (e.g., physics, physiology, biology, etc.) which are also involved in voice identification. Those of us in these academic areas are still searching for the features necessary in isolating the processes we employ to recognize individual speakers. All of us, whether in auditory, spectrographic, or computer-based research on language and speech are still in the very fundamental stages of trying to unravel the mysteries of speech production, perception and verification and identification. We are still searching for those intrinsic versus extrinsic features involved in speech or voice identification. Whole books have been devoted to these particular and complex problems (Nolan 1983).

Our work in the police has taught us to constantly look for new features in each case. What was crucial in case A may be peripheral in case B or totally irrelevant in case C. Thus, each case presents us with a tabula rasa, a new adventure, a new challenge. We learn more about the traditional features and how they may work and help us. We have encountered cases where individual sounds were crucial. Others where the intonation patterns were significant. In some cases the background noise was less of a deterrent than in others. In certain cases non-identical texts hindered us less than expected. In some examples, the voices sounded similar but the spectrograms were less similar than we would have liked. In other cases the spectrograms of the policeman were more similar than we would have liked after hearing the differences in the voices as the policeman recorded the actual suspect. We have sometimes been able to achieve good results from poorly recorded material as well.

For all of these reasons, we have adopted an attitude of sober realism with regard to forensic voice identification. Our knowledge of the theoretical and methodological problems of speech perception and production and the state of the art of the sciences affiliated with them prevent us from having undue and naive expectations in this area. The fact that we have worked together for over ten years and have developed a system which is operative and has been successful both in making positive identifications and eliminations as well as having helped the police narrow down the number of suspects in particular cases prevents us from being unduly pessimistic or iconoclastic as well. By respecting the limitations of the system and viewing each case individually and separately, we have learned a great deal and know how much there still is to be known in this difficult and controversial area of forensic expertise. Our sober realism combined with our desire to learn

more from the traditional auditory, spectrographic and
computer methods may allow us to further develop our theoretical
and working knowledge and improve the modest achievements we
have made together in the area of voice identification in the
Israel Police.

## References

Nolan, Francis. 1983. The Phonetic Bases of Speaker Recognition.
Cambridge and London: Cambridge University Press.

Tosi, Oscar. 1979. Voice Identification: Theory and Legal
Applications. Baltimore: University Park Press.

Tobin, Yishae and Sima Segev. The Spectrographic Method of
Voice Identification: From Theory to Practice.
Classified CID Report. 1982. Israel Police. (In Hebrew).

Tobin, Yishae and S. Segev. The Functional Load of Phonemes
in Modern Hebrew as Cues to Speaker Identification:
Articulatory Parameters. 1983. Classified CID Report 10.
Israel Police.

Tobin, Yishai and Sima Segev. The Functional Load of Modern
Hebrew Phonemes in Voice Identification: An Acoustic
Analysis. 1983. Classified CID Report 11. Israel Police.

Tobin, Yishai and Sima Segev. Roman Jakobson's Distinctive
Phonological Features as Potential Parameters for Spectrographic
Speaker Identification. 1984. CID Report 1. Israel Police.

Tobin, Yishai and Sima Segev. The Chomsky-Halle Feature
System as Potential Parameters for Spectrographic Speaker
Identification. 1984. CID Report 2. Israel Police.

# FORENSIC APPLICATIONS OF AUTOMATIC SPEAKER VERIFICATION

Professor Arnon Cohen
Electrical and Computer Engineering Dept.
Ben Gurion University
Beer-Sheva, Israel


Computer based automatic and semi-automatic schemes for speaker identification and verification have been described in recent years for commercial and forensic applications. This paper reviews the problems associated with forensic speaker verification and the state of the art of verification algorithms and systems and gives some recent results from the research work done at the BGU in Israel. The conclusions of the paper are that with current technology (and with the technology expected in the near future) the problems presented by the forensic applications cannot be completely met by automatic machines. Computer verification of speakers will have to remain an assist device, coupled with the more conventional methods of trained listeners and manual examination of spectrographs.

Speech is the natural means for human communication. The speech signal is produced and comprehended by the brain, in a manner still not completely understood.

For many years now efforts have been made to produce (synthesize) and to comprehend (recognize) natural speech by machine. Such efforts, if and when successful, will have an impact on all man-machine interfaces and will revolutionize the way in which man and machine "converse". In recent years, mainly due to the advancements in computer technology and signal processing methods, the field of speech processing has been receiving a lot of attention. Systems that can synthesize a limited vocabulary of speech with various degrees of intelligibility are commercially available. Systems that can recognize a limited vocabulary of isolated words are also commercially available. More sophisticated systems that can recognize limited vocabulary of continuous speech are under investigation in various research centers around the world.

Inspite the large efforts in terms of budget allocations and manpower, the results achieved until today are still remote from the goal of constructing a machine that can process the speech signal in a manner comparable with the processing done by the human brain.

The various aspects of speech processing are depicted

in Figure 1. From forensic point of view the most interesting aspects are those of Emotional State analysis and Speaker Identification and Verification.

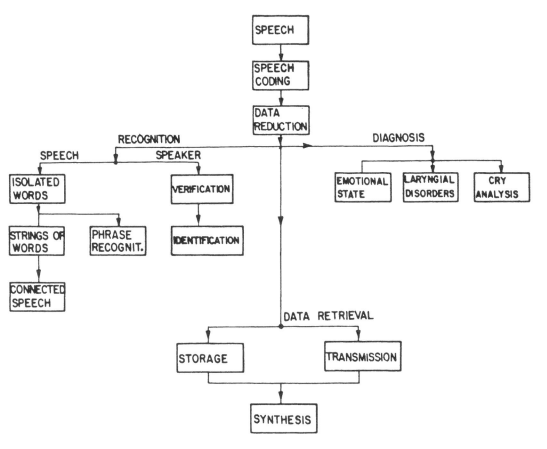

FIG. 1: Speech Processing Application.

It is well-known that the human speech conveys not only the intended message but additional voluntary and non-voluntary information concerning the speaker. If the human listener is familiar with the speaker, he can recognize the speaker's identity by analyzing the utterance, even if the speech signal is burried in background noise and is distorted by a transmission channel (i.e. telephone). Information concerning the speaker's identity is thus inherently present in his speech. One can also determine, to some extent, the emotional state of the speaker from various clues in his speech. It is believed that stress causes some involuntary physiological changes in the speech producing mechanism [1-3]. These may result in variations in acoustical parameters such as amplitude modulation or pitch.

Several "lie detector" types of instruments have appeared on the market which claimed to be able to detect psychological state of stress in humans by means of voice analysis. This phenomenon is however not well established. At least some researchers[4] could not find statistical, meaningful acoustical parameter changes related to stress.

The problems of speaker verification and identification are of extreme importance in forensic investigations. In many cases (kidnapping and blackmailing attempts, bomb threats, etc.) the only clue to the criminal's identity is a strip of recorded voice. The problem is then to use this given evidence in order to identify the speaker or verify the hypothesis that a certain suspect is indeed the speaker.

Speaker verification is defined as follows[5,6]: given two speech utterances one by an unknown speaker and the other by a known speaker, determine whether the two speakers are the same person.

Speaker identification (recognition) is defined as follows: given a speech utterance, from an unknown speaker, determine his identity. Usually the identification problem is restricted to a given list of suspects.

The complexity of both speaker identification and verification schemes is determined by the constraints imposed on the problem. The main constraints to be considered are briefly discussed here:

A. Text Dependence

The utterances to be compared may be identical in text or may contain different texts. Schemes that require identical texts are known as "Text Dependent" while those based on different texts are termed "Text Independent".

B. Speaker Cooperation

The speaker to be verified or identified may or may not be cooperative. In some commercial applications of access control or banking, the speaker is cooperative and wishes to be correctly identified.

C. Speech Quality

The given utterance may be noisy and distorted or presented in high quality. Background noise, transmission interferences and distortions may become decisive factors in the accuracy of verification and identification.

D. Processing Time

The process of machine verification or identification requires many calculations, some are time consuming like matrices multiplications. The amount of time allowed for calculations can restrict the accuracy in applications such as verification for access control.

E. Cost of Hardware

The verification and identification procedures are usually performed by means of a digital computer. The type of application may imply constraints on the cost of hardware (computer and associate peripherals). In some commercial applications such as, for example, credit card verification, the verifying machine has to be placed at every store thus, must be simple, compact and inexpensive.

Forensic applications of speaker verification [7-9] place severe constraints which render the problem of automatic verification extremely difficult.

Most often in police practice, verification cases involve text independent, uncooperative speaker and poor quality speech. The available speech segment is usually recorded over the telephone lines. The speech is thus subjected to unknown frequency distortions that depend on dialing connections. The unknown speaker usually makes his call from some public location such as a central bus or train station. Background noise is thus introduced into the recording rendering poor signal to noise ratio.

The speaker in forensic applications is by definition uncooperative. He may disguise his voice by putting something in his mouth while talking. The suspect person, whose voice is to be compared with the recording, may also be uncooperative and intentionally falsify his voice.

Many researchers have addressed themselves to the problems of verification with poor quality speech [10-17] and with mimickry and falsifications [18-20]. These still remain severe problems which most often render automatic verification systems unapplicable for forensic work.

Speaker verification problems encountered in police work are usually text independent. This is often the result of the refusal of the noncooperative suspect to repeat the given incriminating text, or due to the fact that it may not be advisable to discover the original text.

The text independancy constraint exerts a heavy burden on the verification system. Since the texts of the two utterances to be compared are different, one can use only "average" characteristics of speech. To achieve meaningful "averages", utterances of at least 15 seconds must be available. This is not always practical in forensic applications.

In terms of processing time and hardware cost, forensic applications pose no constraints. The processing is done off line. Processing times of even several hours are acceptable in most forensic application. Such time periods may be considered infinitely long for the signal processing required. The processing is done in a central laboratory where a large computer and all necessary peripherals are available.

SPEECH AND SPEECH MODELS

In speaker verification and identification methods one tries to extract from the given utterance some clues which uniquely relate to the speaker (but not to the uttered text). An understanding of the human speech production mechanism is required in order to achieve this goal.

In this section a brief review of the speech signal and speech production models are given. The interested reader is referred to the vast literature on the subject [21-24].

The speech signal is the product of the voluntary motions of the respiratory and masticatory systems [24]. Through learning, the central nervous system can control the time motions of these systems in order to generate the required sound at a required rate, intensity and intonation.

The production of an utterance is controlled by the lung pressure, type of excitation and the structure of the acoustical tract. Three types of vocal excitation are common. Phonation is the production of voiced sounds by the vibratory action of the vocal cords. The air flows through the vibrating vocal cords, excites the acoustical tube with a train of pulses at a fundamental frequency or "pitch" in the range of about 80 to 300 Hertz. The second type of excitation is produced by turbulent air flow, generating unvoiced sounds. The third excitation is produced by the abrupt release of pressure build-up at some point of closure. This produces a transient excitation of the vocal tract, generating voiced or unvoiced plosive sounds. The structure of the acoustical system is dynamically changed during excitation. The coupling between vocal and nasal tracts, cross areas of the tracts and end point constrictions are all controlled by the central nervous system to produce the desired utterances.

The anatomy of the acoustical system and its activation are unique to each individual. Estimation of the characteristics of both the anatomy and dynamic activation of the various parts of the articulatory system can thus be used in order to determine the identity of a speaker.

Typical segments of voiced and unvoiced speech with their spectra are depicted in Figure 2. Note that the voiced segment has a more structured appearance with the

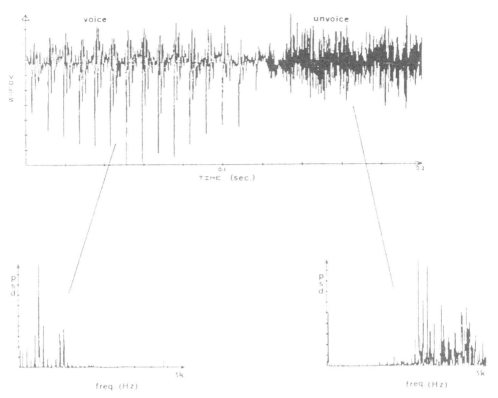

FIG. 2: A Typical Speech Record, Time and Frequence Domains.

pitch period clearly observable. The unvoiced segment resembles a noise signal with almost flat spectrum.

Many types of models have been suggested to describe the speech production mechanism. Few linear time variable models are briefly discussed here:

A. Formant Model

The vocal tract represents an acoustic cavity. Resonant frequencies of the cavity causes peaks in the power spectrum of the speech signal. These peaks, known as formant frequencies, are characteristic to the shape of the acoustic cavity, thus to the utterance generated by the cavity and to the speaker. Four formants are usually used to represent the vocal tract.

B. Acoustic Tube Model [21]

The vocal tract is modeled as a set of interconnected acoustic tube sections of equal length, but varying cross sections. The parameters of this model, namely the cross sections of parts of the vocal tract, have direct physiological meaning. The values of these parameters are functions of both utterance and speaker.

C. Linear Prediction (LPC) Model [25]

In this model the vocal tract is assumed to be linear, time varying all pole filter (LPC). This filter provides the modulation of the incoming air flow. The input to the filter can be either white noise (unvoiced) or a train of pulses generated by the vocal cords (voiced). The description of the model is given in Figure 3. The LPC coefficients (the ai in Figure 3) are calculated every 10-20 milliseconds to provide the time varying parameters of the speech. The LPC's depend on the utterance and on the speaker.

Figure 3

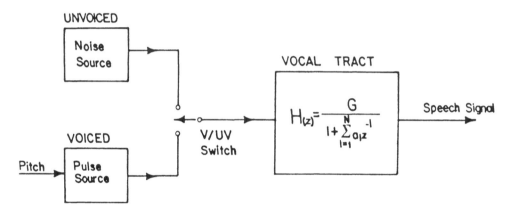

FIG. 3 : The Linear Prediction Model of Speech Production.

## AUTOMATIC SPEAKER VERIFICATION

Speaker recognition for forensic application is mainly performed by means of one of three methods.

A. Human Listeners

A number of experimental studies of speaker verification and identification by human listeners, have been made[26]. Human listeners have been used in criminal verification cases. According to McGehee[27] the first application of speaker recognition by auditory perception in public might have been in the 1932 kidnapping case of Lindberg in the U.S.A. Many of the more recent experiments evaluate the differences in performance between human listeners and some automated method. Rosenberg[6], for example, has shown that verification accuracy of 96 percent was achieved by a group of human listeners. In his experiment listeners were presented with a 2 second long, all voiced utterances from a population of 40 speakers. The same set of utterances was verified by an automatic method using formants, pitch and intensity. The automatic verification system provided verification accuracy of 98 percent. Shorter speech utterances show verification accuracies of 40-98 percent depending on the length of the utterance, the text and the elapsed time interval between test and training session.

Human listener verification has several disadvantages when considering forensic applications. The method requires the availability of a trained listener. It is a subjective method which highly depends on the listener. One of its main disadvantages is that it cannot be automated and thus cannot be applied to cases where large amounts of data are to be handled.

B. Spectrographic Methods

Spectrographic methods use the visual comparison of the spectra of speech utterances. Since the speech signal is highly non-stationary its power spectral density function changes with time. The power spectrum of the signal is estimated by means of a bank of filters, by means of the Fast Fourier Transform (FFT) or other efficient estimation algorithms (for example time series analysis methods). The power spectrum, which is the distribution of the signal's power in the time-frequency domain, is presented in terms of gray scale or color images. These are known as "Spectrographs", "Voice Prints", "Sonograms" and others. [18,19,26,28]

According to Potter[28] what was considered the first study of speech spectrogram was developed during the second world war and was reported at 1944. Since then the method has been investigated, further developed and applied to criminal investigations.

When considering spectrographic methods in forensic applications, several disadvantages become apparent. Two voiceprints can be compared if they belong to the same utterance. Hence the method is inherently text dependent. When the available texts are different, one may still find some identical words or portions of utterances and try to compare it. However, it is well-known that the characteristics of the utterance depend on the phonetic environment - a phenomenon known as coarticulation. There may be significant differences in the spectrograms of the same words, even when spoken by the same speaker, when they are inbedded in different texts.

The visual comparison of two spectrograms is a subjective process. It requires and depends upon an expert. Recently[12] some experiments have been made with automatic comparison of spectrograms by computer in an attempt to provide objective evaluation. Results were encouraging when applied to high quality text dependent speech. The method has not been evaluated with non-cooperative speakers, text independent speech such as required for forensic applications.

C. Machine Verification of Speakers

The availability of digital computers and sophisticated signal processing methods have made possible the automatic and semi-automatic speaker verification and identification systems. Most machines require "training" before the verification process is activated. The machine has to "learn" the characteristics of the speaker's voice before it can make a verification or identification decisions.

Machine speaker verification is performed with two main phases: Feature Extraction and Hypothesis Testing. Features are first extracted from the utterance. These may be mean features evaluated from the given utterance (in text-independent systems) or local features corresponding to the various phonemes (in text dependent systems) The desired optimal characteristics of the features as were outlined by Wolf[29] are:

1. Representing effectively the speaker dependent information in the utterance
2. Stable over time and insensitive to speaker's physical and psychological states
3. Easy to measure
4. Occurring naturally and frequently in the speech used for the application at hand.
5. Changing little from one speaking environment to another.
6. Not susceptible to mimicry and falsification
7. Insensitive to background noise and channel distortions.

Unfortunately there is no set of features which is optimal with respect to all the above qualities. The problem of features selection is therefore an important problem in any automated system. Various schemes have been suggested[30-31] for the sub-optimal selection of features. Probably one of the most effective is the method of dynamic programming[30].

After the features have been extracted, from the unknown speaker's utterance, the problem has been transferred into the following one: given a set of measured features, determine whether they "belong" or are "sufficiently close" to the features generated by the speaker whose identity is claimed (or hypothesized). This is usually done by calculating the "distance" between the two feature vectors and determining whether the distance is small enough such that the two utterances have the same characteristics.

Various definitions for "distance" are used, as well as methods for determining what is to be considered "small enough" distance.

## SURVEY OF SOME WORKING SPEAKER VERIFICATION SYSTEMS

Research efforts in universities, research institutions and industry have provided a variety of speaker verification and identification systems. Most of these systems are still under development[32-34] stages. Speaker verification for access control applications, where the constraints are somewhat relaxed, is simpler to implement. The most advanced systems (from commercialization point of view) are thus access control systems. As of today, there is no commercially available system for forensic applications.

In this section a short review of speaker verification and identification systems is presented. We do not claim to review all reported experimental systems but rather some, probably typical ones, so as to give an impression of the state of art.

## AUROS - AUTOMATIC RECOGNITION OF SPEAKERS BY COMPUTER[7,8,35]

This system was initially developed by Philips Research Laboratory and the Heinrich Hertz Institute and later used and furthur developed by Federal Republic of Germany's police.

The AUROS is a modular experimental system for the analysis of speaker verification and identification under various constraints on speech, text and quality and speaker cooperation. The system contains impressive computer power and special hardware processors. The system was checked with a large data base of 2,500 utterances of 41 male and 9 female cooperative speakers. Both text dependent and text independent tests were performed with high quality utterances lasting from 2 seconds and up. Results show that speaker verification and speaker identification, with high quality speech and cooperative speakers, can be achieved with error rates of less than one percent.

No results are available on system performance under noisy low quality speech with uncooperative speakers.

## SAUSI - SEMI-AUTOMATIC SYSTEM FOR SPEAKER IDENTIFICATION[36]

This system is under development at the Institute for Advanced Study of Communication Processes, University of Florida. The ultimate purpose of the system is to permit field identification of unknown talkers. The system utilizes four feature vectors consisting of 11-45 features each. The currently used vectors are:
1. The Speaking Fundamental Frequency Vector
2. The Long Term Speech Spectra Vector
3. The Vowel Formant Tracking Vector
4. The Temporal Analysis Vector

The system was tested under laboratory conditions. Identification accuracies of almost 100 percent were reported for a test consisting of large subject population and limited passband noisy speech. To simulate a more realistic test condition, the"Simucrime" procedure was suggested. Here speech materials representing a series of "crimes" were generated by an unknown talker, who extemporaneously produced the spoken material on the basis of his experience with that particular type of case. The "criminal" calls were made over a telephone circuit and the recordings were made using a standard suction cup telephone pickup coupled to a "typical" cassette type tape recorder[36]. Detailed results of the "Simucrime" tests were not published.

## THE TEXAS-INSTRUMENTS ENTRY CONTROL SYSTEM[37]

This system was designed for access control purposes, namely for high quality, cooperative speaker applications. The analysis is mainly based on short-term spectra as measured by a 16 channel filter bank. In over 44,000 verification attempts, the total number of rejected attempts was 416 for an average rejection rate of 0.9 percent. For imposters trying to "fool" the system the statistics were even better with only 0.7 percent of the persons fooling the system. Using a 4 phrase sequential decision strategy a false rejection rate of 0.3 percent and false acceptance rate of 1 percent was achieved[33].

## THE BELL LABS SYSTEM[10,38,39]

This system has been used primarily for conducting investigations aimed at making it possible to verify speakers over their own telephones. The problem is thus dealing with telephone quality voice. The features used by the system were dynamic contour measurements of pitch and intensity which were found to be less sensitive to transmission lines distortions. Error rates of about 10 percent were reported. After longer use and continuous adaptation the false acceptance and false rejection error rates dropped to about 4 percent. Further development of the system was reported by Furui[10]. With the use of cepstral analysis verification error rate of one percent or less were obtained for telephone quality speech.

## LOW COST SPEAKER VERIFICATION DEVICES [40,41]

Due to recent advances in microcomputer technology and in signal processing methods, speaker verification systems can be implemented on low cost hardware. Such a system was developed by Philips Research Laboratories in Hamburg. The low cost system requires, on the average, 8 seconds for verification. Preliminary experiments suggest that the error rates will be one percent false reject and 2 percent false accept.

The system is intended for access control application with cooperative speaker and high quality voice.

## THE BGU SPEAKER IDENTIFICATION SYSTEM

An interactive system for speaker verification and identification has been developed[9,34,42] at the Ben Gurion University, Beer-Sheva, Israel in cooperation with the research and development unit of the Israel police department.

The system was designed to operate as a text dependent as well as text independent identification system. Figure 4 depicts the block diagram of the system. The system operates with a general "library" of 80 features. That is to say, each speaker is represented in the system by means of 80 mean features representing his voice. The operator can manually determine the number of features he wishes to

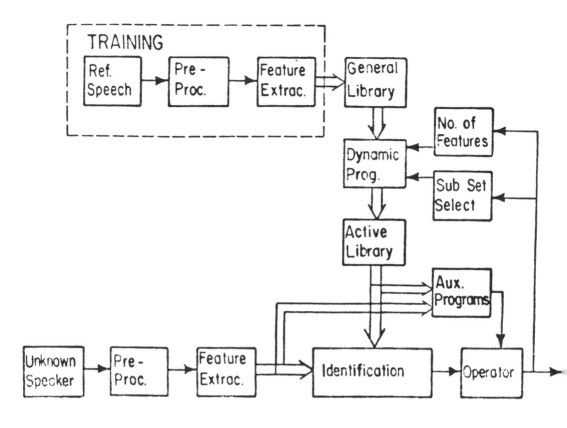

FIG. 4: Block Diagram of the BGU Speaker Identification System.

work with and can dictate some or all of them. In case the operator does not specify the types of features he wishes to use, the system selects (by means of dynamic programming[30]) the set of (sub) optimal features out of the 80 given features.

Two main modes of operation are available:

A. Text Independent Mode

Here the system matches the mean features of the speech utterance of about 15 seconds. During "training", segments of speech are preprocessed by filtering and by segmentation into voiced, unvoiced and silent sections. Mean features of the voiced and unvoiced speech are calculated as well as the estimated covariance matrix. These are stored in the "General Library" memory. The operator determines the number of features he wishes to use, and may also dictate to the system type of features he wishes be part of the final set. The system automatically determines the optimal set of features and stores their mean and inverse covariance matrix in the "Active Library".

The unknowns speaker's utterance is subjected to preprocessing which may include filtering, adaptive noise elimination and segmentation. The appropriate features are extracted and the distance measure calculated.

The system also provides auxiliary programs which allow the operator to monitor histograms, pitch contours, spectograms and other functions.

DISTANCE (IN DB).

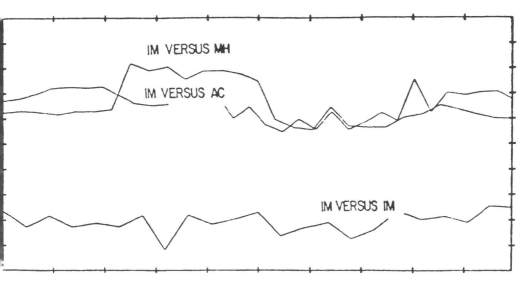

VERIFICATION TEST -- FEATURES SELECTED BY DYNNAMIC PROGRAMING (VOICED ONLY)

FIG. 5 : Text Independent Speaker Identification Distances of Speaker IM From Other Speakers.

Some experimental results of text independent identification are shown in Figure 5. The "distance" from an utterance, spoken by IM to templates of speakers AC, MH and IM itself are plotted. Note that along the complete utterance, the distance from IM to itself is much lower (distance scale is logarithmic!) than the distance between IM and other speakers. The machine thus easily correctly identifies the "unknown" speaker as IM.

B. Text Dependent Mode

In this mode the system compares speech characteristic of two utterances - when the text is identical. This mode is usually applied in access control applications when the speaker is cooperative and can be asked to utter the same text as that of the unknown speaker utterance. It is, however, sometimes applicable to forensic cases when the suspect agrees to cooperate or when segments of the uncooperative speaker contain text (words) that are also found in the unknown utterance.

One of the main problems in text dependent speaker identification is that of time warping[42-43]. When a speaker utters the same word several times, he does not repeat the word exactly. Time changes, compression and alongation, occur during the utterance. One must bring the words into a common time base when comparing their characteristics. Efficient, dynamic programming algorithms are used in order to estimate the non-linear "time warping" transformation. Figure 6 depicts the time warping process.

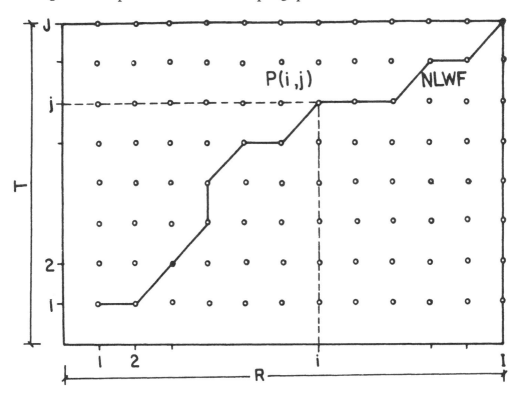

FIG. 6: Time Warping.

T- Test Word with Duration J ;   R- Reference Word with Duration I ; NLWF - Non Linear Warping Function.

After time warping the features of each segment of the utterance are extracted and their distance from the corresponding segment of the template is calculated. We, therefore, use here time dependent features rather than mean ones. Text dependent identification has several advantages over the text independent mode. A special text is chosen that contains the utterances best representing the speaker. For each segment optimal features are used.

The system was checked with high quality speech. Both text dependent and text independent experiments yielded close to 100 percent correct verifications. In text independent experiments speech records of 15 seconds were used. In text dependent experiments the text "Rasham Kol" (Tape Recorder in Hebrew) was used. No attempts to find the optimal text for each speaker were used in these experiments.

Experiments with low quality speech are under investigation. A simulated environment of transmission lines (telephones) with typical frequency distortions and noise has been developed. The system is being tested with speech that has been subjected to the simulated environment as well as speech that has been recorded from real telephone network. No statistically significant results are yet available.

CONCLUSIONS

Various aspects of speech processing are being extensively researched and developed in research centers around the world. The commerical appeal of automatic speech and speaker recognition and the expected impact of such systems, when available, ensures the continuation of increasing research and development efforts. It is expected that better hardware and more sophisticated algorithms be developed and be commercially available for speech and speaker recognition.

Forensic applications of speech and speaker recognition do not have commercial appeal. This usually means that research and development funds will be hard to get. However, advances in other related applications, both in terms of hardware, software and processsing algorithms will no doubt have their impact on forensic applications.

For the time being, and for the foreseeable future, fully automated speaker verification and recognition systems for forensic applications, will probably not be available. It is our conclusion that research and development efforts should be directed towards the developments of highly interactive systems, operated by experts. The goal of such systems should be to provide the linguistic expert with a sophisticated tool that will be used in conjunction with current verification methods (listening, spectrograms). The system therefore must be very flexible allowing the operator to use his own judgements as to what segment of speech to use, what type of features he desires and what method of comparison is to be applied. The operator must have the option to monitor various speech characteristics such as pitch contours, histograms of features, etc.

We note that such an interactive system, though may be termed "Semi-Automatic", does not have the desired advantage of effectively processing large amounts of speech data. It does require an expert operator and does rely on his subjective decisions. It does not seem, however, that with present technology and state of the art, fully automatic speaker identification or verification systems for the tough forensic applications are implementable.

## REFERENCES

1. Scherer, K. R., Nonlinguistic Vocal Indicators of Emotion and Psychopathology, in Emotions and Psychopathology, Izard, C. E., (ed.), Plenum Press, N.Y. 1979, pp. 493-529

2. Levin, H. and Lord, W., Speech Pitch Frequency as an Emotional State Indicator, IEEE Trans. Syst., Man and Cyber., Vol. SMC-5, pp. 259-273, 1975

3. Inbar, G. F. and Eden, G., Physiological Evidence for Central Modulation of Voice Tremor, Biolo. Cyber., Vol. 47, pp. 1-12, 1983

4. Streeter, L. A., Macdonald, N. H., Apple, W., Krauss, R. M., and Galotti, K. M., Acoustic and Perceptual Indicators of Emotional Stress, J. Acoust. Soc. Am., Vol. 73, pp. 1354-1360, 1983

5. Atal, B. S., Automatic Recognition of Speakers from their Voices, Proc. IEEE, Vol. 64, pp. 460-475, 1976

6. Rosenberg, A. E., Automatic Speaker Verification: A Review, Proc. IEEE, Vol. 64, pp. 476-486, 1976

7. Bunge, E., Speaker Recognition by Computer, Philips. Tech. Rev., Vol. 37, pp. 207-219, 1977.

8. Bunge, E., Automatic Speaker Recognition System AUROS for Security Systems and Forensic Voice Identification, Proc. of the 1977 Int. Conf. on Crime Countermeasures, July, 1977

9. Cohen, A. and Froind, I., Software Package for Interactive, Text Independent Speaker Verification,

Proc. of the IEEE Medit. Elect. Conf. (MELECON), Tel-Aviv, Israel, 1981

10. Furui, S., Cepstral Analysis Technique for Automatic Speaker Verification, IEEE Trans. Acoust. Speech Sig. Proc., Vol. ASSP-29, pp. 254-272, 1981

11. Hunt, M.J., Yates, J. W. and Bridle, J. S., Automatic Speaker Recognition for Use Over Communication Channels, Proc. of the IEEE Acoust. Speech Sig. Proc. Int. Conf., pp. 764-767, 1977

12. Ney, H., Gierloff, R. and Frehse, R., An Automatic System for Verification of Cooperative Speakers Via Telephone, Carnahan Conf. on Crime Countermeasures, Lexington, Kentucky, pp. 97-101, 1981

13. Shridhar, M., Baraniecki, M. and Mohankrishnan, N., A Unified Approach to Speaker Verification with Noisy Speech Inputs, Speech Commun., Vol. 1, pp. 103-112, 1982

14. Doherty, E. T., and Hollien, H., Multiple-Factor Speaker Identification of Normal and Distorted Speech, J. of Phonetics, Vol. 6, pp. 1-8, 1978

15. Hall, J. L., Auditory Discrimination Among Speakers in the Presence of Masking Noise, IEEE Trans. Acoust.

16. Furi, S. and Rosenberg, A. E., Experimental Studies in a New Automatic Speaker Verification System Using Telephone Speech, Proc. of IEEE Int. Conf. Acoust. Speech Sig. Proc., pp. 1060-1062, 1980

17. Hollien H. and Majewski, W., Speaker Identification by Long Term Spectra Under Normal and Distorted Speech Conditions, J. Acoust. Soc. Am., Vol. 62, pp. 975-980, 1977

18. Reich, A. R., Moll, K. L., and Curtis, J. F., Effects of Selected Vocal Disguises upon Spectrographic Speaker Identification, J. Acoust. Soc. Am., Vol. 60, pp. 919-925, 1976

19. Endres, W., Bambach, W., and Foster, G., Voice Spectrograms as a Function of Age, Voice Disguise and Voice Imitation, J. Acoust. Soc. Am., Vol. 49, pp. 1842-1848, 1971

20. Reich, A. R. and Duke, J. E., Effects of Selected Vocal Disguises Upon Speaker Identification by Listening, J. Acoust. Soc. Am., Vol. 66, pp. 1023-1028, 1979

21. Flanagan, J. L., Speech Analysis, <u>Synthesis and Perception</u>, Springer Verlag, <u>Berlin</u> , 1972

22. Schafer, R. W. and Rabiner, L. R., Digital Representation of Speech Signals, Proc. IEEE, Vol. 63 pp. 662-677, 1975

23. Schafer, R. W., and Markel, J. D., (eds.), <u>Speech Analysis</u>, IEEE Press, N.Y., 1978

24. Fant, G., <u>Acoustic Theory of Speech Production</u>, Mouton, The Hague, 1970

25. Makhoul, J., Linear Prediction - A Tutorial Review, Proc. IEEE, Vol. 63, pp. 561-580, 1975

26. Stevens, K. N., Williams, C. E., Carbonell, J. R. and Woods, B., Speaker Authentication and Identification: A Comparison of Spectrographic and Auditory Presentations of Speech Material, J. Acoust. Soc. Amer., Vol. 44, pp. 1596-1607, 1968

27. McGehee, F., An Experimental Study in Voice Recognition, J. Gen. Psychol. Vol. 31, pp. 53-65, 1944

28. Potter, R. K., Kopp, G. A. and Green, H. C., <u>Visible Speech</u> , Van Norstrand Co., N.Y., 1947

29. Wolf, J. J., Efficient Acoustic Parameters for Speaker Recognition, J. Acoust. Soc. Amer., Vol. 51, pp. 2044-2055, 1972

30. Cheung, R. S. and Eisenstein, B. A., Feature Selection by Dynamic Programming for Text-Independent Speaker Identification, IEEE Trans., Acoust., Speech Sig. Proc., Vol. ASSP-26, pp. 397-403, 1978

31. Sambur, M. R., Selection of Acoustic Features for Speaker Identification, IEEE Trans., Acoust., Speech Sig. Proc., Vol. ASSP-23, pp. 176-181, 1975

32. Jesorsky, P., Principles of Automatic Speaker Recognition, in Speech Communication with Computers, Bloc, L. (ed.), McMillan Press, London, 1978, pp. 93-137

33. Shridhar, M. and Mohankrishnan, N., Text Independent Speaker Recognition: A Review and Some New Results, Speech Communication, Vol. 1, pp. 257-267, 1982

34. Cohen, A., Speech Recognition and Synthesis for Man-Machine Communication, Proc. of the 4th Conf. on CAD/CAM, Tel-Aviv, Israel, paper 5.2.1, 1982

35. Bunge, E., Hofker, U., Jesorsky, P., Kriener, B. and Wesseling, D., Statistical Techniques for Automatic Speaker Recognition, Proc. of the IEEE Int. Acoust. Speech and Sig. Proc. Conference pp. 772-775, 1977.

36. Hollien, H., Childers, D. G., and Doherty, E. T., Semi-Automatic System for Speaker Identification, Proc. of the IEEE Int. Conf. on Acoustic, Speech and Sig. Proc., pp. 768-771, 1977

37. Doddington, G., Voice Authentication Gets the Go-Ahead for Security Systems, Speech Tech., pp. 14-23, Sept. - Oct., 1983

38. Rosenberg, A. E., and Sambur, M. R., New Techniques for Automatic Speaker Verification, IEEE Trans., Acoust., Speech Sig. Proc., Vol. ASSP-23, pp. 169-176, 1975

39. Rosenberg, A. E., Evaluation of an Automatic Speaker Verification System Over Telephone Lines," Bell System. Tech. J., Vol. 55, pp. 723-744, 1976

40. Kuhn, M. H., and Geppert, R., A Low Cost Speaker Verification Device, Proc. of the Carnahan Conf. on Crime Countermeasures, Lexington, KY., pp. 57-61, 1980

41. Geppert, R., Open Sesame - The Access Control Device of the Future?, Int. Security Rev., pp. 44-63, 1980

42. Shalom, I. and Cohen, A., On Time Warping Algorithms for Speech Recognition, Proc. of the 14th Conv. of Elect. and Electron. Eng. in Israel, Tel-Aviv, 1985

# "HITLER DIARIES"
## CASE HISTORY, EXAMINATION RESULTS, HANDLING IN COURT

Dr. Wolfgang Steinke
Bundeskriminalamt
Viesbaden, Germany

When the West German weekly news magazine, Der Stern, published the Hitler Diaries in 1982, the Bundeskriminalamt requested the assistance of the Federal Archives of Germany in Koblenz to provide information and standards of Hitler-era documents. This enabled examination of the newly surfaced documents to determine their authenticity. Various examinations were conducted, particularly in light of the possible great historical significance of the diaries. This paper details the various technical examinations conducted, and it gives scientific support to the conclusion of forgery which has been so widely publicized. This conclusion is based upon a number of factors including the use of a particular whitener in the paper which was first introduced well after World War II.

## CASE HISTORY

In mid-1982, the German Federal Archives at Coblenz contacted Bundeskriminalamt (Federal Criminal Police Office) with a request to test the authenticity of several historically very important documents. These documents, allegedly written by Hitler, had been offered to "Stern", a West German weekly magazine, who were principally interested in buying them. The Federal Archives were told by "Stern" that, after a journalistic campaign, the documents could be provided to them for free, if they established expert opinion that would leave no doubt about the authenticity of the Hitler documents. Bundeskriminalamt were given nine individual documents and five comparison documents from the stocks of the Federal Archives which definitely originate from Hitler. The nine documents to be examined were drafts of mostly one-page letters and captions. One of the nine individual documents was a (dateless) "official party statement" which later turned out to be a page removed from a "Hitler Diary" (the so-called 1941 Hess Volume).

During a further meeting held at Bundeskriminalamt, representatives of "Stern" and of the Federal Archives were told a cursory ultraviolet light examination had shown that, in all probability, four of the nine documents in question must have been forged, because even macroscopic inspection had revealed a whitener (for example Blankophor) which undoubtedly had not been in use at the time when the documents were supposed to have been written. As a result, the examination of the nine individual documents was deferred for the time being. "Stern" offered three Hitler diaries to the Federal Archives for examination purposes, who, in turn, supplied them to my Office on 28 April, 1983, for expertising. These diaries included:

- a notebook consisting of black binding and lined paper as well as a typewritten label bearing the date 1934;
- a notebook consisting of black binding and lined paper as well as a typewritten label inscribed "Streng Geheim ..." (Strictly Confidential) and bearing the date 1941 as well as two red seals (Hess Volume);
- a notebook consisting of black binding and lined paper with a red seal without label, and bearing the handwritten date "September 1943".

## EXAMINATION RESULTS

The examination of the nine individual documents turned out the following results:

Five documents contained different blue and black ink colors. None of the papers showed any water mark. In part, it was paper which to the naked eye appeared to be greyish and old. By contrast, two documents appeared as optically white in daylight. Procedures of fluorescence technology and emission spectroscopy revealed that the paper material of these documents, tested under UV light, disclosed fluorescent characteristics which clearly pointed to the content of so-called "optical brighteners". Although the first optical brighteners or fluorescent white dyes of a certain chemical composition have been known since about 1941, they have been used on any large scale for manufacturing paper only since after World War II.

267

Under UV light the paper material of the other three individual documents disclosed a very weak fluorescence which however is typical of white dyes.

To answer the question whether or not the white dyes identified were actually put on the market after World War II or, possibly, in a certain chemical composition, before that time, a well-known German chemical company manufacturing white dyes was requested to identify, on the basis of paper samples, the type of these agents in paper samples and to determine, when they were manufactured, as the company referred to has had much experience in this field and has also been observing the international market over many decades.

An initial close examination revealed that all the paper materials viewed in daylight showed a markedly lesser white effect than it is found in common writing paper today. Under UV light, all the paper samples disclosed fluorescence typical of white dyes but which was remarkedly different. As a result, our chemists have found three types of white dye, namely;

1. Bis-(diethanolamine-phenylamine-triazinylamino) stilbene disulfonic acid derivate;
2. Bis-(methoxy phenylamine triazinylamino) stilbene disulfonic acid derivate;
3. Bis-(ethanolamine sulfanile triazinylamino) stilbene disulfonic acid derivate.

These types are products that were not available before about 1955. None of the products that were available prior to 1945 have been found.

The chemists used thin-layer chromatography.

An examination of four printed matters and pictorial documents from the individual items have yielded the following results:

A black printing found on a "certificate of appointment" was an offset printing product of inferior quality imitated by means of reproduction. By contrast, the authentic certificates of appointment, which serve for comparison, and other authentic documents taken from "Reichskanzlei" (Chancellery of the former German Reich), files were principally made by means of relief printing.

What is also remarkable with the emblem in the top part of the document is that the eagle, seen from its own view, turns its head to the left while it always looks to the right in authentic comparison documents. It is obviously a reversed image.

It has also been established that in one case the disputed document lacks the seal which now as before is usually impressed on all certificates of appointment. In addition, the black/white red colored ribbon originally affixed to the document and the document itself bore residue of adhesive material. It is a synthetic adhesive produced on isoprene basis, as for instance "Pattex". Such adhesives appeared on the market only after World War II.

The edges of a certificate of appointment pasted on cardboard showed non-linear cutting which is clearly a trace of manual trimming.

Three of the disputed pictorial documents bearing handwritten dedications by Hitler did not constitute photographs, but rather scanned printed matters produced by letterpress printing. One pictorial document bears printing on the reverse, which suggests that it is a picture originating from a magazine. To establish their authenticity, the three "Hitler Diaries" provided by "Stern" have been tested according to the following criteria:

1. Evaluation of typewriting on the labels affixed to the 1934 and 1941 volumes;
2. Examination of bookbinding method;
3. Quality of the material used;
4. Composition of the inks used;
5. Period when the inks were used to write the diaries.

## RE ITEM 1

The texts of the labels affixed to the 1934 and 1941 "Diaries" were written on an "Adler Klein 2" typewriter which was equipped with Adler "pica" typefaces ("push type bar machines). The typewriters equipped with this design of types were manufactured from 1925 to 1934. On account of the characteristics found, there is every indication that the writing on the labels was performed on the same typewriter. The individual type faces shown on both labels also disclose characteristics which did not change over a period of seven years. Therefore, it is assumed that the labels affixed to the 1934 and 1941 volumes were inscribed immediately after the other.

## RE ITEM 2

The bookblock of the 1934 volume contained twelve quires comprising four sheets each. This kind of paper is commercially available only as quires of five sheets each under the designation of "Kanzleipapier" or "Kanzleibogen" (register or foolscap paper). The quires were connected by thread stitching fitting in a shirting strip. The back of the bookblock was sized. The front and rear-end papers were stuck on, the projecting shirting strip was the connection to the book covers. Evaluation from the point of view of fluorescence technology by means of UV light and the subsequent chromatographic examinations with comparison specimens of optical brighteners produced by an industrial establishment revealed that the end papers contained an insignificant proportion of optically brightened single fibres and that a paper strip that was to a high degree optically brightened and intensively blue fluorescent, had been worked into the book cover. The composition of these whitening agents can be compared with that of optical brighteners which appeared on the market only after World War II but probably not before 1955.

The binding method of all the three volumes was identical. The end papers of the 1941 volume contained blue fluorescent single fibres, while optically brightened fibres portions could not be discovered in the end papers of the 1943 volume. The book covers of the 1941 and 1943 volumes, however, contained intensively blue fluorescent paper strips. On the basis of these facts it is safe to conclude that the covers of the three "Diaries" were manufactured only after World War II and probably not before 1955.

RE ITEM 3

All the paper pages found in the 1934 volume had blue fluorescent white dye but, as with all the three volumes, only certain proportions of the fibrous material mixture showed some sort of "dyeing". The fluorescent strength in all the pages of the 1934 volume was almost the same. This also applied to the paper used for the 1941 volume. Only the bookblock of the 1943 volume contained very differently brightened paper, besides paper with no white dye. Comparison examinations, made by thin-layer chromatography, of the paper on all three volumes disclosed that all the white dye contained in the paper corresponded to optical brighteners that were not commercially available before 1955.

Subsequently, paper samples were taken from the individual "Diaries" at random and their fibrous material, which had been dyed by means of micro-preparation, was evaluated under the microscope on the basis of morphological conditions. The following are the results obtained:
    a. 1934 "Diary": The specimen contained exclusively coniferous wood pulp - spruce, pine

b. 1941 "Diary": Same results as with the 1934 one. From this latter volume another sample was taken which consisted of coniferous wood-pulp, grass pulp (grain straw) and hardwood pulp. According to an appropriate reflex paper company, straw pulp has no longer been manufactured in the Federal Republic of Germany since about 1972. However, several Eastern Bloc countries reportedly continue to supply straw pulp.

c. 1943 "Diary": This sample contained coniferous wood pulp
- spruce, pine -,
grass pulp - grain straw - and hardwood
pulp - poplar, beech, birch.
Compared with the dominating two other kinds of pulp, the proportion of hardwood pulp was small.

Altogether, the paper used was of inferior quality with little resin sizing and bad ink solidity.

## RE ITEM 4

Four different dye inks were used for the three volumes. The so-called ferro-gallic ink, which had normally been in as general use as document ink during the war, was not found.

By means of thin-layer and paper chromatography, the four inks were compared with some of those originating in the USSR, in Czechoslovakia and East Germany. None of the inks in question was identical with those manufactured in Eastern Bloc States. As, however, only few samples of Eastern Bloc inks were available for comparison, this is merely a relative result. One of the black inks concerned, which was used on all the three "Diaries, however, showed such characteristical zones that it could be identified as a mixture of two inks, namely "Pelikan Schwarz 4001" and "Pelikan Blau 4001", which are both available on the market in the Federal Republic of German.

## RE ITEM 5

The "Mezger - Rall - Heess" method was employed to determine when the "Diaries" were handwritten.

What was tested was the rate of migration of the chloride ions contained in the handwriting so that it was possible to determine within a limit of two years when the "Diaries" were handwritten. The ink examination had the following results:

1. The inks used for the 1934 volume had exceeded the final stage of chloride migration. Thus, the volume must have been written more than two years before the test.
2. The inks on the 1941 volume had not yet reached the final stage of chloride migration. The writing must consequently have been done about two years prior to the test.
3. The inks on the 1943 volume showed a migration of chloride ions which determined that it must have been written about one year before the test.

As a result, the three "Diaries" were written consecutively according to their years.

The tests also answered the question of whether the "Diaries" had been written when they were already bound or rather initially on loose leaves. As congruent writing was often encountered between a considerable number of ink traces on the left-hand side with copied text fragments and the respective text passages on the right-hand diary pages, it must be concluded that the 1943 "Diary" pages were inscribed when the "Diary" was already bound. By contrast, the 1934 and 1941 "Diary" pages failed to show any copied ink traces or text fragments. Thus, the initial question cannot be answered, as far as these two volumes are concerned.

TEXTILE EXAMINATIONS

The three volumes were also examined as to determine whether and where they contained any structural textile fabrics and threads and, if so, what fibres these parts consisted of.

In the "Diaries" the following textile parts were established:

red sealing threads affixed to the 1941 and 1943 volumes,
threads to sew the sheets of all three volumes
fabric strips to reinforce the link between book-block and cover equally in all three volumes.

The red sealing threads were two-step plied yarns with the corresponding 6Z/3Z/S structure. The material was non-mercerized cotton. The color and dye of the sealing threads were identical. Fluorescent brighteners could not be applied.

The binding threads of all three volumes constituted similar single yarns with no identifiable twist.

Corresponding round non-delustered filament fibres made of polyamide 6 = perlon were used as fibre material. The fibres were not optically bleached.

The fabric strips consisted of undyed fabric which is known as double thread book binder gauze (linen weave), with the warp containing two folded single yarns (Z-twist), while the weft consisted of doubled just a single Z-twisted yarn. The threads of the pick system in all three volumes revealed only non-delustered viscose fibres of identical thickness. As far as the 1934 and 1943 volumes are concerned, the threads of the weft system also contained non-delustered viscose fibres only. By contrast, the 1941 volume contained, besides the proportion of viscose fibres, a second fibre component, namely the polyester fibres.

In order to determine the age of the material, not only the presence of the two types of synthetic fibres (polyamide 6 = perlon and polyester) was of importance but also the fact that polyester fibres together with viscose fibres formed blended fibre yarn Unlike viscose fibre or cotton, the two types of synthetic fibres were neither discovered nor in usage prior to 1934. According to experts specialized in synthetic fibres, perlon was spun as a fibre the first time in 1938. As from 1940, there was a plant in Germany to produce silk-type perlon filaments for parachute silk.

Polyester fibres are a British-developed product. It was first spun in 1941, but its production was begun only after the end of the war; in Germany the companies styled "Glanzstoff" and "Hoechst" started production in 1953. During the war, it is reported, there was no polyester fibre material, not even for research purposes. The technology to produce polyester blended fibre spun yarns was developed in the mid-50s.

The examination results all tied in with the statements made by the forger, who was later identified as Konrad Kujau. A search of his apartment revealed, among other things, brown cardboard paper which was later examined as to whether there were any cutting traces in relation to the cardboard of a pictorial document. A stereomicroscope examiantion disclosed that the brown cardboard paper showed corresponding traces, in the area of the cut, in the form of matching and/or continuous trace designs.

Also black cardboard was seized from Kujau which was subsequently compared with the cardboard of another pictorial document. Examination revealed that there were also corresponding and matching trace characteristics.

In addition, a book cover was found which proved to be of the same material as that of the 1934 "Diary", according to the findings of the chemical-physical paper comparison examination, the microscopic fibre material determination and the thin-layer-chromatographic comparison of the optical brighteners contained in the material concerned.

The examinations of the "Hitler-Diaries" handwriting substantiated the initial suspicion that the "Diaries" presented to Bundeskriminalamt had been written by Konrad Kujau himself. Herr Hecker will now make some additional remarks on the details of the handwriting comparison expertise.

# HITLER DIARY FORGERY

M. Hecker
Scientific Director
Head Handwriting Laboratory, BKA

Let me say something in more detail about the handwriting aspects of the Hitler diaries, whereby, to begin with, I want to sketch the situation that presented itself to the handwriting experts of the Federal Criminal Office (BKA) at the time they were given the task. At the time that the race for the exclusive publishing rights was in full progress loud voices were also to be heard from the ranks of other handwriting experts. A renowned university professor deemed it appropriate to state in a radio interview, that the Hitler diaries could not, alone on the basis of the already known volume, possibly be forgeries, in other words they must be genuine. A short time later however the same institution declared the books to be forged. At this point the opinions of a well-known Swiss expert, a highly thought of American expert, and a German handwriting expert, had been known for some time, and all three had come to the conclusion that identity of origin existed between the samples of Hitler's handwriting and the diary excerpts presented for comparison. The fatal error that all three experts made lay in the fact that together with some few authentic exemplars of Hitler's handwriting, their employers had presented such materials as genuine, that also stemmed from the pen of the later self-confessed forger. The three experts, in part at least, had compared forgeries with forgeries. A serious reproach from which none of three experts can be excluded is that from a methodical point of view all of them failed to carry out material critical internal comparison of the alledgedly genuine Hitler material. Such an examination would have led to the result that a considerably larger affinity existed, in terms of shape and form, between parts of the material presented for comparison and the diaries, than amongst the individual complexes of the comparison material itself. Even if such a material critical examination had not aroused any suspicions, the obligatory physio-technical examination carried out within the framework of every handwriting examination would have shown that on the basis of the material used, it could not be authentic. The experts referred to however, were unable to carry out such an examination since they had, contrary to duty, agreed to examine copies which, naturally enough, cannot be subjected to such analysis.

Let it be said here that these erroneous judgements were presented between May and June 1982.

In contrast, the Federal Criminal Office carried out it's examination in the right sequence, that is to say, the material element was checked for possible anachronisms. These inter-disciplinary analyses led to the following conclusions:

1. Typed labels found on two of the diaries, carrying a date difference of 7 years, were written on the same typewriter dating from that time. Since no time-specific wear and tear could be determined in the type face, it was concluded that the labels had been typed shortly after one another and not with a time interval of 7 years.

2. The flourescent-technical and chromatographical examination of the bindings led to the confirmation that the fly-leaves and the paper backing of the binding contained white dyes which were only available after the 2nd World War, that is, after 1955. These results were, in the main, also found to apply to the paper of the diaries.

3. The inks used in the diaries presented for examination were identified as "Pelikan Black 4001" and "Pelikan Blue 4001". The date of manufacture of the ink used in at least two of the examined diaries was 1981/1982 at the earliest. Further examination of the ink showed that the diaries had obviously been written in the same sequence as the years they were dated.

4. Examination of the textiles used in the bindings showed the presence of polyester fibres, the technology for the production of which was only developed in the mid 50's.

In view of these clear analyses the question as to why a handwriting comparison was carried out must be asked, since at this time no one would have seriously wanted to come to the hypothesis that, although the materials used were of a later origin, the handwriting of Hitler was genuine. In addition, at the time that the Federal Criminal Office began its examination of the handwriting, a media spectacular confession, with a circulation of millions, by the suspected forger had already occurred.

This question could be easily answered:

1. In sensational investigations and criminal proceedings of this kind it can be assumed that a confession will be withdrawn on the grounds that it was extorted with the promise of a mild or reduced sentence.

2. It could not be excluded that a few of Hitler's notes were available around which the whole complex of the forged diaries could have been written.
3. It could not be excluded that several writers were involved, considering the bulk of the forgeries.

Since the examination of handwriting is one of my specialities, let me briefly say something about the particular methodical problems of this case. Every handwriting examination that has authenticity as its aim must concern itself, in the first instance, with the qualitative and quantitative aspects of the material to be compared. In this connection the first difficulties arose since, without doubt, authentic samples of Hitler's handwriting are very few and far between in Germany. The Federal Archive itself has only very few examples of original material. Even Hitler's will, dated 2 May 1938, is only available in the Archives in the form of a copy. A significant side effect of this case was that, as a result of our extremely difficult investigations, we were able to determine the where-abouts of this historically very significant original document, and to pass this information to the Federal Archive. The document, comprising several pages, was available to us during the time of the investigations. The necessity to examine original material is briefly pointed out:

Although numerous manuscripts of Hitler have been published, for example in Maser's book "Hitler, Letters and Notes" or in Fest's "HITLER", this type of reproduction does not provide a suitable basis for comparison since too many significant details of the handwriting are lost during the reproduction process. In a recent publication I referred to this problem and used the following example in connection with the Hitler diaries.

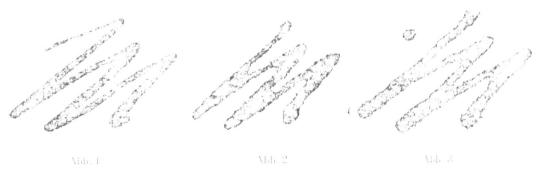

In these pictures you can see 3 different versions of reproduction of one and the same letter, namely the "M" in the title "Mein Testament" of Hitler's will.

Picture 1 is a photographic reproduction of the original; picture 2 is a copy resulting from the technical printing procedure in Maser's book and picture 3 a copy obtained through the technical printing procedure from the magazine "Archiv Fur Krimilogogie". The here obvious differences in detail speak for themselves and underline again the necessity of examining the original material.

The second big difficulty lay in the fact that the available known material from Adolf Hitler did not meet the requirements of conformity with chronological development. The incriminating diaries under consideration alledgedly cover the period 1934 to 1943.

It is well known that a person's handwriting undergoes changes in the course of a life-time analogous to his development, as well as being dependent on particular situation, specific influences, especially endogenously variable situations such as illness, injury and similar conditions. Considering the public announcement concerning Hitler's health, it becomes clear how important the knowledge of these conditions is on the acute form of the handwriting, primarily from the point of view as to whether the manuscripts in question originated at a time when the symptoms were evident or not. A short quotation from FEST seems to confirm this, "that since the end of 1943, he (Hitler) suffered a breakdown of his nervous stabilising system, which could only remain undetected by an act of emmense and desperate self-discipline". In another passage (p. 921 ff) we read: "Morell, Hitler's doctor, was naturally forced, in the course of time, to resort to increasingly stronger means in ever shorter periods of time, in order to maintain Hitler's capacity for work, after which antedotes of a sedative nature were administered in order to quieten the excited nerves, so that Hitler was subject to a constant strain.

The result of the permanent intervention with at times up to 28 different drugs first became evident during the war, as the exacting events, the lack of sleep, the monotony of a vegetarian diet and the Lemur-like life in the bunker-world of the headquarters increased the effects of the medication. In August 1941 Hitler complained of fainting fits, nausea and ague . . . . it cannot be ruled-out that this was one of the first reactions to the years of artificial control of his body; in any event from this time onwards the states of exhaustion increased. Since Stalingrad he took anti-depressive medication every two days .... complained, among other things of a disturbed sense of balance .... The difference of opinion concerning the effects of the strychnine element of the medication given by Morell reaches its limit at this point. Similarly, the question which the quoted source leaves open, whether Hitler suffered from Parkinson's disease or whether the tremor of his left arm and the bowed stature, as well as the lack of physical coordination could be found in psychogenic origins, is only of minor ..... interest".

If the condition of Hitler's health has been mentioned in some detail, then not only because a series of changes in handwriting, due to the effects of medication is known, but additionally that definite proof is available showing that the minimal administration of certain medicines, for example neuroleptica, lead to noticeable changes in the fine handwriting motoricity. This condition makes use of the ambulant psychiatric practice wihh the so-called "method of the creeping dosage to cross the neuoleptical threshold" insofar as it serves to prevent the appearance of extra-pyramidical inhibition symptoms from acting as a dosage criterium when using stronger latent neuroleptica to prevent the onset of course motoricitical Parkinson's symptoms. HAASE (1972) was able to determine that "in most cases of writing ability, extra-pyramidical symptoms were recognisable, although the patient's gait showed no abnormality" by using 25 various neuroleptica and 20,000 hand- writing specimens of the same text. (P. 114) It would seem probable to determine, from Hitler's authentic written material - if such were available in the unbroken form of diary - how the medication and/or illness phenomenon manifested itself. Con- versely, every missing characteristic, even those of an unspecified nature, can be an indication for the non-authenticity of the diaries in question. What sense was there in comparing the alledgedly authentic specimens of Hitler with the diaries in question, when the results of the investigations of the neigh- bouring fields were already known?

As you all know, the peculiarities of a writer can be determined from the discrepancies of script characteristics. This does not as a rule apply to very short forgeries such as a signature; here however, we were concerned with hundreds of pages, whereby the forger most certainly did not have the quantitative equivalent available. He had therefore, per force, to quasi "phantasise" concerning script characteristics and introduce self-constructed script elements. These latter had to be isolated when comparing them with authentic material from Hitler, and later to analyse them for similarity with script material from the suspected forger.

This presented a further problem, namely that whilst the suspected forger was cooperative in providing script specimens, he could produce only a fraction of the amount of the diaries. It was therefore impossible to cover the complete variations of the manuscript, especially as the forger's impartially produced material was unusable since it did not as habitual script, contain the mixture of Latin and German script elements of Hitler's own writing.

A further difficulty lay in the fact that only such specimens were available which quasi represented the final stage in the endeavors at forgery, that is, they represented the highest degree of penmanship in an incompatible script, whereas the diaries contain the elements of continuity. When later, during the court proceedings, the judge requested the forger to demonstrate his ability, the latter had great difficulty to recapitulate or reproduce signatures from particular parts of his forgeries. In this connection the forger confirmed that there were signatures "from the beginning of his era as a forger and others from his mature period". For this reason it was necessary, in a first attempt, to test the questioned documents in an internal comparison in order to ascertain to what extent the incriminating scripts came under the aspect of continuous improvement through practice by a single writer.

The results of this procedure can be summarised as follows:

1. A clear differentiation is to be made between the copies in question and the authentic writings of Adolf Hitler. The general overall impression of similarity of the Latin-German script mixture under course analysis only serves to veil the discrepancies at the individual characteristic level.

2. The copies in question are, amongst themselves, on the whole homogeneous and contain no indication that further writers were involved.

3. The discrepancies between the authentic Hitler material and the diary scripts conform in a high degree with the script idiosyncrasies of the forger.

Please allow me a few more comments on the often discussed "clumsiness" forgeries. As far as the signatures "Adolf Hitler" are concerned that are to be found under many diary entries with the probable intention of lending additional authenticity, these can be described as having been done very well. Due to the relatively few letters contained in the signature of Adolf Hitler they do not make particularly high demands even on an only averagely talented forger like myslef.

As far as the other written copies are concerned, I have already stated that they only make a genuine impression when looked at superficially, unless one compares them with products from the same source.

I have tried, with this fleeting excursion into a specialist report of 400 pages, to give a superficial impression of the events. Thank you for your attention.

# TECHNIQUES FOR DETECTING DOCUMENTS CREATED BY PHOTOCOPY MACHINES

Dr. David A. Crown
Examiner of Questioned Documents
Fairfax, Virginia

> Because of the "best evidence" rule, photocopies of documents are encountered in civil and criminal cases. The various types of fraudulent photocopied documents are discussed. Techniques for the examination of photocopied documents and proof of forgery are detailed.

With the tremendous growth in sales of photocopy machines has come a concurrent increase in problems for the Questioned Document Examiner. The Examiner is frequently asked to examine photocopies to determine if:

a. there ever was an "original" document from which the photocopy was made,

b. portions of two different documents have been combined by the montage technique to create a new, spurious document.

The literature makes frequent reference to the dangers of accepting photocopies of documents at face value without a searching evaluation. (1-9) Years ago, Conway (10) pointed out that "writing produced by an accused after evidential writings have come into dispute and solely for the purpose of establishing his own contentions should always be exposed to careful scrutiny and received with extreme caution".

Hilton and Cromwell (11) refined this concept and set up the following criteria for judging the possibility of fraud by photocopy:

a. Where photocopies exist in situations where there was no need to make such a photocopy,

b. Where there is a lack of independent documentation or supporting documentation bolstering the contentions of a proferred photocopy,

c. Where the photocopy concerns the type of transaction or activities which would not normally be engaged in by either of the parties involved,

d. Where the photocopy, if believed, would provide the significant evidence or proof of a contention, and without which, the case would be lost.

In any of the above scenarios, the "phantom original" or the montage photocopy are to be found. The techniques to detect these two different types of fraudulent documents differ however.

In the case of the "phantom original", the proponent offers the photocopy as evidence of some contention with some type of explanation as to why the original is not to be found such as "I sent the original to you on ... and this is my file copy of the document". The proponent of the document will try to have everything correct on his master prior to the photocopying and subsequent destruction of the master. The proponent of the photocopy can only get correct the facets of the document that he is aware of. Rare, however, is the individual with a thorough knowledge of the general availability of certain types of typewriters, pens, letterheads, copiers, etc., and a knowledge of the specific availability of specific typewriters, pens, letterheads, copiers, at the time the alleged document was created.

In a simple situation where the same typewriter, letterhead, copier, etc., have been in use in an office for a long period of time, it may be easy to find the "correct raw materials from which a document may be created. However, there are temporary situations which can interrupt such planning. Typewriters develop temporary individuality by a build-up of dirt in keys at a certain time; photocopy machines have distinctive trash marks on the glass platen during a certain time span. It is imperative for the forger to get the correct materials with the correct characteristics for a specific time period.

This throws a great burden upon the creator of a "phantom original". He might have the appropriate typewriter for the letter, and an appropriate letterhead for the date of the letter but have the initials of a typist in the lower left corner of the document of an individual who was not hired until two weeks after the date on the alleged document.

The proponent of a document must invariably "take a position" when questioned about the preparation and location of the alleged original of a document. When the proponent does not know the answer to a question, he will have to provide an answer whether he knows the correct answer or not. It is the function of the document examiner to evaluate every aspect of the document that can be checked against the general date-of-introduction (DOI) files in the laboratory and against contemporary documents from the office proferring the alleged authentic document.

DOI files exist on the introduction of mechanical devices such as typewriters and photocopy machines although there may be difficulties in differentiating the specific makes and models of machines. On the other hand, if the proponent of a document claims that the document was prepared on the office IBM Selectric typewriter and then copied on the Canon photocopy machine, it may be possible to demonstrate that those specific machines were not available in general or in that specific office on the date claimed. Purchase or lease invoices can usually substantiate the date office machinery was acquired in an office. It is the careful delineation of each and every evidentiary aspect of a document that results in determinations of fraudulent preparation.

The author was involved in a case in recently which involved the examination of two photocopies which warned of a certain condition vital to a contention in a civil lawsuit for very consequential damages. It was alleged that the original had been sent to the other party but a copy had been retained in the files of the proponent. A careful examination of the photocopy of the alleged original revealed that:

a. the specific typewriter used to prepare the original was not available in the proponent office until several months after the date on the alleged original,

b. the letterhead used contained a slight flaw and the flawed letterheads were not available until at least a year later than the date on the document, and

c. the document was not copied on the Xerox copier which was in use in the office in question on the date alleged.

In short, the summation of evidence was such that the original could not have ever existed, given the conditions of preparation described by the proponent or established by laboratory examination.

In any case, where there is one clear-cut incompatibility with the correct general DOIs and specific DOIs, basis exists to claim that the document cannot be authentic. Naturally, correct, authenticated DOIs must be used. There may be aspects of a case where there is insufficient data to establish accurate DOIs. In such a case this must be noted. There may be instances where it may not be possible to definitely establish what type/brand of photocopier was used to copy a document, but if it is not the type/brand that was claimed to have been used, or should have been used, it does not matter that the specific type used cannot be pinpointed. The burden is on the perpetrator to get everything right and nothing wrong. It is up to the questioned document examiner to check every aspect of the document that provides dating or timing significance.

The techniques for differentiating typewriters by both class characteristics as well as individual characteristics for purposes of dating are well known and do not bear repeating at this time. Photocopies and photocopy machines can be differentiated by:

a.  Type of process involved:
Plain paper indirect electro-static
ZnO coated paper direct electro-static
Dual spectrum
Diffusion transfer
Dye transfer
Stabilization process
Thermo-fax
b.  Marks on the photocopy:
watermarks or printed proprietary symbols
gripper marks
band marks
c.  Text deletions in margins:
missing side text
missing top and bottom text combinations
d.  Degree of expansion/contraction of the text:
positive
negativee
Zero change
e.  Toner differentiation:
X-ray spectrometry
TLC of sensitiving dyestuffs
Coated paper- UV response
IR spectrometry of binder resins

DOIs of some of the photocopiers in use are listed in Kelly's 1983 monograph on office copiers (12). Others will have to be derived from the contemporary office machine litera- ture and from the photocopier manufacturers.

· In a recent case, a plain paper photocopy of a "phantom original" was submitted for examination. The proponent of the document, when pressed, stated that the document had been copied on the office copy machine, either a Pitney-Bowes or a Monroe photocopier. With consideration for the alleged date on the document, it was determined that the Pitney-Bowes photocopier available at the time in question used ZnO coated paper and that the Monroe photocopiers available had different coefficients of expansion than that displayed by the questioned photocopy. It was concluded that the photocopy could not have been prepared as claimed by the proponent of the document.

The creation of montage documents requires other skills of the perpetrator. The text from two documents must be com- bined or a portion of a document must be removed so that it can be filled in again with original typing/handwriting. To be successful, the perpetrator must combine the two units so that:
a.  both units are in correct alignment, and
b.  there are not tell-take junction lines.

284

It is the function of the document examiner to make an in-depth examination of the proferred photocopy to determine evidence of the above conditions. Just as it is impossible to re-align typing after a sheet of paper has been removed from a typewriter, the same problem exists when two units of typing are pasted together for photocopying. The photocopy should be checked for incongruous units of typewriting, unusual spacings for signatures and line junctions that have no rational explanation. If the proponent of a document states that the document was produced in the ordinary course of business and all in one typing operation, this contention can be evaluated.

When two units are placed together for copying, invariably there are junction lines on the first generation photocpyy. If "White-Out" or other similar product is used, the second generation photocopy may not have the "offending" outline lines. It may take several generations to achieve a photocopy acceptable to the perpetrator. All portions of the documents should be checked for unaccountable lines which could indicate that a portion of the photocopy was extracted from another document which contained a line crossing not completely obliterated. Finding the original document from which a signature was lifted makes for an excellent courtroom display.

All typewritten units of a proferred photocopy should be checked for actual unit spacing. The various typewriter testplates available, such as those previously sold by the American Society of Questioned Document Examiners, can be used to determine typewriter pitch. The spacing determined on the photocopy must be compared with the unit spacing for the specific make and model of typewriter used.

Specific degrees of expansion/contraction can be determined by using an accurate ruler such as the Schaedler Precision Ruler produced by John N. Schaedler, Inc. which measures in increments of half millimeters or the Universal Diagnostic Plates produced by Forensic Research, Suite 9B, 207 Duke Ellington Blvd, New York, NY 10025 which give accurate readings of spacings to within 10 microns. When there are differences in degrees of expansion/contraction in typewritten portions of photocopies with malalignment of the typewritten units basis exists to conclude that the document was produced by the montage process. The degree of expansion/contraction for each model of photocopy machine can be established from company data and from test runs made with a specific machine. Expansion/contraction measurements are not affected by dark/light controls on the machine. Machines with zero expansion/contraction will have the same spacing regardless of the generation involved. Specific calculations can be made of the expansion/contraction of a specific generation of photocopy.

Each model of photocopy machine has a different rate of image degradation. The rate is affected by the settings of the dark/light image control on the machine and the density of the initial image. Image degradation studies should be run to at least twelve generations or more without adjustments to the dark/light control. Separate generational studies can be made with the control set to make darker images or lighter images. Degradation of image may vary from corner to corner on a specific photocopy machine. Where there is a significant difference in the images of two portions of a document, that cannot be accounted for otherwise, basis exists to conclude that a document is a montage. The breakdown of background to a pebble grain effect is an indication of multi-generation copying.

In a recent case, a photocopy of a document was produced which allegedly proved that the corporate headquarters of a defendant in a civil suit was located in Maryland. Examination of the documents involved revealed that a portion of a photocopy of an authentic document listing the corporate headquarters in Virginia was blanked out with "White Out" and successive photocopies were made to eliminate the tell-take outline. A new corporate address was typed onto the document and then photocopied again. It was possible to demonstrate the difference in alignment of the typewriting and the gross differences in image degradation.

In another case, a woman offered a photocopy of a change of beneficiary form to substantiate her claim that she was entitled to the proceeds of an insurance policy. It was determined that that signature on the change of beneficiary form was identical with the signature of the decedent on his will. A photocopy of the will signature had been pasted onto a change of beneficiary form and then re-photocopied.

Using both the statements made by the proponent of a photocopy and what can be revealed from careful examination of all aspects of a photocopy, determinations can be made that a photocopy is a frabrication.


Bibliography:

1. Osborn, "Photocopies: The Most Dangerous Pitfall Of Document Examination Today", paper, ASQDE Conference, 1980.

2. Keckler and Moore, "A Case Study Of The Dangers Of Office Machine Copies: Beware Of Self-Serving Standards", paper, ASQDE Conference, 1983.

3. Hilton, "Detecting Fraudulent Photocopies", Forensic Science International, Vol 13, p. 117, 1979.

4. Masson, "Caught In A Generation Gap", paper ASQDE Conference, 1981.

5. Moore, "The Identification Of A Office Machine Copy Of A Printed Copy Of A Photographic Copy Of An Original Sales Receipt", Journal Of Forensic Sciences, Vol 27, No. 1, p. 169, 1982.

6. Nemecek, "Copier Copies Can Tell", paper, Eighth International Meeting of Forensic Sciences, Wichita, 1978.

7. Kelly, "Identifying The Copying Machine Used In Preparation Of Simulated Forgeries", Journal of Forensic Sciences, p. 410, 1973.

8. Totty and Baxendale, "Defect Marks And The Identification Of Photocopy Machines", Journal of the Forensic Science Society, Vol 21, p. 23, 1981.

9. Carney, "Fraudulent Transposition Of Original Signatures By Office Machine Copiers", paper, ASQDE Conference, 1983.

10. Conway, "Evidential Documents", Charles C. Thomas Publishers, p. 108, 1959.

11. Hilton and Cromwell, "Fraud By Photocopy", Case & Comment, p. 34, March - April 1977.

12. Kelly, "Classification and Identification of Modern Office Copiers", American Board of Forensic Document Examiners, 1983.

# SURVEILLANCE UNDER ADVERSE WEATHER CONDITIONS: WAVELENGTH FILTERING CONSIDERATIONS

N. S. Kopeika
Dept. Electrical and Computer Engineering
Ben Gurion University of the Negev
Beer-Sheva, Israel 84120

Image quality in long range surveillance is generally limited by atmospheric effects rather than by equipment limitations. In locations whose ground or sand particles are not adhesed to the ground, such as desert and beach areas, significantly wavelength dependent multiple forward scattering by relatively large particulates noticeably limit image resolution. Changing the climate to suit our surveillance requirements is beyond our capability. However, often, suitable wavelength filtering permits improvment in image quality. Multi-variable correlation coefficients from over 2500 measurements of atmospheric modulation contrast and meteorological parameters in the Northern Negev were computed. In winter, image quality was seen to improve with humidity increase particularly in the visible. Increased temperature had a degrading effect upon resolution, with no noticeable wavelength dependence. These measurements and calculations suggest that in low humidity and/or high wind conditions, noticeably improved image quality is obtained in the near infrared. This was also found to be true after rain. However, for high relative humidity and/or low wind conditions, it is preferable to image at visible wavelengths. In summer the opposite conclusions apply. Explanations base upon the meteorological dependencies of airborne particulate size are presented.

Imaging through desert and non-desert atmospheres is compared from the standpoint of interactions of optics and meteorology. Modulation transfer function (MTF) criteria for image resolution are presented to describe atmospheric image degradation deriving from atmospheric background radiation, turbulence, and aerosols. Regression coefficients with which to ascribe relative roles in experimentally observed image quality are calculated for relative humidity, air temperature, and windspeed. The last is particularly important in desert atmospheres because of its role in causing desert dust to be airborne. Analysis of regression coefficients in the spatial frequency domain permits quantitative determination of effects of each meterological parameter on atmospheric background, turbulence, and aerosol MTFs separately. In this way insight is gained as to not only the extent to which each metereological parameter affects imaging resolution, but also the mechanism of the effect. In general, near infrared as compared to visible imaging can significantly improve image resolution except under dry weather desert conditions, such as in the summer and during khamsin and sharav conditions.

The interaction of optics and meteorology in determining image quality obtained from seeing through the atmosphere is complex. When the atmosphere is that of a desert the complexity of interaction is considerably greater as a result of the airborne desert dust particulates.

In non-desert atmospheres image quality is governed primarily by atmospheric background illuminance and by atmospheric turbulence (1 & 2). The former serves to decrease contrast in much the same way as background illuminance from ceiling lights decreases image contrast on the movie screen in a movie theater. The atmospheric effect is essentially independent of spatial frequency but does vary strongly with wavelength. Atmospheric illuminance results from scattered sunlight and thermal emmission of atmospheric gases[3]. The first is primarily visible light whose spectrum is determined by that of the incident solar light and spectral light scattering and absorption properties of the atmosphere. The spectrum of thermal emission of the atmosphere is in the infrared and is determined by air temperature and atmospheric spectral absorption. The scattered sunlight and thermal emission spectra, both of which comprise background atmospheric illuminance or radiance, intersect at about 3 - 4 um wavelength under normal daytime conditions[3]. It is here that atmospheric background radiance is least and, as a result, so too is image degradation caused by such atmospheric background radiance[2]. In non-desert atmospheres this degradation decreases as wavelength increases from the middle of the visible into the near infrared spectrum. We shall see that in the desert this wavelength dependence is different.

Atmospheric turbulence describes the common situation where atmospheric refractive index fluctuates randomly, thus causing random refractions of light. Light propagating from a point source should be ideally imaged into a point image. However, refractions of the beam, which are random in both time and space, cause the beam finally incident on the receiver to arrive from many different angles, thus smearing or spreading the image of the point source. This spreading is called the system "spread function" and it characterizes the resolving capability of the imaging sygem including the intervening atmosphere[4]. The spatial Fourier transform of the spread function yields the optical transfer function (OTF) of the system, which decreases monotonically as spatial frequency increases. It is customary to normalize the OTF by its maximum value, so that the normalized OTF varies between unity and zero. The magnitude of the optical transfer function is called the "modulation transfer function" or MTF. For a sine wave object (rather than point source or object), the system MTF can be shown to be equal to the system modulation contrast transfer function (MCF) (ratio of image plane modulation contrast to object plane modulation contrast)[5]. The decrease of MTF with increasing spatial frequency signifies contrast degradation at higher spatial frequencies. At some relatively high spatial frequency, system MTF has decreased to such a low value of contrast, that it is below the threshold contrast function of the observer. This means that such high spatial frequency content of the image cannot be resolved by the observer because of the poor contrast. The spatial frequency at which system MTF is just equal to the threshold contrast of the observer defines the maximum useful spatial frequency content of the system. We will call it here $f_{r_{max}}$. Often the threshold contrast of the observer is taken to be 2%, although there is some evidence that it really increases with spatial frequency[6] as shown in Fig. 1. If x and x' are uncertainties in the object and image planes respectively, and if s and s' are object and image distances respectively, then on the basis of similar triangles:

$$\frac{\Delta x}{s} = \frac{-\Delta x'}{s'} \propto -\frac{1}{f_{r_{max}}s'} \qquad (1)$$

where the minus sign refers to image inversion. Since optical magnification $\underline{M}$ is equal to the ratio of s' to s, the minimum size of resolvable detail in the object plane is:

$$\Delta x \propto (f_{r_{max}} M)^{-1}. \qquad (2)$$

The greater the useable spatial frequency contact $f_{r_{max}}$ provided by the imaging system, the smaller the object plane detail that can be resolved and the better the imaging system.

For relatively long propagation paths through the atmosphere, system spread function and MTF are limited primarily by atmospheric - rather than instrumentation-limited phenomena[1].

The contrast degradation deriving from background atmospheric radiance can also be considered from the standpoint of spatial frequency domain. Such background illuminance contributes towards dampening of MTF uniformly across the spatial frequency spectrum, as will be shown below. Since MTF decreases monotonically with spatial frequency, such dampening causes the intersection of MTF with threshold contrast to take place at a lower spatial frequency. This decrease in $f_{r_{max}}$ deriving from the dampening causes an increase in $\Delta x$ in (2) and thus a worsening of resolution[1,2].

Spatial frequency domain analysis shows that overall system MTF is equal to the product of the MTFs of each individual component in the imaging system[4]. This means that the atmosphere can be approached as any other component in the imaging system and an MTF assigned to it. In particular, the MTF describing image degradation resulting from background atmospheric radiance $N_A(\lambda,T)$ is 1, 2, 7

$$M_B(\lambda,T) = \frac{N_O(\lambda,T)}{N_O(\lambda,T) + N_A(\lambda,T)} \quad \tau(\lambda,T) \qquad (3)$$

where $N_O$ is object scene radiance, $\lambda$ is wavelength, and T is thermal emmission temperature. $\tau(\lambda,T)$ is atmospheric transmittance over path length z and is equal to:

$$\tau = \exp\left(-\int_O^z \alpha(\lambda,T,z')\,dz'\right) \qquad (4)$$

where is the atmospheric extinction coefficient, which is equal to the sum of the atmospheric scattering and absorption coefficients $S_A$ and $A_a$, respectively. Equation (3) shows that $M_B$ is not a function of spatial frequency. If $N_A$ were zero, then (3) would be unity and there would be no dampening. Since atmospheric background is non-zero, (3) is less than unity, and multiplication of other MTF's by it represents MTF dampening uniformly across the spacial frequency spectrum.

Turbulence phenomena are generally characterized with a refractive index structure coefficient $C_n$. The MTF to describe relatively long exposure plane wave imaging through atmospheric turbulence is often given by 8, 9, 1

$$< M_T(\lambda,f_r)> = \exp\left[(-59.19\,(f_r\,f_r)^{5/3}\lambda^{-1/3}\int_O^z C_n^2 dz'\right)$$

where $f_\ell$ is imaging system focal length and $f_r$ is spatial frequency. It can be seen from (15) that the wavelength dependence of turbulence MTF is quite negligible. As a result the wavelength dependence of seeing through a non-desert atmosphere is usually determined by (3) which, in turn, is affected strongly by the wavelength dependence of the atmospheric pathance $N_A$ described above(1) (2). For high glare and/or long atmospheric path lengths imaging at even 0.9 um offers significant improvement in resolution over that obtainable at visible wavelengths [1].

Background aerosols are normally on the order of half a micrometer radius or less[10]. Light scattering by them is typically at large angles relative to direction of propagation prior to the scattering because the small size of the scattering particulate relative to incident wavelength limits diffraction effects. As a result of the large scattering angle, the effect of the scatter is essentially attenuation with regard to the initial direction of propagation. However, as scattering particles grow in size, much of the light is diffracted in the forward direction. This is manifested as forward scattering at very small angles relative to the initial direction of propagation. Multiple forward scattering effects cause some forward scattered radiation to be received and imaged together with the unscattered light. This means that the multiple forward scattered component is incident on the receiver from random small angles of arrival with respect to that of the unscattered component. The effect on spread function and resolution is qualitatively similar to that of atmospheric turbulence. Quantitatively, however, scattering exhibits strong wavelength dependences according to the ratio of scattering particulate size to wavelength. The aerosol MTF for the object beam is given by 11:

$$M_a(f_r) = \exp(-A_a z)\ \exp[(-(f_r/f_c)^2 S_a z),\ f_r < f_c$$
$$= \exp(-a z) \qquad\qquad\qquad f_r \geq f_c.$$

$f_c$ is a high spatial frequency cutoff, whose value is
$$f_c = a/(\lambda f)\ ,$$
where a is scattering particulate radius. Expressions similar to 6 have been developed independently by Yura [12] and Ishimaru [13] for underwater imaging limitations imposed by particulate scatter. These differ from other theoretical developments based on single-scattering approximations that are not limited by a high spatial-frequency cutoff [14,15] It is assumed in eqn. 6 that light received from the object is scattered many times $(\int_6^z S_a(z',\lambda)dz' \gg 1)$ before reaching the receiver. The spatial-frequency dependence of image

292

degradation by small-angle aerosol scattering is essentially a low-spatial-frequency process, with the high-spatial-frequency cutoff $f_c$ in (6) being proportional to the ratio of particulate size to light wavelength. For ordinary background aerosols $a \approx 0.2 - 0.4 \mu m$, and $f_c$ is consequently too small for the aerosol MTF to be observed with ordinary topics. Very little visible and near infrared light scattering is then in the forward direction. However, soil-derived particulates such as desert dust lifted by the wind usually have a radius of the order of 2 - 4 um (10), (16), thus increasing $f_c$ by an order of magnitude and enabling the aerosol MTF not only to be easily observed at visible and near IR wavelengths but also to play a dominant role in the wavelength dependence of imaging through the atmosphere [16-18]. The wavelength dependence of the scattering coefficient can often be expressed as [19],

$$S_a \propto \lambda^{-n} \qquad (8)$$

where n is its maximum value of 4 for pure Rayleigh scattering. The wavelength dependence of (2) is then

$$M_a(f_r, \lambda) \propto \exp(-\lambda^{(2-n)}) \qquad (9)$$

where (7) and (8) have been substituted into (6). Eqn. (9) thus suggests considerable wavelength dependence according to the value of n. For n 2, $M_a$ favors imaging at shorter wavelengths where fall-off with increasing spatial frequency is less rapid. In very clear weather n 2, and consequently $M_a$ then falls off less rapidly with spatial frequency at longer wavelengths. In this situation, better resolution is obtained at longer wavelengths. The wavelength dependence of the scattering coefficient in (9) is very much a function of meteorological conditions with regard to both soil and the atmosphere. If the soil contains moisture, for example, the resulting adhesiveness of soil particles to one another prevents many from being airborne in the wind, particularly as regards the larger and heavier particles. Good correlations have been observed under dry desert soil conditions between (6) and the time-integral of wind strength in experiments involving imaging through desert atmosphere in both horizontal[16,17] and near-vertical directions [18]. The time-integral of wind-strength plays a large role in determining both the size distribution and concentration of soil-derived particles that are airborne. Expression (6) affects image quality propagated through the atmosphere particularly in areas where the soil is dry and bare so that particulates can be uplifted by the wind. Hence, it is particularly significant in desert climates.

The three known atmospheric mechanisms of image quality degradation are described quantitatively by (3), (5) and (6). In the visible and near infrared wavelength regions the background atmospheric radiation is also affected largely by aerosol scattering properties. When scattering particulate radius $a$ is on the order of wavelength size, the magnitude of the scattering coefficient is generally maximum. For $\lambda < a$, the wavelength dependence of $S_a$ displays various maxima and minima. For $\lambda > a$, $S_a$ generally decreases with wavelength according to (8), where n increases with increasing wavelength. It is clear, therefore, that (3) and (6) are both strongly wavelength dependent, and they essentially determine the wavelength dependence of imaging through the atmosphere. We will now proceed to compare imaging in desert with imaging in non-desert atmospheres.

The wavelength dependence of (3) is determined by the ratio $(N_A/N_0)$ and a. For a background deriving primarily from scattered radiation, $N_B$ itself is affected, too, largely by a, although wavelength dependence is determined too by that of the background source, which often is the sun. Thus, for nonarid areas where aerosol radii are normally on the order of a fraction of a micrometer, $(N_A/N_0)$ and a are maximum at approximately 0.45 um. (16), (19), (20). In this situation, atmospheric resolution improves as imaging wavelength increases beyond this range, particularly in high glare situations [1]. Image degradation stemming from (3) is least at wavelengths where atmospheric background is minimum. Normally, when aerosol sizes are small as indicated above, optimum background contrast is in atmospheric windows between 2 - 4 um wavelength [2].

When the atmosphere contains large concentrations of soil-derived particulates such as desert dust [10, 16] a peak in aerosol size distribution is also seen at 2-4 um radius. Such particles scatter near-infrared radiation much more than they do visible radiation [16, 19]. Under such conditions, (3) is higher at visible than at near IR wavelengths, thus indicating resolution improvement at shorter wavelengths [16]. This means that when concentrations of airborne desert are relatively high, better resolution is obtained at visible than at near infrared wavelengths - the very opposite result of that typical of non-desert atmospheres [16]. In other words, if near infrared sensors which are advantageous in non-desert atmospheres are utilized in desert atmospheres, they are most likely to be disadvantageous in dry season.

The small size of background aerosols can be used to explain why the sky is blue in clear weather. Because for such small particulates $a < \lambda$, there is less scattering at longer wavelengths. Hence, in the visible spectrum it is the short wavelength blue light which is scattered most, thus causing the sky to appear blue to us. However, as particulate size increases through haze and fog, their light scattering becomes more spectrally neutral and the sky appears to us to become grayer and whiter. Finally, in the desert where soil derived particles are so large that $a = \lambda$ in the mid-infrared light scattering in the visible is maximum at longer wavelengths and the sky appears to us to be brownish and even reddish in dust storms.

The complex interactions of imaging and meteorological properties of the desert atmosphere are compared further with those of the non-desert atmosphere in the following experiment.

EXPERIMENT

Modulation contrast functions (MCF) at visible and near infrared wavelengths over a 4.15 ground level near-horizontal path (elevation varied from 1 - 5 m) were measured in the northern Negev desert in Beer Sheva, Israel, during a three year period. The target was a collection of black and white stripes forming normalized spatial frequencies of 4, 9, 10, 13, 20, 28, 40, 83, and 104 lines per milliradian, as described in [16]. Long wavelength-pass filters with varying short wavelength cutoffs were used to measure MCF spectral dependence. The long wavelength cutoff was that of a 700 TV line enhanced infrared response silicon vidicon TV system, at about 1 um wavelength. Irradiance at the receiver was maximum at about 450 nm wavelength and fell off strongly as wavelength increased, being at 750 nm only slightly more than 10% of its peak value at 450 nm. Thus, for shorter wavelength cutoffs most of the detected video current was derived from the visible rather than IR portion of the passed light. Neutral density filters were used to attenuate where needed so that for the lowest spatial frequency, video signal was equal at all wavelengths. Measurement of MCF at the various higher spatial frequencies then yielded to a first approximation the wavelength dependence of imaging through the atmosphere, as described in more detail elsewhere [16]. (Since the target was square wave rather than sin wave MCF did not equal MTF, but was close to it.) Meteorological parameters at the times of measurement were obtained from the local branch of the Israel Meteorological Services, which was situated only about a kilometer from the experimental line-of-sight. Such measurements include surface air temperature, air pressure, wind speed and direction, relative humidity, clouds, etc. Multiple partial regression coefficients between the imaging (MCF) and meteorological parameters were computed [21]. In the calculations the parameters are assumed to be normally distributed. Over 3000 measurements were taken. The required averaging or summation of MCF over wavelength or spatial frequency yields 60 - 70 separate cases.

The data was treated as type 1 in the nomenclature of Crow, et al. [21] because of the possibility of non-independence of some of the time sequential meteorological measurements. In the type I method the independent variable is taken as measured and only the dependent variable (MCF here) is required to be a stochastic variable. This allows for regression but not correlation calculations, since the latter require independent, normally distributed dependent as well as independent variables. The f-test allowed the examination of the significance of the regression formulae. Because climatic conditions are so different between winter and summer the data have been divided according to season. Winter is cooler, more damp, and rainy at times. Summer is hotter and the soil is quite dry. Moisture in the soil in winter plays a major role in decreasing soil-derived airborne particulate size and concentration. The summer or dry season thus permits an excellent opportunity to study effects of soil-derived particulates upon imaging through a desert atmosphere. The winter season is essentially comparable to a non-desert atmosphere since the atmosphere is freer of desert dust. Winter measurements preclude rain conditions since resolution was too poor then for any measurements.

RESULTS AND DISCUSSION

As a single-value criterion of image resolution, the MCF area (MCFA) is a number convenient to use in much the same way as MTFA [6]. MTFA is the area bound by the MTF and threshold contrast function curves in Fig. 1. Here the summation of MCF measurements at a given wavelength are used as single numerical criterion for image quality at that wavelength. The greater the spatial frequency at which MCF measurements can be obtained, the higher the sum of such measurements. This is proportional to MCFA and is labelled here $\Sigma MCF (\lambda)$. Regression coefficients for temperature (T), relative humidity (RH) and windspeed (W) were calculated.

For the winter or rainy season, it was found that
$$\Sigma_{f_r} MCF_w(\lambda) = a_w(\lambda) \ T + b_w(\lambda) \ RH + c_w(\lambda)W + d_w(\lambda) \quad (10)$$
Fig. 2 shows the values of the regression coefficients as functions of wavelength.

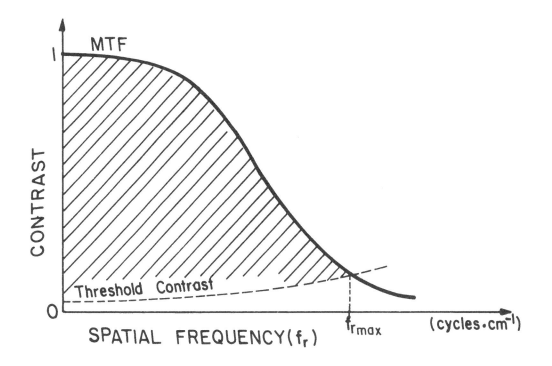

Fig. 1. Image resolution as defined in the spatial frequency domain. Shaded area is MTFA.

Thus, for 780 nm wavelength
$$\sum_{f_r} MCF_w(780) = -2.92 \times 10^{-2} T_w + 0.69 \times 10^{-4} RH_w + 3.76 \times 10^{-2} W_w + 1.48 \qquad (11)$$

where $T_w$ is in °C, $RH_w$ is in % and $W_w$ is in knots. For summer the subscript s is used instead of w. This figure includes standard error of the mean estimate for the regression coefficients. Solid lines are used for winter and dotted lines for summer.

To calculate regression coefficients of temperature, relative humidity, and windspeed for each spatial frequency, MCF data at each spatial frequency averaged over all wavelengths was used as the criterion for image quality at each spatial frequency. In this way, regression coefficients of these meteorological parameters were calculated at each spatial frequency $f_r$, i.e. for winter

$$\overline{MCF_w(f_r)} = a_w(f_r) T + b_w(f_r) W + d_w(f_r). \qquad (12)$$

where the overbar refers to averaging over all wavelength intervals. The regression coefficients as functions of spatial frequency for winter and summer respectively are plotted in Fig. 3. In many cases, MCF at higher spatial

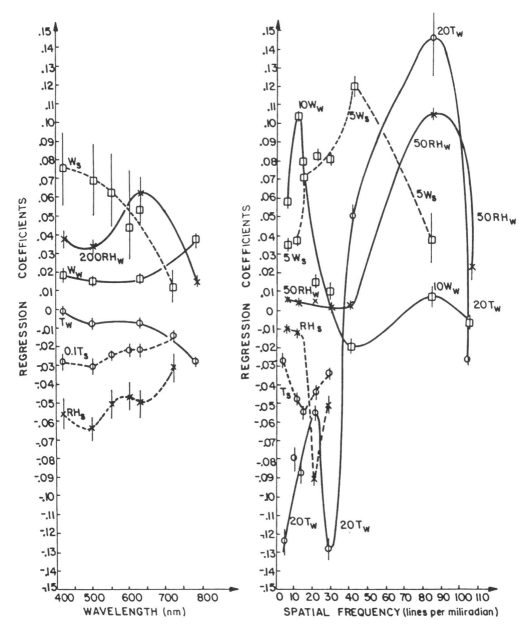

Fig. 2. Meteorological regression coefficients vs. wavelength.

Fig. 3. Meteorological regression coefficients vs. spatial frequency.

frequencies was zero, particularly at mid-day in the summer when turbulence was high. Consequently, some of the regression coefficients for summer in Fig. 3 do not extend out to high spatial frequencies.

The strong changes in Fig. 3 indicate the existence of the different MTF mechanisms in the different spatial frequency intervals. This information is obtained in the following way. Background contrast degradation and aerosol MTF are both highly wavelength-dependent, while turbulence is very weakly wavelength-dependent. However, turbulence degrades atmospheric MTF over the whole spatial frequency spectrum [10-12], while aerosol MTF refers only to spatial frequencies less than $f_c = a/\lambda f$. Background contrast degradation is manifested as a uniform dampening over the whole spatial frequency spectrum. As such, background contrast degradation affects adversely resolution of both large and small objects, while turbulence degrades resolution or primarily small objects. Forward scattering degrades resolution of medium-size objects in particular. Thus, at very low spatial frequencies overall atmosphere MTF is limited primarily by background contrast, since turbulence and aerosol MTFs both start at unity at zero spatial frequency. At slightly higher spatial frequencies aerosol MTF begins to make its presence felt. At spatial frequencies higher than aerosol MTF cutoff, overall atmospheric MTF is affected primarily by turbulence. This spatial frequency variation between the various atmospheric imaging degradations makes it possible to utilize spatial frequency information to determine how various meteorological parameters affect imaging through the atmosphere. The aerosol MTF high spatial frequency cutoffs in these experiments is on the order of 17 - 20 lines mrad $^{-1}$ [16-18].

In winter, Fig. 2 indicates relative humidity increase and windspeed increase are seen to yield improved imaging through the atmosphere, since these regression coefficients are positive, while air temperature increases are seen to lead to worsening of image quality propagated through the atmosphere. Our measurements and calculations involving relative humidity effects upon imaging through the atmosphere here are opposite to those obtained at microwave frequencies on the basis of turbulence alone [22]. They might, without Fig. 3, imply some role for forward scattering upon imaging through the atmosphere, as explained in the introduction. However, Fig. 3 indicates that it is particularly at high spatial frequencies that the regression coefficient for relative humidity is most positive. This means that imaging resolution improvement brought about by relative humidity increase in winter is a result of decreased turbulence degradation in particular. However, turbulence should affect all spatial frequencies, including low ones. The strong dip in the $RH_W$ curve in Fig. 3 at low spatial frequencies indicates relative humidity increase also increases image degradation via increased atmospheric background and forward scattering effects. This is attributed to increased haze and particulate size as relative humidity increases and should not be surprising. However, the decrease of turbulence degradation in winter with relative humidity increase, is opposite to that obtained in [22]. The reason is discussed below, after the temperature data are analyzed.

The negative temperature regression coefficient in Fig. 2 indicates temperature decrease yields improved resolution. As pointed out above this implies decreased temperature gradient improves imaging resolution. This is consistent with turbulence-related phenomena. Temperature decrease, if absolute humidity does not change, implies relative humidity increase. Thus, the negative temperature and positive relative humidity regression coefficients in Fig. 2 appear to be connected with each other and point to turbulence as a common mechanism is limiting image resolution through the winter or rainy desert atmosphere. However, Fig. 3 indicates that at low spatial frequencies the regression coefficient for temperature Tw is negative while at higher spatial frequencies it is positive. Thus, at higher spatial frequencies the $T_W$ and $RH_W$ curves are similar rather than opposite. The very low spatial frequency result implies that increased winter temperature increases background degradation by increasing the background radiance. This shows that the evaporation rate of soil moisture into the air tends to be greater than condensation of haze droplets back into water vapor, thus increasing the number of haze droplets and atmospheric scattering background radiance. This is supported by the second dip of $T_W$ in Fig. 3 at about 30 lines mrad$^{-1}$, corresponding to additional image degradation by forward scattering effects. Similar phenomena seem to characterize summer temperature effects and suggest the negative regression coefficients for temperature stem from forward scattering primarily. However, the higher spatial frequency results in Fig. 3 indicate image degradation due to turbulence decreases as winter temperature increases. In view of the low spatial frequency $T_W$ results, this may well suggest a decrease in humidity gradient resulting from the known increase in the absolute number of haze droplets as winter temperature increases.

This would also be consistent with the rise in the $RH_W$ regression coefficient at higher spatial frequencies. The latter implies that increase in relative humidity leads to decreased image degradation by turbulence [22]. Thus, the similar higher spatial frequency characteristics of both $T_W$ and $RH_W$ in Fig. 3 suggest the two are related in the manner described here. The spectral dependence of both these curves in Fig. 2 are not too different either. This result is the opposite of that of [22] for microwave fading and suggests that in that case turbulence was affected largely by temperature rather than humidity gradient.

The sharp positive peak of winter windspeed regression coefficient at very low spatial frequency in Fig. 3 indicates that the primary effect of wind on imaging in winter is to disperse haze droplets and thus decrease atmospheric background. This indicates the effect of windspeed in winter is mostly on background and not on turbulence, and that the spectral effect of the $W_W$ curve in Fig. 2 must be evaluated accordingly. This latter curve indicates background contrast degradation in the near infrared is less than in the visible. This is a common result and indicates airborne desert dust does not play so significant a role in winter imaging. Although the $T_W$ curve in Fig. 3 indicates some forward scattering effects as discussed above, these are attributed to increased particle size via humidity increase rather than picking up of large desert dust particles by the atmosphere. That the origin of this forward scatter is humidity is supported by the low value of the $RH_W$ regression coefficient at low spatial frequencies as compared to that at high spatial frequencies in Fig. 3.

While increased windspeed is seen to be favorable to imaging through background haze dispersal, the high spatial frequency dip in Fig. 3 indicates increased windspeed increases turbulence degradation. This too is opposite to the result in [22] and is attributed to increased humidity gradient via decrease in number of haze droplets brought about by wind dispersal, and is thus consistent with the $RH_W$ and $T_W$ data in Fig. 3.

To summarize, in winter increased windspeed and decreased air temperature and relative humidity tend to improve background contrast particularly in the near infrared, while at the same time increasing image degradation via turbulence effects. Forward scattering degradation is attributed to humidity rather than soil-derived aerosol effects. The background contrast improvement in the near infrared is typical of conditions where soil-derived aerosols do not play major roles, and results from the relatively small size of common background aerosols which scatter much less near infrared than visible light [1]. This description is typical of non-desert atmospheres in the absence of rain.

The summer results in Fig. 2 show that increased windspeed improves resolution while increased relative humidity and temperature degrade resolution at short wavelengths in particular. Fig. 3 indicates strong forward scattering effects involving all three meteorological parameters since they decrease at low spatial frequencies. The fact that the $W_S$ curve in Fig. 2 is positive rather than negative would appear to result from increased air mixing and reduction of turbulence MTF by wind, as discussed in [22]. The significant effect of windspeed on atmospheric turbulence is indicated by the positive values of $W_S$ at higher spatial frequencies in Fig. 3. This is in agreement with the microwave results [22] and is consistent with the winter model presented above. In winter, it is suggested above that increased windspeed increases image degradation through turbulence because wind disperses haze and thus increases humidity gradient. In summer, however, although the early mornings are quite humid relative humidity decreases very quickly to very dry conditions by about 9 - 10 a.m. [16]. Windspeed picks up around noon[16]. Thus, in summer windspeed has little if any effect on humidity gradient and its main effect is only decreased turbulence effects through increased air mixing. Consequently, while the winter result for wind speed disagrees with that of [22] regarding turbulence, the summer result is in complete agreement and reflects the complexity introduced by desert dust conditions.

The wavelength dependence of $W_S$ is determined primarily by forward scattering effects. Fig. 2 shows strong degradation of resolution in the near infrared since $W_S$ there drops so sharply. Extension further into the near infrared might even result in a negative regression coefficient despite the positive effect of windspeed on imaging via turbulence reduction. The forward scattering effects in summer brought about by increased windspeed are thus quite significant. This is quite consistent with comparisons of visible and near infrared imaging presented previously for these desert conditions [16,17]. The average airborne desert dust particle radius in summer is 3-4 um [16]. Because of the large size such particles scatter near infrared radiation much more than they do visible radation[19]. The curve for $T_S$ in Fig. 3 indicates that increased temperature decreases background contrast and leads to increased image degradation through forward scattering, as in winter.

However, Fig. 2 indicates that while in winter such degradation is primarily at infrared wavelengths, in summer the degradation via temperature is primarily at short wavelengths. The curves for $RH_s$ in Fig. 2 & 3 are similar to those for $T_s$ and suggest the effects of temperature and relative humidity on imaging are related also in summer. Increased humidity in summer degrades short wavelength resolution primarily. In the introduction it was pointed out that the size of haze droplets increases with time for high humidity conditions. Thus, in winter when it is humid for long periods of time the droplets tend to be larger than in summer, when it is humid only for short periods in the early morning. As temperature increases as the day wears on, evaporation of early morning dew is in the form of very small droplets primarily. The dry conditions as the day wears on prevent the size of such droplets from growing in summer. Consequently, background and forward scattering temperature and humidity image degradation tend to be at shorter wavelengths in summer. The long duration of high humidity in winter causes the droplets to grow in size, thus affecting longer wavelengths in particular.

However, the strong winds beginning typically at mid-day in summer [16] uplift many dry soil-derived particles into the atmosphere. Their large size (3-4 um radius) causes forward scattering image degradation of near infrared wavelengths in particular, as described above and by the $W_s$ curve in Fig. 2.

The negative relative humidity regression coefficients for summer in Figs. 2 and 3 are opposite from those to be expected from turbulence. In view of the above the main effect of humidity in summer on image degradation is seen to be short wavelength forward scattering effects as can be seen from the strong dip at about 20 lines·mrad$^{-1}$. Fig. 2 indicates regression coefficients for relative humidity in summer and winter are of opposite sign. With Fig. 3 we can see that there is no contradiction since the spatial frequency analysis indicates that the primary effect of relative humidity is on turbulence (high spatial frequencies) in winter and on forward scattering (low spatial frequencies) in summer.

In summary, in desert atmosphere (summer) increased windspeed and decreased temperature and relative humidity improve background contrast particularly at shorter wavelengths. This spectral result is opposite to that of winter (non-desert atmospheres). Increased desert windspeed decreases image degradation via turbulence; however, it increases image degradation significantly via forward scattering effects, particularly in the near infrared, as a result of the relatively large size of soil-derived particulates.

The wavelength dependence of imaging in summer (desert atmosphere) tends to be opposite to that in winter (non-desert atmosphere) over the spectral region used in these measurements. This is attributed to the role of the large soil-derived desert dust particulates airborne in the dry summer season. Their size and concentration increased with windspeed. This causes both background contrast and aerosol forward scattering degradation of image quality to be worst at near infrared wavelengths during periods of high concentration of such particles, such as in the afternoons when windspeed is relatively high. Earlier in the day, when windspeed is low, background contrast and aerosol forward scattering image degradation is worst at shorter wavelengths, as is typical of non-desert environments, because of the small size of aerosols.

Using Figures 2 and 3, substitution of typical values of temperature, relative humidity, and windspeed into (10) indicates overall image quality as determined by the MCFA criteria tends to be somewhat better at near infrared wavelengths in non-desert and at shorter wavelengths in desert atmospheres.

A start has been made on predicting imaging resolution in accordance with meteorological prediction inputs, using regression coefficient calculations. These calculations have been carried out to show both wavelength dependent and spatial frequency-dependent effects of air temperature, relative humidity, and windspeed. Analysis of spatial frequency regression coefficients permits individual determination of effects of each meteorological parameter on background contrast, forward scattering, and turbulence. Thus, we know not only the effect of each meteorological parameter on imaging resolution but also the mechanism of effect. This interplay between wavelength and spacial frequency dependences permits development of a model on a quantitative basis to describe the interrelationships of meteorological and imaging resolution parameters. Although some of the results here disagree with those in literature [22] which pertain to non-desert atmospheres, the Fourier spatial frequency analysis permits quantitative explanations here as to the reasons and circumstances for the deviations in behavior from those recorded in the literature. This diagnostic tool should be useful in understanding the interactions between optical and meteorological parameters under different climatic conditions.

Here, they have been compared for winter and summer which correspond to non-desert and dry desert atmospheres respectively.

## REFERENCES

1. N. S. Kopeika, Appl. Opt. 16, 2422 (1977), 1162 (1978).

2. N. S. Kopeika, Appl. Opt. 20, 1532 (1981).

3. N. S. Kopeika and J. Bordogna, Proc. IEEE 58, 1571 (1970).

4. L. Levi, Applied Optics/Volume 2, Wiley, New York, 1980.

5. G. B. Parrent, Jr. and B. J. Thompson, Physical Optics Notebook, Society of Photo-optical Instrumentation Engineers, Bellingham, WA. 1969, p. 21.

6. H. L. Snyder, "Image quality and observer performance," in Perception of Displayed Information, Plenum, New York, 1973, pp. 87-100.

7. N. Jensen, Optical and Photographic Reconnaissance Systems, Wiley, New York, 1968, p. 44.

8. R. E. Huffnegel and N. R. Stanley, J. Opt. Soc. Amer., 54, 52 (1964).

9. D. L. Fried, J. Opt. Soc. Amer. 56, 1372 (1966).

10. E. M. Patterson and D. A. Gillette, J. Geophys. Rev. 82 2074 (1981).

11. R. L. Lutomirski, Appl. Opt. 17, 3915 (1978).

12. H. T. Yura, Appl. Opt. 10, 114 (1971).

13. A. Ishimaru, Appl. Opt. 17, 348 (1978).

14. M. V. Kabanov, Atm. and Ocean Phys. 4, 478 (1968).

15. P. Y. Ganich and S. A. Mukarevich, Atm. and Ocean Phys. 8, 462 (1972).

16. N. S. Kopeika, S. Solomon, and Y. Gencay, J. Opt. Soc. Amer. 71, 892 (1981).

17. N. S. Kopeika, J. Opt. Soc. Amer. 72, 548 (1982).

18. N. S. Kopeika, J. Opt. Soc. Amer. 72, 1092 (1982).

19. E. J. McCartney, Optics of the Atmosphere, Wiley, New York 1976, ch. 6.

20. S. T. Henderson, Daylight and its Spectrum, 2nd ed., Adam Hilger, Bristol, England, 1977 ch. 9.

21. F. L. Crow, F. A. Davis and M. W. Maxfield, Statistics Manual, Dover, 1958.

22. J. A. Schiavone, Radio Sci. 18, 369 (1983).

23. N. S. Kopeika, A.N. Seidman, I. Dinstein, C. Tarnasha, R. Amir, and Y. Biton, "Meteorological effects on image quality: reconnaissance considerations," in Airborne Reconnaissance VIII, Paul Henkel and F. R. LaGesse, Editors, Proc. SPIE, vol. 496 in press 1984.

# ANALYSIS OF EXPLOSIVES IN THE ISRAEL FORENSIC SCIENCE LABORATORY

S. Zitrin
Criminal Identification Division
Israel Police HQ, Jerusalem, Israel

This paper reviews 15 years of activity in explosives analysis in the Israel National Police Analytical Chemistry Laboratory. Until the late 1960's only a limited use of explosives in criminal activity in Israel was recorded. After 1967 there was an increase in the criminal use of explosives, mainly in politically related terrorism but also in internal disputes in the Israeli underworld. Today more than 300 cases of explosives are handled in the laboratory each year. Two types of analysis are perfomed: 1)identification of explosives which were not detonated, and (2) identification of explosives after a blast. Results from the first group are used primarily for court evidence, while those from the second group constitue an aid to the investigator. Identification of undetonated explosives is made by the usual methods employed in modern analytical chemistry --- chromatographic (TLC, GC, HPLC) and spectrometric (IR,MS) for organic compunds, and "wet" chemistry, IR spectrometry, SEM/EDX, and XRD for inorganic compounds. The most challenging cases are those where one has to identify a "totally unknown" compound whose analytical data do not appear in available literature. In post-explosion analysis the crucial step is the extraction and purification of the explosive residues from the debris. Analysis is often based solely upon chromatographic methods.

This article reviews fifteen years of activity in the field of explosives analysis. The work has been done in the analytical laboratory of the Israeli police. Until the late sixties, the use of explosives in criminal activity in Israel was rare. It was limited mainly to few cases involving illegal fishing with explosives. The six-days war in 1967 was followed by a sharp increase in the illegal use of explosives. Today more than 300 cases per year are being handled by the explosives analysts in our laboratory.

Explosives have been employed in two general types of cases:

1. politically-related terrorists acts.
2. settling disputes among Israeli criminals.

As will be shown later, one of the purposes of an explosive identification is to help the investigator to decide which of the two types of the crimes had occurred.

The analysis of explosives in the laboratory could be classified as follows:

1. identification of an unexploded explosives.
2. identification of explosives after an explosion had occured.

Obviously, the first type is technically much easier. The amount of the sample is usually sufficient for the analysis and problems of contaminations are minimal. Results from this type of analysis are mainly used for court evidence - to prove that a suspect material contains an explosive. The second type- post explosion analysis - is technically much more complicated. The amount of the original explosive in post-explosion scenes is often very small and its exact distribution among the debris is unknown. The debris usually contains highly contaminated items, thus making extraction and purification procedures very difficult. Results from post-explosion analysis are rarely needed for court evidence but they could be important for the investigation, helping to decide the motive or background of the explosion. Some explosives-either home-made mixtures or from Eastern-European origins-have been almost exclusively connected to terrorist acts related to the Arab-Israeli conflict. Explosives employed by criminals of the Israeli underworld are usually stolen from the Israeli Defense Forces.

Identification of unexploded explosives is performed by the usual methods of modern qualitative analytical chemistry. For organic compounds these include chromatographic (thin-layer; gas; liquid) and spectrometric (infrared; mass spectrometry) methods. For inorganic compounds we use "classical" spot tests, SEM-EDS (scanning electron microscopy combined with energy dispersive spectroscopy) and XRD (X-ray diffraction). The most challenging cases in the identification of unexploded explosives are those where one has to identify a "totally unknown" compound whose analytical data do not appear in the available literature. Examples are some exotic organic peroxide which have been identified by us.

In post-explosion cases, a most important step is the clean-up of the explosive residues. This step often includes extractions by organic solvents and elutions through chromatographic columns. Following this, the analysis is often based only on chromatographic methods (mainly TLC). The small amount of the sample and the high degree of contamination usually prevent the use of IR spectrometry. There is no doubt that if one is to use a reliable method combined to the chromatographic methods, mass spectrometry will be the method of choice. In principle, the on-line combination of liquid-chromatography and mass spectrometry (LC-MS) seems most promising. Unlike gas chromatography (GC), LC operates in room temperatures so that thermally labile explosives do not decompose.

Mass spectrometry is the best method available for the identification of sub-microgram amounts of organic compounds. The "on-line" combination is now commercially available. Nevertheless we feel that the state of art of LC-MS makes it unsuitable for use in routine cases of post-explosion analysis. This conclusion is not based upon our own experience (we do not have an operating LC-MS system) but on information from other groups.

We have been recently trying a combination of capillary column GC-MS for post-explosion identification of explosives. It is true that certain explosives - especially some nitrate esters and nitramines - undergo thermal decomposition under G C conditions. However, these decompositions could often be minimized by using gentler conditions (lower temperatures; "on-column" injection). Also, the use of shorter capillary columns will decrease the extent of decomposition, though on the expense of the chromatographic resolution. Obviously, the state of art of capillary column GC-MS is better than that of LC-MS.

If one does not want to base his results only on chromatographic method, we believe that capillary column GC-MS could be successful in routine analysis of most organic explosives in post-explosion cases.

# RECENT ADVANCES IN LASER LATENT FINGERPRINT DEVELOPMENT

E. Roland Menzel
Center for Forensic Studies
Texas Tech, University
Lubbock, Texas   79409, USA

Recent advances made in development of latent finger-prints by laser at Texas Tech University's Center for Forensic studies will be presented.  These include:

1. Development of physical and chemical treatments for difficult surfaces such as brown paper, cardboard and wood, that lend themselves to utilization of the UV output of Ar-lasers.  These treatments include vapor staining with 9-methylan-thracene and chemical treatment with dansyl chloride.

2. Exploration of physical and chemical treatments tailored to the use of frequency-doubled Nd: YAG lasers.  These include solution staining with 3,3' - diethyloxadicarbocyanine iodide and chemical treatment with benzo (f) ninhydrin.  (Work done in collaboration with Dr. Joseph Almog, Israel National Police.)

3. Use of hydrolytic enzymes (mainly trypsin) that break down inert constituents of fingerprint residue into aminoacids for purposes of enhancement of fingerprint development.

4. Computer image processing of developed latent fingerprints in conjunction with video recording with image-intensified TV cameras.

## THE BASIS FOR LASER LATENT FINGERPRINT DEVELOPMENT

Laser detection of latent fingerprints is often regarded as a procedure on equal footing with, for instance, cyanoacrylate ester fuming, ninhydrin treatment, or dusting. I should like to state from the outset that I regard laser fingerprint development as a general method that differs fundamentally from the conventional ones, one that constitutes a different general approach to latent fingerprint detection.  To see why this is so, let us consider, for example, a latent print on a white surface developed with black powder.  Ambient light is reflected (scattered) from the paper surrounding the fingerprint and ridges, but not the ridges themselves because the black powder absorbs the incident light. Absorption/reflectance thus constitutes the essence of conventional fingerprint development. In case of a faintly developed print, when very little powder adheres to the fingerprint, ridge sites reflect incident light only very slightly less than the surrounding paper. Thus, the detection of the print amounts to detection of a small difference between two large signals, and this is as a general rule a poor detection technique. Consider now the opposite situation, namely that in which no light is seen by the eye (or camera) as coming from the surroundings of the latent print, but only light from the ridges reaches the eye or camera. In this situation, detecting a weakly developed print means detection of a small signal. This is far easier to accomplish than the detection of a small difference between two large signals. The human eye attests very clearly to this.

Laser induced fluorescence, in which the laser light scattered from the examined surface is blocked by a filter that, however, transmits the fingerpring fluorescence is a way of approaching the situation in which light only from the fingerprint ridges reaches the eye or photographic camera, thus necessarily providing vastly enhanced sensitivity over the absorption/reflectance approach. Similarly, fluorescence detection in, for instance, chromatography is more sensitive than absorption detection.

Let us now consider the main conventional procedures for latent fingerprint detection that have been developed in this century, as well as some promising recent procedures. The main ones are ninhydrin (developed in 1954 by two Swedish biochemists), used primarily on paper, cyanoacrylate ester fuming (developed in Japan in the mid-seventies) for latent prints mainly on smooth (non-white) surfaces, and gentian (crystal) violet (developed by the Italian police in the late sixties) for latent prints on the sticky side of adhesive tapes. Procedures for very specific instances include the iodine/silver plate procedure for latent prints on skin and benzidine or o-tolidine for fingerprints in blood. In the last decade, a number of promising procedures have been developed in England. They include autoradiography with $SO_2$ vapor, vacuum evaporative deposition of zinc, solution deposition of molybdenum disulphide, and a solution development system that involves silver, a ferrous/ferric redox system and a detergent. This last procedure, designed for development of latent prints on paper that has been wetted, is particularly interesting. A very promising electrochemical procedure for development of latent prints on brass cartridge cases was recently developed in Israel.

All of the above-cited procedures have one aspect in common: they are procedures designed for specific situations, i.e., they are not general methods aimed at development of latent fingerprints on all surfaces. Laser latent fingerprint development, which should more generally be called fingerprint development by photoluminescence, on the other hand, is a general method. It involves a range of procedures, namely development by inherent fingerprint fluorescence (which has no conventional analogue), cyanoacrylate ester/dye staining (the analogue to conventional ninhydrin treatment), and a host of procedures for special instances, including an o-tolidine procedure for fingerprints in blood, vapor staining for fingerprints on skin, a time-resolved procedure that exploits delayed fluorescence or phosphorescence to eliminate fluorescence background, etc. To date, lasers have been necessary to induce the fluorescence resulting from these treatments with sufficient intensity for the detection of latent prints. However, since the early 80's, there have been attempts to replace the laser as the source for fluorescence excitation with conventional lamps. Because a very small portion of the lamp spectrum must be isolated, which presents many problems, these lamps have so far not been shown to be competitive with lasers in sensitivity. However, this may yet change. In any event, it has by now been amply demonstrated that fingerprint development by luminescence, using laser excitation, provides much superior sensitivity over the conventional procedures. Thus, the laser-luminescence method is surely this century's most significant advance in latent fingerprint development methodology.

CURRENT LASER PROCEDURES

The three most widely applicable laser procedures that have reached the maturity for routine use are detection by inherent fingerprint fluorescence,[1] solution dye staining after cyanoacrylate ester fuming [2] and ninhydrin/$ZnCl_2$.[3] Dusting with fluorescent powder is only rarely employed in laboratory examination but is of interest at crime scenes. At first, only Ar-lasers were used in fingerprint work. In the last three years, however, Cu-vapor and frequency-doubled Nd: YAG lasers have started to see use as well.[4] The latter laser is of particular interest because it is portable, hence useful at crime scenes. Because of power and flexibility in terms of the available lasing wavelengths (near UV, blue, green) and ease of pumping of dye lasers, the Ar-laser continues to be very attractive.

## RECENT ADVANCES

The above-cited three procedures for laser detection of latent fingerprints render the laser method useful for a large majority of surfaces one usually has to contend with. However, certain surfaces fluoresce very strongly under blue-green illumination and are thus not amenable to these procedures. They include brown paper and cardboard, certain leathers and wood. These surfaces do not show strong fluorescence under UV illumination, however. Accordingly, we have explored procedures compatible with examination by Ar-lasers operating in the near UV or even ordinary UV lamps. Two procedures have been developed, namely vapor staining (after cyanoacrylate ester or together with it) with 9-methylanthracene and chemical treatment with dansyl-chloride. The former is an analogue to vapor or solution staining with rhodamine 6G, while the latter is the analogue to the ninhydrin/$ZnCl_2$ procedure. The details of these procedures are presented in an upcoming article in the Journal of Forensic Sciences.[5]

The operating wavelength (532 nm) of the frequency-doubled Nd:YAG laser is not well suited to the ninhydrin/$ZnCl_2$ procedure (which works well, however, with Cu-vapor and Ar-lasers). To remedy this shortcoming, we have investigated a series of ninhydrin analogues which are as good as ninhydrin in the sense of reaction with aminoacids of fingerprint residue with the aim of tailoring the spectroscopic properties for compatibility with the Nd:YAG laser. Benzo (f) ninhydrin was found to be excellent in this respect.[6] At times, replacement of $ZnCl_2$ by $Cd (No_3)_2$ can also be effective together with ninhydrin or ninhydrin or ninhydrin analogues.

In instances in which background fluorescence is prohibitively strong when rhodamine 6G or rhodamine B solution or vapor staining is used together with the frequency-doubled Nd:YAG laser, solution staining with 3,3'-diethyloxadicarbocyanine iodide (DODC) can be effective.[4]

Even the very sensitive ninhydrin/$ZnCl_2$ method is often not able to develop faint latent prints on porous items such as paper. Thus, we have continued to search for procedures to enhance the sensitivity of this procedure. Also, certain surfaces, including skin and cloth, continue to be generally intractable. It appears that latent prints on such surfaces will likely have to be transferred to more tractable surfaces (in the manner analogous to iodine/silver plate lifting) for subsequent chemical treatment. Because the lifting step will leave most of the fingerprint residue behind, sensitivity is a critical issue in the subsequent treatment, i.e., there is considerable similarity in the situation to that of very faint prints on paper. We have thus explored the use of hydrolytic enzymes to enhance the sensitivity of ninhydrin treatment. In our earlier preliminary study,[7] we encountered problems when developing old prints on paper. These problems have now been overcome and enzyme enhancement of latent print development can now be achieved also for old prints. The details will be presented in a forthcoming article.[8] Figure 1 shows an example of laser fingerprint development by ninhydrin/$ZnCl_2$ and shows the enhancement achieved by enzyme (trypsin) pre-treatment.

In some instances, latent fingerprints developed by laser-induced fluorescence are too weak to be seen by eye but can be detected by image intensified TV camera.[4] This form of electronic fingerprint recordation lends itself quite naturally to digitization, hence computer image processing. The Center for Forensic Studies of Texas Tech University has just initiated a research project dealing with fingerprint detail enhancement by computer. Preliminary results indicate that adaptive binarization may be a very suitable approach.

REFERENCES

1. E. R. Menzel, Fingerprint Detection with Lasers, Marcel Dekker, N.Y., 1980.

2. E. R. Menzel, J. A. Burt, T. W. Sinor, W. B. Tubach-Ley, and K. J. Jordan, J. Forensic Sci. 28(2), 307 (1983).

3. D. W. Herod and E. R. Menzel, J. Forensic Sci. 27(3), 513 (1982).

4. E. R. Menzel, J. Forensic Sci. 30(2), 1985.

5. J. A. Burt and E. R. Menzel, J. Forensic Sci. 30(2), 1985.

6. E. R. Menzel and J. Almog, J. Forensic Sci. 30(2), 1985

7. E. R. Menzel, J. Everse, K. Everse, T. W. Sinor, and J. A. Burt, J. Forensic Sci. 29(1), 99 (1984).

8. K. Everse and E. R. Menzel, to be published in J. Forensic Sci.


This material is based upon work supported by the National Science Foundation under Grant CHE 83 13527. Any opinions, findings, and conclusions or recommendations expressed in this publication are those of the author and do not necessarily reflect the views of the National Science Foundation

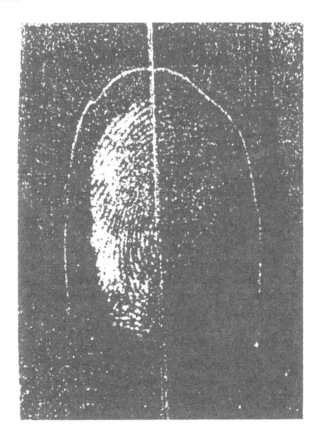

Fig. 1  Latent fingerprint under laser illumination after ninhydrin/$ZnCl_2$ treatment (right half) and after trypsin/ninhydrin/$ZnCl_2$ treatment (left half).

# SPEEDOMETER EXAMINATION FOR
## TRAFFIC ACCIDENT RECONSTRUCTION

Ilya M. Zeldes, Ph.D.
Supervisor, Criminalistics Laboratory
Office of Attorney General
Pierre, South Dakota 57501, USA

A very important factor to be determined in any traffic accident investigation is the speed of the vehicle at impact. One of the methods to determine vehicle speed at impact is to examine the speedometer. The laboratory examination of the speedometer consists of observation, microscopical analysis under normal lighting conditions and ultraviolet light, and microphotography. In cases when skidmarks are available and the vehicle involved in traffic accident collided with another object, speedometer examination is a sufficient and necessary step in determination of the actual speed before sliding began.

A very important factor to be determined in any accident investigation is the speed of the vehicle at impact. It can be established in a few different ways, among them, an examination of the vehicle and estimation of the damages it sustained from the collision is used frequently. In practice, these estimates are made by comparing the damages with those observed in other accidents in which vehicles collided with fixed objects at known speeds (1). However, in such cases estimations depend more on the officer's guess, experience and familiarity with the results of similar collisions than on objective calculations.

One of the methods used to determine vehicle speed at impact is to examine the speedometer. All automobiles are equipped with a device that indicates speed in either miles per hour (MPH) or kilometers per hour (KMH) and is easily viewed by the driver (2, 3). The visible part of this instrument consists of a numbered dial and needle or indicator. Usually, the scale and numbers on the dial's background are white, but they can also be multicolored, particularly on the newer models designed to indicate both mph and kmh. The needle is coated usually with an orange or red luminous paint.

The above mentioned instruments have been installed in vehicles in one form or another since their origin, yet they are seldom used to determine the speed of vehicles involved in accidents. By examining the speedometer, the speed of the vehicle at the time of impact may be determined, but it should be remembered that a direct speedometer reading of a stuck needle after an accident may or may not be the impact speed of the vehicle. Many times the indicator became jammed or stuck indicating a speed but it is usually at or near zero. The amount of damage to the speedometer and the vehicle may suggest that the direct reading is or is not valid (4).

In some instances, head-on or fixed-object collisions may be so severe that the speedometer needle makes a mark (stamp) on the dial as it pushes against the face of the speedometer during impact. This stamp or mark (so called "speed mark") sometimes can be seen with the naked eye.

There are also other marks which could be used for speed determination even though the needle does not stay at the point it struck the dial. These marks are the paint smears on the dial which the needle may have left at the time of impact. If the vehicle is involved in a collision from the front or either side, there may be enough forward momentum to cause these pain smears. However, these pain smears are not usually detected by the naked eye or a magnifying glass; laboratory examination is necessary.

The laboratory examination consists of observation, microscopical analysis under normal lighting conditions, ultraviolet light, and photomicrography. During the laboratory examination, the speedometer is initially observed and photographed under normal light. Examination under binocular stereoscopical microscope in some instances could reveal some indentations or scratches on the dial of the speedometer. Usually, no superimposition of foreign paint can be seen on the dial during this observation. The next step is examination under ultraviolet light. If there are any transfers of luminous paint particles from the needle to the speedometer dial, they can usually be seen quite easily when observed under ultraviolet light through the stereoscopical microscope.

Sometimes a different "speed mark" can be found on the speedometer dial. This is a "polishing sign" produced by the plastic needle when it touches the painted surface of the dial. This mark can be detected by oblique reflected light at various angles.

A laboratory method of a speedometer examination for determination of vehicle speed at the time of impact was developed in the South Dakota Criminalistics Laboratory (5, 6, 7). This method has been used successfully since 1979 and we have testified on many cases in municipal, state, and federal courts (8).

As our experience shows the success of any speedometer examination in the laboratory, and its use as evidence is going to be valid only if the speedometer is properly removed from the damaged vehicle by the investigating officer. Occasionally, the speedometer can be cut out of the wreckage easily so that it can be taken to a laboratory for examination.

In some instances, when paint particles are spread on the large part of the dial, it is impossible to determine the position of the needle and speed at the time of impact. In many other cases, when the paint particles are distributed on the dial as a straight line or as a row of dots from the pivot point of the needle outward to the edge of the dial, it is easy to determine the place of needle-dial contact, and consequently, the reading of the speedometer or the speed of vehicle at the time of impact.

In cases, when skidmarks are available and the vehicle involved in the traffic accident collided with another object, speedometer examination is a sufficient and necessary step in determination of the actual speed before sliding began. The speedometer examination can determine the vehicle speed immediately prior to an impact. Therefore, this speed should be used to estimate how far the car would have had to be going to continue to slide to a stop without hitting anything. Then these estimated "additional skidmarks" must be added to the original prime skidmarks and the value of the combined extended skidmarks should be substituted into a well-known formula for speed determination (9, 10) or nomograph (11) for actual speed determination.

A word of caution must be added. This speed calculation is, of course, merely an estimation. But it is a scientific estimation, based on well-known laws of physics and modern sophisticated laboratory examination. Therefore it is much more accurate and reliable than guesstimation, still common in some traffic accident reconstructions.

## REFERENCES

1. Traffic Accident Investigation and Physical Evidence, by D. R. McGrew, Charles C. Thomas, Publisher, Springfield, Illinois, 1976.

2. Society of Automotive Engineers Handbook, 1981.

3. Automobile Engineer's Reference Book, George News Ltd., London, England.

4. Highway Collision Analysis, by James C. Collins and Joe L. Morris, Charles C. Thomas, Publisher, Springfield, Illinois.

5. Speedometer Examination: An Aid in Accident Investigation, by Dale Stoner and Ilya Zeldes, FBI Law Enforcement Bulletin, March 1980, pp. 11-15.

6. New Twist in Application of an Old and Not so Old Technology, by Ilya Zeldes. Paper presented at the Midwestern Association of Forensic Scientists Meeting, October 16, 1981, Overland Park, Kansas.

7. Examination of Tool Marks on a Speedometer Dial, by Ilya Zeldes. Paper presented at the Association of Firearm and Tool Mark Examiners Meeting, May 11, 1982, Orlando, Florida.

8. U.S. v. Larry L. Archambault, 670 F. 2d No. 2, 800-802.

9. Autotechnical Expertise, by V.A. Bekasov et al, Juridical Literature, Moscow, 1967.

10. Traffic Accident Investigation Manual, by J. Stannard Baker, The Traffic Institute, Northwestern University, Evanston, Illinois, 1976.

11. Simple Estimates of Vehicle Stopping Distances and Speed from Skidmarks, by J. Stannard Baker, The Traffic Institute, Northwestern University, Evanston, Illinois,,1981

# DETERMINATION OF FIRING DISTANCE BY TOTAL NITRITE

Mark Ravreby
Criminal Identification Division
Israel National Police Headquarters
Jerusalem, Israel

Modifications of the Walker test in the physical arrangement of transferring the gunshot residue to photographic paper are described. In addition to regular cloth exhibits, these modifications make it possible to determine firing distance on semi-permeable and impermeable objects such a military cloth belts, thick coats and wood without damaging the exhibit. Alkaline hydrolysis of the unburned and/or partially decomposed smokeless gunpowder is also discussed, which significantly increases the sensitivity of the test. In some cases the sensitivity of the test. In some cases the sensitivity of the firing distance is increased to three meters where the regular Walker test has no sensitivity even at near contact range. Reactions, limitations, interferences and applications are also discussed.

One of the most common methods for determining firing distance based on the nitrite distribution pattern is the Walker test[1], which was first reported in the literature in 1937. Two major disadvantages to this method are that it requires easy access to the exit side of the bullet entrance hole and the target material must be readily permeable to acetic acid. In cases where the bullet entrance hole is in the chest region of a shirt or in the central back portion of a shirt no difficulties are encountered. However, when the bullet entrance hole is near the shoulder or on thick sweaters and coats, difficult access to the rear side of the bullet entrance hole and/or lack of permeability of the exhibit to acetic acid may make it virtually impossible to perform a Walker test.

The Walker test is sensitive to inorganic nitrite ion. Certain types of smokeless powder ammunition do not contain inorganic nitrite as an oxidizing agent in the primer and as a result no nitrite distribution pattern is obtained with the Walker test even at near contact firing distances. With test shots fired at close range, gunpowder particles are clearly visible on the cloth target which contain organic nitro groups. Alkalin hydrolysis of these particles decomposes the nitrocellulose and/or nitroglycerine to a variety of products, amongst them inorganic nitrite ion. As a result the total nitrite is determined, i.e. inorganic nitrite ion plus hydrolyzable nitrite ion.

## EXPERIMENTAL

Reagents - A solution of 8% alcoholic KOH, sulfanilic acid 5 g/l in 30% aqueous acetic acid, and napthylamine 1 g/l in 33% aqueous acetic acid. Photographic paper is stripped of its silver salts by washing in a sodium thiosulfate solution followed by thoroughly washing in water.

Procedure - The exhibit containing a bullet entrance hole is sprayed with 8% alcoholic KOH and placed in a drying oven at 110 - 120° for fifteen minutes. Simultaneously photographic paper which has been stripped of its silver salts is sensitized with Griess reagent for 5 - 10 minutes by placing the paper in a plastic tray and adding two parts of the sulfanilic acid solution to one part of the napthylamine solution. The exhibit is placed on a clean white cloth with the bullet entrance hole facing up. The moist sensitized photographic paper is placed with the emulsion side down onto the exhibit. A clean white cloth is placed above the photographic paper and the sandwich arrangement is ironed at moderate heat for approximately five minutes. The photographic paper is then removed and bright red orange spots develop where nitrite ions were present.

Figure 1 shows the physical arrangement for the classical Walker determination and the modified arrangement. The principles involved in the classical Walker arrangement are that the heat from ironing causes the acetic acid to permeate the cloth exhibit from the rear side of the bullet entrance hole. The nitrite particles around the bullet entrance hole are in firm contact with photographic paper which has been stripped of its silver salts with a thiosulfate solution and sensitized to nitrite ions with a reagent such as Griess reagent. This dried, sensitized paper is generally stocked in advance. A combination of the inorganic nitrite ion, acetic acid and Griess reagent results in diazotization and coupling to produce an azo dye.

In the modified arrangement the freshly sensitized, moist photographic paper has absorbed a sufficient amount of acetic acid to permit the diazotization and coupling reactions to occur. Under heat and pressure from the iron, the nitrite ions around the bullet hole are in firm contact with the sensitized photographic paper and an azo dye develops. Using this modified arrangement nitrite distribution patterns were obtained on exhibits such as thick cloth belts used by military and police personnel (figure 2) and on thick wooden planks (figure 3). This would be impossible to do with the classical Walker arrangement.

The reactions involved in diazotization and coupling with Griess reagent are illustrated in reactions 1 and 2. Reaction 1 proceeds rapidly but sometimes an undesirable side reaction occurs and the naphthylamine undergoes diazotization and self-coupling to produce a brown azo dye (reactions 3 & 4). This undesirable side reaction can easily be prevented by adding a large excess of sulfanilic acid. Generally the sulfanilic acid solution and the naphthylamine solution are prepared in advance as stock solutions. The optimum ratio of the sulfanilic acid solution to the naphthylamine solution can readily be determined by a simple spot test using one drop of a 10 ppm nitrite solution. Numerous other reagents have been proposed and used for nitrite detection [2-4] but almost all of them are based on the general reactions of diazotization and coupling.

There are several sources of inorganic nitrite ion in gunshot residue. One source is from the barium nitrate frequently used as an oxidizing agent in primers. Its decomposition is illustrated in reaction 5. Black powder consists of potassium nitrate, carbon and sulfur. A similar decomposition of the potassium nitrate produces nitrite ion.

Most types of modern gunpowder consist of smokeless powder. Single base smokeless powder contains nitrocellulose and double base smokeless powder contains nitrocellulose and nitroglycerins. When these compounds decompose the products are gaseous and primarily consist of carbon dioxide, carbon monoxide, water, oxygen, nitrogen and various nitrogen oxides (reactions 6 & 7). When a cartridge is fired, in addition to these gaseous decomposition products, there are partial decomposition products and gunpowder particles which have not decomposed. Nitrocellulose and nitroglycerine which contain organic nitro groups are a partial source of inorganic nitrite ion. Reactions involving diazotization and coupling are only sensitive to inorganic nitrite ion and do not react with these organic nitro groups. However, alkaline hydrolysis of nitroglycerine and nitrocellulose will result in nitrite ion being liberated.

As can be seen from the hydrolysis reactions 8 and 9, the reaction products are varied but do not yield glycerine and nitrate salts of the cation of the base. What is of primary interest is that inorganic nitrite ion is amongst the hydrolysis products.

Nitrocellulose is essentially a hybrid between dinitrocellulose and trinitrocellulose. Under alkaline hydrolysis the products are numerous and varied including complete breakdown of the cyclic rings[5]. Similar to nitroglycerine hydrolysis, cellulose and nitrate salt of the cation of the base are not the reaction products (reaction 10). Again what is of primary importance is that inorganic nitrite ion is amongst the hydrolysis products.

A good example which illustrates the advantages of the total nitrite determination consists of test shots fired at 50 cm from an Uzi submachine gun at cloth targets using old Israel Military Industries 9 mm parabellum ammunition. This type of ammunition which was produced on a large scale until the late 1970's used potassium chlorate as an oxidizing agent and was a double base smokeless gunpowder. For reasons not fully understood the decomposition products yield essentially no inorganic nitrite ion and even at very close firing distances no nitrite distribution pattern is detected when the regular Walker test is performed (figure 4a). This is true even in cases where the gunpowder flakes are clearly visible on the target material. Using the total nitrite method a very distinct nitrite pattern is obtained at 50 cm (figure 4b) and a nitrite pattern is detectable at firing distances of 2-2.5 meters. As a result of this observation all firing distance determinations are routinely performed in Israel using the total nitrite method.

Interferences consist of certain types of blue jeans which react with the Griess reagent, certain types of shoe polish and nitrocellulose lacquer. Inorganic nitrite ion fron non-gunshot residue sources and organic compounds which hydrolyze to produce nitrite ion but are unrelated to gunshot residue are additional limitations to this method.

As a result of modifications in the physical arrangement for transferring nitrite residues to photographic paper and modifications in the method of sensitizing the photographic paper it is possible to determine firing distances on thick, impermeable objects. Hydrolysis of the gunshot residue can significantly increase the sensitivity of the test.

REFERENCES

1. Walker, J. T., "Chemistry and Legal Medicine", New Eng. J. Med., 216, 1024-1037, 1937

2. Walker, J. T., "Bullet Holes and Chemical Residues in Shooting Cases", J. Crim. Law and Criminology, 31, 497-521, 19

3. Sawicki, E., Stanley, T. W., Pfaff, J., D'Amico, A., "Comparison of Fifty Two Spectrophotometric Methods for the Determination of Nitrite", Talanta, Vol. 10, 641-655, 1963

4. Maiti, P. C., "Powder Patterns Around Bullet Holes in Blood-Stained Articles", J. of Forensic Science Society, Vol. 13, 1971, 1973

5. Urbanski, "Chemistry and Technology of Explosives", vol 2, Pergamon Press, 304, 1965

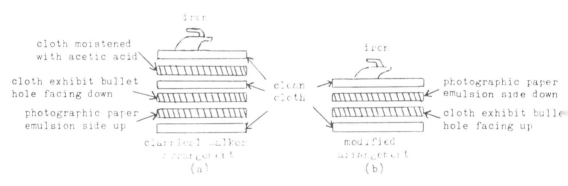

Figure 1 The physical arrangement of the exhibit for nitrite determination by (a) the classical Walker arrangement and (b) the modified arrangement.

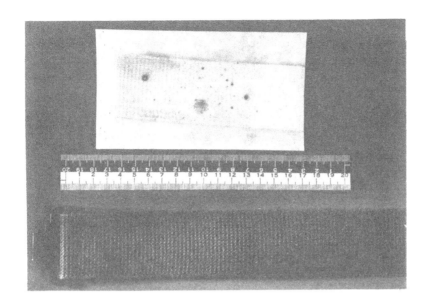

Figure 2  Nitrite determination on cloth belt.  Test shot fired using a Webley Mark IV revolver with 0.38 Browning S & W ammunition at a range of 40 cm.

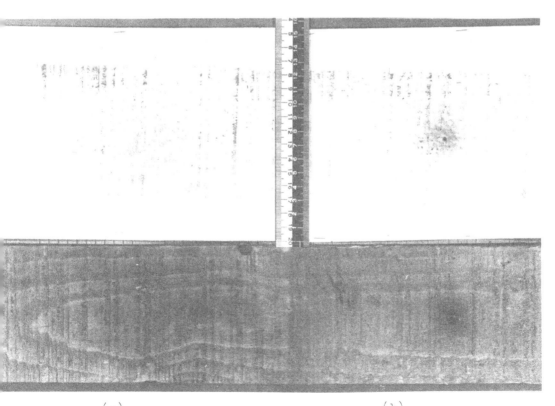

(a)                                                (b)

Figure 3  Nitrite determination on wooden plank.  Test shots fired using a Star pistol with 9mm parabellum Luger W-W ammunition at a range of (a) 5 cm (b) 20 cm

(a)                                   (b)

Figure 4  Test shots fired on white cloth using an Uzi submachine gun with 9 mm parabellum Israel Military Industries ammunition manufactured in 1968 at a range of 50 cm:  (a) nitrite determination without hydrolysi (b) nitrite determination with hydrolysis.

Reactions

$$NO_2^{\ominus} + \text{(}\alpha\text{ napthyl amine, }-NH_2\text{)} \xrightarrow[\text{slow reaction}]{CH_3COOH} \text{(diazonium salt, }-N\equiv N^{\oplus}\text{)} \qquad (3)$$

nitrite ion   $\alpha$ napthyl amine   diazonium salt

$$\text{(diazonium salt, }-N\equiv N^{\oplus}\text{)} + \text{(}\alpha\text{ napthyl amine, }-NH_2\text{)} \longrightarrow \text{(}-N=N-\ -NH_2\text{, brown azo dye)} \qquad (4)$$

diazonium salt   $\alpha$ napthyl amine   brown azo dye

$$Ba(NO_3)_2 \longrightarrow Ba^{++} + 2NO_2^{\ominus} + O_2 \qquad (5)$$

nitrite ion

$$4C_3H_5(ONO_2)_3 \longrightarrow 12\ CO_2 + 10H_2O + 6N_2 + O_2 \qquad (6)$$

nitroglycerine

$$C_{12}H_{14}O_4(ONO_2)_6 \longrightarrow 3CO_2 + 9CO + 7H_2O + 3N_2 \qquad (7)$$

trinitrocellulose

$$\begin{array}{c} CH_2ONO_2 \\ | \\ CHONO_2 \\ | \\ CH_2ONO_2 \end{array} + 5KOH \xrightarrow[C_2H_5OH]{\Delta} KNO_3 + 2KNO_2 + CH_3COOK + HCOOK + 3H_2O \qquad (8)$$

$$\longrightarrow \text{aldehyde resins} + \begin{array}{c} COOH \\ | \\ COOH \end{array} + NH_3 \qquad (9)$$

nitroglycerine   oxalic acid

nitrocellulose

$$\xrightarrow[C_2H_5OH]{\Delta\ KOH} \begin{array}{l} NO_3^{\ominus} + NO_2^{\ominus} + CN^{\ominus} + NO + \\ NO_2 + CO + CO_2 + NH_3 + \\ \begin{array}{c} COOH \\ | \\ COOH \end{array} + HCOOH + HOOCCH_2CHOHCOOH + .. \end{array} \qquad (10)$$

malic acid

# A SIMPLE ADAPTATION OF THE MICROSPECTROPHOTOMETER DOCUSPEC TM/I FOR THE COMPARISON OF SMALL QUANTITIES OF LUMINESCENT MATERIALS

A. Zeichner
Toolmarks and Materials Laboratory
Criminal Identification Division
Israel Police Headquarters
Jerusalem, Israel

A simple method was developed to adapt a DocuSec TM/1 microspectrophotometer for miscrospectrofluorometry work in the visible range. The quartz halogen lamp provided for microspectrophotometry in the reflectance mode serves in combination with a Kodak 18A filter as an excitation source in the near UV range. The emission luminescence spectra may be obtained in the intensity versus wavelength mode. The software of the system may be adapted for quantitative matching of visually similar spectra.

A considerable number of studies were published recently, concerning the use of microspectrophotometry in the comparison and identification of small quantities of paints, inks and fibers ( (1-6) ). It seems, however, that much room is still left for studies of forensic applications in the field of microspectrofluorometry (7, 8).

The importance of such a technique in forensic investigations may be very significant in the comparison of small quantities of luminescent materials, e.g. fluorescent invisible detection materials, fluorescent color markers (highlighters), glass, fibers, optical whiteners etc. (9).

The purpose of this work was to demonstrate a simple way to adapt a microspectrophotometer Docuspec TM/1 for recording emission luminescence spectra, and, the discriminating power of this technique in comparing small quantities of luminescent materials.

EXPERIMENTAL

Instrumentation

The instrument used in this study was the recently introduced Nanometrics, Docuspec TM/I microspectrophotometer computerized system. The modified Olympus BHT microscope with bright and dark field (BF/DF) optics and with quartz halogen lamps for both reflectance and transmission work is used in the system. The system is equipped with a fixed measuring aperture resulting in a measurement area of 18x126 microns for the 20x objective and 9x63 microns for the 40x objective. The wavelength range of the system is 380 - 764 nm.

Excitation source

A standard attachment for fluorescence work may be available from Olympus Corp. It also includes a high pressure mercury vapor arc lamp illumination, which provides much more power in the U.V. range than a quartz halogen lamp. Our purpose, however, was to perform as few as possible modifications so as to enable a quick interchange of the system between the spectrophotometry and spectrofluorometry modes. It appears, that the quartz halogen illumination of 50W (provided for reflectance spectrophotometry) filtered by a Kodak 18A glass filter, supplies enough near U.V. intensity to record emission luminescence spectra with the Docuspec TM/I.

The important feature of the 18A filter (which is ordinarily intended for the photography of reflected U.V.) for our purpose is that it transmits all the near U.V. spectrum while cutting off the visible part (Figure 1). As may be seen, it also transmits some I.R. radiation. Since we were not interested in the luminescence in the I.R. range, additional barrier filters were not applied. Due to the low intensity of U.V. illumination from quartz halogen lamps, the advantage of 18A over narrow band transmission filters is self evident. Of course, it must be emphasized that in using this method, the emission is due to a broad band excitation which is not the regular operational mode of the spectrofluorometer (10).

## RECORDING AND PROCESSING OF SPECTRA

The software of the Docuspec TM/1 dictates that the spectra of the sample (controls and unknowns) in the transmission or reflectance mode can be measured only against a reference. The usual procedure for microspectro-photometry in this system is to measure a spectrum of a reference which is recorded on the chart as an intensity of light versus wavelength. Then one of the samples is deliberately chosen as a control (standard) and its spectrum is measured relative to a reference. It may be presented on the chart only as an absorbance (O.D.) for transmission work or log reflectance for reflectance work. It is also stored in the RAM of the computer. The other samples are run as unknowns. Their spectra are also measured relative to the same reference and presented in the same form as the standard. The areas selected should not be too highly absorbing since measurements will be subject to noise at high absorbance values. An area is too absorbing if strong peaks in the spectrum are above 2.0 absorbance units.

This would show as an off scale flattening on the top of the scan. The software can compare quantitatively the spectra of unknowns to any standard that is stored in the RAM in the whole spectral range (380-764 nm) or any part of it. However, there is no option to record a spectrum only in a part of the range. The measure of similarity is shown by a match number (mn). The lower the number the better the match; zero corresponds to the best match. In order to make the above correlation possible the software normalizes the spectra of unknowns to that of the standard, thus eliminating effects resulting from differences in concentration. Such normalized spectra may also be recorded on a chart.

Care must be exercised when samples are less absorbing (or more reflecting) than the raference. This will produce negative O.D. values and normalization factors. In such cases quantitative comparison of the spectra will not be possible.

The spectra of references cannot be subject to the above processing and the only processing that can be accomplished is a change in the amplification of the signal by the "gain" of the photomultiplier and the recorder.

SAMPLES
===

The samples were prepared according to the quantity and characteristics of the lumminescent materials. Fluorescent invisible detection powders (Fargo Corp.) were mounted on SEM stubs coated with double side adhesive. In real cases when the quantity of material is limited, the same stub can be examined in the SEM/EDS for elemental composition following the luminescence analysis.

For fluorescent markers two types of white paper served as substrates. The possible contribution of the substrate luminescence was checked by inspecting the obtained spectrum. All the samples were viewed and measured with the 20x objective.

## RESULTS AND DISCUSSION

There are several approaches one could consider for the adaptation of the Docuspec TM/I to obtain and compare luminescence spectra.

The straightforward approach would be to apply the reflectance mode of the microspectrophotometer. In this mode, the reference could be a spectrum of a white standard obtained with unfiltered quartz halogen illumination. Then, the spectrum of a luminescent material would be obtained relative to the reference using 18A filter in the -log reflectance mode. Of course, the pattern formed in such a way is not the regular method used for presenting luminescence spectra. Also, due to the relative low intensity of U.V. radiation given by the quartz halogen lamp, resulting in a weak luminescence signal, and the off scale flattening of the system for absorbance 2 it was found that it would be preferable to use a gray standard (e.g. Kodak gray scale) of about -log/reflectance = 1 as a reference (Figure 2). However, even then because of the usual large variation of luminescence intensity versus wavelength of luminescent materials, the phenomena of off scale flattening could not be avoided, and the spectral recognition feature of the system was not efficient.

A much more useful approach appears to be as follows: the luminescence spectra are obtained in the reference mode and the intensity of a signal may be varied by a gain of the photomultiplier and the recorder. The spectrum recorded in this way is a convolution of luminescence intensity, diffraction efficiency of the grating and spectral response of the photomultiplier. Since the response of a gallium arsenide photomultiplier (the photomultiplier of the system), in the 400-700 nm range is nearly flat (12), the obtained spectrum represents luminescence intensity modified by diffraction efficiency. Since the variation of the diffraction efficiency versus the wavelength is not very large (13), the spectrum generally represents the color of luminescence perceived by visual observation. Figure 3 shows the reflectance spectrum of the white standard (supplied with the Docuspec TM/I, which does not exhibit luminescence in the visible range) illuminated by a filtered (Kodak 18A filter) quartz halogen lamp. The spectrum was recorded in the reference mode. It confirms that a 18A filter is indeed a barrier for visible radiation (see also Figure 1). Although there is some transmission in the region of 660 nm, it is very small relative to that in the U.V. and I.R. ranges and practically does not at all interfere in the comparison of emission luminescence spectra in the visible range. Obviously, in all such spectra there will be a contribution of reflectance in the U.V. and I.R. ranges and only the visible range should be considered for luminescence spectrum evaluation.

Figures 4, 5 show the luminescence spectra of invisible detection powders and two types of white paper that served as substrates for fluorescent markers in this study. The powders are nonhomogenous materials and therefore exhibit a variation of luminescence color. The spectra presented here show the average characteristics of each powder.

Figures 6, 7 show the characteristic spectra of fluorescent markers which can be distinguished from each other without the need of spectral recognition processing. The luminescence of these markers is indistinguishable when observed visually. They also show no visual difference in color when observed in reflected light, however their reflectance spectra are distinguishable (Figures 8,9). As shown, the difference is quite small in the case of the two yellow and green markers. It was mentioned previously that the software of the system cannot be used for quantitative comparison of spectra in the reference mode. Nevertheless, the following method for objective comparison of visually similar luminescence spectra (recorded intthe reference mode) may be useful.

One of the spectra is arbitrarily chosen to be a reference. Then, the material chosen as a reference is recorded as a standard (O.D. mode) using a neutral density filter (e.g. Kodak Wratten gelatin filter No. 96, O.D.=0.3). The neutral density filter is necessary to prevent a situation where luminescence intensity of a sample will be higher than that of the reference, which could cause software problems.

The other materials are recorded as unknowns in the same way as the standard and then quantitatively compared to it by the software.

Using this method for the quantitative matching of visually similar luminescence spectra, one can prevent the problems of off scale flattening mentioned previously. Figures 10,11 show the application of this technique in the case of yellow and green fluorescent markers. As can be seen a good discrimination is obtained in these cases: in the case of the yellow markers, the match number (m.n.) of (b) and (c) relative to (a) was 4.7 and 2.3 respectively; the variation in (a) in terms of m.n. was only 0.06. In the case of the green markers the m.n. of (b) relative to (a) was 2.7 and the variation in (a) was only 0.2.

CONCLUSIONS

It was demonstrated that the microspectrophotometer Docuspec TM/I may be adapted for microspectrofluorometry work simply and quickly. Thus, an objective comparison of minute quantities of luminescent materials may be carried out, providing as we believe to be a significant contribution in forensic evidence examination.

REFERENCES

1. R. Macrae, R. J. Dudley and K. W. Smalldon, The Characterisation of Dyestuffs on Wool Fibers with Special Reference to Microspectrophotometry. J. Forensic. Sci., 24 (1979) 117-129.

2. D. K. Laing, R. J. Dudley and M. D. J. Isaacs, Colorimetric Measurements on Small Paint Fragments Using Microspectrophotometry. Forensic Sci. Int., 16 (1980) 159-171.

3. D. K. Laing, R. J. Dudley, J. M. Home and M. D. J. Isaacs, The Discrimination of Small Fragments of Household Gloss Paint by Microspectrophotometry, Forensic Sci. Int., 20 (1982) 191-200.

4. H. H. Hausdorff and V. J. Coates, Color Matching by Microspectrophotometry, a New Dimension in Document Examination. SPIE - Electro-optical Instrumentation for Industrial Applications 411 (1983) 54-59.

5. D. K. Laing and M. D. J. Isaacs, The Comparison of Nanogram Quantities of Ink Using Visible Microspectrophotometry, J. Forensic, Sci. Soc., 23 (1983) 147-154.

6. D. R. Cousins, C. R. Platoni and L. W. Russell, The Use of Microspectrophotometry for The Identification of Pigments in Small Paint Samples. Forensic Sci. Int., 24 (1984) 183-196.

7. J. B. F. Lloid, Fluorescence Spectrometry in the Identification and Discrimination of Float and Other Surfaces on Window Glasses. J. Forensic Sci., 26 (1981) 325-342.

8. T. A. Cubic, J. E. King, Ira S. Dubey, Forensic Analysis of Colorless Textile Fibers by Fluorescence Microscopy. The Microscope 31 (1983) 213-222.

9. P. F. Jones, New Applications of Photoluminescence Techniques for Forensic Science, ACS Symposium Series 13 (1975) 183-195.

10. T. J. Johnson, New Developments in Spectrofuorometry, International Laboratory (1984) 20-25.

11. Kodak Filters for Scientific and Technical Uses, Kodak Publication No. B-3 First Ed. 1970.

12. L. Levi, Applied Optics, vol. 2 John Wiley & Sons 1980 p. 462.

13. G. Schmahl and D. Rudolph, Progress in Optics 14 (1976) 223-242.

Acknowledgements

The author is most grateful to Mr. E. Springer, Dr. S. Kraus and R. J. Almog for much useful discussion.

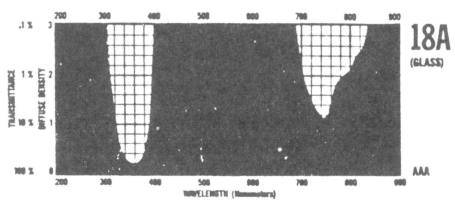

Glass filter. Only transmits ultraviolet radiation between about 300 and 400nm (e.g., 365nm line of mercury spectrum) and infrared radiation. Used for ultraviolet reflection photography.

Figure 1

Transmittance characteristics of a Kodak 18A glass filter (11).

# FORGERIES OF THE USSR DRIVERS LICENSE

Benjamin Perelman, M.A.
Examiner of Questioned Documents
Jerusalem

During the past ten years the Israel National Police has examined several hundred forged USSR drivers licenses. Although many of these documents contained alterations, the large majority were total forgeries produced from more than thirty different printings. This paper discusses aspects of the genuine USSR drivers license, then it examines various faults and points of identification found in the forgeries. The problem of known standards for comparison is also discussed.

## INTRODUCTION TO THE SOVIET DRIVERS LICENSE

In 1971 the Soviet Union began a process of issuing a new national drivers license. Until that time, there were numerous types of drivers licenses in use in the Soviet Union. The 1971 program was an attempt to adopt a standard format for the entire country.

The situation prior to 1971 was particularly complicated. Different licenses (in totally different printing and format) were issued not only for type of vehicle, but even according to the occupation of the driver. Thus, examination of the licenses was quite problematic, since there was a severe problem of obtaining exactly appropriate authentic comparison materials.

The current license is totally different from its predecessor. Although the licenses have already gone through several printings, it has remained a standardized document that is now issued to all drivers in the country, regardless of occupation. On the license there is a check-off for various types of vehicles permitted, a procedure quite common in the West but new to the USSR.

From the point of view of the questioned document examiner, the current Soviet license is a document with a high level of security. One might compare this level to the one in a well designed currency note. For example, the document contains a detailed background pattern with an infra-red visible security feature.

FRAUDULENT LICENSES

During the past ten to twelve years at the Israel Police, numerous fraudulent licenses have been encountered:
Type 1 - Genuine Licenses
Changes of driver's personalia: name, father's name, date and place of birth, residence photograph. Changes in issuance details: date and place of issuance, class of vehicle permitted, authenticating seals (particularly over photograph).
Type 2 - Total Forgery
Forged printing of the entire document. Fraudulent issuance with fraudulent cachets.
Type 3 - Combination
Authentic cover pasted on forged inner page. (Infrequent).
This paper will concern itself with Types 2 & 3 of fraudulent licenses, since Type 1 is already well covered in standard questioned documents literature.

A DETAILED LOOK AT THE GENUINE LICENSE

All Soviet drivers licenses are printed by the government of the USSR. From information available outside the USSR it appears that most if not all of the licenses are printed at the official government printing facility in Perme, a city in the eastern portion of European Russia.
From printing dates noted on the licenses it is clear that there have been several printings of the license. These, however, have been standard in form and quality (as mentioned above).
A. Cover & Binding
The cover is made of red coloured synthetic material adjoined to a cloth webbing. Thus, the cover is quite durable and resistant to cracking when bent.
The symbol of the USSR and the titling on the cover are imprinted by a pressure technique (similar to letterpress) which is effected with the aid of heat and a plastic single-use ribbon which conveys the black colour. In this manner, the printing is not only clear, but it also maintains its quality even after the document has

seen considerable use.

In order that the document can be opened and closed easily, an impressed groove (Rus. "falc") is present.

(Note: Minor variation has been observed in the shade of red on the cover. It has also been observed that the ends of the document can fray.)

B. Inside of the document

The inside of the document is printed on a security paper and is pasted with synthetic-base glue to the cover. The security features of the paper are:

1. The text "X CCCP" is visible with the aid of IR.
2. The page contains a complicated security background which is disturbed when chemical or mechanical erasures or alterations are made.

The text of the license, including the alphabetic series indicator, is printed by letterpress. The actual serial number is impressed with a numerator after printing is completed. The series indicators started in 1971 with AAA, AAB, etc.; they have continued progressively over the years.

C. Document Fill-in

The fill-in of the personalia and issuance particulars is accomplished with black writing ink or India ink. The licenses are issued in those numerous cities in the Soviet Union where there is an office of the Automobile Inspection Authority; even though the issuance is effected throughout the country, the use of black ink is standard. Every office of the Automobile Authority maintains its own rubber cachets. In larger cities, such as Moscow, the cachets are numbered in the text according to the group effecting issuance. In smaller places with only one issuance "team", these numbers are not necessary. From examination experience it can be said that the cachets are usually stamped into the licenses with a violet ink, however the exact shade of that ink has been observed to vary. The cachets are not made at a central point, hence they come in various sizes with different text and format. In all cases, however, they are made of rubber.

A photograph is glued to the license over an area where the Russian word for photograph is printed. It has been my experience that as a result of license use, there have been instances where the photograph has become detached, then reattached by

337

the rightful document owner.

D. Warning Card
Together with the drivers license, every Soviet driver must be in possession of a "Warning Card". This card contains the "points" for traffic violations committed by the driver. Whenever a driver is stopped for a violation, the police officer punches a perforated hole in an appropriate box. The document must be carried by drivers; it is an integral part of the licensing documentation. The number of the Warning Card is always written on the lower right of the license. Likewise, the number of the drivers license is always recorded on the Warning Card. As usual, black ink is used. The Warning Card is printed on relatively thin clear brown cardboard. The document contains a green printed security pattern.

## TOTAL FORGERY OF THE LICENSE

During the past ten years I have examined USSR drivers licenses and have found no fewer than twenty-five (25) different types of totally forged licenses. Some of these types also have several "sub-types". In a number of the types I have found numerous forgeries -- in certain cases amounting to more than one hundred.

## DETECTION POINTS

A. Cover
One of the first details that should be examined is the printing of the letters on the cover. In a number of forgeries they are not printed in the proper front.
In all of the forgeries that I have examined, the text on the cover has been printed without the aid of a thermographic process. The ink has always been usual printers ink rather than special security ribbon. As a result it is not infrequent to find that the black ink in forgeries does not lay uniformly on the cover, flakes off, wears thin, or is printed in globs. In many cases I have even found spelling errors on the cover (particularly in the French translation of the Russian text).
In the authentic license the symbol of the USSR and the titling are always well centered. In numerous

forgeries these details have been printed off-center and askew.

B. Internal Page

The quickest detection of forgery can be done by the document examiner with the aid of an IR viewer. In my experience there is no total forgery of the license that has succeded in reproducing the IR security tint.

In all but one of the types of forgery that I have examined, the background pattern of the document has not been reproduced accurately.

In the forgeries which I have examined there have been many defects in the printing of the text. For example, in some forgeries the length of printed lines has been different from the genuine.

There have also been forgeries in which the front used has varied from the genuine in both size and formation of letters. This has the resultant effect of sometimes altering the placement of the text.

In several forgeries the serial number has been printed into the document instead of being entered with a numerator. Thus, more than one license with the same serial number has been "issued". (This, obviously, never happens with genuine licenses.) In one total forgery it was even found that the serial number was entered with a typewriter.

The Soviet drivers license contains several straight lines, but in forgeries these are sometimes broken. The reason for this seemingly basic error is that in letterpress printing the lines will have these defects if proper arrangement and closing of the master plate is not accomplished. There must also be even pressure on the plate. These are some of the "tricks of the trade" of the experienced printer.

C. Cachets

In the license there is an authenticating cachet from the local issuing office. Since these cachets vary from place to place, and since it is not possible to determine when older cachets are replaced with newer ones, comparisons are particularly difficult to effect. The most practical examination is to determine if the cachet was made from metal (never used in genuine cachets but common in forgeries) or contains hand-drawn text/designs.

D. Cutting

Although the cutting of the license appears to be a simple matter, in several cases it has been a key to the determination of forgery. In the genuine, a single straight blade is used ot make each of the perimeter cuts. In some forgeries scissors have been used, thus resulting in uneven cutting lines.

CONCLUSIONS

This paper has been a general introduction to the USSR drivers license. Although it might not be a commonly examined document in the case load of American document examiners, it is commonly encountered in Israel

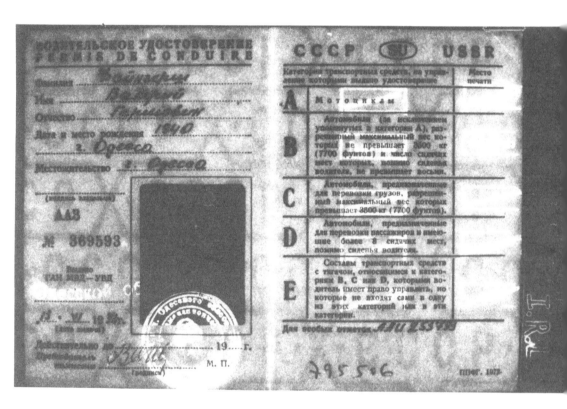

SECURITY FEATURE.

X     CCCP     X
    X     CCCP     X

This feature is visible under IR. Good imitations have not been found in forgeries.

1. COVER. Above is genuine; below are forgeries. Note background pattern in documents, differences in printing fonts, and different methods of printing.

## ВОДИТЕЛЬСКОЕ УДОСТОВЕРЕНИЕ
## PERMIS DE CONDUIRE

**CCCP** (SU) **USSR**

Фамилия ......

Имя ......

Отчество ...... *Абрамович*

Дата и место рождения ...... *1946,*
*г. Москва*

Местожительство ...... *г. Москва*

(подпись владельца)

**ААБ № 034324**

Выдано ГАИ МВД – УВД

г. МОСКВЫ
25 . 7 . 19 72 г.
(дата выдачи)

Действительно до ...... 19 ...... г.
Председатель
комиссии ......
(подпись) М. П.

| | Категории транспортных средств, на управление которыми выдано удостоверение | Место печати |
|---|---|---|
| **A** | Мотоциклы | |
| **B** | Автомобили (за исключением упомянутых в категории А), разрешенный максимальный вес которых не превышает 3500 кг (7700 фунтов) и число сидячих мест которых, помимо сиденья водителя, не превышает восьми. | Разрешено |
| **C** | Автомобили, предназначенные для перевозки грузов, разрешенный максимальный вес которых превышает 3500 кг (7700 фунтов). | |
| **D** | Автомобили, предназначенные для перевозки пассажиров и имеющие более 8 сидячих мест, помимо сиденья водителя. | |
| | Составы транспортных средств с тягачом, относящимся к категориям B, C или D, которыми водитель имеет право управлять, но которые не входят сами в одну из этих категорий или в эти категории. | |

Для особых отметок  ААБ- 977622    25-7-72

827032

---

## ВОДИТЕЛЬСКОЕ УДОСТОВЕРЕНИЕ
## PERMIS DE CONDUIRE

**CCCP** (SU) **USSR**

Фамилия ......

Имя ......

Отчество ...... *Срулевич*

Дата и место рождения ...... *1940*
*Москва*

Местожительство ...... *Москва*

(подпись владельца)

**ААВ № 022394**

Выдано ГАИ МВД – УВД
г. МОСКВЬ
23 XI 19 71 г.
(дата выдачи)

Действительно до ...... 19 ...... г.
Председатель
комиссии ......
(подпись) М. П.

| | Категории транспортных средств, на управление которыми выдано удостоверение | Место печати |
|---|---|---|
| **A** | Мотоциклы | |
| **B** | Автомобили (за исключением упомянутых в категории А), разрешенный максимальный вес которых не превышает 3500 кг (7700 фунтов) и число сидячих мест которых, помимо сиденья водителя, не превышает восьми. | Разрешено |
| **C** | Автомобили, предназначенные для перевозки грузов, разрешенный максимальный вес которых превышает 3500 кг (7700 фунтов). | |
| **D** | Автомобили, предназначенные для перевозки пассажиров и имеющие более 8 сидячих мест, помимо сиденья водителя. | |
| **E** | Составы транспортных средств с тягачом, относящимся к категориям B, C или D, которыми водитель имеет право управлять, но которые не входят сами в одну из этих категорий или в эти категории. | |

Для особых отметок  ААБ 123693  23/XI 71

834844

2.    INSIDE PAGES.   Examples of genuine licenses.

3. INSIDE PAGES. Forgeries. Note differences in background tint, size, font of numbers in serial. In title of upper forgery, note handwritten circle around "SU".

4. INSIDE PAGES. Forgeries. Printing date is fictional. (It should also appear nearer to bottom of document.)

# HANDWRITING CHARACTERISTICS OF ARABS WRITING HEBREW

Yaakov Yaniv
Examiner of Questioned Documents
Jerusalem

The purpose of this paper is to review the difficulties which are presented to the Examiner of Questioned Documents by certain aspects of script writing. Understanding these difficulties may assist examiners in assessing the relative importance of handwriting features or individualities in case work. The paper begins by summarizing the technical difficulties of writing in any language and cites specific examples from the Hebrew script. Ways which have been suggested to solve these difficulties are also mentioned.

This paper is based on a study of the handwriting of 100 Arabs writing Hebrew at various levels of proficiency. A number of questions arose during the process of classifying and analyzing these manuscripts:
1. Are the typical characteristics of Arabic script expressed in each case of Hebrew script, and to what extent?
2. Do these characteristics decrease in relation to an increase in the writer's level of intelligence, and in his use of Hebrew script?
3. Do the graphic characteristics of Hebrew written by Arabs differ in various regions?
In an effort to answer these questions, I undertook a methodical analysis of the material, giving attention to various features of handwriting, such as: conjunction of letters in Hebrew script which are similar in form and movement to conjunctions in Arabic; forms of vocalization similar to vocalization in Arabic writing; the frequency of vocalization in Hebrew script compared to the existence of diacritical marks in Arabic; letter construction in Hebrew reminiscent of letter construction in Arabic, particularly in regard to the letter's form and to handwriting movement.

The conclusion of the study is that in most of the manuscripts of Arabs writing Hebrew, the specific characteristics of Arabic script were manifest in the Hebrew script, e.g.: conjunction of letters, initial and final strokes, similarity in handwriting movement, diacritical marks, etc.

Hebrew and Arabic are Semitic languages, written from right to left, and one is therefore likely to find a similarity in the handwriting of a person who has achieved mature graphic expression in both languages.

Understanding the process of development of handwriting will allow a more basic understanding of this similarity: when a child begins to write, he tries to imitate a model set before him, and he is therefore incapable of writing with an "automatic" movement of his hand.[1] As his writing becomes more fluent, it diverges further and further from the school model, and the writing becomes individualized in accordance with the person's physical and intellectual capabilities. Once the writer has attained graphic maturity, he will always write in the same personal and specific way in various alphabets. Therefore, an expert, with adequate knowledge of various alphabets, can compare the Arabic and Hebrew written by the same person.[2,3]

Upon analyzing the Hebrew handwriting of 100 Arabs, I perceived recurring characteristics, which I will call "group traits". These include graphological features, for example: letter conjunctions; use of phonetic symbols, such as vocalization; graphic similarity between letters, etc. There were also linguistic features recurring frequently, such as transliterations and direct translations, syntactic formations, and indications originating in differences of pronunciation.[*]

Arabs which were demonstrated in this study are important as an aid to the examiner of documents who wishes to identify the origin of the writer; they also serve for the purpose of comparison between Hebrew and Arabic script written by the same hand. According to the quantity and quality of these characteristics, one can ascertain the degree of the writer's fluency in Hebrew, and also the degree of his intelligence. As the writer's level of intelligence decreases, there is a decrease in "group traits", and an increase in specific, individualized signs which are not typical of Arabic script.

This study digresses from the subject of comparison of handwritings, which is the field of work of an expert examiner of documents, but I believe it will interest the reader, and point up an interesting development in handwriting during the interim period between one language and another.

## FOOTNOTES

[1] R. Saudek, Experiments with Handwriting (Sacramento, California, 1978 reprint), p. 73

[2] I. Haggag,"Comparison of texts in languages with different alphabets," International Criminal Police Review (Oct. 1968).

[3] J. Levinson, "Questioned Document Examination in Foreign Scripts," Forensic Science International, Vol. 22, No. 2-3 (1983), pp. 249-252

\* Some of these group traits occur also in the handwriting of Jews from Arab countries, and a separate study is required to answer the question whether one can differentiate between the Hebrew writing of an Arab and that of a Jew from an Arab country.

Some examples of "group traits" are presented here, from the classification of 100 manuscripts, arranged in tables according to the principle features of each category:
1) Similar conjuctions of letters and handwriting move - ments

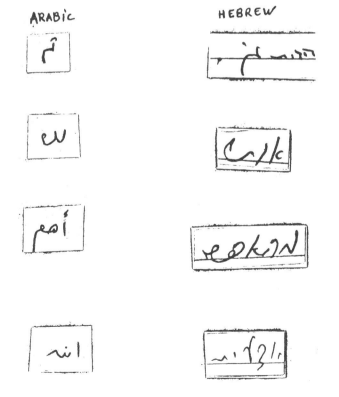

In Hebrew, it is not the rule to join letters. In Arabic, however, all letters are connected (except ‏أ, د, ذ, ر, ز, و‎ ) and the Arabic writer will carry over the conjunctions into Hebrew.

2) Exaggerated use of the diacritical dot

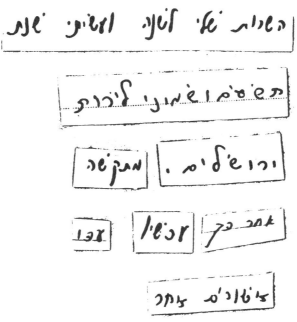

The Arab writer views the dot as an integral part of the letter, as it is in Arabic a) because he does not differentiate between diacritical marks which preserve various forms of Proto-Semitic consonants;

1) In Hebrew there is ת ת ; in Arabic: ت ث
2) In Hebrew: ד ד ; in Arabic: د ذ
3) There is a similarity in the form of the letter ج in Hebrew and Arabic b) because of the similarity in form of some letters in Hebrew and Arabic (see fig. 3/3).

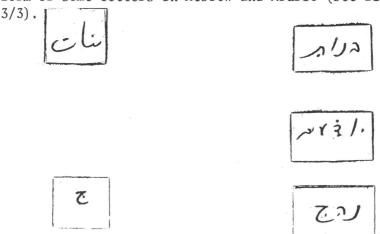

3) Hebrew vocalization which is similar graphically to Arabic vocalization

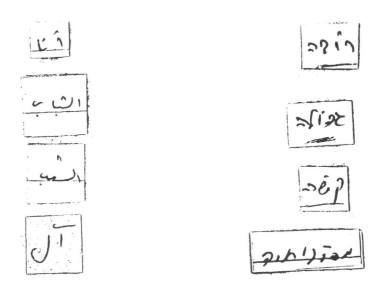

4) The letter "י" is relatively higher or much lower than the other letters in the word, and it would seem that the writer regarded this letter as a diacritical mark.

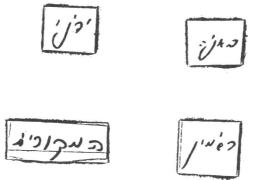

5) Transliteration from Arabic to Hebrew
In the right-hand column, the words were transliterated from the Arabic, and are not in accordance with the Hebrew spelling and pronounciation.
6) Forms of style which are peculiar to Arabic, and which occur when the writer is thinking in Arabic while writing Hebrew
This form is called "Maful Mutlak" in Arabic, and is used to confirm the certainty of an action.
7) Exaggerated use of the letter "י", due to the absence of the vowel ָ in Arabic, for example: חלבי instead of חלב; מין instead of מן.

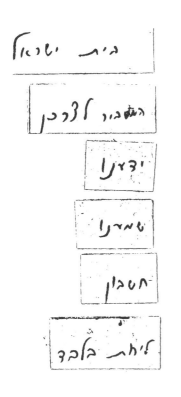
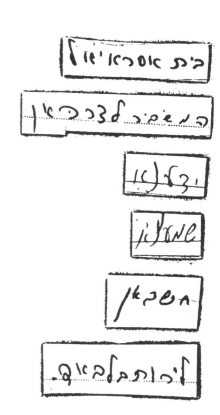

8) Similarities of letter construction in Hebrew and Arabic

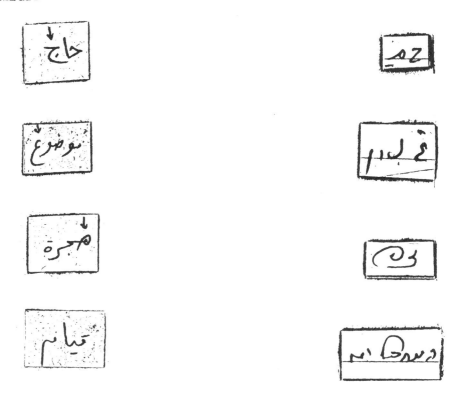

# IDENTIFICATION OF THE DEAD
## CAN CHIROPODISTS HELP?

I. E. Doney and P. H. G. Harris

It is universally accepted that when identification of the dead is difficult, the forensic odontologist is one of the key members of the identification team. He relies very much on records supplied by the deceased's personal dentist. However, in cases of decapitation or head mutilation his skills are limited. This paper draws attention to the type of accurate records of foot charting available in the offices of chiropodists and podiatrists throughout the world and suggests that where lower limb identification is required, the identification team could benefit from enlisting the help of local chiropody services. Slides and methods of charting foot lesions will illustrate this vast pool of neglected professional information available to the investigating identification team. It could be of great help in situations of terrorist massacres, mass disasters or in individual cases of missing persons.

The place of the forensic odontologist in assisting with identification of victims in mass disasters is universally known and many would regard him as the most important member of the identification team. In the D.C. 10 Mount Erebus (New Zealand) disaster, for instance, 115 of the 214 victims finally named were identified by dental comparisons.

The importance of the dentist's work at such a scene related to the availability of accurate records from the victim's personal dentist for comparison.

In this paper, the authors point out that other medical and paramedical personnel also keep accurate records of their work and, in particular, draw attention to the chiropodist and discuss the possible usefulness of chiropody records in identification of lower limbs in mass disasters. They also discuss how greater awareness of the value of their records by chiropodists themselves could make their profession an asset to the disaster team. Both common and unusual identifiable lesions are discussed. It is doubtful if such items would be recorded in any such detail by any other medical department nor by the victim's own personal physician.

## FOOTCHARTING

Chiropodists have standard chiropody foot charts which are basically the same throughout their profession whether they are in private or in hospital practice. On the charts the chiropodist records the patient's history, notes abnormalities, plans treatment, all in an approved manner, and this is roughly the same world wide. Such records, therefore, contain valuable, accurate professional information.

It may be argued that the preponderance of people attending chiropody clinics are elderly and the chiropodist would only be able to help in the identification of older people. This is only partly true. Many travellers overseas are tourists and are in the older age group and there is therefore a preponderance of older people at risk.

It may be asked whether young people ever bother to go to a chiropodist at all. They do. More and more young people are becoming foot conscious and approach chiropodists for advice on foot care, foot lesions, ingrowing toenails, verruca treatment.

Furthermore, young people often attend hospital chiropody clinics as part of their general medical out-patient routine supervision. These include cases of foot deformities, diabetics, patients with vascular disorders (Raynaud's, scleroderma), neurological disorders, congenital abnormalities, dermatological problems, trauma.

## COMMON CONDITIONS

Corns and calluses are common the world over; often they occur in common situations and many investigators would feel that a mere description of such lesions would identify nobody. Nor would it be of much value if a particular chiropodist could identify only his own work as it is unlikely

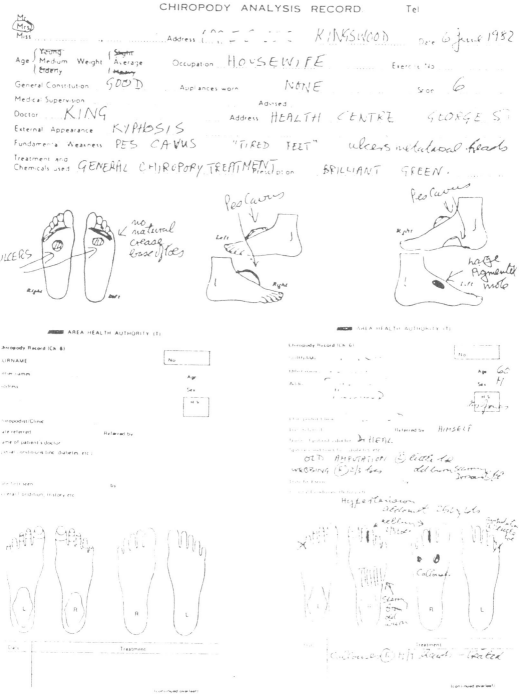

that he would be prepared to travel far to identify it.
If, however, corns or calluses had been recently treated
with some particular medicament such as a dye or a particular
dressing which could be identified (and chiropodists have
individual traits in the type and shape of the pads they
use), this might usefully narrow down the field, where
there is doubt about identification. A decapitated body,
for instance, thought to belong to a Mr. X having had
corns recently treated in some distinctive way, might be
identified by a report from his own private chiropodist
confirming the treatment. It might be as useful a report
as a dental surgeon's. Indeed, in the case of the
unfortunate decapitated Mr. X, a much more useful record
than a dental chart!

In addition to these common conditions, chiropodists
also chart other items which could be of vital importance.
Obvious items such as major or minor degrees of talipes,
amputation or webbing of toes are recorded, but also less
obvious yet distinctive lesions such as haemangioma,
infected bunions, cysts, gouty nodules, a pigmented mole
which a chiropodist may have actually measured in case he
felt one day it might become malignant. It is very
unlikely that such lesions would ever have been accurately
described in any other medical records. Skin conditions,
eczematous and fungal, are recorded in detail together
with treatment prescribed. It is doubtful if, for instance
in the case of a fungal condition, the patient's general
practitioner would have recorded anything more than
"tineapedis" in his records, whereas the chiropodist would
almost certainly have entered the actual toe affected and
recorded them on his charts.

APPLIANCES

Other items that chiropodists record are special appliances such as shoe supports and plastic arches to correct
flat feet or poor arches. Many thousands of these are made
and sent out to shoewear firms and would by themselves
provide no identification. If, however, such arches bore
an identifiable mark or the name and address of the chiropodist,
it might well be a means of providing a referral source
from which further enquiries could be made. The chiropodist,
while thus helping disaster teams, might also benefit from
this sneaky form of advertising! Other small appliances
such as plastic toe separators, if labelled or marked, could
be traced to what is, in effect, an accurate and professional
source of reliable information.

It goes without saying that larger orthopaedic appliances and surgical shoes should be traceable through relatives or through local hospital orthopaedic departments, but chiropodists also record these things and therefore have records which would make their discovery a vital peice of information - at the very least, they would provide corroborative evidence where there is doubt or dispute.

## FOOTWEAR AND FOOTPRINTS

There may, of course, be other forensic implications when considering professionll records kept by chiropodists, e.g. injuries recorded, trace evidence involving medicaments There have been some papers written and forensic work carried out on the possible value of footprints. Indeed, it could be argued that Robinson Crusoe, discovering the footpring of Man Friday on the desert island, was, in fact the first forensic chiropodist! Dr. J. D. DeHaan's paper draws attention to other ways in which feet and footwear have a place in forensic science.

## POTENTIAL UTILITY

The authors have prepared this short paper to draw attention to the type of records kept by chiropodists and to suggest they they may provide a very useful source of untapped information for investigation teams. The success of dental identification by reference to already available professional records is universally accepted. Another group of enthusiastic record keepers are chiropodists. The disaster team might well enlist the help of a local chiropodist to assist in identification by charting foot lesions particularly in cases where only legs or feet are recognisable. His help could be vital and in court his professional expertise might make him an expert witness.

## BIBLIOGRAPHY

Treadwell, W. J., Aircrash on Mount Erebus, November 1979 Operation Overdue. The Police Surgeon 1981: 20,21

DeHann, J.D., Footwear evidence: 1983, ICFS, Sacramento Calif.

Lucock, L. J., Identification from footwear. Medicine, Science and the Law 1979: 19, 225.

# THE IDENTIFICATION OF THE SERIOUSLY DAMAGED BODY USING NON-DENTAL DATA

Dr. M. Rogev, Consultant in Forensic Medicine
Department of Pathology
Tel Hashomer, Israel

A study of the literature revealed that in aircraft accidents, 30% to 35% of the dead are buried without identification. This results from the very serious degree of damage sustained from the effects of the accident. In these reports reliance is placed on dental data and the identification of personal effects. The dental data in those unidentified bodies was destroyed when the face and teeth were totally damaged and unidentifiable. In this paper attention is drawn to the fact that the addition of non-dental parameters to the examination reduces the percentage of the unidentified to a minimum or eliminates it completely. Evidence is based on case records and experimental work and consists of the following parameters: (1) the diagramatic reconstruction of the immediate vicinity of the body; (2) the use of anatomical data such as age, sex and height as a classifying procedure; (3) full recording of clothing and personal posessions, including photographs; (4) x-ray examination of the frontal sinuses of the skull; (5) full body x-ray where the skeleton is still covered by tissue; (6) fingerprints; (7) the limited use of forensic serology. Special attention will be paid to the value of the x-ray examination and fingerprints.

In 1928, acting on available knowledge, Carter and Cavendish discovered the tomb of Tutenkhamun and identified his remains.[1,2] How was this possible after a lapse of over 3,000 years? These explorers based their determination of identity on the comparison between the information available from historical sources, tomb wall paintings, and the results of archeological and pathological examinations.

The following criteria enabled the identification:

1. Place of Burial
   The tomb was found to be consistent with historical records[1].

2. Method of Embalming
   The pathological examination confirmed the method of embalming the pharoah as recorded by Herodotus[1].

3. Anatomical parameters
   Historical records indicated that the pharoah was of slim constitution, he ascended the throne at the age of 12 years, and died at the probable age of 19 years. The tomb wall paintings showed the figure of Tutenkhamun standing by a table[2]. The height of Tutenkhamun was compared with the height of the table in the painting. This gave the probable ratio between the height of Tutenkhamun and the table. As the same table was found with the funeral furniture and its height could be measured, the application of the Tutenkhamun height table height ratio was deduced from the painting. Assuming this ratio to be reasonably correct, the estimated height of Tutenkhamun would be between 170 to 175 cm. Examination of the body gave a height of approximately 170 cm, an age of 19 to 21 years and male of slim build.[2]

4. Jewelry
   Court and personal jewelry found on the mummy between the layers of bandage were identical to drawings of the same jewelry portrayed on the tomb walls on funeral furniture, and on the ceremonial throne.[2]

5. Amulets
   Amulets carrying the name of the pharoah were found between the bandages

6. The Name of Tutenkhamun was found on the outer surface of the gold coffins in which the mummy was found.[2]

Clearly, the compulsion was felt by the ancient funeral directors to ensure the correct identification of Tutenkhamun on his admission to the Afterlife!

The criteria for the non-dental identification of severely damaged bodies are discussed in this paper. The case of Tutenkhamun is a good example of the application of this identification methodology. This should form the basis of the identification in all circumstances.

There can be no doubt that dental evidence on its own, and when available, is the single most useful peice of evidence.

In recent years reports have appeared that indicate that between 35 to 40% of victims in mass disasters could not be identified. H. R. Muhlman et al[3] surveyed reports of identification results collected over a ten year period from 1963 to 1974. These reports deal with the identification examination of 1,189 fatal casualties that resulted from 12 mass disaster aircraft accidents. Forty-four percent of these victims could be identified by non-dental data alone, whereas using dental data alone, or in combination with non-dental data, 41% could not be identified.

In these collected surveys 14% of the victims could not be identified at all. J. H. Woolcott and C. A. Hanson[4] reported in connection with the Teneriffe air disaster 212 out of a total of 326 remains, leaving 110 bodies unidentified. Four passengers did not belong to the American passengers, but to the KLM aircraft with which the American Pan American aircraft had collided. That means that 33% of the bodies could not be identified using mainly dental data.

B. J. Rumsch[5] reported the identification of 31 bodies out of a total of 37 fatal victims using all methods of identification, including dental data, anatomical parameters, x-rays and fingerprints. Six were identified by non-dental measures, and confirmed by personal identification.

C. C. Snow et al[6] refer to the failure of the identification procedures adopted in dealing with the Teneriffe air disaster. The use of anatomical criteria, such as sex and race on a computerized basis, was investigated by these works to provide non-dental diagnostic data.

J. R. Hill[7] reported a 67% success rate using dental data alone in an aircraft mass disaster. In these reports, attention was paid mainly to the identification of bodies by dental procedures of identification, with less attention being paid to non-dental measures.

The identification of the aircrash of the New Zealand DC 10 on Mount Erebus (1981) is a further example. In all, 257 fatal victims were involved. It was possible to identify 213 bodies, but 43 bodies, i.e. approximately 16%, were not identified. In this accident non-dental methods were employed extensively, reducing the percentage of the non-identifiable to 16%.

It is apparent from the study of these reports that the use of dental procedures was negated in those cases where the damage to the face and jaws was so severe that the normal anatomical structure was disrupted. Loose teeth in fragments of jaw bone that can not be reassembled prevent the accurate evaluation of dental data. It is assumed in this paper that all the antemortem dental data were available for comparison.

Injuries to the head and facial region that damage the jaws leading to the scattering of bone fragments and teeth, will occur in a wide range of traumatic events. These are a few examples:

A. Aircraft Mass Disasters
   In these cases the deceased may sustain multiple injuries with destruction of body regions and disruption of the head and face. Secondary fire will destroy what is left.

B. Explosions
   These cause disruption of body tissue on direct exposure to explosive effects. Buildings or mine tunnel walls that collapse as the result of explosions destroy tissue by crushing. Again, secondary fire aggravates the damage. Battle injuries caused by explosive devices can cause severe destructive effects on tissue, both soft tissue and bone.

C. Earthquakes
   These will cause damage mainly by causing the collapse of buildings.

D. Traffic or railway accidents
   In these circumstances the damage to the body may be very severe as the result of the massive force involved. Secondary fire will damage tissue more severely.

In all types of cases, the following procedures of identification is recommended:

A. Characterisation of the deceased's body
B. Specific identification techniques other than dental.

The characterisation of the body involves the following:

1. Site orientation of the body.
   This involves the examination of the body in site. Attention is paid to the damage sustained by the body and the evaluation of the cause of the damage. These two factors can help to site the individual at the moment of the accident. E.G., a burnt body

360

found on a burnt seat in a fire area in the aircraft can be said to represent the possible passenger who sat in the seat at the time of the accident. If a record of passengers and their seating arrangements are known, this could provide the first part of the identification procedure.

2. The anatomical orientation of separated parts of the body.
This is done according to anatomical principles. It must be possible to reconstruct each individual in full compliance with the normal anatomical structures and morphological appearance of the human body.

3. Anatomical parameters
These are: age, sex, height as determined by anatomical examination.

The value of the characterisation of the body using above mentioned data was tested in a survey carried out by the author in 1966, Nairobi, Kenya (unpublished data).

In this survey, 398 exhumed bodies were examined. Antemortem details, including grave identification, were compared with postmortem data.

Antemortem information consisted of the following:
a. Grave identification by family or police.
b. Sex, age, height, provided by family. The latter two aspects were provided according to the cultural criteria of the family.
c. Details of injury provided by police.

Postmortem results consisted of the following:
a. Grave identification during exhumation. This was done by the family or police.
b. Age and sex. This was determined using methods described by Krogman[10].
c. Height as determined by the methods described by M. Krogman[10], Trotter and Glezer[11].

The results of this comparison showed that both antemortem and postmortem information were consistent in 162 cases. In a further 107 cases, although full antemortem details were present, inadequately exhumed bodies or skeletal parts prevented the determination of all three parameters of age, sex and height.

In this group the results could have been improved with more care in the exhumation.

In 23 cases the antemortem details and the postmortem anatomical parameters were inconsistent.

Finally, in 106 cases, consistency could not be tested as the antemortem information was either totally absent, or inadequate.

Once the basic characterisation has been achieved, more specific methods should be used.

## SPECIFIC IDENTIFICATION TECHNIQUES

A. Fingerprints

In most countries, the only records of fingerprints are those kept in the central criminal record department of police forces. The population at large is not fingerprinted as a routine procedure. Fortunately, technical procedures are available for the development of latent fingerprints found on personal effects and in the victims' homes. The routine collection of fingerprints for filing in the personal files of potential accident victims is of distinct value. In a recent survey carried out in the Israel Defence Force, 120 consecutive fatal casualties whose bodies were intact, were subjected to fingerprint examination. Positive comparison between fingerprints filed in the victims' personal file, and those taken after death was possible in 107 cases. In the remaining 13 cases, no fingerprint records were filed in the casualties' file [12].

As long as the body is intact and the hands are attached to the body, the characterisation of the body as described above is sufficient to provide a positive basis for identification (The specific identification using fingerprints is then a deciding factor). When the hands are separated from the body, they have to be correctly assigned to the body before fingerprints can be used for confirmation of identity.

B. X-ray methods of identification

X-ray photography can be used in different ways in identification:

1. Comparison between x-ray pictures of suspect deceased with x-ray pictures taken during life. This method demonstrates the similarity between anatomical abnormalities before death with those found after death, such as spina bifida, callus in healed fractures, osteoarthritis, chronic or healed bone lesions of tuberculosis, and deformity of bones.

2. The determination of age, especially in the spinal column.
   Where this will be of paramount importance. Age determination will then depend on the presence of osteoarthritic changes. The age determination in the age group 35-45-55-65-70+

depends on the presence of osteophitic changes in the various parts of the spinal column. The accuracy of this method is such that a range of 10 to 20 years must be allowed, i.e. assessed age ± ten years.

3. The determination of the architecture of the walls of the frontal maxillary sinuses, and sphenoid sinuses[14]

A recent survey carried out by the Medical Corps of the I.D.F. illustrates the possible variations in frontal sinus architecture[13].

Based on analysis of 5,000 x-ray photographs taken of the frontal sinuses for diagnostic reasons, the following conclusions are valid:

1. No two sinuses were the same.
2. Architechturally, the sinuses could be divided into four types:
   a. No sinus frontalis present at all. The sinuses seen are extensions of the ethmoid sinus anteriorly to either left or right, or to both the left and right;
   b. Sinus frontalis present on the left and extends into the right;
   c. Sinus frontalis present on right and extends into the left;
   d. Sinus frontalis present in both right and left. Each of these sinuses can be divided into three groups.

Medical-legal reports exist on the identification of the single skull by comparison of its frontal sinus x-ray, with x-ray pictures taken during life[14,15,16].

Krogman[17] quotes Culbert and Law (1927) and Law (1934) as presenting cases of identification by "sinus prints." These cases show 13 points of comparative identity in respect of the frontal sinuses.

No previous work has been carried out to prepare x-ray pictures in advance in high risk personell. This is a project that could be very profitably investigated as a definite method of identification[13].

X-ray and ultra-fluoroscopic methods exist for the correct association of skeletal parts. These methods are of especial value in the correct association of skeletal elements to make up individuals in a random assembly of skeletal parts[18].

C. Blood group serology
   The use of blood group serology is of value mainly in the allocation of body parts to make up

individuals. In the case of the soldier referred to below, blood group serology was used to confirm the correct association of the body parts found to constitute one individual.

The following case demonstrates the identification procedure recommended:

## THE IDENTIFICATION OF THE VICTIM OF AN EXPLOSION

A soldier was fatally injured while standing close to an explosion. The body suffered total disintegration and the various body parts were scattered over a wide area.

The various parts were x-rayed, and examined by dissection. The following parts could be identified:

a. Vertebrae from the cervical and thoracic spine;
b. Thoracic soft tissue;
c. Left hand and fingers;
d. Left metatarsal area and assorted tarsal bones;
e. Pieces of long bones;
f. Fragments of ribs, scapulae, skull bone;
g. Soft tissue from the skin and muscles.

The correct assignment of the various parts of the body to constitute one body was based on the following criteria:

1. Anatomical features of long bones consistent with one individual.
2. Vertebrae, long bones and soft tissue showed similarity of blood group, i.e., group A, Rhesus (+).
3. All tissues were equally charred.
4. X-ray examination of all body parts revealed the same metallic fragments, confirmed by chemical analysis of fragments.

On the basis of the above data it was clear that we were dealing with one body. A study of the antemortem data available on a number of individuals who were believed to have been in the area at the time or tne explosion revealed the probable identity of the missing soldier. Further comparisons between the anatomical data of the missing soldier and those of the reconstituted body indicated that we were dealing with a male adult, probably aged between 35 to 40 years. The left hand could be fingerprinted, and comparison with the fingerprint record in the missing soldier's file confirmed the identity.

The value of the methods described is also indicated by the identification of the late Mrs. Dora Bloch, who was murdered in Kampala in 1975.

# THE IDENTIFICATION OF THE LATE MRS. DORA BLOCH[19]

As isknown, Mrs. Dora Bloch was murdered in Kampala, Uganda, in 1975, following the Entebbe rescue by an Israeli army unit. Death was caused by severe injuries that resulted from blows on the head, body and limbs, with a panga. After death the body was partially burnt on an open fire. The body was buried in an identifiable grave, with a civilian eyewitness. The deceased was described in the available medical records as a white Caucasian female, aged over 70. Her height was 156 to 160 cm. There was a medical report of osteo-arthritic changes in the cervical, thoracic and lumbar spines. There was also fusion of the thoracic 8-9 vertebrae due to osteo-arthritic spondlyosis. The x-ray examination also revealed marked anterior curvature of the cervical spine, and postero-lateral curvature of the thoracic and lumbar spine. Records were available of the upper and lower dentures prepared by a Tel Aviv dentist as recently as 1974.

The comparison between this information and the results of the postmortem examination confirmed the identification.

The remains were identified on the basis of the two stage approach described above.

A. Group characterisation of the remains:
1. Remains were found in an identified grave by eye witnesses to its burial;
2. The remains were those of an elderly female caucasion. The age was above 70 years;
3. The height was assessed as approximately 157 cm;
4. The injuries present on the skull were consistent with the information supplied by eye witnesses to the murder.

B. Specific identifying features:
1. Osteophytic lipping of all spinal vertebrae in the body consistent with the appearance of x-ray changes in these vertebrae shown during life;
2. Osteoarthritic spondylosis with complete fusion of thoracic vertebrae 8-9, consistent with x-ray picture during life;
3. Assembling the vertebrae during the examination restored the spinal column curvature as demonstrated in the x-ray photographs taken during life;
4. Dentures were found loose in the grave. They were identical with the description provided by the Tel Aviv dentist who prepared them.

# REFERENCES

1.  Encyclopaedia Britannica, 1975.  Encyclopaedia Britannica, Inc., U.S.A.

2.  Treasures of Tutenkhamun.  I. E. S. Edwards.  Ballantine Books, New York, 1978

3.  Identification of Mass Disaster Victims.  The Swiss Identification System.  H. R. Mulman, E. Steiner, N. Brandestini, Journal of Forensic Sciences, 24/1:173-181, 1979.

4.  Summary of the means used to positively identify the American victims in the Canary Island Crash. J. H. Woolcott and C. A. Hanson.  Aviat Space Environ Med. 51(9):1035-1035, 1980.

5.  Medical Examiner's Report of a Boeing 727-95 aircraft accident.  B. S. Rumsch.  Journal of Forensic Sciences, 22/4:835-844, 1977.

6.  Sex and race determination of craniary calipers and computer.  C. C. Snow, S. Hartman, E. Giles, F. A. Young.  Journal of Forensic Science, 24/3 448-460, 1979.

7.  The dental identification in fatal aircraft accidents. I. R. Hill.  Aviat Space Environ Med. 51/911:1021-1025 1980.

8.  Aircrash on Mount Erebus.  F. J. Cairns, B. Herdson, G. C. Hitchcock.  Med. Sci. Law 21/3:184-188, 1981.

9.  Unpublished data.  M. Rogev, 1966.

10. The human skeleton in forensic medicine.  W. M. Krogman 1962.  Charles C. Thomas, Publisher, Springfield, Illinois, U.S.A.

11. Estimation of stature from long bones of American Whites and Negroes.  H. Trotter, P. Glesser.  A.J.P.A. NS 10(4):463-514, 1952.

12. Unpublished data.  Israel Defence Forces.  M. Rogev, 1984.

13. Unpublished data. Israel Defence Forces. M. Rogev, 1984-1985.

14. Ravina A. L'identificationdes corps pare le V-Test. Le Presse Medicale 68:178, 1960.

15. A. Schuller. Note on the identification of skulls by x-ray pictures of frontal sinuses. Med J. Australia 1:554-556, 1945.

16. A. Schuller. Das Rontgengram der Stinholhe. Ein Hilfsmittel fur die Identilatsbestimmung von Schableln. Monatschr. F. Ohremn. 55:1617-1620, 1927.

17. W. M. Krogman. Quotes case history presentation by Bulbert al Law 1927 and Law 1934. The human skeleton in Forensic Medicine. Charles C. Thomas, Springfield Illinois, USA 1973 (Second Edition).

18. Unpublished data. Israel Defence Forces. M. Rogev, 1984-85.

19. Unpublished data. Israel Defence Forces. M. Rogev, 1979-80.

## An Approach to Laboratory Automation
E.C. Tulloch, G.J. Kupferschmidt

Abstract

   The Royal Canadian Mounted Police (RCMP) Laboratory System consists of eight disciplines in each of eight regional laboratories; therefore, the scientific equipment and commensurate data handling for forensic investigation is diversified. Based upon what we considered to be our unique forensic requirements, and recognizing the already established resources within our EDP Departmental Responsibility Centre, various automation concepts were assessed for suitability within the RCMP. Automation criteria were established resulting in a decision to adopt centralized processing wherever possible. Since the historical development of the RCMP Laboratory System was centred around dedicated processing it was necessary to develop implementation criteria in order to ensure a smooth transition to the centralized approach. Such things as site preparation, service contracts, operator selection, training, performance specifications etc. are considered.

Fig. 1 - Royal Canadian Mounted Police Forensic Laboratories

Introduction

   Canada is a vast country, about 5,000 miles from coast to coast with a population of 25,000,000 people. There are ten provinces and two territories (Fig. 1). The Royal Canadian Mounted Police provides a national network of eight forensic laboratories in support of law enforcement. Each laboratory is divided into the following disciplines or areas of expertise:

| Alcohol | Serology | |
|---|---|---|
| Chemistry | Toxicology | |
| Documents | Analytical Services | |
| Firearms | Central Bureau | Central Forensic |
| Hair & Fibre |    for Counterfeits | Laboratory Only |
| Photography | Radiography | |

As with any laboratory, a forensic service depends upon a multitude of techniques some of which are highly sophisticated and require a great deal of computer control and data handling as well as data base development. The following is a categorical list of equipment used by the RCMP Laboratories.

Category A:

Atomic Absorption Spectrophotometers
Differential Scanning Calorimeters
Emission Spectrographs
Fluorometers

Category B:

Gas Chromatographs
High Pressure Liquid Chromatographs
Infra-Red Spectrometers
UV/VIS Spectrophotometers

Category C:

Computerized Fourier Transform Infra-red Spectrophotometers
Computerized Gas Chromatography Mass Spectrometry
Microspectrophotometers
Scanning Electron Microscopy/Energy Dispersive X-Ray Systems
X-Ray Spectrophotometry
Glass Refractive Index Measurement System

Category A represents the scientific equipment receiving less and less emphasis in the Forensic Laboratory. This has come about either because exhibit materials are now viewed differently in the overall analytical scheme of things, or because better, more sensitive techniques have been developed replacing them. Category B represents that equipment considered to have general application to a number of forensic disciplines. As a result, large numbers of these instruments will be found in any one laboratory fulfilling a number of analytical requirements. Finally, category C represents the scientific equipment present as single installations, one per lab. This is usually as a result of the specialized nature or the sophistication of the technique involved. In many cases category C equipment has eliminated, automated or combined category A and B equipment.

Historical Perspective

Even though the electronic digital computer became available in the early fifties it was not until approximately the last ten years that its capability to make very rapid control decisions or to communicate at high speeds with other devices, such as laboratory instruments was fully recognized. The early applications of digital computer methods focused on data-logging techniques, whereby some type of digital or analog data-acquisition device was attached to an instrument and the data collected transferred to the computer at some later date for further manipulation. As technology advanced, digital integrators and small mini-computers began to appear that were capable of direct data-acquisition from instruments, along with the appropriate devices for the display or listing of data thus obtained. Interfaces were being developed that were capable of controlling the instrument. Up to the mid 1970's the scientific instrument and the computer were considered as separate entities. At about this time, manufacturers of scientific equipment realized the potential in interfacing the two components and as a result, began to incorporate microprocessors into their equipment for the purpose of controlling instrumental parameters. Some vendors extended the capability of the microprocessor and developed a fully operational computer around the microprocessor incorporated into the instrument (Intelligent Instruments). Other manufacturers decided to use the microprocessor incorporated into the instrument solely for parameter control and utilized a second microprocessor with a fully operational computer in a device called a data station. This device was a specialized microcomputer. Still other manufacturers decided to develop small main-frame computers capable of servicing a large number of instruments simultaneously, from one central location utilizing a single processor.

Forensic Science has gradually evolved from the traditional wet chemical and microscopic techniques to highly sophisticated instrumentation. In the past, analytical endeavours consisted of a series of manual steps, beginning with separation and isolation followed by identification and perhaps quantitation. Each technological change was essentially an effort to enhance sensitivity and specificity. Probably the greatest advancement occurred with the development of the microprocessor and its incorporation into scientific instrumentation, providing for rigid control of instrumental parameters and therefore greater precision and reproducibility. The development of an operational computer around the microprocessor fulfilled the data handling requirements of the specific technique and resulted in the birth of intelligent instruments. Concurrently, analytical chemists, researchers and manufacturers were attempting to combine traditional stand-alone techniques with the aim of increasing the separation and isolation efficiency using one entity, and coupling it with a highly specific fingerprinting technique.

Because of the various combinations, more complicated controllers and data handling devices were required due to the inherent sophistication and massive data generating capability of such equipment. In other words, the combination instruments such as GC/MS - Gas Chromatographs/Mass Spectrometers, GC/FTIR - Gas Chromatographs/Infra-Red Spectrometers, LC/MS - High Pressure Liquid Chromatographs/Mass Spectrometers, Microscope/UV-VIS Spectrophotometers and Scanning Electron Microscopes/Energy Dispersive X-Ray Systems were developed only because of the incorporation of a powerful computer. In general, these computers are designed for a specific analytical purpose utilizing sophisticated hardware and software and therefore have an inherent ability to provide a general purpose processing capability.

In the late 1970's and early 1980's the RCMP Labs possessed equipment with varying degrees of automation. To complicate matters further, this equipment was purchased from different suppliers and as a result instrument to instrument or more properly computer to computer communication was not feasible without considerable hardware and software investment. The data generated was in general not compatible since it is manufacturer-oriented.

When the long term requirement for data manipulation, data handling flexibility, data exchange and the development of Forensic data bases is analyzed, consideration must be given to standardization of the scientific instrumentation, the data handling devices and all of the hardware and software associated with them.

The present work describes the approach taken by the RCMP Laboratories in developing an automation plan to meet our forensic requirements.

Automation Elements

When laboratory automation is considered, numerous avenues are available. Before a particular configuration can be chosen, the elements of automation must be defined. These elements include:

1) Instrumental Control –

parameter control such as gas flow rates, pressures, temperature zones, ionization current, etc;

2) Automatic Sample Preparation/Automatic Sample Introduction –

this eliminates repeated manual steps in an analytical procedure, and allows 24 hr. continuous usage;

3) Data Capture and Control –

the ability to collect and convert analog signals into a digital format commensurate with the requirements of the analytical technique;

4) Data Editing/Display/Graphics –

the ability to represent digital data in an analog format during analysis in order to monitor the analytical event, and in addition allow for the massaging and manipulation of the digital data (i.e., reintegration, elimination of background, peak stripping, etc.);

5) Preliminary Processing –

the ability to provide standardized information reflecting the technique being utilized i.e., peak tables, integration characteristics, relative abundance, mass to charge ratios, etc;

6) Extended Processing/Special Purpose Computing –

the ability to utilize the results of preliminary processing in order to develop additional analytical correlations or to perform a statistical evaluation on accumulated analytical results;

7) Instrument Specific Data Bases –

the ability to provide a data base with respect to the parameters being measured in a given analytical technique;

8) General Data Bases –

the ability to provide a data base with respect to the parameters measured by a multitude of unrelated analytical techniques or simply general information about a given subject area;

9) Multiple Access –

the ability to distribute information to other interested users within the same laboratory and to users in other laboratories; and

10) General Purpose Computing –

the ability to develop non-specialized programs having general application to a laboratory system.

371

Upon analyzing the various elements, it is obvious that the first seven elements are "on-line" functions and as such must remain in close proximity to the analyst. The latter three can reside anywhere because they are acted upon only when an analysis is completed, therefore they do not have a "real-time" need.

Within the RCMP, there is an EDP facility consisting of a large mainframe network of hardware and software and is primarily responsible for management and police information systems. The RCMP Laboratories have access to these resources via terminals within the respective laboratories. After considerable discussion it was decided that general data basing, multiple access and general purpose computing would be provided by the EDP facility and that the laboratories would remain responsible for the "on-line" functions previously described.

Automation Concepts

In today's analytical laboratory, three main types of configuration utilized for instrumental control, data acquisition and data handling are commonly seen:

(i) <u>Dedicated Processors</u> incorporated or in close proximity to the instrument;

(ii) <u>Distributed Processor</u> networks comprised of data stations from which information is channelled through a hierarchical network to a host computer; and

(iii) <u>Centralized Processors</u> in which data acquisition, instrument control, integration, storage, etc., are performed by a single central processor.

To add to the complexity, each of these configurations gives rise to several variations as shown in the following table.

Type of Configuration - Variation

| <u>Dedicated</u> | – | INSTRUMENT ---- INTEGRATOR |
|---|---|---|
| <u>Centralized</u> | – | INSTRUMENT ---- COMPUTER |
| <u>Centralized</u> | – | INSTRUMENT/MICROPROCESSOR CONTROL ---- COMPUTER |
| <u>Distributed</u> | – | INSTRUMENT/MICROPROCESSOR CONTROL/DATA HANDLING ---- -- COMPUTER |
| <u>Distributed</u> | – | INSTRUMENT ---- DATA STATION ---- COMPUTER |
| <u>Distributed</u> | – | INSTRUMENT/MICROPROCESSOR CONTROL ---- DATA STATION ---- COMPUTER |
| <u>Centralized</u> | – | INSTRUMENT ---- INSTRUMENT/MICROPROCESSOR CONTROL ---- COMPUTER |

All configurations existed within the RCMP Laboratory system, which made the move towards standardization difficult to implement.

The Category A instruments, as noted earlier, are either being phased out of the system (i.e., spectrograph) or are to be replaced with instruments which would fit into the standardization plan as Category B or as Category C instruments.

The Category B instruments require far less precision and instrumental control than Category C; and have general processing requirements and low volumes of data storage. The vast majority of the laboratory instruments fall within this category. For example a particular lab may have 20 instruments of this type. At some point in time, this Category may include benchtop Fourier Transform Infra-Red spectrophotometers and mass selective detectors which do not require the degree of storage and data handling of the Category C instruments. For these reasons, only Category B instruments were deemed suitable for central automation at this time.

The Category C instruments, as mentioned previously, include the highly specialized combination instruments which require:

a)  high data sampling rates;

b)  large volumes of analog data usually at 16-32 bit precision or greater;

c)  extensive dedicated software;

d)  foreground/background operation;

e)  large single purpose libraries, dedicated vendor supplied peripherals (i.e., x-y plotters); and

f)  complex instrument control.

These instruments are of a research quality and normally require a dedicated processor to generate the necessary speed and precision to cope with their data generation capabilities.

The first step in standardizing Category B instruments was an analysis of our present and future instrumental requirements:

a)  Number one priority was the acquisition of data at a rate and accuracy essential for meaningful integration.

b)  The second involved the flexibility of integration of this data to accommodate a wide range of instruments and methods.

c)  Thirdly, post integration processing was required, involving statistical calculations, data base search routines and the correlation of data from more than one instrument.

d)  The fourth requirement involved non-standard instrumentation, void of data handling such as a microspectrophotometer.

e)  The final requirement identified was the transfer of data and methodology between laboratories.

With the requirements identified, the cost of adopting each of the three configurations had to be examined. Factors such as the initial cost of buying a centralized minicomputer against the constant obsoletion of integrators/microprocessors with changes in technology of instrumentation had to be weighed. Consideration also had to be given to absorbing or re-distributing existing resources in the system.

An assessment of centralized laboratory automation offered the advantages of flexibility such as:

a) in-house software development;

b) wider choice of vendor software packages;

c) Software revisions to capitalize on changes in instrument technology;

d) greater selection and better utilization of shared peripheral devices (plotters, CRT terminals, modems etc.);

e) memory expansion (CPU and disc storage);

f) hardware expansion to accommodate normal growth;

g) time sharing to allow for efficient use of CPU time;

h) capability of interfacing non-standard devices and existing resources;

i) networking capabilities within the existing RCMP mainframe facility;

j) purchase of less expensive analytical instruments void of data handling;

k) capability of building a distributed networking system if and when required.

To accommodate both present and future requirements the centralized automation concept provides cost effectiveness, flexibility and system growth as well as solutions to potential specialized analytical problems.

Implementation

Our first implementation of a central laboratory system occurred in the Central Forensic Laboratory, Ottawa, in 1982. This pilot installation, provided a protocol for implementing subsequent purchases. This includes in order of priority:

(1) imparting the philosophy of centralized lab automation systems to the end users emphasizing the flexibility and the unique capabilities of central automation;

(2) inventory of existing analytical instruments and data handling devices:

a) to determine existing peripherals that could be integrated into the system;

b) to identify special interfacing requirements;

c) to re-deploy non-compatible resources for backup purposes where applicable;

(3) determination of building requirements including space, security, utilities and location of user sections to be serviced;

(4) preparation of the purchase order for central automation system to include:

a) hardware/software packages;

b) peripherals;

c) cables;

d) connectors;

e) manuals;

f) software packages; and

g) CPU and associated hardware storage devices with performance specifications, terms and conditions to be met by vendor, site preparation including building renovations for electrical requirements (power line conditioners/filters, power stabilizers), air conditioning, environmental control, (static, humidity and dust control) and pre-wiring of laboratory for peripherals.

(5) appointment of system manager who is responsible for:

a) management of hardware and software resources

b) implementation of installation of equipment:

c) interfacing of analytical instrumentation and system peripherals;

d) regular software backups of system for archival purposes;

e) specialized analytical software development;

f) liaison with vendor and general hardware/software upkeep.

(6) system installation with performance testing to ensure vendors' specifications have been met;

(7) training of System Manager by vendor and training of user sections by vendor and by System Manager;

(8) initiation of hardware service contract to commence when warranty terminates and software subscription for update of software revisions; and

(9) projection of future requirements to include expansion of system and hardware/software replacement within the budget cycle.

Central computers tend to be dynamic in growth as opposed to static and once installed the system expands with normal Laboratory growth.

To date three central automation systems have been purchased and are at various stages of implementation. It is expected that all RCMP Laboratories will be equipped with similar systems by 1987.

## Conclusion

In conclusion, it is our opinion that central automation is the most appropriate approach at this time. It is recognized that as communication technology changes, there will be a greater tendency to proceed toward distributed processing. By standardizing the central automation system first, the distributed portion can be implemented as needed avoiding any interfacing pitfalls.

# CENTRAL COLLECTIONS OF PHYSICAL EVIDENCE
## AND POSSIBILITIES OF SUPPORT THROUGH USE OF COMPUTERS

Dr. Wolfgang Steinke
Bundeskriminalamt
Viesbaden, Germany

A breakdown of the BKA structure dealing with the receipt and handling of evidence is provided in this paper. Terrorist materials are handled separately, and statistics are given for the various crimes which terrorists have committed. Information about arson and bombing incidents is computerized, and based upon the modus operandi and weapons/chemicals involved. It is possible to construct investigative leads by associating similar incidents. In 10 years, for example, there were 5200 cases of arson and bombing attacks, thus it was decided in 1979 that computerization would be more effective than manual filing for information retrieval. Computerization was then applied to other problems such as narcotics cases, use of alias names and questions involving handwriting identification.

If one speaks about collections compiled by the BKA and knows about their enormous volume, one also inevitably thinks about a total computerization, since the BKA is, according to law, the central point of the Electronic Data System and in fact has advanced the employment of computers by the police decisively. Our search systems - persons and objects - operate since more than ten years with absolute accuracy.

Dokumentation of tracing systems for big cases are build up temporarely. The "police observation" is supported by computers and for some special fields of offences, case data are set up and functioning. Thereby it is possible to affix - over the modus operandi - similar committed offences as well as to recognize, if offences committed by unknown persons are performed after the same method.

Only one thing, however, could not be accomplished so far, to build up a global offence/criminal data base which will allow investigations concerning all or single fields of offences according to similar methods. Concerning such a data pool the catalogue - like filing of descriptions of offences and offenders were leading to rough generalizations, whereby the characteristics of offences would not be recognized and consequently integrations not take place. Efforts are therefore made to find another method of presentation in lieu of a catalogue like form in order to still find a system of investigation which will be useful in reference to linking crimes and identifying criminals instead of just satisfying statistical requirements. Every single case of course will be numerically registered by the computer, whereby possible connections are established with cases already compiled. So in every aspect where the computer might be helpful, use is being made of it.

The following account is given with special emphasis of central collections of physical evidence (including finger-prints) in respect of computerisation in order to give you a close view, under the aspect of common international interest, regarding the range of application of this mass project.

## REGISTRATION OF PHYSICAL EVIDENCE CONCERNING EXPLOSIVES AND INCENDIARY DEVICES

Under the impression of a series of explosive-assassina-tions, the local police departments will first inform the designated central evaluation centre point of the BKA by telephone, teletype and later on give specific formal information regarding the incident, including technical details and measures taken at the scene of crime.

These compulsory incident reports also include the safe-guarding of misused industrial and military explosives and incendiary devices, pyro-technical devices, dummys as well as written instructions concerning the production of unconven-tional explosives and incendiary devices.

After conclusion of inquiries and investigations, the local police authorities will send all materials to the evaluation center.

The BKA then will proceed investigations as to place of origin and direct all measures necessary concerning identification of traces, means of crime or proof of evidence. (explosives, ignition devices, military ammunition, ducks, fire extinguishers etc.)
These reports are pertaining to
type of devices,

container and connection,
filling,
ignition device,
type of ignition,
additional parts (wires, switches etc.)
other parts of device (tape etc.)
carrying device,
deposit or placement of device,
if known to the committer, admittance of crime,
finger-print recognition and
criminal-technical examinations.

Since the numbers of incidents did increase considerably during the early years after the installation of the center, (more than 5.200 known incidents within 10 years), an electronic data-system was installed, compiling all incidents since 1975. In addition, for the time before this date, all earlier incidents of special interest for comparison purposes were added to the system. The data-pool "Explosives and incendiary devices" is divided into four groups, which can be compiled by a number of references.

A respective file is established under this number, so one may talk of a FILE-REFERENCE-SYSTEM.

The first data-group contains the type of incident, time of incident, special behavioral patterns and motives.

Data-group 2 contains the name of the established delinquent or the institution (no suspected cases) sex and date of birth of the established persons.

The 3rd data-group contains information regarding the place of crime, type and name of attacked objective.

Finally, the 4th data-group designates the object, type, model and manufacturer - importer, distributer -, color, number, material, measures and weight of object and space for special characteristics, in which - in manner of a thesaurus - unusual aspects of a case may be maintained catchword-like.

This amount of information has been sufficient so far, in order to rapidly relocate comparable incidents and their attached files.

## COLLECTION OF HAND-WRITINGS

A second central collection holding hand-written documents in connection with the interstate active offender is being maintained at the BKA, with especially numerous documents in the fields of terrorism, fraud, prescription forgery and threats extortion.

Every year, approximately 50.000 questioned documents

are submitted by the Federal States for the purpose of identifying the writer or establishing connections between crimes. The handwriting classification system proper is based on features which in the literature on handwriting examination are described as general characteristics of writing. This system, developed by the BKA, is orientated at relatively stable elements of script, such as: system of writing, type of connection, size, emphasis, loop shape etc., and allows a classification into certain categories. It offers a relatively high degree of selectivity in search against the collection.

The collection purging period of the data-pool is limited to ten years.

Besides the purely graphical points of view, additional data, such as fictitious names are compiled in order to minimize the time of investigation and at the same time to increase the rate of retrieval. The rate of identification achieved by this service is approx. 30%. The evaluation of documents of terroristic origin secured in conspirative apartments and depots even ranges to an identification rate of 75-100%.

This conventional system of classification shall shortly be replaced by a computerized application called FISH (Forensic Information System Handwriting). Detailed information regarding this project will be delivered by Mr. Hecker if it is possible.

## COLLECTION OF CRIMINALLY UTILIZED AMMUNITION

The BKA further more maintains a central collection of ammunition parts, (cartridges, cartridge cases, projectiles) in connection with fire-arms, compiled throughout the Federal Republic. Purpose of the collection is the recognition of possible criminal connections (connecting scenes of crime, in case a weapon is not available, and relate the weapon used for crime to ammunition by comparison of traces with compared ammunition). This collection at present amounts to nearly 8000 cartridge cases and 5000 projectiles out of approx. 5200 unsolved cases.

The collection is growing at a monthly rate of 60 to 80 cases and is adjusted through identification or cleared in accordance with the time limits subject to the statute of limitations. The collection has proved itself as very effective. About 100 cases are solved during a year and 50 to 60 connections between crimes, committed by unknown offenders, are established. To achieve even more effectiveness, an attempt of computerizing the system has been made in the past. The computer however so far has been unable to select with the necessary precision all pieces of evidence essential for a comparison. Therefore, the computerization has to be delayed, until digital image processing in this field has been further developed.

## COLLECTION OF KEYS

In the struggle against terrorist-inspired crimes of violence we were compelled to provide a selection of keys secured by the apprehension of terrorists and from conspirative apartments and depots. Thereby, we were able to recognize which person had admittance to a certain known or unknown object. The collection contains 900 keys at present, although the rate of increase is negligible. After a period of 10 years, the respective items will be sorted out. The effectiveness however, especially in recent times, has diminished. In view of the relatively minor stock maintained, there are no problems concerning classification or investigation.

## PRINTINGS AND SEALS

Not only by the terrorist-activities during the early 70s we were obligated to establish facilities of recognition as a central collection for printings and seals.
These collections contain:
approximately 3000 forged german driving licenses,
approximately 2000 german automobile ownership-
 licenses,
approximately 100 securities (such as shares, cheques,
 stamps etc.)
approximately 50 printings of documental character
 (such as certificates, testimonials or official
 documents of personal status),
approximately 600 publications out of the fomenting
 sphere.
First of all, the classification of the items to be inserted into the collection will take place according to purely organizational, superior criteria, such as imprints of driving licenses, textual contents of agitatorial publications or according to picturial or figurative contents for example as the RAF-logo.
The forensic differentiation follows fixed evaluation-criteria (printing-procedure, contents of picturial information) and analysis-data (for instance one or two component-toner in fotocopies). In case the forgeries

appear for the first time, the deviations from the authentic
document will be registered and maintained as characteristic
of the specific group for future comparison. If a forgery
of the same kind should appear again, an identification
will be possible within a short period of time, merely by
comparison of the characteristic-matrix. Thereby, supra-
regional connections of at first looking independently
committed crimes may be established through this factual
proof. In view of the relatively low quantities of items,
the collection is not computerized.

## CENTRAL COLLECTION OF TYPESCRIPTS

This collection contains incriminated and comparative
scripts accumulated by acts of crime. The respective
scripts are classified and inserted with a system developed
by the BKA. Precondition for the integration of a script
into the collection is the presence of facial-characteristics,
which allows the identification and possibly recognition
of the specific typewriter. The main purpose of the collection
is the ascertainment of alignment and being able to give
references pertaining to search and investigation. At present,
the collection has a volume of approx. 20.000 scripts.

The continuation may become problematic however, when
in future daisy wheels (printwheels) instead of type-bars
and elements will be used. They are made of cheap synthetic
material and are often exchanged because they wear out
rather rapidly. Since worn out wheels are usually destroyed,
they are not available for comparative-examinations. It
would be possible to computerize the collection, however,
priority was given to more important computer-projects.

## CENTRAL COLLECTION OF IDENTITY DOCUMENTS

This collection presently consists of approx. 500
specimen, divided into:
200 German Passports and
100 German Federal Identity Cards.
Alien identity documents amount to approx.
100 Passports
200 ID-Cards
100 Driving Permits and
70 other identification documents.
The collection serves as a foundation for examination
of items produced on a reproductive-, printing- and

processing base with the aim of finding connecting cases of crime especially on the supra-regional level and to relate falsifications to the forgers responsible.

In view of the limited volume, the collection is not computerized.

## COLLECTION OF ROUNDS

During the past 10 years in about 550 cases metal-rounds in the size of 5,-- DM, 2,-- DM and 1,-- DM pieces were submitted to the BKA for examination in order to gain informations concerning the composition of this devices and thereby establishing possible connections of cases.

The presentation of coins in foreign currencies (France, Great Britain, Greece, Belgium, Mexico and Poland) is relatively rare.

The rounds produced for german automates will have to be prepared with magnetic materials in order to pass the magnet-tester of the automat. In some cases, rolls filled with leadet rings instead of coin-money rolls were presented to financial institutions. The culprits exchanged genuine coin-rolls on a large scale to such an extent as it was deemed necessary to establish a certain degree of trustworthiness. Then, at a given time, the manipulated rolls are offered to the bank for exchange into bank-notes. On the base of the achieved confidence, the so presented rolls instead of being opened and counted are only weighted. In recent times, the BKA has also established Expert-opinions on the grounds of total falsifications of 20 US-Dollar-gold coins, as well as 1,-- DM and 5,-- DM coins, and old silver 5,-- DM. Cases have occured, whereby the dates of year were changed by a quicksilver-amalgam-procedure in order to multiply the collectors value.

So far, the automation of the rounds-collection has not been realized. If, however, the rate of increase is developing to the same extent as it did in the past, the processing will have to be supported by computer.

## FINGERPRINT-COLLECTION

The BKA - together with the State Crime Labs - has created a fingerprint classification-system, by which investigations within a collection of fingerprint leafs numbering about one million, are possible. This collection was created and is centrally maintained at the BKA. Otherwise, 11 different collections spread over the various

State-Criminal Offices would have to be consulted in order
to identify fingerprints of the supra-regional offender.
Such a procedure however, would be uneconomical. By
integration of all regional collections, the ten-fingerprint
collection of the BKA reached an amount of about 1,8
million leafs during recent years.

The classification formula for this collection, divided
into males and females, contained three main classes and
three sub-classes.

Since there are fraction-formulas, which in their main
classes and some sub-classes appear quite frequently,a
large scale classification concerning the so-called
"Standard-Fractions", leading to an acceptable reduced
number of fingerprint leafs in search against the collection,
was not possible. The collection of Standard-Fractions
had increased to such an extent, that in an average case,
200 to 300 fingerprint leafs had to be visually examined
by the investigator.

Even investigations of about 600 leafs, keeping the
examiner occupied for an entire day, were not unusual.
In some cases - although very exceptional - up to 13.800
leafs had to be compared with each other. All this was
leading to unacceptable search times. So a more disting-
uishing method had to be found. The aspects suggested a
computerized system, able to memorize and re-trace a
substantially extended formula. A second, vital point for
installation of a computerized fingerprint collection
derided from the fact that single fingerprints secured on
the scene of crime, could only be  locally evaluated, since
there was no centrally located unified single fingerprint
investigation-System available, not even in the various
Federal States. Therefore, plans were made to formulate
all ten fingerprint leafs of those offenders liable to leave
their fingerprints in the course of further offences,
whereby a formula was to be affixed to every single
fingerprint and that formula filed in a single fingerprint
data bank. Such a system would have made it possible for
instance to establish a connection between fingerprints
of a Munich resident secured in Bremen. Under the
instructions of the BKA an order was placed with a renowned
manufacturer for the creation of such a system. After a
development of several years a model was produced,
presenting itself as follows:

The new System developed jointly by the Federation and
the Federal States represents a combination of old,
proven classification features (Abb. 1) and of new ones.

For the first time, it enables a system-oriented use to be made of ten print collections for the identification of fingermarks (crime-scene prints), makes it possible to perform searches within an extremely short time, and reduces the material to be visually compared by the fingerprint technician to a minimum thanks to a high degree of selectiveness. It further leads to the unification of all classification systems in the Federal Republic and provides decentralized availability of the central fingerprint data base kept at the Bundeskriminalamt (Federal Criminal Police Office) to 11 State Criminal Police Offices.

## TOOLS

Fingerprints and fingermarks are analysed by means of a classification unit which displays the fingerprint enlarged by factor 7.1 (linear) on the back of a screen using the principle of the overhead projector. The screen is divided into 24 sectors and can be rotated about its axis, and using the steering table, the print can be moved in any direction. The screen is pivoted in its centre, which in combination with a reference point allows the print to be properly positioned.

A line which also can be rotated and runs through the center of the display facilitates ridge counting and the locating of certain characteristics (Abb. 2)

By means of a visual display unit the analytical results obtained are fed directly into a central data processing system which controls the interactive operation, searches the data base, and prints out hit lists via a high-speed printer.

## ELEMENTS OF CLASSIFICATION

Total information contained in a fingerprint data record is composed of the following elements, which in combination with each other, make for a high degree of selectivity.

1. Finger designation
   In about 50 percent of all cases, it is possible on the basis of a fingermark lifted from a crime scene to tell which finger of the perpetrator produced the latent print. This is valuable information which is stored for further use.
2. Basic pattern classes
   Fingerprints are grouped in 5 classes.
3. Basic patterns
   Abbildung 3

4. Basic pattern compliments
   Loop patterns, which account for about 60 percent
   of all cases, and other patterns having an
   innermost loop are further classified by certain
   structures (e.g., islands or rods) present within
   a defined area to enhance selectivity.
   Abbildung 4
5. Locating the deltas
   The location of deltas in loop, and whirl, patterns
   is recorded by sector and by distances, i.e., by
   counting the ridges crossed by the locator line
   between the given delta and the center point.
   Abbildung 5
6. Locating the characteristics
   Within a 9 mm circle in the center area of the
   pattern, aberrations from continuous ridge flow
   (the anatomical characteristics) are located and
   recorded as beginning or ending ridges (B or E).
   The locating is performed clockwise - as in locating
   the deltas - by direction (sector) and distance
   between center point and characteristic.
   Abbildung 6

## RECORDING, STORAGE, AND COMPARISON

The fingerprint technician locates by an electronic
stick the individual points, and the computer transforms it
into a formula and stores the formula.

A distinction is made between short records having about
80 - 100 characters (ten-finger formula) and long records
having some 800 - 1000 characters (one-finger formula).
(Abb. 7)

## CONCLUSION

In view of the experiences gained so far, the fingerprint
data processing system operated by the BKA has proved itself
efficient and expeditious:

In order to cope with the incoming workload, over 84.000
ten-fingerprint leafs had to be visually compared within
the manually operated system. With the help of the computerized system, this number was reduced to 1/70.

In the past, the BKA, within the Federal States System,
has registered ten-fingerprints for identification purposes
of about 930.000 persons, 430.000 of them with single-finger
assortment. Since the introduction of the system
over 8000 persons using false names or refused to

reveal their identities,
300 unknown dead persons and
4800 prints caused by unknown persons
could be identified. The rate of success is increasing.

From the technical point of view, the computer supported system is available for 24 hrs. daily without any functional restriction. At the present time of utilization the answer-time ratio substantially meets the police demands. Complete utilization of the system however will be achieved, if the entire fingerprint stock within the system will be available. So far, this is the case by only 50% of the persons registered by the BKA identification service. Therefore the highly personal intensive concurrance of the old and new system is necessary for the time being. Even after a complete change to the new system, at a high level of efficiency and speed of investigations in the field of classifications, there will remain a comparatively high time and personal consuming effort which should be reduced in the future. At present all efforts are directed towards this goal.

## COMPUTERIZATION OF FRAUDULENT CHEQUES COLLECTION

Shmuel Kraus, Ph.D., Chief Superintendent
Israel National Police

Peter Tytell
Tytell Questioned Document Laboratory
New York City

Stolen checks can be linked to their passers by handwriting comparison. The Questioned Documents Laboratory operates a stolen check collection in which those checks are kept. The collection has more than 7000 checks written by some 3599 different persons. New checks were routinely searched with the existing checks for common account numbers and aliases. Comparisons based on handwriting were made only occasionally, when the expert remembered and recognized the handwriting. Computer assisted searching of the checks became the most viable way of handling the ever-growing collection. The Hebrew alphabet lends itself to relatively simple classification, since it is comprised of unconnected letters only, whether they be script or block printing. Two classes of handwriting variables were selected from each check. Six letters and six digits which are found on most checks were chosen for classification. The second group of variables was that of habits in filling out forms. The idea was that people under pressure will adhere to old habits even when they are aware of the need to change their handwriting. Eleven features of writing, such as line position, signature placement, slant, the way in which the date is written, etc.,

> were also classified. The variables were categorized in a way which made it possible for an inexpereienced lay person to input the information into the computer quickly and reproducibly. To date, 5000 checks of 2500 writers have been encoded. An internal search of the file revealed 4 cases of checks which were linked to the file of known writers.

I should like to present a pilot project for computer assisted stolen cheque collection handling. This is a joint project of the Israel National Police Questioned Documents Laboratory and Mr. Peter Tytell of the Tytell Documents Laboratory of New York.

All of us appreciate the fact that a good handwriting comparison is second only to fingerprints comparison in connecting a person to a crime.

The use of stolen cheques is a perfect example of a case where a criminal will deposit the incriminating evidence to his crime in the hands of the police only to have it wait for him for a later date. About ten years ago, parallel to the increase in fuel prices, the Israel Police started experiencing a problem of stolen cheques being passed, especially in gas stations. A decision was made at that time and has not been changed since, that all stolen cheques brought to Police attention, regardless of the sum involved, be collected and stored in the Questioned Documents Laboratory.

At the beginning, cheques were filed in albums. Sections were made holding the cheques of the same person, stored chronologically by date of submission. The file comprised four parts: "known" and "unknown" both subdivided into male and female passers. The differentiation between a male and a female was based just on the assumed names used. We have not found cases involving a man writing a cheque and a woman cashing it for him.

In the early days each new cheque was visually compared by handwriting experts to the file, and if no match was found, the cheque was just added to the collection as an unknown. As the collection grew in size, some sorting system was needed. A card file of account numbers and assumed names was created in the mid-1970's.

To computerize just this card file would have been a major waste of effort, hence it was decided to find ways to computerize the handwriting search.

In the early 70's Varda Tamir and Sima Yagen of the Questioned Documents Laboratory proposed a system for the classification of letters, numerals and handwriting features.

The Hebrew Alphabet lends itself to a rather easy classification as it comprises separately written letters. This applys both to the **block letters us**ed in printing and to the handwritten cursive letters.

Their system was to be implemented on the IBM punched cards sorting machine, but because of the very comprehensive classification of all letters and all numerals and also many writing features, it took a long time to punch a single cheque and the results were not encouraging. The system was abandoned for some years but not forgotten.

In 1982 the stolen cheques collection contained more than 7,000 cheques prepared by about 3,500 writers. Visual searches of the files became impractical and were only seldomly performed, usually when the expert felt he recognized and remembered the handwriting.

We felt that this approach was very unsatisfactory, and it was decided to revive the computerization project.

After exploring what was done in some other laboratories, we decided to base the new program on a minimal number of parameters of habits and handwriting.

The idea behind using writing habits was based on the concept that while under pressure of committing the crime, a person will tend to adhere to his habits of writing and form filling even if he is aware of the need to disguise his handwriting.

Peter Tytell, Jay Levinson and Shmuel Kraus chose six numerals, six letters and eleven writing habits to be coded. The parameters were chosen and defined so as to enable the lay person to classify them easily, accurately and reproducibly. Each parameter can assume one of three or four possible definitions which are as evenly spread among the population as possible (this regretfully is not always the case).

The first few hundred cheques were coded and fed into the computer by Dr. Jay Levinson. The results were very encouraging so we proceeded to the next stage.

An unqualified yet very bright young lady was briefly trained in coding the cheques. So far she has coded more than 4000 cheques of about 2,000 writers. Some of the writers have a single cheque in the data base and some have more than 20. We think it is advisable to enter as many cheques of the same writer as possible as this will improve chances of a new cheque coinciding with at least one of those present in the data base. There is another important reason for this in that we are now trying to apply statistical operators to the multi-cheque samples in order to assess the significance and weight of the various parameters.

The data base is currently searched in three alternative modes:

1. All of the new cheques' parameters are compared to the whole data base. Every match scores one point while contradiction or lack of information score zero.

2. The percentage of each parameter definition in the data base is calculated relative to the other definitions of the same parameter. A grade for each definition is then calculated by dividing 100 by the percentage. A rare quality will so receive a high grade while a common one will score only a few points. The search is then carried out as before, and each match scores its respective grade.

The inherent drawback of this grading system is that it may give a very high grade to an insignificant rare quality.

3. In order to overcome this flaw, a third grading system was devised based on QD expert's feelings as to the importance of the qualities. A set of multiplication factors was applied to the second system to form new scoring weights.

When the comparison of the cheque to the data base is finished, the computer sorts the possible matches in decreasing order.

When we began this project we aimed at finding the correct cheque among the best 20, so far we usually find it at the top of the list.

An internal search that was carried out on the data base revealed more than 70 groups of 2 cheques or more of the same writer of which we had no previous knowledge. Moreover, 5 cheques were linked to the "known" collection and made the prosecution of the criminals possible.

A search of a single cheque takes about four minutes. This is a result of the sequential nature of the file and also a problem of time sharing on the departmental PDP 11/70 mini-computer.

In the future we plan to base the grading system on statistical evaluation of the parameters and also to dedicate a micro-computer to this project. We believe that this will shorten the search time to seconds.

The next step in the evolution of this project as we envisage it is the application of a read/write Video-disc player as mass storage for the photographs of the cheques. This will make the search in the file a fast and easy task.

# A COLLECTION OF TOOL MARKS MADE BY SELF-LOCKING PLIERS ON BROKEN CYLINDER LOCKS

Nicki Agron, Superintendent
Toolmarks & Materials Laboratory
Division of Criminal Identification
Israel National Police

In Israel a common method of breaking into apartments and businesses is to grasp the protruding cylinder lock on the entrance door with a pair of self-locking pliers. With several swift horizontal movements of the pliers, the cylinder lock breaks at the central screw hole into two halves. The outer half of the lock is removed with pliers and a screw driver; a beetlenosed pliers or other suitable instrument is used to operate the lock mechanism in the door to gain entry. Each self-locking pliers, especially the VISEGELP pliers manufactured by the Pererson Manufactoring Co. of De-Witt, Nebraska, USA leaves toolmarks identifiable by class and individual characteristics. Because of the wide geographic distribution of re-occuring identified individual toolmarks on broken cylinder locks collected at the scenes of crimes, it was decided to organize a nation-wide collection. The collection is organized according to the various police precints. The broken cylinder locks are arranged within each precint's drawer according to the date of break in. Regardless of their geographic origin, locks on which are found toolmarks made by the same pliers are kept together as numbered groups, in separate drawers. Self locking pliers which are found in the possession of suspects are sent to the laboratory for a comparative examination with the collection. There have been numerous convictions in Israel courts based upon toolmark evidence reulting from this collection. In one particular case we were able to show that one person was responsible for no fewer than thirty-six different break-ins.

In Israel it is the common practice to install locks in the doors of dwellings and offices that are constructed essentially of two identical pin-tumbler cylinder locks set back to back in a brass housing. Between the two cylinder locks is a small bridge of metal in which is a screw hole and by which the lock is fastened securely to the door. Above the bridge is the cam which transmits the rotation of the lock core to the bolt mechanism.

Figure 1 is a cross section of a double pin-tumbler cylinder lock with a key inserted in one side. One can see how the profile of the key depresses the tumbler and driver pins to the correct level, thus allowing rotation of the lock.

These locks, when installed in a door, generally protrude from the plane of the door by approximately one to two centimeters. The protruding locks are frequently covered by cylinder guards, thick metal housings which cover the locks such that the locks outer edge is flush with the outer surface of the housing.

One common method of forced entry in Israel is by breaking and extracting the protruding cylinder lock by using self-locking pliers such as the Vise-Grip Self-Locking Pliers.

Figure 2

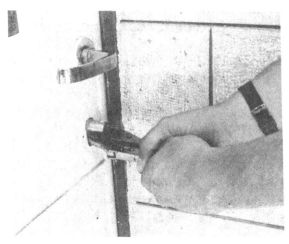

The locking mechanism is operated by means of another tool such as a screw driver, to open the door. Burglars tend to prefer those locks not protected by an adequate cylinder guard. Cylinder guards can be removed with a crowbar or a large screwdriver but the time necessary to break in and the consequent noise involved increase, thus making detection and capture more likely.

In the late Seventies this method of forced entry became popular among burglars in Israel. The number of case files requesting comparisons between tool marks on the outer half of the cylinder locks and those made by a self-locking plier taken from suspects, increased greatly. It was noted that broken cylinder locks from widely scattered geographical locations bore tool marks made by the same plier. This led to the establishment of a nation-wide collection of broken cylinder locks. The collection is housed in the Tool Marks and Materials Laboratory of the Division of Criminal Identification at the Israel National Police Headquarters in Jerusalem.

Broken locks are organized in shallow file-drawers according to geographical location and the date of break-in.

Figure 3

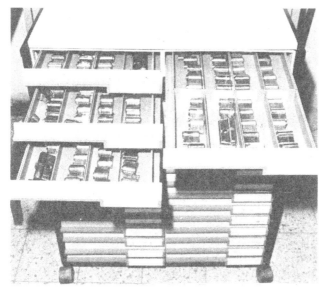

Those locks bearing tool marks made by the same pliers are organized separately into numbered groups. Tool marks from all suspect pliers are compared to those on the grouped locks and those from the same geographical districts in which the suspect was captured and in which he lives.

It is a generally accepted axiom that tools can produce marks with class and individual characteristics. Numerous articles in the professional literature give examples of various tools that were tested and found to support the above axiom. In an attempt to increase the weight of court testimony concerning the individuality of marks made by self-locking pliers on cylinder locks a study using twenty newly manufactured Vise Grip 7R Self-Locking Pliers was made. The jaws of ten of the pliers were broached sequentially while the other ten pliers were constructed from randomly selected broached jaws and finished by the same operator on the same abrasive wheel. In both groups the jaws were found to have unique topographical surfaces that produce unique (individual) tool marks.

# AN EXPERIMENTAL VIDEO-DISC BASED FINGERPRINT RETRIEVAL SYSTEM

Arye Aperman, Criminal Identification Division
Israel Police National Headquarters
Jerusalem, Israel

Lawrence Pfeffer, Media-Tech, Ltd.
9 Haganah Street
Jerusalem, Israel

> Video-discs provide an effective medium for storing large, computer-managed image data bases. This capability provides law-enforcement and security agencies an opportunity to rethink the way in which image files are managed. The paper describes a proto-type video-disc based fingerprint search system in use at the Israel National Police Criminal Identification Laboratory.

Criminal investigation is characterized by analysis of various types of primarily visual evidence that accumulates at the scene of the crime and is provided by witnesses. Recent availability of low-cost optical video-discs make it attractive to develop work-stations capable of rapidly searching, retrieving and analyzing large computer-based visual and audio data bases.

The best known criminal investigation files are:
a. the latent fingerprint file, used to identify fingerprints left at scenes of crime
b. the Mugshot (Criminal Album) file,
c. cartridge case file, used to identify the gun from which a bullet has been fired
d. forged check file, used to analyze handwriting characteristics and identify forgers
e. typewriter specimen file used to trace typewritten notes
f. miscellaneous handwritten note file

At the Israel Police Criminal Identification Laboratory the files are maintained as follows:
a. Latent prints: fingerprint forms in file drawers
b. Mugshots: photographs in file drawers
c. Cartridge cases: both as cartridge cases drawers and as photographs

d.  Forged checks:  in folders
e.  Typewriter specimens:  an impression of each character on an index card
f.  Handwriting specimens:  in folders

Media-Tech, Ltd. and the Israel Police Criminal Identification Laboratory jointly designed a system called the Integrated Criminal Identification System (ICIS) assisting in complex visual file organization and search. The ICIS architecture is based on function specific work-stations integrated around a video-disc based multi-media (digital, voice, video) data base.  Initially a MARK-I fingerprint analyst work-station was prototyped and is in operational use at the Laboratory since the summer of 1983.

Prototype work-station software is being developed for mugshot identification and other applications.  A MARK-II system would consist of a set integrated hardware and software tools for storing, retrieving, correlating, enhancing and abstracting all symbolic, image and audio documents related to criminal identification.

## FINGERPRINTS AND PERSONAL IDENTIFICATION

There are three fingerprint identification related tasks, namely:
1.  access control (e.g. to secure sites)
2.  identity certification (comparing an individual's ten fingerprints against a library of print forms)
3.  latent print identification (comparing a fingerprint image found at the scene of a crime against a library of print forms)

In a typical access control task a person requesting entry must identify himself by insertion of an identification card in a reader and placement of a finger on a scanner. Since the individual is cooperative, the system is informed via the card of his presumed identity and can compare parameters of the scanned fingerprint with that of a single print selected from the library.  If the two prints are reasonably similar than access is granted.

Most law-enforcement agencies certify the identity of booked individuals.  For this purpose suspects are fingerprinted, and their ten prints are checked against the form library.  If the individual's personal details are correct and if he was previously booked, then the prior form is easily found and the prints on the two forms visibly match.  If no prior form is found, then the suspect may be a first time offender in the region or may be attempting to establish an alias and the form(s) of past identities may be in the files. Subsequent to coding the fingerprint the files are searched for fingerprints similar to the suspect. If any are found then the claimed identity is fraudulent.

Fingerprints are unique to an individual and are difficult to gorge and conceal. A proven methodology has been developed to identify an individual based on a latent print: the print inadvertantly left at the scene of crime. Latent prints are regarded by courts of law as the best evidence that a suspect was present where the latent has been found, thus they effectively link a criminal to the scene of crime.

## THE WORK-STATION

The MARK-I ICIS fingerprint search work-station was designed for interactive latent print search. It is compatible with the present fingerprint coding and search methodology at the Israel Police, which is based on the FBI-Code (3). The work-station was expected to raise the departmental identification count at the current staffing level. This expectation turned out to be correct.

In operation, a latent print is placed under a TV camera and is displayed on a black and white monitor. An analyst determines the print's FBI codes(s) which is entered via a terminal as a search key. The key is used by the computer to filter the fingerprint album causing elimination of all obviously unmatched prints. The software presents the remaining prints one-by-one to the analyst, with manual or automatic advance between images. Figures 2-4 show examples of displayed fingerprints and of the work-station in operation.

Assuming that finger number four is the only latent print found at the scene of the crime and that it is a type 3 (Right Loop) print, the search key is ***3*,*****

The key is specified in right then left hand sequence. ***3* requests selection of all individuals who have a type 3 print on the right hand fourth finger. The * acts a "wild card" and is a "don't care" search criterion. According to the above example the selected individuals can have any type of print on their left hand, and on right hand fingers 1, 2, 3 and 5. Should the left hand fifth finger be of type 4 (Left Loop) then the search key would become ***3*,****4

## THE IMPLEMENTATION

The work-station consists of a bank of video disc players, two B&W TV monitors, a TV camera, a computer controlled video switcher and a frame grabber connected to a PDP-11/70 mini-computer (Figure 1). The mini computer could support multiple work-stations, which can be regarded as a multi-media terminals.

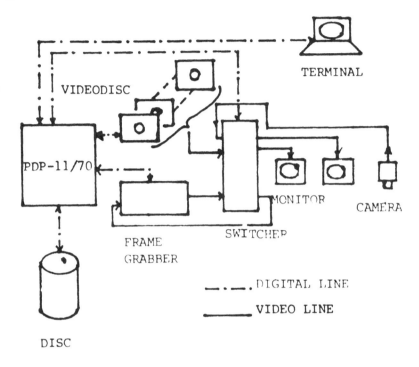

Figure 1: ICIS MARK-I Fingerprint Search Work-Station Schematic Diagram

The frame grabber is a device capable of digitizing a video image in real-time (1/30 second) at 512x512 spatial resolution at a depth of 64 gray levels (6 bits per pixel). It supports image processing tasks, such as contrast enhancement.

The video-switcher is an 8x8 video switch. Any input may be routed to any output under computer control. The switcher was developed to the project's requirements. It is used to connect the output of a selected video disc to a monitor, or to switch the TV camera from a monitor to the frame grabber input for image processing.

Optical video-disc players have been available in the industrial and consumer markets for a few years. Discs can be recorded in Constant Linear Velocity (CLV) or Constant Angular Velocity (CAV) mode (1). In CAV mode the disc is rotated at a constant angular speed of 1800 rpm. The disc is organized in such a manner that a full, two-interlace video-frame is recorded per track along with digital control information. The latter enables frame-accurate addressing. Up to 54,000 frames can be recorded on one side of a CAV laser-disc. The average frame-search time is player dependent, and ranges from 3 to 10 seconds. Information is recovered from the disc via a laser beam, thus there is no mechanical contact with the read-head. The laser-disc player can be stopped on a single frame for extended periods without any damage to the disc. Players may be controlled manually or under computer control. Some players have a built in RS-232C port allowing direct connection to an external ("outboard") computer. CLV discs have constant linear velocity and rotate slower when retrieving information from the outer tracks. They can store approximately twice as much information as in CAV mode (1 hour of video per side vs. 30 minutes). CLV discs don't easily lend themselves to frame-accurate random-access. CAV and CLV discs are two different recording formats onto the same 12" diameter read-only medium. Discs are mastered (produced) at a number of mastering plants (factories) in the USA, Europe and Japan.

A variety of video-disc players are marketed. In the initial phase of the project the following players were used:

Pioneer 7820-II (originally DiscoVision 7820-II)

Pioneer 8210

SONY LDP-1000

Since the purchase of these players more advanced models became available.

In the course of the project a two-sided video-disc was mastered (2). One side contains a regional fingerprint file, the other side a Criminal Album. The fingerprint forms and the mugshots were photographically converted to 16 mm movie film on an animation stand. One fingerprint or mugshot is stored per frame, and unlike in movies there is no visual continuity across frames. After photography, development and edit, the film based image master files were transferred to 1" type C video-tape in a professional video studio according to mastering plant specifications. The tape became input to the mastering plant's production process.

A video disc player/recorder is recently being marketed. It provides a one-time write capability to any of 10,000 or 15,000 frames depending on the model. Frames may be retrieved as often as desired. This system can also be connected to a computer.

The software is based on a bit-vector indexed data-base manager capable of high-speed retrieval on a large number keys, some unspecified by an analyst's query. A key is defined as a single character position in the query. If it has N possible values, and if there are M records in the data base, then an NxM bit matrix is defined. Suppose that the key designates the right-hand index finger FBI-code. The key values range over the set (1 2 3 4 5 6 7 0 ), where 0 designates an undefined fingerprint type. Thus there are eight bit vectors for this key. If the i-th individual has a type 5 right-hand index finger, then bit i in bit vector 5 of this key is set to 1 (true), else it is 0 (false). A set of bit vectors is similarly defined for each key. A search in this type of data base selects the appropriate bit strings, and logically AND-s them. Each bit in the resulting Section Vector marks the corresponding data base record as SELECTED. For example, if bits (2 7 46 167 7132 81342) are TRUE then records (2 7 46 167 7132 81342) fit the search criteria. Data base records are random accessible by record number, and contain symbolic data and pointers to the video-disc image data base. The pointers designate frame numbers.

## EXPERIENCE WITH THE SYSTEM

Operational use of the MARK-I Work-Station pointed to the following advantages:
1. reduced search time
2. increased analyst concentration due to a more relaxed working environment (reduced eye fatigue, elimination of form search and replacement in filing cabinets)
3. elimination of form misfiling
4. fully backed up forms file feasible
5. elimination of form wear thru use

The above translates into a significant increase in the number of identifications made by analysts.

## FUTURE PLANS

The Criminal Identification Laboratory plans to install a number of work-stations for the fingerprint as well as the other image album based applications. The work-stations would be linked via a multi-media local network capable of digital, audio and video data switching. The work-

ations would be based on independent micro-computers, such
the Motorola 68000. Network servers would include a
otographic imager and a read/write image store. One work-
ation has been designed for effective semi-automatic
ansfer of multi-image documents such as finger-print forms
the image archive.

The operational paper-based latent fingerprint file
uld be transferred to a large video-disc library. Both
e image and the related symbolic data bases would be
-line accessible to each work-station.

During MARK-II development the fingerprint coding
uld be made more effective. A code has been developed
lowing an operator to point to major comparison points
.g. deltas). The image processing software will count
tervening ridge lines. The resulting value would augment
e basic FBI count, thereby rendering the file search
gnificantly more effective than currently. The MARK-II
stem would support both ten finger and latent print
arch.

## REFERENCES

LDP-1000 Interface Manual, SONY Video Communications (1982)

ICIS Laser-Disc Table of Contents
Media-Tech ICIS technical Note 7 (November 1983)

Fingerprint Coding Used at the Israel Police Criminal
Identification Laboratory, Media-Tech ICIS Technical
Note 8 (November 1983)

| | |
|---|---|
| re 2: A Fingerprint Retrieved from the Video-Disk and Displayed on a TV Monitor | Figure 3: A Fingerprint with Video-Disc Command and Frame Number Overlay |

# AUTOMATIC DIGITAL DEFOCUS RESTORING FILTER

N. Ben-Yosef, S. Lashansky and G. Feigin
Applied Physics Division
School of Applied Science and Technology
The Hebrew University of Jerusalem
Israel

> For strong dis-focusing, the degradation function can be found automatically by machine operation only. Using a modification of the inverse filter, the restoring filter can be calculated and applied. These resotrations are not optimal and have the advantage of machine separation only. Real time restoration using this technique is feasible.

An extensive bibliography of image restoration filters and techniques can be found in a paper by Rajala and De-Figueiredo (1). Most of these techniques share a common disadvantage, namely a priori knowledge of the original image is needed. In most cases at least the following information is required; (a) The power spectrum of the undegraded image, (b) the power spectrum of the noise and (c) the degradation function. It is not always possible to obtain all of the above information, even in cases where the information is at hand it may prove to be quite a tedious task to reconstruct the image. Today, a large emphasis is being placed on real time processing, however not many of the existing techniques are suited for this purpose. For example, in a paper by Cannon (2), the degradation function of a defocused image is obtained using the cepstrum technique (3, 4). In the presence of noise, attempts to locate the structure of the degradation function are often frustrated, consequently it is necessary to divide the image into a number of subimages and to average the results in the hope of mitigating the effects of both the signal and the noise in determining the parameters of the degradation function. Quite evidently, this type of process is rather lengthy and somewhat removed from real time processing.

In the present communication an automatic defocus restoring filter will be shown. The main requirements fulfilled are that no prior knowledge of the image is needed and no operator intervention is required. The only restriction is that the image is strongly defocused.

A defocused image can be described in the spatial Fourier domain as follows:

1.  $I(u,v) = (S(u,v) + N(u,v)) \cdot H(u,v) + N_1(u,v)$

Where $I(u,v)$ is the two dimensional Fourier transform of the image, u and v the spatial frequencies, $S(u,v)$ the Fourier transform of the non-degraded image, $N(u,v)$ the "Fourier transform" of the spatial noise preceding the optical system, $H(u,v)$ the degradation process optical transfer function and $N_1(u,v)$ the "Fourier transform" of the noise after the optical system (electronic, film etc.). Numerous restoration techniques and filters are available (1). In the present case we assume that the functional shape of $H(u,v)$ is known (defocus) but not the quantities involved. Further, we assume that $N_1(u,v)$ is not too large and that $(S(u,v))$ is close to possessing a radial symmetry, i.e. it is assumed that the original image is nearly isotropic (no preferred direction is present).

By transforming the spatial frequencies to polar coordinates; $w^2 = u^2 + v^2$ and $\theta = arct\ ^v/u$, and averaging the absolute value squared of the previous equation over all $\theta$ for each w one obtains the Radial Mean Power Spectrum (RMPS) of the image

2.  $P(w) = (P_S(w) + P_N(w))\ H^2(w) + P_{N_1}(w)$

The cross terms with the noise terms cancel out due to the random properties of the noise. In obtaining this relation the assumed radial symmetry of the image transform was used. The radial symmetry of $H(u,v)$ is inherent in the defocus OTF itself.

For the assumed degradation process, strong defocus, the OTF is well-known:

$H(w) = 2\dfrac{J1(x)}{x}-;\ x = 2HWR$

with R being the radius of the defocus PSF, $J_1(x)$ is the Bessel function of the first order. $H(w)$ strongly affects the image in the neighborhood of its zero crossing point due to the fact that it changes sign, i.e. phase change occurs.

The main task in restoring the image is finding the value of R without prior knowledge about the system. By inspecting equation 2, one observes that if $P_S(w)$ does not change too fast in the neighborhood of the first zero of $H(w)$ then the behavior of $P(w)$ is determine mainly by H itself. Consequently, by comparing $P(w)$ with $H(w)$ (best fit) one finds the first point of zero crossing which determines in a unique way the degradation function. The following zeros can be calculated analytically.

Once the degrading function is found the restoring process can commence. The restoration is performed in two steps: (a) Phase correction and (b) amplitude boost. The phase correction is straight forward, once the zero crossing points of H are known one has to change the sign of $I(u,v)$ in the proper spatial frequency domains as follows: let Wn be the zeros of H, then transform:

$$\text{New} \atop (I(u,v)) = \begin{cases} \text{Old } (I(u,v)), & W_{2n}^2 \ U^2 + V^2 \ W_{2n+1}^2 \\ \text{Old } (I(u,v)), & W_{2n+1}^2 \ U^2 + V^2 \ W_{2n+2}^2 \\ \text{for } n = 0,1,\ldots. \end{cases}$$

The amplitude boost cannot be determined in a unique way. In the unrealistic case of no noise the gain function is obvious, the inverse of H. As noise is always present, using the inverse filter will strongly enhance the noise and an unintelligible image will result. We have found that using the inverse filter at the region enclosed by the first zero up to a gain of 5 and then keeping a constant gain up to about $0.5W_{max}$ ($W_{max}$ being the highest spatial frequency available) followed by a smooth decay will result in a good reconstruction. After phase correction and amplitude boost are applied on $I(u,v)$ the inverse transform is used to obtain the reconstructed image.

To clarify the technique some examples will be shown. In figure 1 a defocused image is shown, the defocus was introduced in the optics of the video camera used to digitize the image. The RMPS and the best fit to the MTF are shown in Figure 2. One observes the relative strength of the information and the noise. The $P_{N1}(w)$ term is clearly seen in the high frequency region, Figure 3 shows the restored image after phase correction only was applied. The noticeable enhancement due to this process alone is well-known (5). The gain function constructed according to the delineated procedure is shown in Figure 4. The reconstructed image after amplitude gain is applied without phase correction is shown in Figure 5. The reconstructed image after phase correction and amplitude gain are applied is shown in Figure 6. The need for both phase and amplitude corrections is clearly seen. Figures 7 and 8 show another example, again, a noticeable enhancement is observed.

In conclusion, the delineated procedure can be applied automatically to any defocused image. No operator intervention is needed. The algorithm allows the filter to be calculated and adapted to the particular image to be reconstructed.

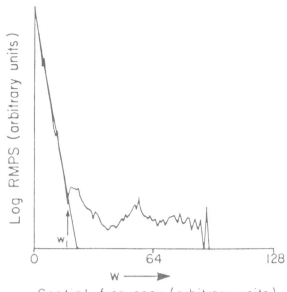

Figure 1: Defocused image. The small and medium size letters are unintelligible.

Figure 2: The RMPS of this image and the best fit of the theoretical defocus MTF are shown.

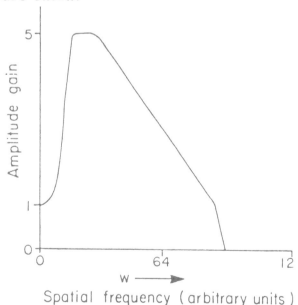

Fig. 3

Fig. 4

Figure 3: Restored image by phase correction only.

Figure 4: The amplitude gains function.

Fig. 5

Fig. 6

Figure 5: Restored image by amplitude boost only.

Fig. 7

Fig. 8

Figure 6: Complete restoration, phase correction and amplitude boost. Most of the letters are recognized.

Figure 7: Defocused image.

Figure 8: Restored image. Notice the numbers.

## REFERENCES

1. S. A. Rajala and R. J. P. De Figueiredo, "Adaptive Non-linear Image Restoration by a Modified Kalman Filtering Approach", IEEE Trans. on Acoustics, Speech and Signal Proc., Vol. ASSP-29, No. 5, 1981, pp. 1033-1042.

2. M. Cannon, "Blind Deconvolution of Spatially Invariant Image Blurs with Phase", IEEE Trans. on Acoustics, Speech and Signal Proc., Vol. ASSP-24, No. 1, February 1976, pp. 58-63.

3. R. Rom, "On the Cepstrum of Two-Dimensional Functions", IEEE Trans. on Information Theory, March 1975, pp. 214-217.

4. D. G. Childers, D. P. Skinner and R. C. Kemerait, "The Cepstrum: A Guide to Processing", Proc. IEEE, Vol. 65, No. 10, October 1977, pp. 1428-1443.

5. B. R. Frieden, "Image Enhancement and Restoration", in Topics in Applied Physics: Picture Processing and Digital Filtering", Ed: T. S. Huang, Springer-Verlag, New York, 1975, pp. 177-248

# FUTURE PRIORITIES IN FORENSIC SCIENCE RESEARCH
## AND DEVELOPMENT IN THE FEDERAL REPUBLIC OF GERMANY

Dr. Wolfgang Steinke
Bundeskriminalamt
6200 Viesbaden, Germany

In West Germany each of the 11 local jurisdictions has its own autonymous police which have forensic science laboratories of differing quality. These laboratories concentrate their efforts on case related questions, hence Research & Development has, perhaps by default, become a subject handled almost exclusively by the BKA. The Kriminaltechnishes Institut of the BKA has 200 people employed in its ranks, and of these, 40 scientists from a wide range of disciplines are assigned exclusively to questions involving research. The various subjects under study are listed and discussed in this paper.

Let me first of all say a word on the difficulties encountered in a federal system in connection with co-operation and in particular with the co-ordination of case work and research activities. Such problems are likely to be present in all federally structured countries.

In the Federal Republic of Germany, there are 11 decentralized State Criminal Police Offices having more or less well-equipped forensic science divisions, which in a way are competing with the Forensic Science Institute of the Federal Criminal Police Office (Bundeskriminalamt-BKA). The responsibilities are not clearly delimited. Strictly speaking, the forensic science unit in any Federal State should be in a position to perform all types of examination on their own. The Bundeskriminalamt should lend its support to the States only in the research field, and as far as case work is concerned only in those areas where the States do not have the proper capability in terms of methodology or equipment or in those cases where it does not pay to maintain specialized facilities because work is so rare in the given field.

Basically and apart from few exceptions, this is in fact the way we work. Since case work takes priority and has increased disproportionately as compared with manpower levels, the research demand is not even close to being met. Just as deplorable is the fact that co-ordination in terms of division of labor cannot be achieved between the various institutes. Each institute wants to scientifically surpass the others and therefore needs to keep its fields of research secret. If this were not the case, competition could come off victorious. You will see how much I trust you because I present to you our research priorities and take the risk that you will be quicker and beat us.

The Forensic Science Institute of the Bundeskriminalamt consists of six specialized units:

1. physics
2. chemistry
3. biology
4. documents
5. handwritings
6. and firearms and tool marks

I shall deal with them in this order.

The Institute has a staff of about 200, some 40 of whom are scientists from all fields of natural science plus psychology for handwriting identification.

The equipment at the Institute's disposal has an overall value of approximately 60 million DM. The facilities are in keeping with the state of the art.

THE PHYSICS UNIT

In the physics unit, the focus of interest is on the examination of fires and indoor gas/dust explosions, the analysis of anorganic materials, the examination of firearms evidence and the determination of firing distances. There is a central laboratory.

1A. Fires, Gas/Dust Explosions

Our research activities in this field will have to be extended to all mineral oil products as incendiary agents. Further, we do not yet know which is the most suitable packing material for physical evidence secured from fires.

We are aware that chemical self-heating processes are encountered in many areas. Of quite a number of substances we know the point of self-heating, particularly of those having a sensitive heating point, i.e. substances such as hardened linseed oil, dust, fertilizer, combinations of cleaning agents, cellulose-nitrate lacquers, nitrocellulose for instance in film storage rooms, or the various kinds of wood. Of some substances we do not yet know the point of self-heating. These are areas for our future work, just as the subject of motor vehicle fires, which needs special research attention.

Concerning fires involving electric appliances, we do not yet know if a fire was caused by a short-circuit or a short-circuit by a fire. So far we have been unable to solve this problem by examining the beads of melted conductor metal; therefore we need to draw our conclusions on the basis of other evidence for the time being.

A comprehensive research effort further needs to be made into the risks of fire through electric cables and wires and with regard to arc-type short-circuits and fuses.

1B. Anorganic Materials

In the near future, we shall have the possibility to substantially enlarge our collection of automotive paints, which so far includes only approx. 3,000 specimens relating to vehicles dating back as far as 1978. In the past and based on our fragmentary collection, we have had some excellent success in identifying vehicles.

Our goal is to extend the collection to cover all vehicles types operated in the Federal Republic of Germany and to keep it up to date for a ten-year period.

In our opinion, the analysis of glass is suitable only for high-grade types of glass such as thick window panes, where the production process causes streaks to be formed in the glass which are just as individual as tool marks for instance. However, our research into these materials has not gone very far as yet. We make only general statements in this field and we identify fragments to matching pieces. But we believe that research on a broad basis will make it possible to identify high-grade types of glass by analytical means alone.

1C. Firearms Evidence

For a long time, we have been looking into the determination of firing distances, and in particular, we studied the distribution patterns of residues (lead from the priming charge, nitrocellulose from the propelling charge, and bullet material). As a rule, determination is feasible for distances of up to 2.5 meters, beyond which no definite statements are possible. Of course, we are criticle enough to be aware that for some calibres the realistic distance does not exceed 50 cm, and for those calibres positive research remains to be done; we are confident that atomic absorption will be a successful approach to further results in this field.

We have also made some initial experiments using photography for the determination of firing distances. Possible, further studies will enable the distance to be determined via the position of the rifling.

Another of our problems is to demonstrate the presence of residue on the firing hand. In many cases, proof is possible even where the suspect has washed his hands after firing the shot. We shall conduct research into this field of great interest to police but are very careful about predictions on possible success.

1D. Central physics laboratory

In the central physics laboratory, we need to take a still closer look at the possibilities of using the scanning electron microscope for the examination of documents, and in particular, the problem of the sequence of writing (e.g., ball-pen, typewriter crossings) has not yet been elucidated conclusively.

THE CHEMISTRY UNIT

In the chemistry unit, we have subdivided work into toxicology, organic materials, explosives and explosive devices. We have a central laboratory there as well.

2A. Toxicology

With a big problem we will be faced in the field of environmental toxicology, i.e. deciding the question which pollutant caused a given illness. We have no past experience in this field and therefore have to fall back on specialized institutes where such cases are submitted to us. This applies not only to environmental toxicology, but also to matters relating to the pollution of water, soil and the air. Further problems we encounter in some areas where the task is the quantitative analysis of narcotics, namely, the question if a particular concentration of a drug comes within the provisions of our narcotics legislation or not. Depending on their concentration, amphetamine, cocaine, and methadone may differ in the effect they produce from 1 to 3,000 times as much. To improve our quantitative analysis in this field is our primary research concern. Another problem can be solved methodologically, we are certain; namely, determining the origin of amphetamine, cocaine and cannabis. At the research front, however, we have not had the time as yet to take a closer look at the problem.

2B. Explosives and Explosive devices

In view of the numerous bombings and attacks using incendiary devices in the Federal Republic, which so far however have been aimed at property only, the explosives field is of enormous importance to us.

As far as research activities are concerned, we need to study the changes that explosives undergo under various storage conditions. In the future, the analysis of explosives and propellant powders using high pressure liquid chromatography will need some research attention, and further progress is required in the identification of explosive residues

Some initial results have already been obtained in studying the mode of action of explosives. We do have the necessary equipment. In one case, we examined, on behalf of Dutch Police, the mode of action of an improvised explosive device which was thrown at a referee. I hope that the future will bring us even more accurate knowledge of home-made explosives.

2.C. Central chemical laboratory

The method of nuclear magnetic resonance needs to be explored with regard to the vast potential it holds for use in forensic science. We believe we are far from having sounded out all possibilities of its application and will examine this, but only where case work brings up the question

## THE BIOLOGY UNIT

In the field of biology, we have made a subdivision into the following areas: serology, general biology, microbiology and soils and textiles. 'General biology' as used in this context means anything not covered by the other three areas.

3A. Serology

In the field of serology, we examine all secretions and skin particles and have gathered, sufficient research capacity being available, a great deal of experience. We can handle 15 different systems of blood typing. We know the impact that blood diseases and drug intake have on our analytical results, and we believe that not all systems have conclusively been investigated so far. In view of the tremendous development in the field of research into genes, there may come a time where we can tell for instance a victim's diseases by identifying his antibodies.

At the present time, our research effort in serology focuses on the demonstration of Lewis antigens in blood and secretions, on the use of isoelectric focusing in the analysis of blood and secretions, and on the determination of enzyme polymorphisms in secretions.

3B. General biology

In the field of general biology, one of the priority subjects for research must be hair analysis, of which we largely have no clear perception so far. We have paid in excess of DM 300,000 for a research project in order to make some progress beyond our hitherto microscopic possibilities in the examination of human hair by making use of keratin analysis. Now the sexing of torn hairs is possible and we can determine if the hair is human or not. Based on a torn hair we can determine the blood group in the ABO system for up to seven weeks after it was torn. Necrotic hair, too, is suitable for blood typing.

It is rather depressing that we are not able to positively identify a hair to an individual by analytical means. This is possible only in exceptional cases; namely, in the presence of extreme hair diseases, or where particular shampoos and remedies are used.

Another deplorable fact is our inability to determine if a human hair originates from a leg or from an arm. We feel that looking at hair cross-sections will not take us any further, the only promising way being the study of keratines. The research that we financed has revealed that there may be around 250 components, but so far we have the identification know-how for only a few of them, which means we are at the beginning of an enormous research project whose significance for crime control must not be underestimated, however.

There is no systematic research into feathers, but I believe that in view of the large research need in other areas we can do without it for the time being.

3C. Microbiology and soils

Concerning the collection of plants, we are at square one, and our problem is that frequently the material submitted includes only minute plant particles so that most of the time we can link them merely to a plant family or species. Also when it comes to differentiating pine needles-there are about 40 different species of pines in the Federal Republic of Germany. We are just starting, and the same applies to the determination of grass species, of which alone there are about 200 in the Federal Republic. Because of staff bottle-necks we are presently unable to do research work in these areas.

3D. Textiles

A large-scale study of material presenting cuts and stabs has been done in our institute in which we looked at the arrangement of threads. In the light of our experience, we are in a position to tell the direction in which the stab was executed and also its force if we have the item concerned. But from the trace pattern we can also draw conclusions as to the instrument used.

Some success has also been achieved in determining the age of fibres by examining dyestuffs and other substances contained therein.

In the textiles field, there are two areas that we want to give special research attention, namely the development of micromethods for the analysis of single fibres using infrared spectroscopy and the development of a range of methods of efficiently recovering single fibres and obtaining reference material.

## THE DOCUMENTS UNIT

Our Documents Unit is subdivided into the following areas of specialization: documents laboratory, typewriter identification, printed materials and stamp impressions, and identity documents/document security.

4A. The documents laboratory

Our point of view concerning questioned documents is that today such examinations can only be performed by scientists having undergone university-level training. Time and again we find that foreign identity documents suspected of having been altered are in fact high-quality counterfeits. These can be recognized only by highly qualified chemists, whereas alterations are comparatively easy to demonstrate.

4B. Typewriter identification

Concerning the examination of typewritten materials we are going to face major problems in view of new developments in the field of typewheels as these are relatively cheap mass products that are rather rapidly worn out and therefore destroyed. The entire complex needs to be studied empirically.

4C. Printed material/stamp impressions

In the field of photocopying machines, our research has enabled us to identify an individual photocopy to a particular copying machine via traces on paper. We are also aware of a paper, developed by a Swiss company for the Americans, which because of its dark red color will not photocopy. Unfortunately, this paper cannot be read without additional equipment so that aspects of practibility and also the relatively high costs involved do not recommend it for use in our sensitive areas of activity. Further, we know a possibility of marking paper in such a way that photocopying the relevant documents will not go unnoticed.

It is depressing to see how little research attention has been paid so far to the problem of determining the age of ball-pen inks. It is virtually unpardonable that time and again we have to admit that we are relatively successful in precisely determining the age of fountain-pen inks but have to surrender in the face of other writing instruments. This field of study needs to be given specially high priority.

Further, we think about using laser scanning microscopy to make indented impressions visible.

Also, we want to determine in which sequence crossing strokes were put to paper by making use of the scanning electron microscope and to apply thin-layer chromatography to the identification of inks.

## THE HANDWRITING UNIT

Organizationally, we have subdivided handwriting examination by our psychologists by type of crime as follows: crimes of violence, threats and extortion, cheque fraud, and prescription forgery. Recently we have seen that crime-related writings are increasingly prepared by offenders using stencils, so we have compiled a collection of such items for identification purposes. So far, we have gathered very little experience in this field and are trying to complete our body of knowledge.

No in-depth study has been made so far of the problems encountered in connection with the use of automatic text editing systems, which is a project for future work.

The most intensive future research will no doubt take place in the handwriting field because entirely new methods can be used there thanks to computer support. The computer will also be able to assist us in linguistic text analysis and in the field of dynamic writing parameters, which is a research project in which we want to determine if a given document is an imitation or not by measuring the depth of penetration in the paper.

The computer will also be able to assist us in the analysis of writings made by means of stencils and of machine-produced signatures as well as in the differentiation of high-quality signature forgeries.

## THE FIREARMS AND TOOL MARKS UNIT

In the field of firearms and tool marks we have subdivided our work into firearms identification, ballistics/weapons technology and technology of materials.

6A. Firearms identification

The high standard of technology in the weapons field forces our experts to familiarize themselves with the production methods, to learn new techniques again and again, and often to forget about the knowledge they have previously acquired.

For example, polygonal barrels are presently manufactured as a novelty; they leave only minute marks on the bullets fired, and this will possibly face us with enormous problems in firearms identification, and it may even make this field of expertise eventually become extinct. In order to differentiate between marks that are produced at random, regularly by the production process, or always the same by the firing process we have used high-speed photography, a method which enables a million pictures to be taken per second and thus makes the whole firing process reproducible at extremely low speed. Thanks to this sophisticated technology we know how the marks that have long been familiar to us come about in the first place.

6B. Ballistics/weapons technology

Subjects for research in this field are the ballistic phenomena encountered in firing at hard targets, the propagation of powder at the muzzle, as well as experimental and theoretical studies concerning the behavior of bullets when fired outdoors.

6C. Technology of materials

As far as materials are concerned, the revolutionary developments that take place in private industry frequently confront us with the question if certain marks are individual or not. Often we need to know the entire production process in order to determine if for example a shoeprint presents marks that are individual to it or rather if they are random ones that are due to the production process.

We shall be in for problems when individualizing members will be applied by electron beam, for example chassis numbers by car manufacturers.

In the materials technology field, typical examinations that we are requested to perform include studies of the individual character of general shaped traces, determining the influence that production processes have on the creation of structures, and the morphological investigation of broken glass and metals.

I hope this has given you a summary idea of our present and future research activities. Thank you for your attention

# SHI'ITE TERRORISM

Martin Kramer
The Dayan Center for Middle Eastern
and African Studies
Tel Aviv University

The recent emergence of Shi'ite terrorism has stimulated unchecked apprehension and speculation. This is due above all to the suicidal method successfully employed in a number of terrorist acts attributable to Shi'ites. The suicidal dimension has prompted many questions about the possible motivations and religious commitment behind such acts. Yet this sort of analysis, which draws mostly on psychology and the interpretation of Shi'ite religious doctrine, has been almost wholly speculative, since very little is known about the organizations and persons actually responsible for this terrorism. The aim of this brief note is to look precisely at the lesser-known organizational side of Shi'ite terrorism, and to ask whether an international network of Shi'ite terrorism now exists.

## THE NAJAF CONNECTION

Shi'ism is a minoritarian branch of Islam, with its origins in the very earliest period of Islamic revelation. This is not the place for a discussion of the doctrinal differences which have separated majoritarian Sunni Islam from Shi'ite Islam. Suffice it to say that these differences have left Shi'ite Muslims with an acute sense of historical self-importance, and a separate identity reinforced by Sunni hostility. Shi'ite Muslims constitute an overwhelming majority of the population of Iran, and are 'soft' majorities in the more heterogeneous populations of Iraq and Lebanon. There are also Shi'ite minorities throughout the Arab Gulf states, and in Afghanistan, Pakistan, and India.

These scattered Shi'ite communities are linked by a class of religious clerics -- ulama -- who enjoy a degree of authority over their coreligionists unique in Islam. Until recent years, these ulama were schooled together in the Shi'ite shrine cities in southern Iraq, of which Najaf was the most important. Najaf was the home of the most renowned academies of Shi'ite learning. Great ayatollahs, scholars, and students assembled in Najaf from throughout the Shi'ite world, to study sacred law, theology, and philosophy. Their learning remained medieval in content, as did the method of instruction. In their half-spherical turbans, accomplished and aspiring mullahs engrossed themselves in a tradition which was everywhere under attack and in most places in retreat.

In the 1950's and 1960's, a group of ulama in the shrine cities began to preach a new doctrine: that the process of Westernization, which threatened to obliterate the cultural and religious traditions of all Muslims, could only be arrested by the establishment of truly Islamic regimes, guided by the ulama themselves. The preaching of this idea in Najaf received an important endorsement in 1965: Ayatollah Khomeini, expelled from Iran by the Shah, arrived in the city, where he spent thirteen years in exile. It was in Najaf in 1970 that Khomeini delivered his seminal lectures on Islamic government, in which he argued for the seizure of political power by the Muslim clergy.

The revolutionary atmosphere of Najaf in these years left an indelible imprint on a generation of Shi'ite ulama who studied there, and then returned to their own communities. In addition to absorbing revolutionary ideas about government and society, they also established personal relationships and friendships with Shi'ite ulama from other lands. The connection of revolutionary thought linking the Shi'ites of Lebanon and Iraq with Iran was forged in these student days, in the highly charged intellectual climate of Najaf. Just as dissenting Cambridge of the 1930s ultimately yielded treason, so the unsettled Najaf of the 1960s eventually produced Islamic terrorism. Iraqi security authorities have since purged the academies, but the friendships and commitments forged there remain as binding as ever.

With the success of the Islamic revolution in Iran, Khomeini was catapulted almost directly from exile in Najaf to power in Tehran. Since then, the network of old school affiliations has been transformed into an apparatus for generalizing -- or 'exporting' -- that revolution, especially to Iraq and Lebanon. The Najaf background of Shi'ite ulama gives Shi'ite terrorism its international character. Educated in the same tradition, by the same teachers, in the same mosques, these Shi'ite ulama are the inspirational nuclei of many of the organizations plausibly linked to Shi'ite acts of terror. There is no point here in listing all of these organizations, but the more notable ones are worth naming, especially when their leaders can be identified. Each of the following organizations revolves

418

around a charismatic man of religion, whose inspirational role in terrorist activity is as indispensable as the contribution of the logistical planners and the terrorists themselves.

THE IRAQI BRANCH

Since the Iranian revolution, Iran has offered sanctuary to numerous Iraqi Shi'ite activists who are at odds with their own government. These are permitted to set up offices in Tehran, engage in propaganda, publish newspapers, and recruit members. The most important of these organizations are led by Iraqi Shi'ite ulama, who draw their followings from among the many Iraqi Shi'ite refugees in Iran. Many of the Iraqi clerics knew or studied under Khomeini during his long exile in Najaf. Since the outbreak of war between Iran and Iraq, the émigré groups have grown in importance.

The Iraqi Shi'ite organizations come under the general authority of Hujjat al-Islam Muhammad Baqir al-Hakim, 'spokesman' of the Supreme Assembly of the Islamic Revolution of Iraq (SAIRI). This cleric is the son of the late Ayatollah Muhsin al-Hakim of Najaf, perhaps the leading Shi'ite religious authority of his time. The al-Hakim family is highly regarded throughout the Shi'ite world, and Muhammad Baqir al-Hakim is slated to play the role of authoritative cleric in the Islamic republic which Iran wishes to establish in Iraq. His prominence in the opposition struggle has led the Iraqi regime to attempt to destroy what remains of his family in Najaf. Three of his brothers and three nephews were executed in May 1983, and many other family members of all ages were arrested. Another leading figure in SAIRI is Hujjat al-Islam Sayyid Mahmud al-Hashimi, who bears the title of 'president' of the assembly.

The oldest of the organizations united by SAIRI is al-Da'wa, led by its Najaf-born 'spokesman', Shaykh Muhammad Mahdi al-Asifi. Shaykh Mahdi al-Hakim -- another brother of Muhammad Baqir al-Hakim -- also figures prominently in the organization. Al-Da'wa traces its origins to Najaf of the 1960s, and reveres the late Ayatollah Muhammad Baqir al-Sadr as founder and spiritual guide. Although al-Da'wa attracts mostly Iraqi Shi'ites, it is also active among other Shi'ite refugees in Iran, and among Shi'ite associations and student groups in the West. Several military camps in Iran are reportedly run by al-Da'wa, to train Iraqi Shi'ite refugees for Iran's war with Iraq, and to support its own operations against the Iraqi regime. According to one member, Iran 'gives us no aid other than authorization to be here', but 'the main training base is the Iranian front'. Al-Da'wa takes credit not only for operations in Iraq, but for attacks upon Iraqi institutions and personnel in other countries. On 12 December 1983, this campaign found a new focus, when a group of Iraqi Shi'ites identified as members of al-Da'wa carried out a series of bomb attacks in Kuwait, including the suicidal truck-bombing of the US Embassy. Shaykh Asifi claims that 'we had nothing to do with those attacks'. But a SAIRI resolution declared that the attackers 'have the right to blow up US and French embassies . . .they have the right to take their revenge on the US, because it is America which strengthens and supports [Iraqi President] Saddam [Husayn]'. Members or a faction of al-Da'wa were also responsible for the December 1984 hijacking of a Kuwaiti airliner, during which a demand was made for the release of those convicted of the Kuwait bombings a year earlier.

Another organization, al-Mujahidun, is led by yet another brother, Abd al-Aziz al-Hakim. This group has carried out a number of daring attacks in Iraq, and also regards itself as having a wider mission. 'We are working in coordination with all Islamic movements throughout the Arab world', claims the organization's leading ideologue. But al-Da'wa and al-Mujahidun devote themselves principally to the war against the Iraqi regime. Their targets are usually Iraqi and, on rarer occasions, those whom they deem to be supportive of the Iraqi government.

Another group with a more universal purpose goes by the name of the Islamic Action Organization (Munazzamat al-Amal al-Islami; not to be confused with the Lebanese Islamic Amal). Hujjat al-Islam Muhammad Taqi al-Mudarrisi, the Karbala-born author of numerous philosophical works and a Quran commentary, heads this group. Khomeini himself selected Muhammad Taqi, a personal disciple and former student, to lead the organization. Islamic Action resorts to suicidal bombing operations. According to Muhammad Taqi, 'in one week I can gather 500 of the faithful who are prepared to launch suicide operations. No border will stop them'. Such bombings represent the principal tactic of the organization in hitting targets in Baghdad, as it did successfully on 23 November 1983, and 6 July 1984. Muhammad Taqi preaches the unity of all Muslim movements, and does not hesitate to address appeals to Muslim revolutionaries as far afield as Egypt. Islamic Action reportedly includes Iraqis, Iranians, Bahrainis, Afghans, and North Africans, and works closely with the Tehran-based Islamic Front for the Liberation of

Bahrain, directed by Sayyid Hadi al-Mudarrisi, who is Muhammad Taqi's brother. Muhammad Taqi reportedly opposed the creation of SAIRI, since he regards other Iraqi Shi'ite organizations as lacking in their devotion to Khomeini. The approach of his group is certainly more pan-Islamic than that of the other Iraqi Shi'ite organizations. But little more is known about the issues which divide the Iraqi émigré groups.

## THE LEBANESE BRANCH

The recent political awakening of Lebanon's Shi'ites has combined with influences emanating from Iran, to produce the new assertiveness of this once voiceless community. Part of this militancy has been the resort by some groups to the tactics of terror. Just as the problem of Lebanon is international in scope, so too is the Shi'ite terrorist response. A wide variety of targets -- American, European, Israeli -- have been struck by Lebanese Shi'ite terrorists. But this terrorism is international in another sense, since it benefits from the moral and material support of Iran, and the complicity of Syria.

Lebanon occupies a special place in Iranian strategy. Former Iranian Ambassador to Lebanon, Hujjat al-Islam Fakhr-Ruhani, gives several reasons for Lebanon's importance in Iran's regional calculations. First, there is the weakness of the Lebanese central government. Governmental authority is 'the biggest obstacle to starting Islamic movements in the world', but since the Lebanese government 'does not have much power, there is no serious obstacle in the way of the people of Lebanon'. Second, Lebanon constitutes the 'heart of the Arab countries', from where ideas spread throughout Arab lands. 'We can conclude that the existence of an Islamic movement in that country will result in Islamic movements throughout the Arab world'. Fakhr-Ruhani believes that 'if activities continue as they are, Lebanon will reach the stage of an Islamic revolution'. It is obviously in Iran's interest to see Lebanon reach that stage as quickly as possible.

In each part of Lebanon, Iran has followed a different approach. Iranian involvement is most conspicuous in the Biqa Valley, particularly in and around Baalbek, where about 1,500 Iranian Revolutionary Guards are stationed. There they cooperate with the most openly pro-Iranian factions of Lebanon's Shi'ites: Islamic <u>Amal</u>, led by Husayn al-Musawi, and the Party of God (<u>Hizb Allah</u>), led by Abbas al-Musawi and Shaykh Subhi Tufayli. Husayn al-Musawi claims that 'the Iranian presence in Baalbek is cultural, social, and informational. It has no military purpose or anything like that'. Revolutionary Guards undoubtedly deal in indoctrination, and the contingent includes ulama. But reports of other activities led Lebanon to sever relations with Iran in November 1983, when Iran refused to withdraw the Revolutionary Guards. France and Israel also held Iranian-Lebanese Shi'ite cooperation responsible for suicidal truck-bombing attacks against their personnel in Lebanon, and carried out aerial bombardments against the bases near Baalbek in November 1983.

Since the Biqa Valley is Syrian-controlled territory, and all men and supplies must come through Syria, Iran and Syria cooperate in defining the role of the Revolutionary Guards and their Lebanese Shi'ite clients. The mediatory task falls to Iran's Ambassador to Syria, Hujjat al-Islam Ali Akbar Mohtashemipur, coordinator of Iranian activities in Syria and Lebanon. He lost one hand and three fingers of his other hand upon opening a letter-bomb marked as Islamic literature, but remains at his post in Damascus. Khomeini, the Revolutionary Guards, and the Iraqi Shi'ite organizations also have their own liaison people in Syria. These secure essential political and logistical support, and are frequent visitors to the Biqa Valley.

But the center of Lebanese Shi'ite terrorist activity is Beirut. The religious extremists face a different situation in Lebanon's capital. Here an alternative is provided by a Lebanese Shi'ite organization which seeks redress of specific Lebanese Shi'ite grievances, rather than Islamic revolution. Nabih Birri, the lawyer who heads the mainstream Amal militia, advocates reform of the Lebanese confessional system, not the establishment of an Islamic republic. According to him, Iran severed all relations with his movement back in 1982.

But in the Shi'ite quarters of Beirut, there is considerable sympathy for the Iranian revolution, and much of it has coalesced around one figure: Shaykh Muhammad Husayn Fadlallah. He was born in Najaf to a Lebanese father, and was also schooled there. His preaching, which has earned him a sizeable following in Beirut, constitutes a demand for the eventual constitution of Lebanon as an Islamic republic. Accusations of involvement were leveled at Fadlallah following the bomb attacks on the US and French contingents in Beirut, on 23 October 1983, in which nearly 300 lives were lost. He immediately and consistently denied that he had anything to do with attacks on foreign forces, and still claims to have no connection whatsoever with acts of violence. However, he does believe that 'the Iranian regime, with its mistakes, is the most humane regime in the world', and he visits Iran annually. There he meets with Khomeini, whom he once hailed as 'leader of the world's Muslims, the only person to confront the infidels with all his power and might'. There are many enigmas surrounding Fadlallah's political attitudes and personal involvement in terrorist activities. His disciples, who call themselves the Party of God (Hizb Allah), have been linked to numerous acts of terror against foreigners in Beirut, and to attacks against Israeli forces in south Lebanon. Fadlallah nonetheless has persisted in his dissimulating denials.

## IRANIAN RESPONSIBILITY

Are these many organizations and persons subject to Iranian control and coordination? According to some sources, all of the Shi'ite Iraqi, Lebanese, Arab Gulf, and other organizations, come under the authority of an Islamic Revolutionary Council. This council first met in March 1983, and is headed by the aforementioned Muhammad Taqi al-Mudarrisi. He submits proposals for action to a still higher authority, the Supreme Coordination Council for the Islamic Revolution in Iran and Revolutionary Islamic Movements in the World. Ayatollah Montazeri reportedly presides over this council, which includes Revolutionary Guards Commander Mohsen Rezai, Foreign Ministry Political Undersecretary Husayn Sheikholeslam, Iranian Ground Forces Commander Sayyad Shirazi, and others. Of particular importance is the presence on the council of Sayyid Mehdi Hashemi, a personal disciple of Khomeini, who reportedly conducts the Foreign Ministry's liaison with Muslim movements abroad.

The establishment of such a council had been discussed at length in 1982-83. In its annual report for that year, the Majlis Foreign Affairs Committee mentioned a 'proposal to establish the council for supporting Islamic movements and liberation movements. This proposal was studied in numerous sessions of the Foreign Affairs Committee and in this connection, meetings were held with the Minister and deputies of the Foreign Ministry, and those who had presented the proposal'. This wording makes it apparent that the proposal emanated not from the Foreign Ministry, but from clerics in the Majlis. The debate would have revolved around the tie between such a council and the Foreign Ministry, which does not want to appear to openly support revolution elsewhere. A solution may have been found in attaching the council to

Montazeri's office. But nothing is known about the council's mandate, method of operation, or budget. Its very existence has yet to be confirmed by an Iranian source. ·

Nor is anything known about the telephone callers who style themselves members of an international organization called the Islamic Jihad (al-Jihad al-Islami). None of the known revolutionary Shi'ite organizations goes by this name. This gives rise to the distinct possibility that one or more of the known groups uses the cover name of Islamic Jihad in order to make clear the religious motive of an attack or threat, while nonetheless preserving anonymity.

A wall of denial separates Iran from responsibility for the acts of organizations enjoying Iranian hospitality or support. These organizations, in turn, take shelter behind a cover name, making it still more difficult to apportion responsibility. Yet part of this network is clearly visible: the ulama whose teachings inspire and justify these acts. Shi'ite terrorist groups, like the Iranian regime itself, revolve around men of religion. Their guidance is not simply spiritual, for they would be the first to deny a separation between their spiritual and political message. They have given the Shi'ite struggle its guiding political themes, its anti-Western demonology, and its justification for terrorist violence. Yet they preach openly, and publicly come and go to Iran, where they freely admit to consulting with government and military leaders. The prospect of understanding and perhaps thwarting the network of Shi'ite terrorism lies above all in charting the ideological and political pilgrimages of the militant Shi'ite ulama.